HISTORY OF SOUTHERN AFRICA

Contemporary Southern Africa

HISTORY OF SOUTHERN AFRICA

J.D. Omer-Cooper

Professor of History
University of Otago, New Zealand

Second Edition

David Philip
James Currey
Heinemann

James Currey Publishers
54b Thornhill Square, Islington
London N1 1BE

Heinemann
A Division of Reed Publishing (USA) Inc
361 Hanover Street
Portsmouth, New Hampshire 03801-3912

Agents in Southern Africa
David Philip Publishers (Pty) Ltd
PO Box 23408
Claremont 7735
Cape, South Africa

Maps by Almac
Picture & Map Research by Clare Currey
Edited by Roger Thomas
Design by James Currey and Ingrid Crewdson
Layout and paste up by Tamsin Currey
New edition planned by Nicholas Hardyman

British Library Cataloguing in Publication Data

Omer-Cooper, J.D.
History of Southern Africa. – 2Rev.ed
I. Title
968

ISBN 0-85255-715-9 paper
ISBN 0-85255-716-7 cloth

Library of Congress Cataloging-in-Publication Data

Omer-Cooper, J.D. (John D.)
History of Southern Africa / J.D. Omer-Cooper. -- 2nd ed.
p. cm.
Includes bibliographical references and index.
ISBN 0-435-08095-4
1. South Africa--History. 2. Africa, Southern--History.
I. Title.
DT1787.044 1994
968--dc20 93-40500
CIP

Typeset in Garamond Number 3
by Saxon Graphics Limited, 22 Parker Centre, Mansfield Road, Derby DE21 4SZ
and printed in Great Britain

Contents

Maps viii
Illustrations ix
Preface xi

1 The Khoisan peoples &
   Bantu-speaking settlement 1

   The environment 1
   The earliest peoples 2
     The San - The Khoi
   Iron Age peoples 7
     The Nguni - The Sotho-Tswana - Other Bantu-
     speaking groups - Social, economic and political
     organisation- Chiefdom structure and organisation
     - Patterns of expansion - Bantu-Khoisan relations

2 The establishment & early
   development of the Cape Colony 17

   The first European settlements 17
     The drive towards colonisation - Local
     administration - Conflicts of interest between
     Company and settlers
   The introduction of slave labour:
   expansion in farming 22
     Alternatives to agrarian farming - The loan farms system
   Colonial expansion in the eighteenth century ... 25
     Settlement in the north - Settlement in the east
   Khoisan reactions to the European presence 26
     Development of commandos
   Racial attitudes at the Cape 30
     The rise of the Griqua
   Racial attitudes in the interior 32
   The last years of Company rule 32
     Xhosa resistance wars

3 New wine in old bottles:
   the Cape Colony 1795-1834 35

   The first British occupation of the Cape,
   1795-1802 36
     Attempts to bring peace to the frontiers - Frontier
     revolt and Khoi rebellion
   Christian missionaries 38

   Conflicts of interest
   The rule of the Batavian Republic, 1803-6 41
   The return of the British, 1806 42
     Labour shortages - Labour laws and the Khoi
   Struggle for the zuurveld 44
     The 'ceded' territory
   The drive for closer settlement 46
     The 1820 settler scheme
   Closer ties with Britain: judicial reform 47
     Ordinance no. 50
   Expansion across the Orange 49
     Griqua claims - Frontier relations

4 The mass migrations of the
   mfecane & the Great Trek 52

   The rise of the northern Nguni states 54
     Creation of the Swazi kingdom - Further spread of the
     mfecane - Shaka: the military leader - Northward
     migrations: foundation of the Gaza and Ngoni
     kingdoms - Shaka: the consolidation of power
     - The end of Shaka's reign - Impact of the mfecane
     on Natal and the Transkei - The difaqane: the
     mfecane on the Transorangian highveld - Sotho-
     Tswana upheavals - Moshoeshoe and the establishment
     of the Lesotho kingdom - Mzilikazi and the Ndebele
   The effects of the mfecane 67
     Political change - European observations
   The sixth Xhosa war of resistance 69
     Queen Adelaide Province
   The Great Trek 71
     The progress of the Trek - Military tactics - Early
     trekker groups - Trekker government - Leaders of
     the trek - Ndebele pressed into migration -
     Dingane and Retief - Continued conflict - The
     battle of Blood river - The death of Dingane

5 Boer republics, African states
   & the British 82

   Developments after the Great Trek 82
     British legislation over trekker lands - The
     republic of Natalia - British annexation of Natal -
     Land and settlement schemes in Natal - Conflicts
     of interest in the Vaal/Orange rivers area - British

Kaffraria - The Orange River Sovereignty
The reversal of British policy   88
Abandonment of the Sovereignty
Changes in British policy   91
Sir George Grey: the eastern frontier and the interior
The Orange Free State   93
Formation and early history - Increasing instability
- The question of federation
Consolidation in the Transvaal   95
Unification of the South African Republic   95
Final separation between the Orange Free State
and the South African Republic - Economic
weaknesses in the South African Republic
*War between the Orange Free State and
the Kingdom of Lesotho*   97
King Moshoeshoe urges British intervention - The
political outcome of the war

6 Diamonds & the first British
   attempt to unify South Africa   101

The significance of the diamond fields   101
Increased competition - The beginnings of
migrant labour
Rival claims to the diamond deposits   103
The Keate awards: Britain takes the diamond fields
Responsible government status for the Cape   105
The nature of responsible government -
Continued stress in Griqualand West
The Langalibalele affair   107
The issue of confederation   108
The London confederation conference -
Alternative means of achieving confederation: the
Transvaal - Annexation of the Transvaal
Xhosa war on the eastern frontier   111
The ninth Xhosa resistance war - The escalation of conflict
The Zulu War   112
Imperial desires - Zulu recovery - Faction
struggles in the kingdom - Cetshwayo succeeds
Mpande - Frere seeks war - The British invasion of
Zululand - The battle of Isandhlwana - The
significance of the Zulu victory - The end of the war
Sotho resistance: The 'Gun War'   116
The Phuthi are driven to rebellion - Moorosi
besieged - Sotho disarmament
Parallel resistance to confederation   119
Resentment in the Transvaal
British policy on withdrawal   120
Arrangements with the Transvaal - The Cape
abandons Lesotho

*New era: industrial revolution in the
diamond fields*   121
Amalgamation of the diamond fields - Increased control
of African working conditions - The many ambitions
of Cecil Rhodes - New states, new boundaries

7 Gold & the unification
   of South Africa   126

Initial changes caused by gold mining   126
Reactions in the Transvaal *volksraad*
The nature of the Rand deposits   127
Effects of boom on the industry - The rush to
build rail links
The politics of capitalism: Cecil Rhodes   131
Mining concessions from Lobengula - Rhodes's
'pioneer column' - Political tactics in the Cape -
Changes in Rhodes's fortunes
Organised opposition in the Transvaal   136
Rhodes's plan to overthrow the Transvaal
government - The Jameson raid
Ndebele and Shona uprisings   139
Rhodes profits from peace talks
The South African War   141
Continuation of conflict in the Transvaal - Kruger
consolidates his position in the Transvaal - Milner
and the Transvaal - Agitation for a show of force -
Moderates attempt negotiation - The course of the
war - The Vereeniging peace terms - Betrayal of
African interests
Post-war reconstruction   148
Labour exploitation and social problems -
Importation of Chinese mine labour - White
opposition to Milner's policies
Political developments   151
The foundation of political parties - Elections
Economic developments   152
Increased pressures on Africans in Natal -
Bambatha's rebellion
White political unity   154
The need for a closer union - The draft constitution
- The Cape franchise - Attitudes to the constitution

8 From Union to apartheid:
   the politics of segregation   158

A changing society   158
The politics of migrant labour
The first Union governments   159

The break-up of the South African National Party
- Afrikaner nationalism under Hertzog

The development of African nationalism   160
Early political associations - The establishment of the
African National Congress (ANC) - The 1913 Land Act

Indian protest: the origins of Satyagraha
in South Africa   163

White labour unrest   164

The First World War   165
Afrikaner opposition - The conquest of German
South West Africa - Smuts and the League of
Nations Mandate system

Post-war political developments   167
White party politics - The birth of the
Broederbond - The ANC and the struggle for
African rights on the Rand 1918-20

*The legal foundations of urban segregation
and influx control*   169

The Bulhoek Israelites and the Bondelswarts   169

*Race relations in the Rand mining work
force*   170
Pauperisation of rural Afrikaners: the poor-white
problem - The Rand rebellion - The Labour-
National Party alliance - Increased labour
discrimination

South Africa becomes independent   173
The response of the Broederbond and Afrikaner
nationalists - The 'Black Peril' election - The
formation of the United Party and destruction of
the Cape franchise

Afrikaner nationalism   175
The *voortrekker* centenary

African political activity between the wars   178
The Industrial and Commercial Workers' Union -
Non-whites and the franchise issue - The All
African Convention - The revival of the ANC

South Africa and the Second World War   181
The Afrikaner nationalist response - The
economic impact of the war - Social changes
arising from industrial growth - Afrikaner politics
in the war period - The struggle between the
National Party and the Ossewabrandwag - Smuts's
1943 election victory - African nationalism in the
Second World War: the recovery of the ANC -
African trade union activity - The Natives'
Representative Council protests

The 1948 general election and its background   188
The policies of the United Party - Smuts and the
United Nations - The National Party and its
apartheid policy - The 1948 apartheid election

9   The first two phases of apartheid   193

Baaskap apartheid 1948-61   193
The legal framework of apartheid - The impact of
baaskap apartheid on black and brown South Africans
- White opposition to apartheid - The Torch
Commando - Black-led opposition to apartheid:
the mass defiance campaign - The Congress of the
People and the Freedom Charter - The ANC splits:
foundation of the Pan-Africanist Congress - Other
forms of black protest and resistance - The
Sharpeville massacre - The opening of armed
struggle - South Africa becomes a republic and
leaves the Commonwealth

From baaskap *apartheid to separate
development*   211
New policy for the Bantustans - Constitutional
development of the Bantustans - Economic
development of the Bantustans - The outward-
looking policy - The other face of separate
development: forced removals and tightened
labour controls - Heightened police repression -
White opposition in the period of 'separate
development' - The division of Afrikanerdom: the
first split in the National Party - Black opposition
to separate development - Steve Biko and the rise
of the black consciousness movement - Changes in
the central-southern African region

10 The final phase &
collapse of apartheid   223

The revolution in Portugal and the strategic transformation
of the central African region - The Soweto explosion -
Repression and militarisation: the martyrdom of
Steve Biko - Changes in policy towards urbanised
Africans - The other side of the co-option policy:
independence for the Bantustans - Black opposition
after Soweto - Government and white opposition
after 1974 - The 'Muldergate' affair: P.W. Botha
becomes prime minister - Botha's managerial style
of government and the new dominant elite - The
development of regional policy - The introduction
of the multiracial constitution

The Township rebellions   237
Faltering reform and tightening sanctions -
Suppression of the townships: origins of inter-
African political violence - Leading white opinion
turns towards radical change - Botha and the

securocrats maintain the total strategy - The
destabilisation strategy - Military stalemate in
Angola: resolution of Namibian issue - Internal and
external pressures combine to force negotiated change -
The abandonment of apartheid

11 Order or anarchy?   243

Towards the new South Africa   243

Appendix 1 The enclave states,
Lesotho, Swaziland & Botswana   252

The kingdom of Lesotho   252
A breakdown in unity: Cape administration 1871-83 -
The return to British administration: development
of the economy - Social inequality - Towards political
reform - The rise of the Basutoland Congress Party -
Independent Lesotho - The 1970 coup

Swaziland   263
The system of government - Frontier losses and
concession hunters - Constitutional change -
Swaziland as a High Commission Territory -
Sobhuza II: first political moves - Economic
development - An absolute monarchy

Botswana   270
From chiefdoms to national politics - Political
parties - The independence era

Appendix 2 Namibia   278

Population   278
*Inter-ethnic conflict and European
intervention*   279
*The German administration of South
West Africa*   280
*South West Africa (Namibia) under
South African rule*   281
The creation of the South African Mandate -
The style of Mandate administration: social
effects - The repression of the Bondelswarts -
South African schemes to absorb or partition
South West Africa - United Nations protest and
its effects - The 1971 strike - Further UN
pressure - Effects of the Turnhalle Conference -
South African reactions to Namibia's future

Bibliography   295
Index   301

Maps

frontispiece: Contemporary Southern Africa   ii

1.1 South Africa, showing relief and rainfall and the
    probable migration routes of the Khoi   2

2.1 Expansion of the Cape colony: approximate areas
    1652, 1710 and the 1798 frontier   27

3.1 The progressive expropriation of the Xhosa,
    1812-20   46

4.1 Approximate directions of major movements
    during the *mfecane* in southern Africa and the
    main directions of movement of the Boer Great
    Trek   65

5.1 The Trekker Republic and the Boer communities
    of the Transvaal   83

5.2 White encroachment on Basutoland (Lesotho)   98

6.1 Rival claims to the diamond fields   104

7.1 The consolidation of white rule and the extinction
    of African independence in southern Africa: the
    situation in 1897   139

7.2 The South African War, 1899-1902   144

9.1 Contemporary South Africa, showing the
    Bantustans (Homelands)   214

Illustrations

The author and publishers acknowledge with thanks the sources listed below for the pictures in this book. Particular thanks are due to the Africana Museum, Johannesburg, the International Defence and Aid Fund, and Hilary Morgan at Longman for help given. The pictures on pages 233 and 243 to 250 are reproduced by kind permission of Reuters, Johannesburg and reproduced from Rich Mkhondo *Reporting South Africa* James Currey London and Heinemann Portsmouth New Hampshire 1993.

Efforts have been made to trace the ownership of all the pictures used, but so far we have failed to trace the owners of the pictures on pages 85, 109, 122, 132, 151, 171, 173, 177, 206, 260, 267, 268, 279 (foot), 281 and 283.

A nineteenth century view of a Tswana town (Samuel Daniell: 'Town of Leetakoo' in *African Scenery and Animals*, 1804), xiv

A San rock painting (Mansell Collection), 3

A Namaqua kraal (Keith Johnston, *Africa*, 1878), 4

Khoi village beside the Orange river (Samuel Daniell, 1804, Africana Museum, Johannesburg), 6

Nguni settlement (Ludwig Alberti, *Account of the Tribal Life and Customs of the Xhosa in 1807*, Africana Museum, Johannesburg), 9

Street in a Tswana town (Keith Johnston, 1878), 10

Detail from picture on page 9, 11

Detail from picture on page xiv, 12

Group of Nguni travelling (Alberti, 1807, Africana Museum, Johannesburg), 13

Nguni couple (Alberti, 1807), 15

Table Bay and Table Mountain (Artist unknown, Africana Museum, Johannesburg), 17

Boer outspan in the Karroo, about 1830 (C.D. Bell, Africana Museum, Johannesburg), 19

Adriaan van der Stel's estate, Vergelegen (W.A. van der Stel, Africana Museum, Johannesburg), 21

Plan of the Vergelegen estate (*Contra Deductie*, 1711, Cape Archives, ref. M. 140), 21

'Cape Dutch' farmhouse (Theal, *South Africa*, 1894), 23

Chief Ngqika meeting General Janssens (Alberti, 1807, Africana Museum, Johannesburg), 42

British settlers arriving on the beach at Algoa Bay, 1820 (Thomas Baines, Africana Museum, Johannesburg), 48

Philippolis, 1834 (C.D. Bell, Africana Museum, Johannesburg), 51

View of Griquatown (Campbell, *Travels in South Africa* 1815), 51

Shaka, king of the Zulus (Nathaniel Isaacs, *Travels and Adventures in Eastern Africa*, 1836, Africana Museum, Johannesburg), 56

Zulu warrior in full regalia (Africana Museum, Johannesburg), 57

Dingane (Gardiner, *Narrative of a Journey to the Zoolu Country*, 1836, Africana Museum, Johannesburg), 61

Moshoeshoe, 1833 (Casalis, *Les Bassoutos*, 1859), 62

David Livingstone (*Last Journeys of David Livingstone in Central Africa*, 1880), 63

Sekonyela (*Diary of Andrew Smith*, 1834, Africana Museum, Johannesburg), 64

Thaba Bosiu (Casalis, 1859), 67

Crossing Cradock's Pass (C.C. Michell, Africana Museum, Johannesburg), 69

Sir Benjamin D'Urban by E. Hareman (Africana Museum, Johannesburg), 70

W.H. Coetzer's picture of Louis Trichardt's party bringing waggons down a mountain (Africana Museum, Johannesburg), 73

The great dance at Mbelebele in 1836 (T.M. Baynes, in Gardiner, 1836), 78

A.W.J. Pretorius (Painting belonging to the government and Republic of South Africa: it hangs in the Old Raadsaal, Pretoria), 80

H.M.S. Southampton covering the landing of the British troops at Port Natal, 1842 (T.W. Bowler), 85

Indian cane-cutters in the sugar cane fields, Natal (Reprinted from Robert A. Huttenback: *Gandhi in South Africa*, copyright 1971 by Cornell University Press. Used by permission of the publisher.), 86

Adam Kok III (Africana Museum, Johannesburg), 87

Sir Harry Smith by W. Melville, 1842 (Africana Museum, Johannesburg), 88

Xhosa ambushing a British patrol (International Defence and Aid Fund (IDAF)), 89

Moshoeshoe, 1845 (Professor Leonard Thompson), 90

Sir George Grey (South African Library, Cape Town), 93

M.W. Pretorius (Africana Museum, Johannesburg), 94

The start of the Kimberley mine, 1871 (from J.T. McNish, *The Road to El Dorado*, Struik Publishers, Cape Town), 100

The diamond fields, 1872 (*Illustrated London News*, 30 March 1872), 102

The sorting table at the diamond diggings, 1872 (*Illustrated London News*, 26 October 1872), 103

Colesberg Kopje before the discovery of Kimberley mine (J.T. McNish, *The Road to El Dorado*, Struik Publishers, Cape Town), 106

Colesberg Kopje twelve months after the start of the mine (J.T. McNish, *op. cit.*), 106

Advertisement from The Diamond News, *Kimberley 1876*, 107

Sir John Charles Molteno, 109

Sir Bartle Frere (Africana Museum, Johannesburg), 110

Pondo warriors (*Illustrated London News*, 22 February 1879), 112

Crossing a drift (*Illustrated London News*, 1879), 114

British troops attacking a Zulu stronghold (*Illustrated London News*, 1879), 115

Zulu attack at Intombi Drift, 1879 (*Illustrated London News*, 1879) 116

British forces using the laager method of defence during the Zulu War (Mansell Collection), 117

Prospecting for gold (Thomas Baines in *Shifts and Expedients of Camp Life*, 1871, National Archives, Zimbabwe), 121

Cecil Rhodes and Alfred Beit (Photograph by E.H. Mills), 122

Punch shows Rhodes as a colossus (*Punch*), 123

Cetshwayo (from a photograph by J.E. Bruton in Vijn, *Cetshwayo's Dutchman*), 124

President Kruger by E. Rinaldi (Africana Museum, Johannesburg), 127

Battery and tramways on a Witwatersrand goldfield (*Illustrated London News*, 6 July 1889), 128

Crown Deep Gold Mine, Witwatersrand, 1898 (BBC Hulton Picture Library), 129

Lobengula and his sister at the great military dance (A.A. Anderson, Africana Museum, Johannesburg), 130

Lobengula reviewing a dance before missionaries (Fr. Croonenbergh, Africana Museum, Johannesburg), 131

Lobengula, king of the Ndebele, 132

The Pioneer Corps on the way to Mashonaland, 1890 (*The Graphic*, 25 October 1890), 134

Jameson's men cutting the telegraph wires, 1895 (Mansell Collection), 138

Nehanda and Kagubi mediums in Salisbury prison, 1898 (National Archives, Zimbabwe), 140

Sir Alfred Milner (R. Chester Master Collection, Weidenfeld & Nicolson Archives), 142

General C.R. de Wet addressing his commando by John Beer (Africana Museum, Johannesburg), 145

Boer women being taken to a concentration camp (National Army Museum), 146

'Camp for undesirables' (Weidenfeld & Nicolson), 147

Returning from the gold mines, 151

General Louis Botha (Brian Willan), 160

J.B. Hertzog (Africana Museum, Johannesburg), 161

Native National Congress Special Conference Programme, March 1914 (Plaatje papers, STP 3/2, School of Oriental & African Studies, University of London), 162

South African Native National Congress delegation to England, 1914 (University of Witwatersrand library), 163

Police charging white strikers, 1913 (IDAF), 165

Jan Smuts, 1922 (IDAF), 166

Rand gold miners (IDAF), 170

Poor whites (E.G. Malherbe), 171

Troops clearing the Johannesburg streets, 1922 strike, 171

The founding committee of the Broederbond, 173

The 1938 centenary ox waggon trek, 177

Clements Kadalie (Africana Museum, Johannesburg), 178

The Nationalist Cabinet, 1948 (Camera Press), 195

The demolition of District Six, Cape Town (IDAF), 198

An example of segregated facilities (Clare Currey), 199

Women leaving jail, Defiance Campaign, 1952, 206

Albert Luthuli (IDAF), 207

Sharpeville, 21 March 1960 (IDAF), 209

Nelson Mandela (IDAF), 210

B.J. Vorster (IDAF), 216

Resettlement camp, Ramatlabama (IDAF), 217

Chief Gatsha Buthelezi and Chief Kaiser Matanzima (B. Temkin, *Gatsha Buthelezi*, 1976), 220

Soweto riots, 1976 (IDAF), 225

Steve Biko (IDAF), 227

Consultations between the South African government and the chief ministers of the Homelands, 1974 (from D.A. Kotze, *African Politics in South Africa 1964-1974*, C. Hurst, 1975), 230

P. W. Botha, 1986 (Link), 232

Eugene Terre Blanche (Reuters) 233

Graffiti in Johannesburg (Link), 236

Archbishop Desmond Tutu (Link), 238

Nelson Mandela and delegates at Soweto stadium after his release (Reuters), 243

Winnie Mandela after a march to the Union buildings in Pretoria (Reuters), 244

Desmond Tutu touring a camp for refugees from township violence (Reuters), 244

Mandela, de Klerk and delegates at the May 1990 talks (Reuters), 245

Arms confiscated from a migrant workers' compound (Reuters), 246

Cyril Ramaphosa (Reuters), 246

ANC supporters in a Natal township (Reuters), 247

Mandela and Buthelezi at a meeting to halt violence (Reuters), 247

Buthelezi and de Klerk (Reuters), 248

Police in Soweto: peace-makers or third force? (Reuters), 249

Zulu migrant Inkatha supporters (Reuters), 249

AWB supporters awaiting their leader (Reuters), 250

Chris Hani (IDAF), 251

Boer attack on Thaba Bosiu, 1865 (IDAF), 253

Sotho weapons (Casalis, Les Bassoutos, 1859), 254

Sotho warrior (Casalis, 1859), 255

Leabua Jonathan, 260

Nguni huts (Illustrated London News, 21 June 1879), 263

Swazi land delegation to London, 1923, 267

King Sobhuza II, 268

Tswana warriors (Keith Johnston, Africa, 1878), 271

Tswana weapons (Campbell, Travels in South Africa, 1815), 272

Moffat preaching to the Bechuana by Charles Bell (Africana Museum, Johannesburg), 273

Sir Seretse Khama (Office of the President, Botswana), 276

Khoi on the beach at Walfisch Bay (Keith Johnston, Africa, 1878), 279

Jonker Afrikaner, 279

Walfisch Bay (Keith Johnston, Africa, 1878), 280

Maharero, chief of the Herero, 281

Margarete von Eckenbrecher and family, c. 1903, 281

Hendrik Witbooi (Bundesarchiv, Bonn), 282

Ovambo workmen during a meal break in the Otavi mines, 1908, 283

SWAPO demonstrators (IDAF), 289

Preface to the second edition

This new edition incorporates important recent advances in scholarship, especially in relation to our understanding of the early history, settlement, and relations of the San, Khoi and Bantu-speaking peoples in southern Africa, and of the causation and course of the nineteenth century *mfecane*. The recent history of Botswana, Lesotho and Swaziland and that of the newly independent Namibia is recorded, and the account is brought up to date with the crucial changes in South Africa that have taken place since 1985. The white monopoly of power is about to pass away, a transitional regime is to be inaugurated and universal suffrage elections are to be held for a constituent assembly with authority to finalise a new constitution. It is my hope that this book will go some way towards illuminating the patterns of development which have brought this situation about as well as the genesis of the fearful social and political tensions which threaten to engulf the nascent New South Africa in a sea of violence before it is even fully born.

Preface to the first edition

My object in writing this book has been to present a clear outline history of southern Africa in the light of recent scholarship for university students and other interested readers who do not have much previous acquaintance with the subject. The most important single theme is the historical explanation of the creation of that peculiar system of systematic racial discrimination, repression and exploitation known as apartheid and the evolution of that system from its original form to 1985 where it appeared to stand on the threshold of disintegration.

I have concentrated on the evolution of the political, economic, legal and social framework. This has meant giving far less attention than I would have liked to the significance of historical developments for families and individuals in various social situations. As I am most acutely aware it has meant failing to give anything like adequate treatment to the role of women of all races.

The effective pursuit of such topics in social history as have been undertaken in van Onselen's outstanding study of Johannesburg, however, presupposes a knowledge of the wider framework within which the various social groups lived and evolved. To keep changing focus from the wider panorama to that of the grass roots, moreover, would have severely complicated the logic of my presentation and made it much harder to follow.

For the same reason I have attempted to present a single interpretation of the historical evolution of the area and have deliberately refrained from interpellating my account with discussion of the differing lines of interpretation and the historiographical controversies in recent scholarship, fascinating and valuable though that would be. My overriding object has been to provide the reader with a clear and definite picture which can then provide the starting point for further questioning, reading and enquiry.

In presenting this account I have attempted to tell the story of the main developments, providing the reader with the necessary framework of narrative detail on the major events and personalities. The account I offer, however, is by no means simply a chronological narrative, but rather a consciously analytical interpretation. The point of view from which it is written is that technological developments and the economic interests and clashes of interests of different social groups provide the main explanation of most historical developments. Thus in South Africa the development of racially discriminatory practices in the Cape Colony before the nineteenth century is to be primarily explained in terms of desire by whites to maintain and reinforce the race/class social hierarchy which gave them economic advantage and social status. In the twentieth century the heightening of racial discrimination in the form of segregation and, more recently, apartheid is to be explained primarily in terms of the economic interests of white farmers, mining magnates, white workers, and poor whites rather than by consciously held doctrines about race or the strength of deep-seated race prejudice important though these have been.

In this regard my interpretation has much in common with the loose group of historians often known as the 'revisionists', most of whom write from an explicitly neo-Marxist point of view. They have, I believe, made far the greatest contribution to our understanding of southern African history in recent years. In many respects they have revolutionised our perceptions. While accepting a very great deal of their conclusions and explanations, however, I do not share their insistence on the use of a specialised neo-Marxist vocabulary. This is partly because I believe the use of this terminology would be more likely to hinder than to help understanding by the readers for whom I am writing. It also reflects the fact that I do not share their theoretical convictions in the a priori certainty of Marxist doctrine.

The emphasis which I place on economic needs and interests, however, does not mean that I regard political issues as wholly subordinate and secondary. Economic activities take place within a political framework and politics can affect economics very fundamentally. Thus the pattern of labour exploitation which developed on the Rand and was of immense importance for many aspects of the development of southern Africa, was crucially influenced by the fact that white workers had political rights and black workers did not. In the same way though the popularity and strength of ideas and beliefs may be explained with reference to economic and social interests, it is only through such beliefs that these interests find expression in public action. An understanding of their content is thus of vital importance to comprehending the resultant developments. Afrikaner nationalism may only have developed as a major political force in the twentieth century because of the economic problems of Afrikaner farmers, workers and poor whites and the frustrated ambitions of Afrikaner professionals and would-be entrepreneurs. An understanding of the historical traditions and philosophical principles which were incorporated in the ideology, however, is quite essential to a comprehension of its appeal and of the nature of the political movement which it nourished. If politics and ideas are vitally important so too are individuals. Southern African history cannot be explained solely in terms of abstract economic forces. Individuals like Shaka, Moshoeshoe, Rhodes and Kruger have vitally affected the way the pattern has developed.

If southern African history cannot be understood without reference to particular individuals neither can developments since 1652 be adequately comprehended through exclusive concentration on the activities of the whites and the development of the white dominated economic system. The history of southern Africa has always been a story of interplay and interaction between different peoples and different economic systems. Though the white minority has, since the latter part of the nineteenth century at least, held overwhelmingly preponderant power, black Africans have never been mere passive material. They have always been vital actors in the history of their country. Thus the very occurrence and course taken by the Boer Great Trek was largely conditioned by the success of the Xhosa resistance on the Eastern Frontier and the opportunities and obstacles to white expansion created by the *mfecane*. Then again the success of African peasants in adopting new crops and technology and developing market-oriented agriculture thus effectively resisting the pressures which sought to turn them into workers for white employers lay behind many important developments. These include the establishment of the Indian community in South Africa, the abortive attempt to unify the country in the 1870s, and the introduction of formal territorial segregation with the 1913 Land Act.

Apartheid also was not only an expression of the common interests of different Afrikaner social groups but also a defensive reaction against the growing outspokenness and effectiveness of African protest both on the political and economic fronts. The evolution of the system away from its original form to the later 1970s and early 1980s pattern of multiracial co-option has likewise been not just an adaptation to the needs of changing technology, the changed strategic situation in Africa and pressures from the wider world, but also a reaction to the escalation of the freedom struggle waged by SWAPO, ANC and PAC, the increasingly uncontrollable anger of the black townships and the economic muscle of black workers. The importance of understanding the positive role of Africans, Indians and Coloureds as well as whites in the development of southern African society becomes ever more obvious as the white monopoly of power begins to crumble and its ultimate transfer to black hands can be seen to be approaching.

A nineteenth century view of a Tswana town
(Samuel Danniel : 'Town of Leetakoo' in
African Scenery and Animals, 1804)

The Khoisan peoples & Bantu-speaking settlement

The environment

In contrast to the tropical lands to the north, the geographical region of South Africa offers a changing and often harsh environment. The greater part of the region is upland plateau. Here it is hot in summer and freezing cold on winter nights when bitter Antarctic air from the south sweeps over the land. Much of the inland plateau tilts gently to the west. Thus the Orange River, forming with its tributaries the main drainage system of the South African highveld, flows westward to the Atlantic. Further to the north, however, the Limpopo, which forms part of South Africa's northern border, flows eastward in a wide curve around the northern limit of the plateau.

Stretching from the north-east to the south, a mountain escarpment separates the highveld from a lowland coastal strip of varying width. The escarpment rises to its greatest heights in the Drakensberg mountain range which separates the highveld of the Orange Free State and southern Transvaal from the coastal lands of the Transkei and Natal. The highest peaks of the Drakensberg range and the associated range of the Maluti mountains are found within the borders of Lesotho.

The central plateau itself presents a varied landscape. Large expanses of open plain known in Afrikaans as the *platteland* are broken by mountain ranges. These include the Magaliesberg near Pretoria and much rugged country in the lands near the borders of the western Transvaal and Botswana. In the far north of the Transvaal lies the Zoutpansberg range and, further south, the Waterberg mountains. In Namibia (formerly South-West Africa), the plateau falls away to an extensive basin in the central Kalahari desert. In the north-eastern Transvaal, the land also drops away to a more low-lying area, the Transvaal lowveld.

Most of the South African region receives its major rainfall between November and April, brought by winds blowing from the Indian Ocean. Rains are heaviest on the eastern coastal strip and the mountainous escarpment, and decline as the winds move westward across the plateau area. A cold current which flows northwards along the west coast causes most of the moisture brought by winds from the Atlantic to fall over the sea, so that very little reaches the land. The climate over most of South Africa thus becomes progressively drier from east to west with semi-desert or desert conditions in the Kalahari.

Near the Cape of Good Hope, however, the climate pattern is different. This southernmost tip of the continent catches winds from the Atlantic

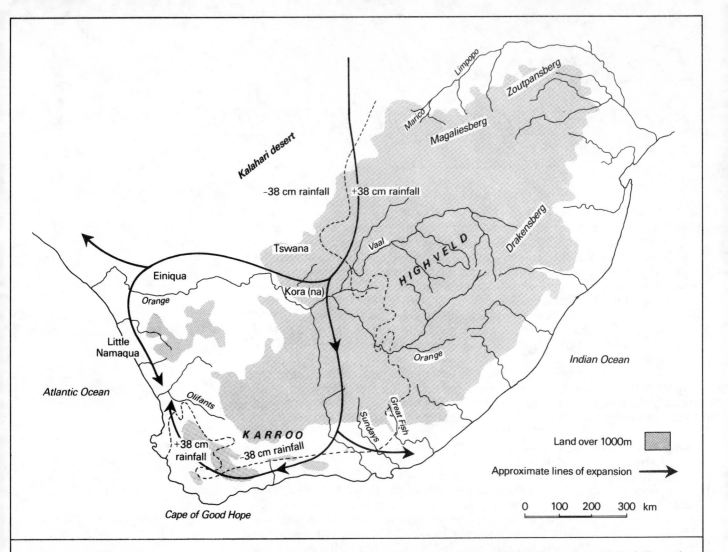

1.1 South Africa, showing relief and rainfall and the probable migration routes of the Khoi

blowing between May and October. The winds bring rain which falls as the rain clouds are forced to rise over the mountains of the Cape. The western Cape thus has cold, wet winters and hot, dry summers similar to those of the Mediterranean countries. The area is well suited to the growing of wheat, grapes and other European fruit crops. The mountains of the Cape series which bring about the winter rain, however, create a rain shadow in the hinterland producing an extensive area of semi-desert known as the *karroo*.

The earliest peoples

South Africa, together with the uplands of central and east Africa, provided a home for the earliest known forms of man and his pre-human relatives. In 1924 the fossilised skull of an ape-like creature with some humanoid features was discovered near Taung in the Transvaal. In later years there were further discoveries at several other sites in the Transvaal. These produced bones and tools which are at least 1.5 million years old and which represent evidence of a very early class of ape man, now classified as *Australopithecus*.

In South Africa numerous finds have been made of the crude so-called pebble tools, possibly the first form of man-made object, and of the more sophisticated stone hand axes typical of the Early Stone Age in Africa. These give way to the more varied stone tools of the Middle Stone Age and again gradually to the carefully shaped, often tiny (microlithic), stone implements of the Late Stone Age.

This late Stone Age culture continued to be practised down to historic times by some of South Africa's most ancient peoples who are known as the San (called the Twa by Bantu-speakers and, derogatively, Bushmen by later European settlers). The San or related peoples were at one time very widespread in central and east as well as southern Africa. This can be seen in the record of stone implements found throughout these regions and in the existence of small pockets of people in east Africa speaking languages containing the click consonants which occur only in Khoisan languages and those of peoples who have been in contact with them. By the seventeenth and eighteenth centuries they had been absorbed into other cultural communities in most of their original territory. They survived, however, in Namibia and neighbouring Botswana, southern Angola and a small area of Zambia, in the hinterland of the Cape up to and somewhat beyond the Orange river, and along the east coast up to the neighbourhood of the Great Fish river. Elsewhere throughout southern Africa, small San communities survived here and there in isolated and barren pockets in territories long occupied by Bantu-speaking populations. San communities survived in the mountains of Lesotho, for example, until the second half of the nineteenth century.

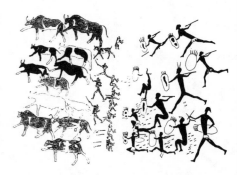

A San rock painting

The San were originally foragers practising no agriculture and keeping no domestic animals other than dogs. In communities which retained or were forced to revert to this way of life the men hunted wild animals using bows and poisoned arrows. The women collected wild bulbs, tubers and fruits, digging up the ground with pointed sticks weighted with heavy stones. They were organised in small communities, hunting bands made up of a few hundred members at most. Political organisation was simple; in many cases decisions were simply taken by discussion and agreement amongst the adult men. In some cases a leader was recognised as chief but his authority still depended on the agreement of the other adults. Each band occupied an extensive but clearly defined territory. Within this territory the band would migrate from waterhole to waterhole in pursuit of wild game and wild-growing vegetable foods. Movement across territorial boundaries into the area of another band, however, required formal consent, and intrusion without permission was met by force.

The San of southern Africa, like some hunting and gathering peoples in other parts of the world, had great artistic gifts. They used natural colours and dyes to decorate the rock faces of many of their caves and shelters. The best examples of their work capture the grace and movement of antelopes and other game with extraordinary vividness and accuracy. Apart from their artistic value, these paintings provide an important historic record. They show not only the animals the San hunted but also scenes of San

3

meeting Bantu-speaking peoples. In some of the most recent paintings white farmers make their appearance.

In contrast to the stereotype formerly portrayed, San culture has been shown by recent research to have been neither self-enclosed nor impervious to change. When contact was established with other peoples they commonly entered into trading relationships with them, exchanging game, meat, animal skins and ostrich eggshell beads for other products, such as iron for arrow heads. The development of such trade may perhaps explain the origin of the Berg Damas (Damaras) in Namibia. Their physical appearance suggests kinship with the Bantu-speaking peoples but they speak San languages and follow a predominantly hunting and gathering lifestyle. Originally they may have been descended from small groups of Bantu traders who penetrated deep into San-occupied country and settled there.

Apart from exchanging their own specialised products the San appear to have been prepared to adopt new food-producing methods from other peoples with whom they came in contact. There is now a great deal of archaeological evidence demonstrating that from about two thousand years ago pastoralism, accompanied in many cases by the use of ceramics, had been adopted by numerous Late Stone Age communities over a large part, if not the whole, of southern Africa. Sheep and goats appear to have been most important initially, with horned cattle subsequently playing the greater role.

This development pre-dates the advent of Iron Age peoples in South Africa by several hundred years and presumably arose from contact between the San and a pastoral people (perhaps a section of the Bantu-speaking peoples) further to the north, possibly in northern Botswana or Angola. The adoption of herding did not mean the abandonment of foraging. Initially domestic animals probably merely supplemented the products of hunting and gathering, though where substantial flocks and herds were built up they would assume the predominant role. On the other hand, where domesticated animals were lost to disease, theft by carnivores or human robbers, the community would revert to a purely foraging lifestyle.

A Namaqua kraal
(Keith Johnston: *Africa*, 1878)

4

The latest research thus shows that the previously supposed contrast between hunters and herders is largely a myth, the product of European false identification of race with culture as well as of the intellectual demand for categorisation. There is considerable evidence derived from white travellers and explorers as well as from African oral tradition to show that many communities identified as San possessed domestic animals in historic times. Where exclusive reliance on foraging was observed, it may indicate not the continuance of a tradition unchanged from Stone Age times but a more recent adaptation to being driven into an environment unsuitable for pastoralism, specialisation in an exchange relationship with another community, or subordination in a client relationship to a Bantu chiefdom.

Among the San communities which did adopt pastoralism, the most prominent were a widespread group which spoke dialects of a common language related to the Tshukwe group of San languages. They called themselves Khoi-Khoi and were known to the Dutch by the derogatory name Hottentots. They kept cattle as well as a breed of fat-tailed sheep peculiar to the Cape. Cattle formed the centre of their lives and the basis of personal status. The animals were used not only for milk, meat and clothing but were trained for riding and were even used in warfare: specially chosen and trained war-oxen were used to charge hostile groups. In addition to using the products of their herds and flocks, the Khoi also practised hunting and gathering. Like the San they did not engage in agriculture and apart from their animals their material culture remained very basic. For clothing they had only cloaks (called *carosses* in South Africa) made from the skins of their cattle or of wild animals. As a protection against disease their legs were sometimes laced with garters made by twisting the raw entrails of cattle around them. Their homes were simple shelters woven of branches, twigs and grass which were sometimes carried on the backs of oxen when they moved their encampments.

The origins of the Khoi and the routes of their migration and settlement in southern Africa are still not known with certainty. As most of the San group speaking Tshukwe languages have their habitat in northern Botswana, and it seems unlikely that they would have migrated as a complete group over any long distance, it is probable that it was in this general area that their ancestors first adopted the herding of domestic animals.

Environmental circumstances make it appear likely that the Khoi would have spread eastward and settled in Zimbabwe, northern Transvaal and Natal. Bantu-speaking peoples now living there use words associated with stock which appear to have been borrowed from them. If they did once live there, however, they had been absorbed into Bantu-speaking communities before European observers appeared on the scene. A large part of the Khoi seem, however, to have moved south from their centre of origin. Near the junction of the Vaal and Orange rivers they divided into two groups. The first spread out westward along the northern bank of the Orange River, settling in communities later known to the Dutch as the Korana and Einiqua. Near the mouth of the Orange some spread out southward down the coast as far as the Olifants river (the 'little Namaqua') while others turned north into southern Namibia (the 'great Namaqua').

The second group seems to have crossed the Orange river near its junction

A Khoi village beside the Orange river
(Samuel Daniell: *African Scenery and
Animals*, 1804)

with the Vaal and continued southward, reaching the coast near the
Sundays river. From there, some spread out eastward along the coast as far
as the Great Fish river. Others moved westward settling the coastal areas
down to and around the Cape of Good Hope. They then continued to
expand northward up the west coast until they met the 'little Namaqua'
near the Olifants river. As they spread out, Khoi communities often
absorbed forager bands into their chiefdoms. Sometimes these clients may
have adopted the Khoi way of life and been entirely incorporated into the
Khoi community. There is evidence for the opposite process also, however.
Khoi communities who lost their cattle from natural causes, in warfare or
(after the establishment of the Dutch settlements) through trade or conflict
with whites, sometimes reverted to a hunting and gathering way of life. A
number of such communities lived along the coast, feeding mainly on
shellfish. They have left numerous shell middens along the beaches east of
the Cape up to and beyond the Great Fish river. The Dutch called them
strandloopers (beach walkers). Other Khoi groups living a foraging life style
they called Bushman-Hottentots.

The Khoi were organised politically in chiefdoms considerably larger than
the San hunting bands but generally consisting of no more than one or two
thousand members. Each chiefdom was normally made up of a number of
clans which recognised a relationship to a senior clan. The head of the senior
clan held the office of chief. Each individual clan was made up of the male
descendants of a single common ancestor. Each clan also had a recognised
head or leader and the clan heads together with the chief made up the government of each chiefdom. In the Khoi chiefdoms decisions were made by
the chief in consultation with the other clan heads. The chief had no
machinery through which to enforce his decisions; his power was limited by
the need to obtain the agreement of the other clan heads and for these to
hold the loyalty of their clan members. In these circumstances the authority
exercised by chiefs depended very much on personality and a given situation

and could vary widely. Though normally mainly made up of members of related clans, the membership of Khoi communities was fairly flexible. Families or clans breaking away from one leader would often be received by another and the chiefdoms sometimes incorporated communities of other peoples. For example, San communities and Bantu-speaking groups might be adopted in this way.

As the population of a Khoi chiefdom expanded, the difficulties of herding all the cattle together would lead to the community separating into two or more groups of clans which would set up separate encampments and graze their cattle separately. This was generally the first step towards a break-up of the chiefdoms. The final break was often caused by a quarrel between the chief and some of the clan heads. These clans would then break away and establish a separate chiefdom which, if it flourished, would eventually divide in the same way. Sometimes political disagreement would lead to the earlier division of a chiefdom. The size of chiefdoms could therefore vary considerably. Possession of cattle provided the Khoi with the opportunity and incentive to engage in economic relations with other peoples. Regular trading relations with Bantu-speaking peoples were established in pre-colonial times, and after the Dutch settled at the Cape the Khoi were drawn into trade with them.

As personal standing in Khoi communities depended on possession of cattle, a man who had none was forced to be the client of a wealthier person. Once trade with whites became established, other material goods also became marks of status. Khoi were therefore prepared to make considerable sacrifices to obtain them. They could thus be persuaded much more easily than the San to enter the services of white masters and alter their way of life for material rewards.

Iron Age peoples

Archaeological evidence shows that settled food-producing communities acquainted with the techniques of smelting iron and other metals were established in much of modern Mozambique, Zimbabwe and some areas in the north and north-east of South Africa as early as the third to fourth centuries AD. These peoples made pottery of a general type that was very widespread throughout central and east Africa and has been used to identify the Early Iron Age in this area. Evidence from the area as a whole shows that this Early Iron Age culture was practised in the neighbourhood of the great lakes in east Africa as early as 300 BC. By the second and third centuries AD it seems to have reached the east African coast. It then spread rapidly southward into what are now Malawi, Zambia, Zimbabwe and South Africa in the fourth and fifth centuries. The spread of the Iron Age culture probably involved both the immigration and settlement of new peoples and the adoption of new technologies by some of the established Khoisan population. Intermingling and intermarriage between the newcomers and the earlier population was doubtless common. Over time, however, the language of the newcomers, albeit enriched by borrowings from Khoisan tongues, was to prevail. From the material remains of the Early Iron Age culture it is impossible to identify the languages spoken by the peoples involved. It is most probable, however, that they spoke Bantu languages: otherwise some remnants of their language would have survived in the present Bantu languages of the area, as is the case with the Khoisan click sounds.

From about the eleventh century in southern Africa, as well as in most of central and east Africa, the Early Iron Age pottery tradition rapidly gave way to different forms typical of the Later Iron Age. These later forms remained virtually unaltered until recent times. Though the appearance of the new style pottery might suggest the arrival of a new immigrant population, examination of occupation sites indicates continuity of settlement and general culture. It is now considered most probable that the new style did not involve significant population movement but the spread of the practice of pottery-making by women rather than by the men who had practised the earlier styles.

Early Iron Age communities in the forested areas on the Natal coast appear to have been predominantly dependent on agriculture, whereas in the arid areas near the Kalahari the established pastoralist tradition remained predominant with agriculture playing a minor role. Subsequently, however, cattle-keeping was to become central to the cultural and political life of Bantu-speaking peoples throughout the area. In most of southern Africa the words used for sheep and cattle in Bantu languages are derived from Khoisan words which are not used by Bantu speakers north of the Zambezi. This suggests that the strong emphasis on cattle-keeping may have been derived from contact with Khoisan pastoralists. It is also possible that the development of hierarchically structured chiefdoms by southern African Bantu speakers may have been related to the heightened role of cattle in their culture. The possibilities offered by control of cattle for the extension of political power seem to have been important in the development of the first known large-scale socio-political organisations in southern Africa: at Toutswemogola near the Kalahari in Botswana from perhaps as early as 900 AD and at the twin sites of Bambandyanalo and Mapungubwe in the northern Transvaal between that date and 1250 AD. In both cases a substantial central settlement was surrounded at a distance by several smaller centres, each at the hub of a network of smaller villages or hamlets. Evidence of the bones of animals consumed at the main centres indicates that they could not have all been provided from herds kept locally, and some must have come from tribute from the smaller settlements where consumption was less extravagant. Finds of goods of east coast origin have been made at these sites, both of which pre-date the rise of Great Zimbabwe. Trade with the Indian Ocean coast was thus clearly established by the earlier years of the second millennium AD. It may have been critical to the rise of Bambandyanalo/Mapungubwe where there was a significant trade in gold, but is unlikely to have played a key role in the emergence of Toutswemogola where the evidence of trade goods is more sparse.

Whether the first iron-using communities came into southern Africa in one or two identifiable streams, or in a whole series of small groups over the whole front from the Indian Ocean to the Atlantic, is a matter of current controversy. The groups which settled in South Africa, however, either inherited or developed an essentially common culture, though recognisable linguistic and cultural subgroupings can be discerned.

The Nguni

Along the coastal land between the Drakensberg and the Indian Ocean lived a large number of communities speaking closely related languages to which the name Nguni has been given. These dialects are all mutually

Nguni settlement
(Ludwig Alberti's *Account of the Tribal
Life and Customs of the Xhosa in 1807*)

intelligible though there are considerable differences of pronunciation and
vocabulary between the northern and the southern branches of the group.
All Nguni make frequent use of the three click consonants derived from
the Khoisan. In addition to the common base of their languages, the Nguni
are distinguished from their neighbours by strict exogamy rules, forbidding marriage to any partner whose descent can be traced from a common
ancestor. Many also have a taboo against eating fish. It should be emphasised however that there were significant cultural variations between different communities within the group, and that the differences between them
and the neighbouring Sotho-speaking communities were neither sharp nor
unbridgeable. Where communities belonging to the different linguistic
sub-groupings were in contact they readily learnt and adopted one another's languages and customs. The apparent precision of the divisions
between sub-groupings, as well as the names given to them, are the product of European scholarship's demand for classification. To that extent they
are in fact inventions, although they do reflect real patterns of similarities.

The eastern coastlands on which the Nguni settled are the best-watered
areas in South Africa and also have some of the most fertile soil. This may
have encouraged their population to grow faster and to spread further south
than other groups. Before contact with the whites of the Cape Colony, the
Xhosa, the southernmost of the Nguni peoples, had already settled along
the coastal strip as far south as the Great Fish river. In the eighteenth century they were beginning to occupy the area immediately beyond it.
Nguni-speaking communities also expanded out of the coastal area and settled over wide areas of the Transvaal highveld as well as in the neighbourhood of modern Lesotho.

The abundance of springs and rivers in the territory they occupied may
help to explain why the Nguni lived in small family hamlets. At the southern limits of their settlement the Nguni peoples were settled alongside
Khoi groups. Their neighbours to the north were the Thonga peoples of
southern Mozambique. Their origin has as yet been inadequately studied

9

but they are probably fairly closely related to their Nguni neighbours.

Over the greater part of the central plateau of South Africa (the area now comprising Botswana, the Transvaal, the Bechuanaland districts of the Cape, the Orange Free State and Lesotho) the majority of the Bantu-speaking population belonged to the Sotho-Tswana group. These peoples speak a group of languages that are mutually intelligible with one another though not with Nguni languages. There are considerable differences in dialect, however particularly between those of the westernmost members of the group, who are called Tswana, and the rest who are known as the Sotho. Differences between the dialects of the northern and southern Sotho are also considerable. Unlike the Nguni, Sotho-Tswana marriage rules encourage marriage between cross-cousins, a relationship which the Nguni regard as incestuous.

The lands occupied by the Sotho-Tswana group are less well watered than those of the Nguni and this is particularly true of the areas near the Kalahari occupied by the Tswana communities. Such conditions may explain why the Tswana in particular lived in fairly large towns situated where permanent water was available. The Sotho lived in villages of a size falling between the large towns of the Tswana and the small hamlets of the Nguni. Before the nineteenth century, the Sotho-Tswana had not spread as far to the south as the Nguni. Their southernmost settlements had not yet reached the line of the Orange river where Khoisan communities persisted.

Though the main centres of Nguni and Sotho-Tswana settlement are clearly geographically distinct, the two language and culture groups were by no means cut off from contact with one another. Many Nguni-speaking communities crossed the escarpment in past times and migrated on to the Transvaal highveld, settling amongst Sotho-Tswana communities in many different parts of the area. These communities, known to the Sotho-Tswana as Ndebele or Koni, became acculturated to the language and customs of their Sotho neighbours to varying degrees. Further south another Nguni group known as the Zizi formed the first Bantu-speaking settlers in modern Lesotho. At the northern end of the eastern escarpment where it forms a less serious barrier to human movement, Sotho-speakers and Nguni communities lived alongside one another in the area of modern Swaziland.

Street in a Tswana town
(Keith Johnston: *Africa*, 1878)

Other Bantu-speaking groups

In the extreme north of the Transvaal, the Zoutpansberg area was occupied by a people known as the Venda who are believed to be closely related to the Shona of Zimbabwe. In northern Botswana some communities of Shona origin, notably the Kalaka, migrated from the north in relatively recent times and settled alongside Tswana communities. Beyond the Kalahari Desert in the northern part of modern Namibia two further groups settled. Their languages were distinct from any other in the Bantu-speaking groups of southern Africa. The Ovambo were the northernmost group; in the dryer lands to the south and in direct contact with Khoi groups were the Herero. Partly because of their dry surroundings and partly through contact with the Khoi, the Herero, like their Khoi neighbours, practised no agriculture.

Social, economic and political organisation

From the period when they were first encountered by the European observers, all the Bantu-speaking peoples in southern Africa except the Herero practised a mixed economy. The bulk of their diet was in most cases provided by agriculture. Sorghum and millet were the traditional staples, later supplemented and increasingly replaced by maize after it was introduced to Mozambique by the Portuguese. These cereals were also the chief ingredients of a thick beer which was the main alcoholic beverage. Surplus cereals were stored in storage pits for use during the dry season. Pumpkins, squashes and gourds were also grown and the women collected the leaves of a variety of wild plants as green vegetables. As agriculturalists, the Bantu-speaking people lived a more settled life in more substantial dwellings than the Khoi. Most Nguni peoples built low, dome-shaped huts of woven grass. The Sotho-Tswana, however, built substantial thatched round huts of mud. The lower parts of the walls of these houses were sometimes faced with stone as a protection against rain. Their cattle enclosures were also often built of dry-stone walling. Huts were kept free of dust by treating the floors with a polish made of earth and cow dung. The walls were frequently ornamented with geometric designs drawn in coloured clay.

Vital though agriculture was to the economy of most of the southern Bantu-speaking peoples, it had less importance in their eyes than cattle-keeping. Cattle not only provided milk, meat and skins but constituted a form of capital that could be accumulated and which would increase itself. Most important of all, cattle played an essential role in legitimating marriage. All the southern Bantu-speaking peoples had a patrilineal family system. Marriage therefore involved the transfer of a woman and her potential offspring from the household of her father to that of her husband. This required the transfer of cattle as bridewealth (*lobola*) to the family of her father. A man who possessed many cattle could thus marry several wives. They and their children would build up the economic and political strength of his household. Cattle thus had the highest social value. Their possession conferred status on the individual, the household or the wider community. Their care was the preserve of men while most agricultural work was done by the women. Cattle were essential for ritual sacrifices. The cattle enclosure was the centre of every settlement and often formed the public meeting place for political discussion and ceremonies. Cattle feature in most traditional stories and proverbs.

Detail from Nguni settlement, p. 9

The possession of cattle not only allowed their owner to acquire women as wives for himself or his sons, it also allowed him to acquire the loyalty of other males as clients. He could do this by loaning some of his cattle to a poorer man. The client would be allowed the use of the milk and sometimes a proportion of the offspring. This system (known to the Sotho as *mafisa*) may have been the means by which some lineage groups were able to build up followers to such an extent that the household was expanded into a chiefdom. Alternatively, the chiefly system may have originated in one or two centres such as Toutswemogola and Bambandyanalo/Mapungubwe and diffused from there. Whatever their origin, by the earliest times to which oral tradition or written evidence refers, all the southern Bantu-speaking peoples were organised in such hierarchically structured political communities.

The patrilineal system of the southern Bantu gave rise to groups of persons who could trace their descent from a common ancestor. Each such clan had a common name. Among the Nguni it was often the name of the remembered common ancestor. Among the Sotho-Tswana it was frequently the name of a totem animal. At the centre of each chiefdom there was usually a core of families belonging to such a clan. Their clan name was often used

11

Detail from Tswana
town, facing p. 1

for the chiefdom as a whole. Chiefdoms, however, usually contained many
families who belonged to other clans. Often these might be the majority.
Chiefdoms were in fact political rather than kinship organisations. Chiefs
were generally very willing to accept new members who had broken away
from other chiefdoms. They sometimes even incorporated Khoi or San,
either as full members or as client communities.

Though chiefdoms were essentially political organisations, their administrative structure was based on that of the royal family. This in turn was
based on the normal family pattern of a wealthy man. Such men would normally marry several wives. These wives and their children were each accommodated in separate homes, cultivated their own land and possessed household property. Normally some portion of the family head's cattle would be
allocated to each such subdivision of his total household. The households of
different wives were ranked in an order of seniority. Among the Nguni, the
houses of the first and second wife to be married were built on the right
and left respectively of the central cattle enclosure. In addition to the
'right-hand house' and 'left-hand house', some Nguni also recognised a
'great house'. This belonged to the senior wife. The eldest son of that house
would succeed his father as head of the family and would inherit the greater
part of his father's cattle and other property, but the eldest sons in the
other houses would become the heads of their respective households and
inherit possessions which went with them. The Sotho-Tswana did not clas-
sify households as 'right-hand' or 'left-hand' but wives and their households
still ranked in an order of seniority. The most senior was the 'great house'.

Chiefs' households differed from those of commoners mainly in the number of followers and servants attached to them and the size of the herds
allocated for their support. Sometimes each royal household would form a
significant hamlet in itself. The households were sometimes placed in different parts of the chiefdom and served as local centres of justice and
administration and rallying points in times of war. When a chief died, the
heirs in such subordinate houses would succeed to the headship and property of those houses and to the power of local authority and jurisdiction that
went with it. In this way each chiefdom was divided into a series of administrative divisions, some governed directly by the chief and others by other
senior members of the royal lineage who were themselves lesser chiefs.

In addition to this hierarchy of 'royals', chiefs and sub-chiefs employed
officers known as *induna*, who were appointed on a personal basis and normally chosen from commoner families. *Induna* could be employed in a variety of ways, as messengers, or as envoys to another chiefdom, as comman-
ders of military expeditions or as deputies who acted in the name of the
chief in hearing legal cases or exercising administrative authority. The system of multiple households, which involved frequent movement of the
chief from one to another, meant that an *induna* would often be left to act
in the chief's name during his absence.

Within each chiefdom, the authority of the chief was final. He represented the unity of the community and the living link with its ancestors.
Unlike his Khoi counterpart, the Bantu chief had supreme authority in
administration and law. Appeals would be brought to his court from those
of the other royals who administered divisions of the chiefdom's territory.
He was also the religious head of the community. Rituals of significance to
the whole community, such as the annual first-fruits ceremony, had to be

performed by him in person. The South African Bantu-speaking peoples did have ritual specialists, particularly witchcraft diviners whose job was to uncover those guilty of sorcery and accused of many ills and misfortunes. In some cases there were also specialist rain-makers though in others this was a function of the chief. Such ritual experts, however, exercised their functions under the authority of the chief. In cases of witchcraft the chief held the final authority to order the execution of those found guilty.

To support his position, and in addition to the produce of his own enlarged household's herd and gardens, a chief was entitled to regular tribute from his subjects and a variety of other payments. A family head seeking to join the following of a chief had to offer a gift of cattle. On the death of a man his family had to console the chief for the loss of a subject with a similar gift. Special levies of cattle were made in connection with the chief's marriage to his great wife. Fees were charged and fines levied in relation to judicial hearings. The cattle of those condemned for witchcraft were forfeited to the ruler.

Chiefs and their officers were thus able to take a significant part of the surplus produced by commoner households over and above their essential consumption needs. They could enjoy higher levels of consumption. They could also marry more wives and attract many personal clients, thus reinforcing their power.

Although the chief's authority was unlimited in theory, in practice it was fairly closely restricted. Within a chiefdom there was always potential rivalry between the chief and other important royals who held sway over parts of the chiefdom and the immediate loyalty of the population. Though rules of succession to the position of chief were quite precise, royalty was believed to belong to all close members of the royal family. Any of them could become a chief, and on occasions a technically junior heir would be chosen by general agreement where the senior heir was regarded as incompetent or otherwise unfit. A chief who angered his powerful relatives and a significant proportion of the population could therefore find himself faced with rebellion or with the secession of one or more segments of his community. To maintain his authority it was essential for him to retain the loyalty of the most powerful members of the community. Government was thus conducted by discussion aimed at the achievement of consensus.

On day-to-day matters the chief would consult with senior members of the royal family living at the household where he was staying, as well as with his *induna* and other personal advisers, who might be chosen on a variety of grounds. On more important occasions a wider council would assemble, including the subordinate chiefs responsible for the main divisions of the chiefdom. Among the Sotho-Tswana, where bigger settlements made this possible, matters of great importance to the community would be discussed in public meetings (*pitso*) open to all adult males. At these meetings anyone could express criticisms of the chief's behaviour and government. Apart from the danger of open rebellion or secession of a section of his following under the leadership of the rival royal, a chief who was unsuccessful or unpopular faced the danger of seeing his support simply melt away. Families who abandoned one chief would be readily accepted by another. Their new chief was in that way able to strengthen his following at the expense of his neighbour. For these reasons the South African Bantu-speaking peoples, while maintaining that 'a chief is a chief by birth', also believed that 'a chief is a chief by the people'.

The tension within chiefdoms between members of the royal lineage

A group of Nguni travelling (Detail from Ludwig Alberti's *Account of the Tribal Life and Customs of the Xhosa in 1807*)

13

frequently came into the open on the occasion of the death of a chief and the installation of his successor. The rules of succession themselves heightened the problem. The rightful heir to a chief was the eldest son of his great house. A chief, however, could only marry his great wife after he had succeeded to the chieftaincy. The bride-price cattle for the chief's bride would then be paid by the community as a whole. It was usually the case however that the chief had sons by earlier marriages who were considerably older than the official heir. The heir himself might also be too young to take over the chieftaincy, and in this event a regency would be necessary, through which the chiefdom could be ruled on his behalf; even when this was not so, this was often an ideal opportunity for a rival to snatch the chieftaincy for himself. The uncles and elder brothers of the official heir frequently resented the accession of a young and inexperienced man. Succession disputes were thus very common and frequently resulted in the secession of one or more sections of the community to form a new chiefdom.

This process of division was not just the consequence of tensions within the royal lineage. It was also a reaction to economic circumstances and opportunities. As the numbers of people and cattle grew, the problems of finding adequate grazing and agricultural land would increase until it was advantageous for a section of the population to break away and move with its cattle into new lands. So long as the South African Bantu-speaking peoples were expanding into extensive areas of thinly populated land this process of repeated fission accompanying increases of population was advantageous. It was important to be able to react quickly against attack from another Bantu group, or perhaps a Khoisan enemy. A large army was clearly impractical for dealing with a small skirmish or cattle raid; so under these circumstances political decentralisation into smaller units was more efficient than the development of large-scale centralised systems.

The process of chiefdom division was also an expression of tension between chiefs and commoners and afforded a channel for commoner ambitions. Chiefs naturally wanted to increase their wealth by raising the level of payments for hearing judicial cases etc., or by multiplying witchcraft accusations. The frequent splitting of chiefdoms and the opportunity to transfer loyalty from a grasping to a less demanding ruler limited the capacity of chiefs to exploit their subjects.

Where the economic conditions that favoured division of chiefdoms were altered, an opposite process – the expansion of a chiefdom into a kingdom – could take place. This might be the result of increased trade. It could also happen because there was no longer any easily accessible unclaimed territory within a particular area for breakaway groups to move into. It might take the form of the head of an original chiefdom successfully maintaining, or re-establishing, a measure of effective authority over breakaway sections. It might also arise through one chiefdom conquering others and reducing their once independent rulers to subordinate status in an expanded realm.

An important element in the political organisation of the southern Bantu-speaking communities, as well as in their social and cultural life, was the institution of manhood initiation. When they reached the age of manhood the youths underwent circumcision followed by a period of ritual seclusion during which they were instructed in the customs and tradition of the community and the behaviour expected of an adult man. Initiation ceremonies provided the most significant educational institution amongst the South African Bantu-speaking peoples. Their psychological impact was deep and lasting. Among the Sotho-Tswana, and possibly some Nguni chiefdoms also, initiation schools were organised by chiefs whenever they had a son of age to be initiated. At the end of their instruction, the initiates formed a permanent group or age-regiment, called a *butho*. Members of a *butho* were expected to fight together in times of war under the leadership of their age-mate prince and might also perform other corporate duties when called upon. In some cases the members of this *butho* would provide the initial core of followers for a young prince when first establishing a sub-chiefdomship (or even independent chiefdom) of his own. In some of the Sotho-Tswana communities, girls also underwent a form of initiation involving a period of seclusion and instruction, though no physical mutilation was practised. Female initiates would form a group under the leadership of their age-mate princess in the same way as the men but without the military functions of the male *butho*. Apart from its other roles, the initiation system helped to consolidate the authority of mature men over the youths. It may also have played some role in delaying the age at which young men could marry past the age of physical maturity thus making it easier for the older men to marry more than one wife.

As political communities split, an original chiefdom would give rise to a cluster of units all recognising their relationship to one another and the seniority of the original parent community but partially or entirely politically independent. Sometimes the original name (that of the founder chief among the Nguni and of a totem animal among the Sotho-Tswana) would be retained. On other occasions a split in the community would be followed by the adoption of a new name by the breakaway group. One example of this process can be seen among the southernmost of the Nguni-speaking peoples, the Xhosa. This group underwent a major split when on the accession of Gcaleka his father's 'right-hand' house seceded under Rharhabe. In the following generation the heir to the chieftainship, Ngqika, was still a boy on his father's death and a regency was established under his uncle Ndlambe. On Ngqika's coming of age, however, Ndlambe broke away. In 1800 he moved with his followers across the Great Fish river. The original Xhosa chiefdom thus gave rise to three main communities plus a number of smaller offshoots, all of which recognised their common origin and thought of themselves as Xhosa. Though they also all recognised the seniority of the rulers of the Gcaleka branch, they were largely independent and sometimes at war with one another.

Patterns of expansion

Nguni couple
(Ludwig Alberti's *Account of the Tribal Life and Customs of the Xhosa* in 1807)

In the Sotho-Tswana area the most striking example of this process is the multiplication of chieftaincies ruled by two chiefly lineages, the Kgatla and the Kwena. By the end of the eighteenth century they dominated much of the area of Sotho-Tswana occupation. The Kgatla appear to have originated as a chiefdom in the centre of the highveld, possibly not far from modern Pretoria. From there, breakaway sections spread over a wide area north of the Vaal and eastwards to the Drakensberg. The most successful of the Kgatla offshoots was a chiefdom known as the Pedi which established itself in the Leolu mountains of the eastern Transvaal. In the eighteenth century the Pedi built up a substantial kingdom there by bringing a number of other chiefdoms under their control.

The origin of the Kwena chiefdoms is believed to be a place called Rathateng near the junction of the Marico and Crocodile rivers. Expansion from the centre may have begun as early as AD 1500. By the end of the

15

eighteenth century chiefdoms calling themselves by this name had spread throughout the area of Sotho-Tswana occupation.

The expansion of the Kgatla and Kwena chiefdom clusters was the main historical development in the Sotho-Tswana area from the sixteenth to the late eighteenth century. It cannot as yet be adequately explained. Perhaps it was a matter of the expansion of lineages with many cattle into areas occupied by cattle-poor agriculturists. The cattle-rich lineages were able to acquire more wives, attract clients and expand more rapidly than others.

Whatever the causes, the expansion of these groups seems to have pushed some others into arid country on the fringes of cultivable land. Unable to sustain their political systems in the difficult economic conditions of the Kalahari, these groups became fragmented client communities within stronger Sotho-Tswana chiefdoms forming a major part of what came to be known as the Kgalagadi. Other groups whose chiefdoms were completely destroyed or who may perhaps never have developed a chieftaincy system formed a class of personal dependents known as the Lala.

Bantu-Khoisan relations

Relationships between the expanding Bantu-speaking peoples and the Khoisan populations took many forms. Conflict and the expulsion or elimination of one group by the other undoubtedly took place in some cases; but this was by no means the only pattern. San communities were sometimes absorbed as client communities in Bantu-speaking chiefdoms. Intermarriage was common and even chiefs might marry San wives. The Xhosa chief, Sandile, was the son of a San woman. Descendants of his lineage amputated the top joint of the little finger on the right hand in accordance with San custom as a sign of their royal descent. While Khoi groups sometimes became clients of Bantu-speaking chiefdoms, roles were sometimes reversed and Bantu-speaking communities came under Khoi rule. Intermarriage also gave rise to mixed communities. One such was encountered by the eighteenth-century traveller, H.J. Wikar, on the Orange river. There, so-called 'half people' provided a trade link between the Tswana communities to the north and the Khoi to the south. On the east coast a rather similarly mixed community, the Gqunukwebe, came into existence on the frontiers of contact between Khoi and Xhosa as the Khoi Gonaqua chiefdom broke up and was absorbed by the Xhosa.

The establishment & early development of the Cape Colony 2

The Cape of Good Hope first became known to Europe as a result of the exploring voyages undertaken by the Portuguese in the search for a sea route to India. Bartholomew Dias rounded the Cape in 1487. He first called it the Cape of Storms but the Portuguese ruler, thrilled that a way had been shown round the African continent, changed the name to Cape of Good Hope. After Vasco da Gama's successful voyage to India in 1497–9 it lay on the main route of European commerce with the East. The Portuguese, however, first set up a staging post on the island of St Helena. Then they established their main base in east Africa on the island of Mozambique. Subsidiary settlements were founded at Inhambane and Quilimane on the Mozambique coastline and at Sena and Tete on the Zambezi. The Cape of Good Hope remained relatively neglected. It gained an evil reputation in Portuguese eyes when in 1510 the viceroy, Francisco de Almeida, and a number of his companions, returning from India, were killed by Khoi whom they had robbed in the course of a foraging expedition from Table Bay.

The first European settlements
In the early seventeenth century the Cape came to be used as a regular watering place by English and Dutch vessels on the way to and from the Indies. Letters were frequently left for the next fleet under what came to be

Table Bay and Table Mountain by an unknown artist

17

called 'post-office stones'. In 1620, officers of the English East India Company formally claimed possession of Saldanha Bay in the name of King James, but the claim was not followed up. Eventually, the directorate of the Dutch East India Company decided that it was a more favourable refreshment station than their existing post at St Helena. On 6 April 1652 Jan van Riebeeck arrived with three vessels, the *Goede Hoop*, *Dromedaris* and *Reiger*, to set up the new post. The enterprise was intended to be a very limited one. A small fort was to be built, supplies of fresh water protected and a garden laid out to provide fresh vegetables for the crews of the Company's ships to help reduce the losses from scurvy. Meat supplies were to be obtained by barter from the surrounding Khoi population. The original settlement was tiny and made up exclusively of the Company's servants. It was confined to the small peninsula on which Table Mountain stands. When difficulties developed with the neighbouring Khoi, an attempt was made to surround the entire settlement with a hedge, reinforced by a series of look-out posts. A plan to dig a canal through the Cape flats in order to turn the little settlement into an island was contemplated.

Farming undertaken by full-time employees of the Company soon proved inefficient and expensive, and on van Riebeeck's suggestion it was decided to try the experiment of establishing a number of settlers on farms of their own. They would grow crops and supply the Company's needs for their own profit. Company servants were therefore offered the opportunity to gain release from their contracts by taking up plots of land as free burghers or citizens. They were to concentrate on growing wheat, which the Company needed for supplying bread to the fleets and the garrison. They were also to supply slaughter stock to the Company and to be enrolled in a burgher militia.

There were twelve first free burghers who were settled on small farms along the Liesbeeck river in April 1657. Over the next few years the numbers grew slowly as more of the Company's servants took their freedom. When van Riebeeck left the colony in 1662 to take up a new post as commander at Malacca, the free burghers numbered forty, with fifteen women and about twenty children.

Small though these numbers were at first, the decision to establish free burghers on farms at the Cape was of tremendous importance for the future. It meant the beginnings of a community of permanent settlers rather than of temporarily resident expatriates. As this community increased, both naturally and with the establishment of more settlers, it became the main element in the white population at the Cape. It soon developed a growing sense of its own identity and an awareness of interests different from those of the Company and its servants. Indeed this tendency became apparent almost as soon as the settlers' community was born. On 23 December 1658, a deputation of fourteen white settlers presented a petition to van Riebeeck, denouncing the oppression they claimed to be suffering under the Company. Van Riebeeck took a tough line with the petitioners, who soon gave way and offered apologies.

For twenty years after the departure of van Riebeeck in 1660, the settler community continued to grow very slowly. By 1679 the number of freemen had only grown to 87, of whom 55 were married, and there were 114 children. Slow though the population growth of the Cape community was, it had already expanded its territory beyond the limits of the Cape peninsula.

A Boer outspan in the Karroo, about 1830 by C.D. Bell

In 1672 the Company took possession of Hottentots Holland, False Bay and Saldanha Bay in order to provide land for Company cattle stations and farming, but with the intention of settling freemen in the area also. In 1679, two burghers were granted permission to take possession of land in the Tygerberg area. The same year two others were granted a three-year lease of land on the Eerste river for sheep grazing. The beginnings of the system under which grazing farms were granted on loan had been established.

The drive towards colonisation

A new phase in the development of the colony began in 1679 with the arrival of a new commander, Simon van der Stel. A recent, bitter war against France had made the Dutch East India Company very conscious of the strategic importance of its station at the Cape. It sought to increase the number of free burghers to provide a strengthened burgher militia. Van der Stel set about the task vigorously and efficiently, encouraging so many of the Company's servants to take their freedom at the Cape that he had to be warned against unduly reducing the crews of the Company's ships. His enthusiasm earned him the title 'second founder of the Cape'.

Up to this time the males in the white community had always far outnumbered the females. Van der Stel urged the Company to take active measures to send out more young women to the Cape. Some orphan girls were despatched and the balance of the sexes in the white population gradually began to even out.

The population of the Cape white community was already made up of a number of different nationalities, mainly German and Dutch, with the Germans outnumbering the Dutch. The Dutch language was, however, used by all. In 1688, a new element was added with the arrival of a party of 164 French-speaking settlers; these were French and Belgian Huguenots (Calvinist Protestants) who had taken refuge from religious persecution in Holland and had been despatched to settle at the Cape. The Huguenots constituted about one-sixth of the then white population. They brought skills in cultivating vines which helped to lay the basis for the Cape wine industry. The use of French was discouraged and the Huguenots were

19

encouraged to adopt Dutch and integrate with the rest of the community. This was made easier because as Calvinists the newcomers could be absorbed by the Dutch Reformed Church. This was the official Church of the colony, to which the overwhelming majority of the Dutch and German settlers belonged. Through its rigid puritanical doctrines, it undoubtedly played a major role in shaping the character and outlook of the growing free burgher populations.

Even before the Huguenots arrived, van der Stel had taken steps to increase the agricultural production of the Cape and expand the area of settlement. A village named Stellenbosch was laid out on the mainland and settlers were granted as much land as they could cultivate in the surrounding countryside. Under van der Stel the pattern of local government was also established. The government of the colony as a whole was firmly in the hands of the commander (who after 1691 was elevated to the rank of Governor). He exercised his authority with a Council of Policy which was dominated by officials; however, it also included two burgher councillors who were chosen by the commander from a list of four drawn up by the burghers. Serious legal cases were heard by the High Court of Justice where the two burgher councillors sat together with a majority of officials. Less important cases were decided by a court of petty cases consisting of two officials and two burghers. For the local administration of Stellenbosch and the surrounding district, a servant of the Company was appointed as magistrate (*landdrost*) to be assisted by a board of four burgher councillors (*heemraden*). Regulations governing militia were tightened up and a boys' brigade was established for boys under the age of sixteen. Target practice for the militia was held annually and became a central part of the annual fair at Stellenbosch. To improve military organisation van der Stel in 1693 appointed a local burgher as *veldwachter* to assist the *landdrost* and keep an eye on illicit cattle barter. This office (later known as *veldkornet*) came to play a crucial part in settler military and political organisation. These officers, appointed from, and in effect often elected by, a group of neighbouring farmers, had responsibility for ensuring that official policy was carried out in their area, for reporting local lawbreakers and for mobilising the men of the neighbourhood group for militia duty. The neighbourhood group with the *veldkornet* as its leader was to become the basic unit of white settler political life.

After the governorship of van der Stel, experiments in assisted immigration came to an end. Some Company servants still took their freedom at the Cape from time to time, but for the most part the community grew by natural increase. Already the growth of the community, the expansion of agricultural production and the development of a sense of local identity were generating problems; these came into the open during the governorship of Simon's son, Willem Adriaan van der Stel, who took over office from his father in January 1699.

The main source of the trouble was competition between the settlers and the senior Company officials for the supply of the limited market at the Cape. Willem Adriaan van der Stel, like his father before him, succeeded in personally obtaining a substantial grant of land on which he built up the estate of Vergelegen. Other senior officials, including the captain of the garrison, also acquired substantial properties. In 1705 conflict reached a

Adriaan van der Stel's estate at
Vergelegen
from a sketch by W.A. van der Stel

A plan of the Vergelegen estate
from *Contra Deductie*, 1711

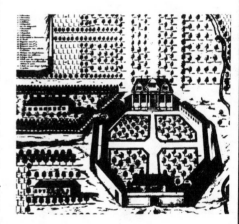

climax when the Governor, acting on instructions from Holland, cancelled the lease which had given the relatively wealthy cattle farmer Henning Hüsing the sole right to supply the Company with meat and to operate a butchery in the colony. The right to operate butcheries was to be leased to four contractors, one of whom must have cattle of his own. Hüsing and his associate Adam Tas organised a movement of protest against the cancellation. The Governor was accused of developing a massive estate with the aid of Company labour and of giving the meat contract to a group of his personal friends. He was also accused of interfering with the wine trade by buying up the wine of the burghers and selling it as his own; in short, of building up a virtual monopoly in certain supplies. The protesters drew up a document which was smuggled on to a ship bound for Holland.

The Directors of the Dutch East India Company, the Council of Seventeen, alarmed at the evidence of disaffection in the colony, acted against the Governor. He was recalled and his estate at Vergelegen was broken up and sold. By this time the settler community in the Cape had begun to think of itself as a community distinct from the Dutch East India Company and its interests. Some settlers now began openly to adopt the name *Afrikaner* to distinguish themselves from the expatriate servants of the Company and subsequently the name came to apply to all white South Africans who were native speakers of Afrikaans, a language that evolved from the Dutch spoken at the Cape. The conflict between settlers and Company also highlighted the growing problems arising from increasing competition to supply a restricted market.

When the first free burghers settled at the Cape it was thought that they would farm very much as peasant farmers did in Europe, mainly employing their own labour. Provision was made for artisans to take their freedom in order to ply their trade for colonists and steps were also taken to provide a certain number of white labourers to assist the farmers. In this way, the freemen were allowed to have the services of some of the Company's

21

employees when they were not needed for Company work and some Company servants were encouraged to take their freedom in order to serve as full-time labourers on the land of established burghers. In 1661, the thirty-one freemen of the colony had forty-two labourers working for them. The services of such hired European workers were, however, soon supplemented and increasingly overtaken by those of slaves.

The introduction of slave labour: expansion in farming

The first substantial batch of slaves was acquired in 1658. Some came from the Dutch East Indies. Many of these were employed as skilled artisans. Along with a number of princes and other important persons from Indonesia brought to the Cape as state prisoners or hostages, they formed the nucleus of the Cape Malay community. Others came from east Africa. By the time van Riebeeck left the Cape the slaves outnumbered the freemen. In 1717 the increasing number of slaves and the effects of slave labour on the character and morale of the colony led the commander of the garrison, Captain Chavonnes, brother to Governor Chavonnes, to have the question of reliance on slave labour and the possibility of its abolition discussed by the Council of Policy. In spite of the captain's arguments in favour of free European labour the decision went against him and the free importation of slaves was adopted as official policy.

At an early stage in the development of the colony, some Khoi began to enter the employment of the freemen. Some did so because they had been deprived of their lands and cattle. Others were attracted by the prospects of material reward. They were naturally well suited to stock herding and their employers often supplied them with firearms to defend the stock.

The continued importation of slaves and the expansion of the non-white labour force available to the white settlers prevented the development of a white labouring class. As visitors to the Cape noticed, it led first to an increasing view that menial labour was beneath the dignity of a white man and, secondly, to a pattern of class distinction which corresponded closely to differences of colour. The growth of the labour force also made possible the expansion of farming enterprises; differences in wealth amongst the colonists increased accordingly. Up to the time of Simon van der Stel's governorship there had been little variation in wealth amongst the freemen; but by the time his son took over, a few individuals like Hüsing and Tas were relatively rich and able to live lives of considerable luxury. Farming in the wheat and wine-growing areas of the western Cape began to involve considerable capital investment. The rude cottages of the first freemen gave way to substantial and attractive houses and in the eighteenth century these were frequently decorated with Dutch gables.

The expansion of agricultural activity also brought about growth in the towns. Cape Town and the peninsula gained a substantial population of freemen. They included innkeepers and lodging-house keepers, shopkeepers and urban property-owners. Both Company officials and prosperous burgher farmers invested in town properties. Among the urban population there developed an elite made up of burgher councillors, militia officers and members of various boards. This group increasingly formed a common social circle with the Company's senior officials. By the middle of the eighteenth century all the members of the Council of Policy were married to the daughters of burghers.

Cape Town and the grape-growing and grain-farming districts of the western Cape contained the majority of the white population. This comparatively stable society did not provide the most dynamic element in the expansion and evolution of the South African white community but its importance in that process was nevertheless fundamental.

The western Cape generally was the main reservoir of white population, continually providing new recruits to the more far-flung areas. It was also the economic base of the white colony. The economic welfare and very survival of the settlers in the ever-expanding areas in the interior depended on the market provided by the denser population of Cape Town and the western Cape, the garrison, the ships calling at the port and the limited export market they provided. The western Cape was also the cultural base of white society. The attractions of its material standards and its life style influenced even the most remote settlers and as a result prevented their integration with the indigenous societies around them. The expansion of the frontier changed the scale and character of the white settlement. At the same time, however, the nature of frontier society and the way race relations developed in those areas were profoundly influenced by the culture of the core area around the Cape.

The economic opportunities provided by wheat farming and wine production in the western Cape, and the businesses of the city itself, were from an early date inadequate for the needs of the growing Cape settler community. The market for agricultural produce at the Cape was a very restricted one, subject to frequent oversupply. The position was made worse by competition between the burghers and senior Company officials. As wheat farming and wine production came to involve increasing investment in slaves and farming equipment, it became more and more difficult for anyone with little or no capital to establish himself. As D.G. van Reenen wrote in 1803:

At present a young man starting to farm cannot expect to make a living on a wine or wheat farm, however hard-working and careful he may be. The high rate of interest and the costliness of all requisites absorb his entire profit. He drudges, toils and moils himself nearly to death but makes no progress whatever (van Reenen, 1937, pp. 139, 141).

The problem was not new; as early as 1717 Governor Chavonnes had reported against further assisted immigration on the grounds that the agricultural conditions and the problems of transporting goods to market made it impossible for a newcomer to make a reasonable living. The importation of slaves and the absorption of Khoi into the labour force ruled out the development of a white labouring class, and business opportunities in Cape Town could not provide openings for more than a small proportion of the growing white population.

Alternatives to agrarian farming From a very early date, therefore, some burghers had sought other ways of living by ivory hunting, the barter trade with Khoi and, most popularly, stock raising in the interior.

The Company itself had at first hoped to secure the meat supplies it needed by barter with the Khoi. It long continued to try to maintain a monopoly of that trade by pushing trading expeditions far into the interior. It was never able, however, to obtain adequate and regular supplies from the Khoi since their society was based on the permanent ownership of cattle and was not organised for market production. Khoi groups were reluctant to part with more than a small proportion of their animals. When they were persuaded to do so and sales outstripped the rate of natural increase, their society collapsed fairly quickly. The impoverished Khoi then either entered colonial society as farm workers or were driven to a hunting and gathering existence similar to that of the San. The Company and the white community at the Cape as a whole was forced to rely to an ever increasing extent on the freemen for its meat supplies.

From the point of view of the freemen, stock raising in the interior offered many advantages. The initial stock could often be obtained by barter with the Khoi. Khoi herders could be employed to look after it in place of expensive slaves. The rancher could live very largely from the produce of hunting and from his flocks and herds. Away from the relatively sophisticated life of the western Cape, his expenses on clothing, furniture, and luxury items could be greatly reduced. His animals could walk to market instead of requiring the expensive transport needed for agricultural produce.

Repeated decrees prohibiting private barter with the indigenous peoples therefore had no effect. Burghers continued slipping away on hunting trips and bartering expeditions into the interior and then settling as cattle farmers. They would settle in ones and twos alongside Khoi groups at first. Later, as more freemen arrived, competition for grazing land developed. The Khoi would be deprived of their land and either be absorbed as cattle herders or forced to withdraw further into the interior. As I. Mentzel, a German who worked at the Cape from 1732 to 1741, put it:

The Hottentots are, as it were, the bloodhounds who smell out the most fertile lands. When their kraals are discovered in such places several European or Afrikanders soon appear and by gifts, flattery and other forms of cajolery wheedle the Hottentots into granting permission for them to settle alongside. But as soon as the pasture land becomes too scanty for the cattle of these newcomers and the Hottentots, the latter are induced by trifling gifts to withdraw and travel further inland (Mentzel, 1921, Vol. 1, p. 36).

The loan farms system As areas nearer the Cape filled up with settlers, the rough wattle-and-daub huts of the pioneer days began to give way to more substantial farmhouses. Fruit trees were planted and a certain amount of grain production was undertaken alongside cattle ranching. Meanwhile the interior continued to be opened up by traders, and farmers followed. By 1714 this process had become so firmly established that the Company decided to take a share of the benefits itself by demanding rents for the farms which freemen staked out for themselves in the interior. The system adopted was to register cattle runs in the interior as loan farms, that is to say on lease from the Company at a low annual rental. The occupier of such a loan farm had no legal right to sell it or pass it on to his heirs. He only had a right to any buildings he had constructed or other improvements he had made to the farm. In practice, however, the Company lacked the means to enforce this system and farms were freely bought and sold. In the more outlying areas many farms remained unregistered and paid no rent at all.

Cattle and sheep raising in the relatively dry conditions of the veld required large areas of land. The normal area of a loan farm came to be fixed by riding a horse at walking pace for half an hour in each of the main compass directions from a central point. The circumference of a circle passing through the four points thus marked would then form the boundary of the farm. With each ranching family occupying at least one such farm of approximately 2500 ha, and with a high rate of natural increase amongst the white population, the frontiers of settlement expanded very rapidly, absorbing part of the indigenous population as farm servants and driving the rest further still into the hinterland.

This process, which got under way in the late seventeenth century and in the eighteenth century when the colony was in contact with only the Khoi and San communities, was to continue through most of the nineteenth century. Its importance as a major dynamic element in South African history only lessened when the growth of mining and industry began to offer significant economic alternatives to the sons of white farmers. Although the wandering cattle farmer (*trek boer*) might move far into the interior there were limits set by his need to sell some of his stock at a profit. His economic independence was only relative. He had to be able to buy some products such as gunpowder and lead to be able to survive at all. The nearer frontier farmers came to the geographical limits of economic viability the less they were able to maintain the European life style of the settled districts of the Cape and the closer they would come in housing, clothing and even culture and social relationships to the African peoples amongst whom they lived. At and beyond these limits they would have to become part of an indigenous society to survive at all. The expansion of the frontier thus depended on the development of the economy of the settled areas which in turn depended on the fortunes of the Company and of the economy of Europe in general. The pace of the expansion can be shown to have varied in close correspondence to periods of prosperity and adversity. The distance over which a product would be profitably taken to market depended on the nature of the product. Ivory was relatively highly priced in relation to weight, and the ivory hunters' and traders' frontier advanced well in front of the cattle farmers' frontier.

Colonial expansion in the eighteenth century

The rate at which the Cape settlement expanded in the eighteenth century was increased by the arid nature of the immediate hinterland. To the north-west and north, farms could only be established where springs, often fed by nearby hills or river courses, provided permanent water supplies. In the whole large area of the *karroo* stretching out to the east behind the coastal ranges, absence of permanent water made settlement impossible. Farmers used the area for seasonal grazing during the period when rainwater, collected in shallow pans and depressions, provided drinking water for their animals. From the Cape, stock farmers spread out to the north-west and north, soon occupying possible sites for farms over a vast area.

Settlement in the east

The largest number of settlers moved eastward along the line of greatest rainfall. They kept along the coast at first. Then, anxious to avoid conflict with the Xhosa on the eastern coastlands, they turned inland, and crossed the *karroo*. Then, as the expansion of settlement in the north-east met increased resistance from San and Khoi, the settlers turned back to the lands nearer the coast.

In 1778, Governor van Plettenberg set out on an official expedition to inspect the eastern and north-eastern districts. Near the coast he found farmers settled alongside Xhosa throughout the area between the Sundays river and the lower course of the Great Fish river known as the *zuurveld* (sour grazing). The Governor entered into discussions with some chiefs living near the Great Fish river and believed he had received their agreement to that river becoming the boundary between the races. The official frontier of the colony was thus extended to the entire course of the Great Fish. The agreement, however, had no effect on the Gqunukwebe Xhosa living on the *zuurveld*. In traditional law no chief had the right to give away the land of his people in this fashion, and in any case the chiefs with whom the Governor talked were not the leaders of the people settled in the *zuurveld* and had no authority over them.

In the north-east the Governor reached the upper valley of the Zeekoe river and established a beacon there, not far from the present town of Colesberg. The whole long frontier stretching westward to the Atlantic coast however was left undefined. A second magistracy was established at the new village of Swellendam in 1747. No further magistratures were created until 1785, and the area of the Swellendam and Stellenbosch districts grew far too large for the *landdrost* to exercise any effective control over the more distant settlers.

Khoisan reactions to the European presence

The rapid expansion of the colony was made easier by the fact that the immediate hinterland of the Cape was occupied by Khoi and San. The relatively sparse population of these peoples could offer only limited resistance to white expansion in its early stages. The presence of the Khoi, moreover, meant the possibility of acquiring stock and labour relatively cheaply; without this such rapid expansion would have been impossible.

Khoi groups generally adopted a friendly attitude to the first whites they met. They saw them as a source of valuable trade goods and were happy to barter with them. They tried to absorb them into their community in the same way as they often absorbed Khoi from other chiefdoms or, more occasionally, families of Bantu-speakers. The white stranger would thus be allowed to stay with the Khoi and encouraged to marry a Khoi woman. Individual whites sometimes made very acceptable members of the Khoi communities but once others came to join them they would often turn on

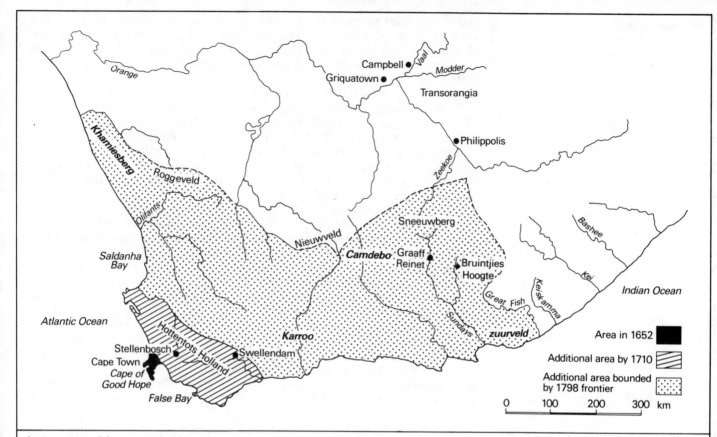

2.1 Expansion of the Cape Colony: approximate areas 1652, 1710 and the 1798 frontier

Legend: Area in 1652 / Additional area by 1710 / Additional area bounded by 1798 frontier

Scale: 0 100 200 300 km

their original hosts and drive them from their land.

As they began to realise what was happening, Khoi attitudes changed. They would reject invitations to barter and avoid contacts with whites. Faced with expropriation they would fight to save their lands and livelihood. Because their own numbers were small and the whites had superior weapons the Khoi did not attempt mass attacks on white settlements. Instead they adopted guerrilla tactics. These tactics could be very effective. Unfortunately for the Khoi, however, the fact that they were divided into many independent chiefdoms meant that they could not combine against the whites on a large scale. Each chiefdom acted separately and while one was in conflict with the settlers others would be on friendly, trading terms.

The Khoi first resorted to war soon after the establishment of the first free burghers along the Liesbeeck river in 1657. Khoi leaders asked where they were to go if the settlers occupied the land where their encampment was. In the absence of a satisfactory answer, intermittent raids and punitive expeditions continued until peace was made in April 1660. The Khoi insisted that the newcomers had been taking more and more Khoi land, and forcefully challenged the settlers. If the land was no longer big enough for both peoples, who should give way, they enquired, the rightful owners, or the foreign intruders? They were bluntly told, however, they had now lost the land on account of the war and that the whites intended to keep it.

Shortly after the Company occupied Hottentots Holland (the first significant expansion of the colony out of the Cape peninsula) the Khoi took up arms again in 1672. The Khoi chief Gonema of the Gorona sub-chiefdom of the Cochoqua kept up the struggle until 1677, when he too made peace and was forced to accept the expansion of the white settlement.

From then on, Khoi resistance was severely weakened by the growing collapse of their society resulting from involvment in trade with the colony. They were also weakened by repeated epidemics of smallpox which drastically reduced their population. In 1717 the *landdrost* of Stellenbosch wrote that there were no more than isolated Khoi families for two or three hundred miles around the Cape. As Khoi society weakened, remaining Khoi chiefs often became clients of the colony, and were awarded staffs of office by the Company's officials.

While many Khoi were absorbed peacefully into the colony's labour force or retired into the interior, without a fight, some who had lost all of their cattle adopted the hunting and gathering life of the San and kept up the resistance struggle by continuing to raid the advancing colonists.

The San, whose way of life involved little contact with other peoples, did not engage in trade with the settlers to the same extent as the Khoi and they were not so readily drawn into economic and cultural dependence on the colony. They fiercely resisted intrusion on their hunting lands, killing herdsmen and raiding stock. In retaliation the colony waged a war of extermination against them and those Khoi groups who similarly raided the settlers' stock. Expedition after expedition went out, killing large numbers. Prisoners were brought to the Cape to endure a life-long servitude in the futile hope of setting an example to the raiders. Children were seized to be raised as apprentices and form a useful addition to the settlers' labour force.

Development of commandos

Military expeditions against Khoi or San were at first made up of the company's regular forces supported by members of the burgher militia in a subordinate role. As the farmers expanded further into the interior, however, conflict with San and Khoi took place on frequent small-scale expeditions. In this kind of situation, the burgher militia began to play the more important part. In 1715 approval was officially given for the first time to members of the burgher militia of Drakenstein to undertake a campaign on their own against San and Khoi who had been raiding the area. Thereafter battles were increasingly fought by burgher commandos acting on their own.

Such commandos were, in theory at least, summoned on the authority of the *landdrost*. The *veldkornets* would then summon the men of their localities to come forward with their horses and guns. The men of one or two such areas might provide enough strength for the matter in hand. Where the threat was more serious two or more whole districts might even put their forces together to form a grand commando. In addition to serving themselves, farmers usually brought mounted and armed Khoi servants with them as auxiliaries. They proved brave and skilful fighters in the service of their masters. According to some accounts, they were often put in the front line when dangerous fighting was imminent.

The commando system was both effective and flexible in military terms but it was also very difficult to keep under official control. As farmers became accustomed to commando service it was an easy matter for private individuals to organise commandos of their own or even for the commandos to turn against the officials of the Company's government.

As the frontiers of settlement pressed outwards to the Roggeveld, Nieuweveld and Sneeuwbergen ranges in the latter part of the eighteenth century, San and Khoi resistance in the northern and north-eastern frontier areas became more desperate. Commando after commando failed to put an end to their raids. By the end of the century it was becoming increasingly difficult to persuade any but the farmers immediately involved in a given area to serve on expeditions. For some time white advance in these areas was checked and in some districts settlers were forced to abandon land they had already occupied.

In the east coast areas the expansion of the settlers saw the breaking up of the Khoi communities lying between them and the Xhosa. In the early days of the colony these Khoi groups had adopted the role of middlemen in trade between the colony and the Xhosa chiefdoms. As hunting and trading parties of colonists themselves pushed right through the area of Khoi settlement and entered the lands settled by the Xhosa, however, the Khoi lost their advantage. As they lost their cattle in trade with the settlers and were increasingly squeezed from their grazing lands, many became farm servants. Others, however, formed roving bands of raiders. Some of these accepted the leadership of a runaway slave named Ruyter and for a brief period dominated the *zuurveld*.

In the area between the Fish and Keiskamma rivers the remaining Khoi chiefdom, the Gonaqua, was absorbed by the Xhosa. This gave rise to the half-Khoi, half-Xhosa chiefdom of the Gqunukwebe. When Governor van Plettenberg made his tour of the frontier districts in 1778 the Khoi had been practically wiped out as an independent group in the eastern frontier areas. Settlers were interspersed with Xhosa in the *zuurveld* and on the upper reaches of the Great Fish river.

Along the northern frontier, where the overall population was much more sparse, the situation was more complex. Between 1700 and 1750 groups of Khoi, retreating before the advancing settlers, filtered into the lower and middle valley of the Orange river and settled alongside others already living there. From this area, the Khoi, known as Kora (or Korana), established contact with the southernmost of the Sotho-Tswana peoples, a group of chiefdoms that had been brought under the temporary rule of the Rolong in the reign of their great chief Tau (*c*. 1700–60). Fighting between the two peoples took place but the military balance remained fairly equal until the death of Tau, who was killed in conflict with the Kora. The Rolong then moved north to settle around the headwaters of the Molopo river, allowing client chiefdoms of the Tlhaping and Tlharo to establish their independence. After the death of Tau's successor, Ratlou, the Rolong themselves split up into five separate chiefdoms. In this more fluid situation, the Kora were able to establish themselves firmly around the confluence of the Orange and Vaal rivers and then move up the Vaal. By the end of the century they were settled around the junction of the Vaal and the Harts.

The northward expansion of the Kora was helped by the activities of Jan Bloem, a German deserter from the Company's service. He succeeded in uniting several Kora clans under his leadership. He led them on a long series of raids against Tlhaping, Tlharo and Rolong, selling captured cattle and receiving supplies of gunpowder and bullets through associates in the colony. He was defeated at last in an ambitious expedition in which he led Kora, Tlhaping and Rolong against the Ngwaketsi. He died soon after this failure but was succeeded by his son Jan Bloem II, who for some time played a prominent part in the history of Transorangia, the area between the Orange and Vaal rivers west of the Drakensberg.

Racial attitudes at the Cape

By the last years of the eighteenth century, when the Kora were settling around the valley of the Harts and its junction with the Vaal, their position on the middle Orange and Vaal/Orange confluence was being taken by new arrivals and those groups of mixed descent who were moving out of the colony in reaction to increasing racial discrimination and prejudice against them.

When the colony was first established there can be little doubt that the Company's servants brought with them some of the attitudes of superiority towards persons of darker skin colour that were developing in Europe as a result of the expansion of European commerce and the growth of the slave trade. Initial contacts with the Khoi produced a most unfavourable reaction from the whites. Open discrimination on grounds of race alone was not, however, the policy of the Company. Van Riebeeck raised an orphan Khoi girl, Eve, in his home. In 1664 she married Pieter van Meerhoff, the surgeon of the settlement, and as a sign of Company approval he was given promotion and a marriage feast in the then Commander's home. Simon van der Stel, most prominent of the colony's early Governors, was himself of mixed descent. As white men long outnumbered white women in the colony, sexual relationships between persons of different race were very common. Three-quarters of the children born to slave women at the Cape up to 1671 were of mixed descent.

This new generation had little difficulty in being absorbed into white society at first. In 1685 Commissioner van Rheede decreed that slaves of mixed descent should automatically acquire their freedom when they became adult. Not only persons of mixed descent but freed slaves without European blood, known as free blacks, at first enjoyed full citizens' rights. As late as 1752, Governor Ryk Tulbagh proclaimed that free blacks should enjoy the same rights and privileges as burghers. By this time, however, the tendency for the whites to convert themselves into a relatively closed racial elite was already well advanced. The continued importation of slaves prevented the development of a white labouring class and this in turn encouraged whites to believe that dark-skinned peoples were inherently inferior. Conflict with Khoi and San which led to attempts to exterminate the San like vermin undoubtedly helped to lower the value of non-European lives in white eyes.

Even more important was the movement towards an even balance of the sexes in white society, begun by Simon van der Stel's vigorous efforts. White women had a strong interest in maintaining the elite status of their own children and denying equal rights and privileges to persons of mixed descent. As early as 1685 Commander van Rheede prohibited marriages between Europeans and freed slaves without European blood even if they were Christian. Church records show that such marriages continued at the rate of about 10 per cent of white marriages registered down to the end of the eighteenth century. By this time, however, the children of mixed unions were normally excluded from white society and increasingly confined to inferior roles. At the same time Khoi and other free non-whites were in practice increasingly denied legal rights and effectively reduced to a position not far from slavery. By the early nineteenth century, whites at the Cape referred to their coloured servants as *skepsels*, meaning living instruments rather than persons entitled to full human rights. As racist attitudes at the Cape hardened, persons of mixed descent, Khoi who had adopted European culture and free blacks found fewer and fewer opportunities open to them.

It was persons of these various origins who made up the groups known as Bastards (Basters) and Orlams. The Bastards were mainly persons of mixed descent who at one time would have been absorbed in the white community. It was, however, as much an economic and cultural category as a racial one and included the economically most advanced of the non-white population at the Cape. Among these were persons who acted as supervisors of other servants and were the confidential employees of their masters. Sometimes these were treated almost as members of the white family. The group also included Khoi, free blacks and persons of mixed descent who had succeeded in acquiring property and establishing themselves as farmers in their own right. The name Orlam was sometimes applied to persons who could also be known as Bastard but was a more general name for Khoi and Coloured persons generally who spoke Dutch and practised a largely European way of life.

In the early eighteenth century it was not uncommon for Bastards to own farms in the colony, but with the growth of competition for land and colour prejudice they came under increasing pressure from their white neighbours and were either absorbed into the Coloured servant class or moved to the fringes of settlement where it was still possible to maintain themselves in independence. From about 1750 the Khamiesberg in the extreme north-west of the colony became the main area of settlement of independent Bastard farmers, some of whom had substantial followings of servants and clients. After about 1780, increasing competition from whites in this area led to the migration of a number of Bastard families to the middle valley of the Orange. Among these were the Kok and Barends families. Shortly before 1800, another group appeared under the leadership of Klaas Afrikaner and his son Jager. The Afrikaner family were of mixed Khoi and San descent and were employed by a white frontiersman named Pienaar, who sent them on raiding expeditions beyond the Orange. In their absence he was believed to have interfered with their wives and mistreated their children. On their return a quarrel took place. Pienaar was killed and the Afrikaner family fled to the middle Orange. Whites now persuaded the Barends family to attack him but Afrikaner drove them off. Barends then moved further up the valley towards the confluence of the Orange and the Vaal.

Missionaries of the London Missionary Society began work amongst these families in 1802. The Kok family, who had also come to blows with Afrikaner, joined forces with the Barends. The two groups under missionary influence took the name Griqua in place of Bastard and established a state around the confluence of the Orange and the Vaal with its capital at

Griquatown. Jager Afrikaner, who took over leadership from his father soon after their arrival on the Orange, built up a substantial following of Khoi and San, beat off all attacks and raided widely in the colony as well as across the Orange.

Racial attitudes in the interior

The expansion of the colony and the movement of farmers into the hinterland influenced the growth of racial attitudes. In the interior, the relationship between a farmer and his dependants came to fall somewhere between that of employer and employees, and that of a chief and his followers. The more isolated the farmer was in the interior, the more this relationship resembled the pattern of an indigenous sub-chieftainship. The difference was that the hierarchy of authority depended on race alone. At the extreme limits of white settlement, the farmer depended a great deal on co-operation with indigenous communities and their authorities. Some frontiersmen were drawn to a greater or lesser extent into indigenous society. They married Khoi-speaking or Bantu-speaking wives and built up personal followings from the indigenous peoples, allying with or becoming the subjects of indigenous chiefs. On the northern frontier such persons as Jan Bloem and a number of others fell into this category. On the eastern frontier Coenraad de Buys, who married Ngqika's mother as well as a number of other Xhosa wives, was the best-known and most influential of a group known as the 'frontier ruffians'.

For most frontier settlers, however, the pull of the more advanced material civilisation at the Cape was stronger in the long run. It was in any case the prestige of European culture and of the white skin associated with it that gave them standing in the eyes of the indigenous peoples with whom they were in contact. Then as more and more settlers moved in from the Cape and as co-operation increasingly gave way to competition and conflict – a development most strikingly marked on the eastern frontier – race feelings were heightened.

The last years of Company rule

In the last years of the Company's rule in South Africa, relations between its officials and the settlers became increasingly strained. In the atmosphere created by the outbreak of the American Revolution, a patriot party of extreme republicans in Holland brought about an alliance with France in 1778 and entered into a treaty with the American colonies. In September 1778 a movement started in the western Cape to demand more relaxed trading conditions and greater burgher participation in government. The leaders of the agitation adopted the slogan 'Unity makes strength' (*Eendragt maakt magt*). A memorandum was taken to Holland by four elected delegates.

The Company, however, rejected the demand for equal political representation of the burgher community. In reaction, a party known as the Cape Patriots emerged which hoped to appeal to the Estates General in Holland to take over the colony from the Company. In 1787, however, the Patriot party in Holland – which might have been favourable to the appeal – was overthrown and any interest the Estates General may have had in the affairs of the Cape lapsed and the Cape Patriot movement died away. While the agitation in the western Cape thus came to very little, a much more significant conflict developed in the eastern frontier area.

Conditions in the easternmost areas of the enormously extended Stellenbosch District were growing chaotic because of increasing conflict with the San in the north-east, and the indiscipline of some of the frontiersmen. In the east-coast frontier area, the advancing colonists were already in contact with the southernmost chiefdoms of the Xhosa. Competition for land and mutual complaints of cattle-stealing soon developed between the Xhosa and their white neighbours. In long-term perspective the history of contact between white farmers and the Xhosa on the eastern frontier is the story of interaction between two different social and economic systems. The social pressures on every young white male to maintain the status of *baas* (master) meant that, as white populations increased, the white dominated society constantly felt constrained to seek to expand, to absorb more land for farms and more of the African population as workers.

The Xhosa communities were also driven to seek more land because of growing population and the social pressures to maintain and expand the numbers of cattle on which their status depended. This is the underlying explanation of the repeated conflicts on the eastern frontier. For a long time, however, the process was not perceived by the participants within the zone of contact itself in terms of outright racial confrontation. Whites and Xhosa did not meet each other drawn up along a clearly demarcated line but in relatively small groups at many different points in a wide zone of contact. In these contacts trade as well as competition for land was an important aspect of white–Xhosa relationships.

Many of the whites living in the frontier zone, moreover, came fairly close in their economic life style and their relationships with their African servants to the pattern of a Xhosa family head or sub-chief. Both Xhosa and whites had conflicts within their own communities which could loom larger in their eyes than their problems with the other race. The underlying process of continuing pressure for territorial expansion by the whites and resistance by the Xhosa thus worked itself out in the short run in a very complex pattern of interactions. Xhosa chiefs often sought white allies in their struggles with one another. Whites also sometimes turned to Xhosa chiefs for help against white enemies. Early in 1780 the *landdrost* of Stellenbosch received a report that three unauthorised commandos had attacked some sections of Xhosa near Bruintjies Hoogte. One of them, under the leadership of Petrus Hendrik Ferreira, had killed a large number of Xhosa and looted a number of cattle. This had been followed by more general conflict and there was a possibility that the settlers in Bruintjies Hoogte, Zwart Ruggens and the Camdebo would be overwhelmed.

On 24 October the Governor appointed Adriaan van Jaarsveld, a hard-bitten leader of expeditions against the San, as commandant of the eastern frontier. He was given instructions to persuade the Xhosa to retire behind the line of the Great Fish river, if possible by peaceful negotiations. After attempts at peaceful persuasion had failed, van Jaarsveld took the field with an armed commando. In July of the following year he carried out a treacherous exercise. He scattered pieces of tobacco for the Xhosa to pick up and, as they did so, ordered his commando to open fire, killing a considerable number of people and seizing about eight hundred cattle. In later attacks he seized further cattle and the Xhosa were temporarily driven from their homes.

This was the first of a long series of wars between the colony and the Xhosa on the eastern frontier. It failed to drive the Xhosa permanently from the lands beyond the Fish. The Gqunukwebe, indeed, were driven deeper into the colony by Ndlambe who was regent of the Rharhabe chiefdom between the Fish river and the Keiskamma. As they fought back against him he allied with the Boers in the colony.

The disturbed and uncertain situation of the settlers in the eastern frontier districts and their quarrels with one another led to repeated requests for a new magistrate's office nearer to the eastern frontier. At the end of 1785, Maritz Hermann Otto Woeke, whose name had been suggested by the local burghers, was appointed *landdrost* for the new magistrate's office. He fixed on a site in the Camdebo roughly midway between the north-eastern districts where conflict with the San was at its strongest, and the *zuurveld*, where the settlers faced the Xhosa. The site was named Graaff-Reinet. Woeke did not prove effective as a magistrate and was soon replaced by his secretary, H.C.D. Maynier.

Maynier, a well-educated, able and energetic official, did his best to carry on the functions of his office and maintain the rule of law on the frontier. He tried to check unauthorised commandos organised by the frontier burghers, insisting that matters of war and peace were the concern of the Company's government, not of private individuals. He opened his court to Khoi who complained of ill-treatment by their masters. In spite of his efforts, the frontier settlers continued their unauthorised activities and in June 1793 a commando drove the Gqunukwebe to retaliate against the whites on a large scale. Maynier took command and with the co-operation of Faure, the *landdrost* of Swellendam, organised a commando drawn from both districts. A large number of Xhosa cattle were captured and the Xhosa chiefs negotiated for peace, while standing firm about their rightful positions on the *zuurveld*. The two officials both knew that they could not raise enough forces to drive the Xhosa from the *zuurveld*, so agreement was reached; the Xhosa would remain on the *zuurveld* subject to 'good behaviour'.

This agreement angered the frontiersmen who were already bitter about Maynier's whole attitude to relations with the Xhosa beyond the border and farmers' rights over their Khoi servants within it. Agitated by confused ideas derived from the French Revolution, they rose in rebellion in February 1795, drove Maynier from his office and proclaimed an independent Republic of Graaff-Reinet. Soon afterwards the burghers of Swellendam drove out Faure and likewise proclaimed a republic. The problems of race relations had thus resulted in the first of a series of conflicts between the settlers and their government. The Company's officials were unable to suppress these rebellions before Company rule was brought to an end by the British occupation of the Cape in 1795.

New wine in old bottles: the Cape Colony 1795–1834

3

By the mid-eighteenth century the expansion of commercial activity had led to considerable social change in Europe. It had also led to the development of new ideas which became widely adopted. In earlier times it had been generally accepted that an individual's rights and privileges depended on whether he was born into a ruling class or came from peasant stock. Now privilege by birth was rejected and it was increasingly believed that all men were entitled to equal rights. This meant that all positions in society should be open to free competition. With this belief went the view that governments should not interfere in economic matters; there should be free competition in the home market and free trade between nations. It was also thought that government should be with the consent of the people and be based on representative democracy. In line with these ideas there was a growing attack on slavery and any other kind of forced labour. In the light of the new ideas, slavery was not only inhuman and unjust, but also economically inefficient. It went against the principle of free competition.

These ideas were most widely held in the world's highly commercial nations such as Britain and France, as well as America. Holland, as an active commercial country, was also affected by them. In France the idea of equality was central to the revolution which broke out in 1789. In England the new ideas were expressed most forcibly in the humanitarian and anti-slavery movements and the evangelical movement. The evangelical movement led to a great expansion of missionary activity in Africa and elsewhere.

Though Britain and France shared the new ideas, their traditional rivalry was not weakened. By 1792 Britain was engaged in a war against revolutionary France which involved almost all of Europe. The wars continued after Napoleon became the leader of France (with only a short break under the Treaty of Amiens of 1802), until Napoleon's final defeat at Waterloo in 1815. As a result of these wars the British occupied the Cape in 1795. In 1803 they handed it back to Holland, but in 1806 retook it, this time to keep it.

Though governments changed at the Cape, the whole period from 1792 to 1834 saw the growing impact of the new ideas on Cape society. The emancipation of slaves in 1834 was perhaps the strongest example of this influence. However, many of the new ideas did not suit the type of society developed by whites at the Cape, based as it was on hereditary privilege of race. The result was a series of conflicts which were to result finally in the mass emigration out of the colony known as the Great Trek.

The first British occupation of the Cape, 1795–1802

In 1794 Holland fell to the forces of the French Revolution. This provoked Britain to take measures to stop a possible French occupation of the Cape which the British knew would gravely endanger their trade with India. On 11 June 1795 a British fleet entered Table Bay. Negotiations with the military commander and the Council of Policy failed, and British troops were landed at Simons Town on 14 July. With the arrival of a second British fleet in September, plans were put in hand for a direct attack on Cape Town. Faced with this situation the military commander and the Council of Policy capitulated and handed over responsibility for the Cape to the British occupying forces.

The newly established British authorities were faced with the problem of continuing opposition in the frontier districts. The Swellendam burghers gave way almost immediately. They capitulated to their previously rejected *landdrost*, Faure, and took the oath of allegiance to the new government. In Graaff-Reinet, however, the leaders of the movements against Maynier expelled the newly-appointed *landdrost* Bresler. They subsequently wrote a letter to the British expressing their willingness to submit but asked to be allowed to enter the Xhosa country to recover stolen cattle. They also demanded permission to settle beyond the Fish river. They insisted that Bresler should not be sent back as *landdrost* and requested the right to elect eight burgher councillors locally. General Craig, leader of the British occupying force, sent a stern reply, strictly forbidding any commando against the Xhosa. He rejected out of hand the idea of taking lands belonging to the Xhosa beyond the Fish. To bring the rebellion to heel he closed the roads from the Cape to Graaff-Reinet, thus cutting off the burghers' ammunition supplies. The burghers speedily submitted, and on 30 July 1797 Bresler was finally re-established in office.

Attempts to bring peace to the frontiers

The British authorities then took up the problem of the frontier of white and Xhosa settlement. They were unable to persuade the chiefs settled on the *zuurveld* to retire beyond the Fish. Their handling of the conflict with the San was more successful. Floris Visser and Jacobus Gideon Louw, two *veldkornet* from the northern districts, had appreciated that the San were near starvation and suggested that farmers be asked to contribute stock to San groups who agreed to live at peace with the colony. This conciliation or peace policy was strongly supported by the British authorities and embodied in a decree (*plakaat*) issued by Governor Macartney on 24 July 1798. It was taken up almost immediately by farmers on the north-eastern frontier, and a surviving collection list of December 1798 shows that some of the farmers there contributed as much as twenty sheep at a time, although their stocks had been seriously depleted by San raids. In addition to providing stock for the San and impoverished Khoi, the practice developed of hunting parties deliberately shooting game for them. This was later made compulsory in a *plakaat* of 1810 which required hunting parties going beyond the borders in the Tulbagh district to share some of their kill with the San in order to maintain their peaceful attitudes towards the colonists.

Frontier revolt and Khoi rebellion

The submission of the eastern frontier farmers had been made under duress. The conflict of interest and attitude between them and the government in

Cape Town had been sharpened by the replacement of the Dutch East India Company by the British. Some of the more restless, led by Coenraad de Buys, plotted to persuade the Ngqika to ally with them in a combined attack on the British. A circular letter was drawn up calling on the burghers to rise. In January 1799 Adriaan van Jaarsveldt was arrested on a charge of forgery. The party taking him to the Cape for trial was overtaken by a group of armed burghers. The prisoner was freed and carried off, and the rebels issued a further circular in the name of the 'Voice of the People' calling for an armed roll-call of all burghers of the district. On 25 January, Bresler was surrounded in his office and forced to sign letters dictated by the rebels.

This time the British authorities decided to react with force. Some troops were sent overland and others by sea to land at Algoa Bay. They included a body of armed Khoi belonging to the Hottentot corps. The rebellion rapidly collapsed, and most of the ringleaders gave themselves up, though Coenraad de Buys and a number of others made good their escape to the Xhosa.

The movement of the troops, however, sparked off a much more serious upheaval. Khoi servants of the white farmers, seeing the British troops accompanied by a Khoi contingent, believed that the British were at war with their masters. Many of them deserted their employers, taking guns and ammunition, and formed three armed bands. Certain sections of the Xhosa had also been disturbed. Rumours had been circulated by de Buys and others who told them that the British intention was to drive them from the *zuurveld*. These allied Khoi and Xhosa groups began pillaging white farms over a wide area. The British expedition withdrew on the completion of its mission and local white commandos proved too weak to combat the combined Khoi and Xhosa forces. The eastern districts of the Colony were subjected to widespread devastation. At almost the same time, on the northern frontier, Jager Afrikaner led his followers from his stronghold on an island in the middle Orange on raids against the colonial farmers of the northern districts.

The British tried to bring about peace by negotiation. Maynier was brought back to the eastern frontier and entered discussions with the leaders of the Khoi and Xhosa groups, who were running short of ammunition and quarrelling over the spoils. He assured the Khoi that if they returned to their employers the government would see that they were well treated and well paid and promised the Xhosa chiefs that they would be allowed to remain on the *zuurveld* so long as they lived at peace with the whites.

Agreement was reached and the disturbances died down, though the position was soon further complicated. In 1800 Ndlambe succeeded in escaping from Ngqika and led his followers across the Fish river onto the *zuurveld*, driving the Gqunukwebe still further into colonial territory. Maynier was appointed Resident Commissioner for Graaff-Reinet and Swellendam districts with overriding authority over the serving *landdrost* officials. He was to supervise the peace and the restoration of the shattered economy of the area. Farmers who had suffered serious property losses were offered some compensation. On the other hand, all employers of Khoi were obliged to register this with the *landdrost*. The district court was to hear charges brought by Khoi against their employers on the basis of equality before the law.

Maynier's efforts contributed to restoring peaceful conditions in the eastern frontier area. The hostility of some of the white frontiersmen towards him, however, remained as strong as ever. Coenraad de Buys and the other fugitives living with Ngqika attempted to alarm the burghers with the threat of an invasion by Ngqika. They also planned to kidnap Maynier and his fellow commissioner, Somerville, and carry them off into Xhosa territory. Commandant van Rensburg of Bruintjies Hoogte travelled to Cape Town to submit complaints against the district authorities, for their prohibition of unofficial commandos against the Xhosa.

The frontier whites were bitter against the use of the church at Graaff-Reinet for church services and instruction for Khoi congregations. They were also agitated by false rumours circulated by Commandant van Rensburg and *veldkornet* Erasmus that farmers were to be conscripted for military service. At the beginning of July 1801 farmers in the *zuurveld* and Bruintjies Hoogte areas openly rebelled again. An armed commando was formed which advanced on the magistrate's office and garrison. Faced with the strong attitude of Maynier and the forces under his command they retired but remained under arms and continued widespread agitation. On 13 July, five of their leaders presented their demands. They insisted that Khoi should no longer be allowed to use the church. They demanded that five Khoi suspected of murdering a farmer should be handed over to them instead of being held for regular trial. They insisted that they be allowed to mount commandos against the Xhosa and be provided with the ammunition to enable them to do so. Faced with refusal and with the strengthening of the garrison by reinforcements brought up from Algoa Bay they once again withdrew. In October they approached the garrison again demanding the surrender of Khoi who had fled there in alarm at rumours promising violence from the farmers. Some shots were exchanged but without loss of life, and the commando once again withdrew.

Faced with the continuing unrest in the eastern frontier districts and a chorus of complaints against Maynier, Acting-Governor Dundas recalled him to face a committee of enquiry and appointed Major Sherlock in his place. The enquiry declared Maynier innocent of the charges brought against him. In the meantime, Sherlock, with troop reinforcements at his disposal, delivered final orders to the farmers to break up their commando, which now at last dispersed. The continuing agitation by the frontiersmen, however, had alarmed and disturbed Khoi and Xhosa living on the *zuurveld*. Once again Khoi fled from their masters and formed armed bands which, in association with Xhosa groups, pillaged a wide area.

Up until the end of the first British occupation in 1803 conditions in the eastern frontier areas remained chaotic. Over four hundred farmhouses were burnt and widespread pillaging continued. Burgher commandos had proved incapable of defeating the combination of Khoi and Xhosa. Far from driving the Xhosa back across the Fish river, the colonists were in danger of being themselves driven back by the advancing Xhosa and their Khoi allies.

Christian missionaries

A development of major importance for South African history in the period of the first British occupation was the beginning of missionary activity on a substantial scale. After the initial efforts at conversion of slaves and Khoi in the earliest days of the Colony, few significant attempts had been made, and the evangelist movement had lapsed. The view was held in the early period that slaves who became Christian were entitled to their freedom. This led to a strong reluctance to baptise slaves. In the absence of Christian evangelisation, the Islamic faith was consolidated amongst the Muslim Malay community of the Cape.

The first attempt to start missionary activity amongst the Khoi was undertaken by a German Moravian missionary, Georg Schmidt, who set up a mission at Baviaanskloof in 1728. Hostility on the part of the burghers, however, led to abandonment of the mission in 1744. In 1792 the Moravians re-entered the field and this time successfully established a long-lasting mission settlement for Khoi at the site of Schmidt's earlier mission at Baviaanskloof, now renamed Genadendal. The resources of the mission, however, were inadequate for more than limited expansion of mission work.

It was only in the period of the first British occupation that the new evangelical missionary movement really established itself in South Africa. The London Missionary Society, founded in 1795, was first in the field, its first party arriving in the Cape in 1799. As the most powerful and influential mission society in South Africa it had twenty missionaries there by 1816, when it was joined by the Wesleyan Methodist Missionary Society and the Glasgow Missionary Society. The Church Missionary Society began its work in South Africa in 1821.

From early in the nineteenth century, missionaries were moving out and settling with indigenous communities beyond the frontiers of the Colony along and beyond the Orange river in the north as well as amongst the Xhosa along the eastern coastlands. The aim of the missionaries to 'convert the heathen' was inseparable in their minds from the task of civilising them, that is to say of encouraging them to adopt a way of life similar to that of nineteenth-century Britain and western Europe. It meant attempting to turn subsistence cultivators into communities of independent commercial producers and craftsmen. It also required development of an indigenous middle class which could maintain and staff churches. Such activity would yield an increased supply of primary products and would generate an expanding market for European manufactured goods. These missionary aims suited the interests of the commercial classes in Britain and Europe who encouraged and supported the movement.

Conflicts of interest

The aims of the missionaries did not necessarily involve bringing African societies under British rule. However, mission staff were naturally attached to their own European roots. They were also dependent on the goodwill of the Cape government. They often experienced difficulties in working within independent African societies; at the same time they felt the need to protect their African converts against the cruelty and exploitation of the white settlers. Sometimes, therefore, they regarded the extension of British authority and control as necessary and desirable.

Missionary aims were in certain respects in direct conflict with white settler interests and attitudes, since these involved converting the indigenous peoples into a subordinate working class within the white-controlled economic system. The work of the missionaries necessarily threatened settler supplies of labour. It also raised the possibility of non-European agricultural producers who might compete with white farmers. It posed a challenge to the essential racial inequality on which the whole structure of

Cape society was based. Hostility from white settlers became evident from the start and was to be a continuing theme in South African history. The missionaries' programme, however, did serve the interests of some members of white society at the Cape. These were the traders and wholesale merchants who specialised in trade with the indigenous peoples. The 'Christianisation' and 'civilisation' of African communities promised them greatly expanded business and profits. They provided the base for a strand of liberal opinion in the Cape which tended to support the missionaries and their ideals.

The missionaries themselves, however, were over time subject to influence by the local white community. This was particularly true of those missionaries who belonged to churches with significant local white congregations. Pressures were greatest where missions were funded largely by the local white congregations rather than from overseas resources. It is not surprising, therefore, that in course of time mission education plans came to concentrate more on inculcating technical skills which white employers wanted in their black workers rather than on the training of an African professional middle class. That ideal was never abandoned altogether, however.

In relation to the indigenous societies amongst which they settled, the missionaries' position was often complex and contradictory. The missionary was often welcomed, sometimes directly invited, as a means by which indigenous peoples could hope to gain access to European arms and other goods and the knowledge believed to be responsible for white prosperity and power. His ability to serve as a diplomatic adviser on problems involving whites was also valued. Because of his relationship to the Cape authorities his presence often provided protection against other African groups or encroaching white settlers.

Missionaries initially found it to their advantage to seek the support of, and work with and through, established chiefs. Their teaching, however, inevitably involved an attack on existing customs and institutions which could result in missionary converts coming into conflict with their own political authorities. Sometimes for this very reason it was groups within indigenous societies that felt already disadvantaged who turned to the missionaries for a new order and formed the majority of their converts. This practice naturally increased the stresses and strains in the missionaries' relations with the chiefs. Where an indigenous ruler was in a weak position there was a strong temptation for the missionary to exploit the opportunity and bring the chief effectively under his own control. Alternatively he might replace the chief with a more co-operative ruler of his own choosing. The missionary's loyalties were thus divided between his mission society, the government of the Cape, the African political unit within which he lived and worked, and his immediate flock of converts within it.

The first party of London Missionary Society missionaries was made up of five members and arrived at the Cape in 1799. The most forceful and controversial amongst them was a Dutchman, J.T. van der Kemp, who had been chosen in the hope that he would prove particularly acceptable to the white colonists. The party split up into two groups. Van der Kemp and his assistant, William Edwards, went to the eastern frontier area and at first attempted to establish a mission station with Ngqika. The others set out to establish missions for the San on the northern frontier and soon began work among the Bastards of the middle Orange whom they subsequently persuaded to adopt the name Griqua.

Van der Kemp's attempt to begin mission work with Ngqika's people involved him in a difficult situation, complicated by the intrigues of Coenraad de Buys and the other white refugees living with Ngqika. He therefore withdrew from the Xhosa community, returned to the colony and began work with the Khoi of the eastern frontier area. It was his work in gathering a Khoi congregation and preaching to them in the church at Graaff-Reinet which provided the basis of one of the white frontiersmen's complaints against Maynier in 1801.

In the light of the Khoi revolt in the eastern provinces in 1799, the British administration was anxious to find ways of reducing Khoi bitterness and persuading them to settle down. It was thought that the provision of some areas of land where Khoi could live without being forced into white employment might help to bring peace. Official support was thus given to van der Kemp for a plan to gather wandering Khoi within the colony and establish a mission station, where they could support themselves. Van der Kemp was given a temporary site for his settlement on a farm in the Swartkops river valley, where he allocated smallholdings to his congregation. His mission station had not time to take root, however. It was destroyed in the upheavals which accompanied the withdrawal of the first British administration at the Cape.

The rule of the Batavian Republic, 1803–6

Under the terms of the Treaty of Amiens of March 1802, the Cape was to be handed over to the authorities of the revolutionary Batavian Republic in Holland. This was finally carried through on 21 February 1803, when Acting-Governor Dundas formally handed over authority to the Batavian Republic's Commissioner-General, J.A. de Mist, and the Governor, General J.W. Janssens.

The brief period of rule by the Batavian Republic was marked by relative calm but saw no significant change in the situation at the Cape. The underlying causes of tension among the settlers, particularly those near the frontier, remained but without the flare-ups of the preceding years. The burghers welcomed the return of a Dutch government and all parties were weary after the prolonged period of disturbance. The new government followed essentially the same lines of policy towards the problems of the frontier as had the British. They maintained the policy of registering labour contracts and requiring the courts to hear cases of ill-treatment brought by servants against their masters. Support was also given to van der Kemp in his attempt to establish a permanent mission settlement where Khoi could live independently of the white farmers. His original settlement had been attacked by frontier farmers and burnt and he was now provided with a new site near the Swartkops river which became the settlement of Bethelsdorp. Unfortunately the area chosen was singularly infertile and quite unsuitable for a viable agricultural settlement. This ensured that the settlement would remain poverty-stricken, justifying its description as 'beggars' town' and providing ammunition to the critics of the mission reserve policy who wished to see it closed down and its members made available as farm labour.

Both Governor Janssens and Commissioner-General de Mist made

Chief Ngqika meeting General Janssens (Ludwig Alberti's *Account of the Tribal Life and Customs of the Xhosa in 1807*)

personal visits to the frontier areas and attempted to negotiate a settlement with the Xhosa providing for the peaceful withdrawal of those settled on the *zuurveld* beyond the Fish. Ndlambe and other *zuurveld* chiefs, however, refused to leave on the grounds that they were afraid of Ngqika. Ngqika tried to enlist the support of the Dutch officials and the colonists for a combined attack on the *zuurveld* Xhosa. He hoped this would drive them back beyond the Fish and bring them under his authority. The officials, however, were painfully aware of their very limited material resources and were determined not to be drawn into conflict with any section of the Xhosa. No action was taken and the Xhosa remained on the *zuurveld*.

The return of the British, 1806

The authorities of the Dutch Batavian Republic had hardly established themselves at the Cape before the Treaty of Amiens broke down and war in Europe was resumed. Much of the brief period of Batavian rule was taken up with the attempt to prepare for the defence of the Cape against a British assault. On 4 January 1806 the long-expected invasion fleet was sighted. It carried forces far too strong for the garrison at the Cape, and on 7 January the authorities in Cape Town gave in. General Janssens retired inland, but as the burghers showed little inclination to support him, he surrendered at Hottentots Holland on 18 January.

The second British occupation, like the first, was initially regarded as temporary, but in the post-Napoleonic settlement of Europe the newly enlarged Kingdom of Holland agreed in 1814 to hand over the Colony permanently to Great Britain in exchange for a grant of two million pounds. This was to be spent on the building of fortresses along the French border in Europe.

Labour shortages

In the early days of the second British occupation the governors at the Cape, representing a Tory government in Britain, had more sympathies with employers than employees. They adopted a distinctly cautious attitude to the activities of the missionaries. Although Bethelsdorp was not closed down and indeed a second mission station for the Khoi in the eastern frontier areas was established at Theopolis, the authorities largely shared the attitude of the farmers towards the mission stations. Like the farmers they saw these as havens of idleness which needlessly barred much-needed labour from the market. This attitude was strengthened as a result of the first major success of the humanitarian and welfare movements, the abolition of the slave trade in Britain in 1807. With the ending of slave imports to the Cape, farmers now suffered from a serious shortage of labour. The British authorities were also having difficulty in finding sufficient recruits for the 'Hottentot' armed force by then known as the Cape Regiment. The mission stations within the Colony were pressured to supply recruits as were the Griqua on the Orange river. When the Griqua refused, trade with their community was officially banned for a time. In 1815 a rebellious secessionist movement developed within the Griqua community in reaction to these government pressures. A section of the Griqua broke away and established themselves on the Harts river, thus gaining the name Hartenaar. They were joined there by Coenraad de Buys.

The revolt finally ended in 1817 when the majority of the Hartenaars were readmitted to the Griqua state. De Buys then moved on northwards and settled in the northern Transvaal near the Zoutpansberg. His mixed-blood descendants, known as the Buysvolk, were later found there by the Boers of the Great Trek.

Labour laws and the Khoi

With a view to eliminating vagrancy and ensuring that Khoi should give their services to the farmers, Governor Caledon issued a series of regulations in 1809. All chieftaincies previously granted by staffs of office were abolished. Every Khoi living within the colonial frontiers was obliged to have a fixed address either with a white employer, or at a recognised mission station. Khoi wishing to move from one district to another were required to carry a pass from the magistrate of the district in which they resided authorising them to do so.

By these provisions Khoi within the Colony were very closely tied to their white employers. They could not move around, either in search of better wages and conditions of service, or to reach a mission station where they could live without working for a white farmer. In 1812 Governor Cradock tightened their bonds still further by ruling that where Khoi children had been born and raised to the age of eight on an employer's farm the children could be apprenticed to serve the employer for a further ten years. On the other hand, the regulations provided for the registration of labour contracts and laid down in some detail the rights to which servants were entitled.

In 1811–12 Cradock responded to complaints sent to London by the missionaries by ordering the Circuit Court to enquire closely into all cases raised by Khoi against their employers. The Circuit Court carried out its task with great thoroughness, and a good deal of abuse was uncovered. Two farmers were even convicted of murder. On the other hand, many of the complaints proved ill-founded or simply mischievous. The very fact that whites could be called to court to answer charges by their own servants threatened to undermine the authority of masters over their employees and challenged the value system on which settler society was built. It aroused such resentment that it came to be known as the 'Black Circuit'.

In 1816, the feelings aroused by the 'Black Circuit' gave rise to a rebellion, the last in the series of frontier uprisings that had begun with the expulsion of Maynier from the post of *landdrost* in 1795. A farmer named Frederik Bezuidenhout was summoned to appear in court on a charge brought by a Khoi servant. He refused, and when a posse which included Khoi soldiers was sent to arrest him he took refuge in a cave, opened fire on the posse and was shot dead. Members of his family then tried to foment an armed uprising in the eastern frontier districts. The authorities responded promptly and most of the ringleaders were arrested and condemned to death as rebels. They were publicly hanged at Slachter's Nek.

Struggle for the zuurveld

Relations between the white settlers and the Xhosa on the *zuurveld* and the San in the north-east were still problematic. The authorities commissioned Captain Collins to tour the eastern frontier areas. He proposed that forcible measures should be taken to drive out the Xhosa from the *zuurveld* and make the Fish river an effective frontier between the races. In 1811–12 the proposal was carried out. War was launched against the *zuurveld* Xhosa and the followers of Ndlambe and the smaller chiefdoms were driven across the Fish river. A series of border posts, the most important of which was Grahamstown, was established to protect the frontier.

The use of British troops altered the balance of power on the frontier, enabling white settler society to pursue its inbuilt tendency to expand which had been temporarily checked by Xhosa resistance. The clearing of the *zuurveld* did not, however, lessen the tension along the eastern frontier as the colonial authorities had hoped. The *zuurveld* Xhosa who had been forcibly robbed of their homelands and much of their cattle were naturally bitter. They formed small raiding parties which slipped across the Fish to seize colonial cattle in revenge for their own losses. The frontier was too long and the terrain too difficult for the colonial authorities to prevent this. The Xhosa raiding parties succeeded in making conditions on the *zuurveld* so insecure for whites that, even though they were badly in need of farms, few were prepared to risk settling on the lands from which the Xhosa had been driven.

The expulsion of Ndlambe beyond the Fish, moreover, produced overcrowding and rising political tension among other Xhosa already living beyond the river. A prophet named Makana (also known as Nxele, 'left-handed'), who had been influenced to some extent by the preaching of van der Kemp, associated himself with Ndlambe and announced that if the Xhosa would strictly adhere to their traditional moral code the heroic ancestors of the past would return, aided by a mighty wind to help them drive the whites from the *zuurveld*. This appeal to religious beliefs to build up a wider unity for a common struggle against the white intruders proved very successful. Makana's preaching roused courage and determination for the resistance struggle and attracted a growing following. Many young men deserted Ngqika, who maintained a policy of friendly relations with the colony, and joined Ndlambe. This embittered relations between the two chiefs. Finally, a triangular struggle between Ngqika and Ndlambe and the senior Gcaleka Xhosa chiefdom was sparked off by conflict over grazing lands, made acute by drought. Ngqika was severely defeated and lost most of his cattle at a battle at Amalinde. It appeared probable that his following would be absorbed by Ndlambe in an enlarged chiefdom inspired by the religious message of Makana.

The colonial authorities acted promptly to stifle this development. In 1818 a colonial force went to the aid of Ngqika and helped him recapture much of his cattle. In response, Ndlambe's forces led by Makana, invaded the colony and besieged Grahamstown. Reinforcements came only just in time to prevent the fall of the town. The Xhosa were then driven back and the struggle was carried across the Fish. In 1819 Makana voluntarily gave himself up in order to prevent more suffering on the part of his people. He was imprisoned on Robben Island and eventually drowned while attempting to escape to the mainland in a small boat. Many Xhosa continued to expect his return as a saviour, and the expression 'waiting for Nxele' became an expression meaning to wait for something that will never happen.

The 'ceded territory'

In the aftermath of the 1818–19 war on the eastern frontier the colonial authorities made a new attempt to solve the problems of frontier tension by keeping settlers and Xhosa apart. Though Ngqika had consistently remained a friend of the Colony, he was forced most unwillingly to surrender the lands between the Fish and Keiskamma rivers. This was to form a neutral strip which was to be kept empty of population of both races. The area included much of the territory of Ngqika's people, including his own birthplace.

Both the European and Xhosa communities were increasingly involved in mutual economic interaction and both were short of land. An attempt to separate them with a strip of no-man's-land was unlikely to succeed for long. In 1821 Acting-Governor Donkin established a fair at Fort Wiltshire which soon became a more or less permanent market. He also persuaded Ngqika to agree to a white settlement at Fredericksburgh in the neutral strip. From the other side, Ngqika's heir in the Great House, Maqomo, returned to the area of the valley of the upper Kat. The neutral strip began to assume the pattern of mixed settlement that had previously marked the *zuurveld*. Though the original agreement forced on Ngqika had been that the area would be an empty land belonging to neither side, it was not long before it came to be referred to as 'the ceded territory' and to be regarded as colonial territory. Africans permitted to live there were regarded as doing so on sufferance and enjoyed no security. In 1829 Maqomo was driven from his lands along the Kat river and a settlement for Khoi was established there. Apart from its welfare function the Kat river settlement was intended to make an

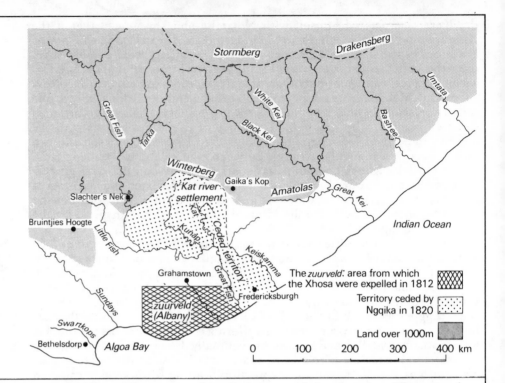

The *zuurveld*: area from which the Xhosa were expelled in 1812

Territory ceded by Ngqika in 1820

Land over 1000m

3.1 The progressive expropriation of the Xhosa, 1812–20

important contribution to the protection of the frontier. The way that Maqomo's lands were seized made Xhosa near the frontier feel very anxious. Maqomo was allowed to come back again on a number of occasions, only to be driven out once more. This harassment of Maqomo convinced the Xhosa that one day the whites would force them still further back on their overcrowded hinterland.

The drive for closer settlement

Following the struggle for the *zuurveld*, a major attempt was made to modify the whole character of the Colony. From at least as early as the period of Batavian administration, it had been clear that many of the problems of the Colony arose from the system of cattle ranching on very large farms. This explained why a white community sparsely scattered over an enormous territory was nevertheless permanently short of land. It also meant that the population of the frontier districts was too small to provide effectively for its own defence. At the same time by inhibiting the growth of towns and other related economic activities, this system produced a vicious circle: it prevented the development of employment opportunities for whites other than cattle farming, and so perpetuated the drive for further expansion. In his report on the frontier situation, Captain Collins had emphasised the need to provide for closer settlement if the problems of security were to be successfully tackled.

A first attempt towards a solution of this problem was made by Governor Cradock in the aftermath of the clearing of the *zuurveld*. This was the introduction of a quit-rent system in place of the traditional loan-farm system. In return for a rather higher rent, farmers would acquire ownership rights to their land. In practice, however, farmers had always enjoyed as much security in their property rights as they felt they needed. It was not the legal aspects of the loan-farm system which prevented the division of farms between heirs or encouraged the wanderings of the trek-farmers but the economic realities of cattle farming in the Colony. Cradock's measures met with little success and merely angered the farmers who saw them as an attempt to raise their rents.

In 1820 Governor Somerset gained approval for an ambitious scheme to bring out and settle substantial numbers of British settlers on the *zuurveld*. Instead of the traditional ranches of about 2500 ha, they were to be established on small farms of 40 ha per man. They would thus provide the closer settlement necessary to ensure the security of the frontier areas and help to introduce a new economic pattern in the Colony. The establishment of a substantial English-speaking population would improve the general security of the Colony by offsetting the doubtful loyalties of the Dutch-speaking majority. At the same time, emigration to the Cape would help to ease the problems of unemployment in Britain. Under the 1820 settlement scheme about 5000 British settlers came to the Cape, the great majority being settled at first on the *zuurveld*, which was now made the new magisterial district of Albany.

The 1820 settlement scheme was based on the false assumption that intensive farming on small farms in the *zuurveld* area would be economically viable. Within a short period the majority of the settlers had given up the attempt to make a living on their holdings and had moved to the towns. Those who remained demanded large farms on the traditional pattern. The 1820 scheme thus largely failed to reduce the need for troops on the eastern frontier. It also added to the existing problems of white land hunger and pressure for further expansion.

Closer ties with Britain: judicial reform

The arrival of the 1820 settlers, however, meant the establishment of a substantial community which had direct links with Britain and was in a position to make its feelings known at home. Its presence was to play an important part in the movement towards the grant of representative institutions to the Cape settler community. A commission of enquiry was appointed in 1823 in response to settler complaints and accusations against Governor Somerset. It recommended the eventual introduction of two representative assemblies, one for the western and one for the eastern district, but these were to be delayed until after the achievement of the emancipation of slaves. In 1828, after a struggle with successive governors, the principle of freedom of the press was extended to the Cape. In the same year English replaced Dutch as the language of the courts and the entire system of justice was revised. Trial by jury was introduced and, although the Roman-Dutch civil law was retained, criminal law was largely remodelled on English lines. In local administration the judicial authority of the *landdrost* was taken over by resident magistrates, while their administrative powers were handled by civil commissioners. The *veldkornet* lost their limited judicial authority and were supplemented by Justices of the Peace, appointments which, however, were little more than ornamental. In Cape Town the burgher Senate was abolished, putting an end to all representative town

British settlers arriving on the beach at
Algoa Bay, 1820 by Thomas Baines

councils. These changes made many Dutch-speaking whites feel that they
were cut off from all contact with government.

By this time too there was a strong political force in Britain pressing for
the emancipation of slaves throughout the British Empire. It also concerned
itself with the welfare of the indigenous inhabitants of land that was now in
British possession. Missionaries in South Africa could now appeal to
powerful friends for support. The lead in this was taken by Dr John Philip,
who had been appointed General Superintendent of the London Missionary
Society at the Cape. In 1828 he published his *Researches in South Africa* in
which he roundly condemned the legal position of the Khoi in the Colony.
The regulations which had been in practice since 1809 made it impossible
for Khoi to improve their economic position, he argued, and reduced them
to a position of serfdom in some ways even worse than actual slavery. The
provision which allowed an employer to hold the services of a Khoi servant
by apprenticing his children for a period of ten years he condemned as
particularly cruel and vicious. He argued that if Khoi were set free to
improve their economic lot and succeeded only in reaching the level of those
at Bethelsdorp, they would still provide an enormously increased market for
British goods.

This combined appeal to humanitarian and business interest assured the
work a tremendous success. Philip travelled to England to seek parliamentary
legislation in the interests of Khoi emancipation. His appeal to parliament
was, however, pre-empted by the Colony's Acting-Governor Bourke who
after consultation with the humanitarian-minded commissioner for the
eastern province, Andries Stockenstroom, issued Ordinance no. 50 in
1828.

Ordinance no. 50   Reinforced by the authority of the British parliament, Ordinance no. 50
introduced a legal revolution in the status of Khoi and other free non-whites
in the Cape. All the restrictive regulations governing their movements were
set aside and they were granted full legal equality with whites. Ordinance no.
50 also seriously affected the settlers' labour supplies. Khoi labour became
more scarce, more expensive and less easy to control. In 1834 Acting-
Governor Wade attempted to reduce some of these problems by introducing
a vagrancy law, but the law was rejected on the grounds that it was contrary
to the principles of Ordinance no. 50.

Apart from its immediate economic effects, Ordinance no. 50 deeply shocked white society at the Cape by directly attacking the whole principle of racial inequality on which that society was based. A further major development in the same direction was soon to follow. The movement towards the abolition of slavery was accompanied by attempts to restrict the spread of slavery, encourage emancipation and limit the rights of slave owners.

When emancipation was finally carried through in 1834, provisions for compensation were badly mishandled. Compensation was made payable only in London with the result that slave-owners had to hand over their rights to agents who could travel to London to collect the sums due. The original owners were frequently badly cheated. Many failed even to attempt to collect their compensation and substantial sums remained unclaimed. More serious in white eyes than even the financial loss involved was the provision that after a period of four years' apprenticeship, ex-slaves would also come under the provisions of Ordinance no. 50 and enjoy full legal equality with their former owners.

Expansion across the Orange

The halt to expansion up the east coast after the war of 1818–19, the creation of the neutral strip, and the occupation of the *zuurveld* lands by the 1820 settlers had already meant increasing land hunger among the white population of the eastern districts. This was now worsened by recurrent droughts, plagues of locusts and moving herds of springbok which destroyed the grazing and forced farmers to seek new lands for their stock.

As early as 1798 farmers in the Sneeuwberg area had succeeded in establishing sufficiently friendly relations with the San to enable them to begin occupying the lands along the Zeekoe river towards the Orange. Though the idea of extending the frontier as far as the Orange was raised in Captain Collins's report of 1809, nothing was done until the 1820s. Farmers, however, continued settling beyond the official boundary in defiance of official prohibition, and between 1800 and 1820 about 130 000 sq km of former San territory in the north-eastern area was fully occupied by white settlers. Between 1822 and 1824 the north-eastern boundary was at last redefined to take account of the realities of the situation. The frontier was extended eastward to the Stormberg Spruit, northwards to the Orange river and as far west as the great bend where the Orange turns north. Hardly had this substantial extension taken place, however, than farmers began settling beyond the new boundary once more. Boer hunting parties had begun crossing the Orange river as early as 1819 and some farmers had found temporary grazing for their cattle in the area of the future Orange Free State as early as 1821. It was only in 1825, however, that this limited pattern of migration began to increase noticeably. In that year, drought and locusts had devastated the grazing in the northern districts. Reluctant consent was therefore given to a petition from the north-eastern frontier farmers to be allowed to take their cattle across the Orange river for a brief period as an emergency measure. Good rains encouraged most of them to return within the frontier in early 1826, but drought in 1827 and 1828 led to renewed migration. This began the process of permanent settlement.

The farmers who began settling across the Orange at this time had no intention of breaking away from the Cape Colony. Their leader, Jan

Oberholzer, collected taxes due from them and paid them over in the Colony. In October 1828 they prepared a memorandum for the Governor pointing out the impossibility of returning to their impoverished lands. Although the government still prohibited movement and settlement beyond the north-east frontier, fourteen requests for the registration of farms along the Modder and Riet rivers were received. In 1829 alone most of these were from farmers who had no land within the Colony.

Griqua claims

Early white settlement in the area between the Orange and the Vaal coincided with the occupation of part of the area by a section of the Griqua. Their population was growing while the western area of their settlement was becoming drier as the result of a general climatic change. This created strains which, together with the political problems of the Hartenaar revolt, led to increasing splits among the Griqua community. The Kok family, led at first by Adam Kok II, left Griquatown to settle at Campbell. Barend-Barends with many of his followers moved to Daniel's Kuil. Finally, in 1820 the community at Griquatown elected a new chief, the mission catechist Andries Waterboer, a man of San descent. His authority was never fully accepted by the followers of the Kok family or by those of Barend-Barends. The Griqua community was then effectively divided into three political units.

In 1822 Governor Somerset, with the aim of bringing the Griquas under closer government control, appointed John Melville as official government agent for the area, and this sparked off a new rebellion in the Griqua community. A group who came to be known as Bergenaars broke away and established themselves on the Modder river. Waterboer was thus faced with the continuing opposition of the old Bastard chiefs and of the Bergenaars as well. In 1824 a rift occurred in the community at Campbell when Cornelius Kok II, favoured by Waterboer and the missionaries, was elected in place of Adam Kok II as chief there. Adam Kok II, however, retained considerable support, and he and Barend-Barends began to think of an alliance with the Bergenaars. Finally, in September 1825, Dr John Philip held a meeting of all parties at Griquatown. It was then agreed that Cornelius Kok II would retain independent authority in Campbell. Adam Kok II, Barend-Barends and the Bergenaars were permitted to settle at the missionary station of Philippolis on the Orange River. This had been initially established for the San in 1821. Three Griqua states were thus established. The first was the settlement mainly west of the Vaal with its capital at Griquatown under Waterboer. The second was the community under Cornelius Kok II based on Campbell further north. The third was the new settlement headed by Adam Kok II in Transorangia based on Philippolis.

Frontier relations

Though relations between the white settlers moving across the Orange from the north-eastern districts of the Cape and the Griqua settling around Philippolis were friendly at first, competition for grazing land and water soon produced disagreement. In 1829 Adam Kok II protested to the Cape authorities at white farmers trekking into lands he claimed belonged to his people and asked for them to be removed. In 1830, with missionary support, he made a determined effort to prevent the encroachment of white farmers, but he was unable to prevent his people from leasing land on long leases in return for immediate reward. In 1835 he went personally to see the

Philippolis, 1834, by C.D. Bell

Governor, asking for the annexation of his territory if no other way of protecting it could be found, but he received a negative reply. He died on the return journey. His successor was to be faced with greatly increased white pressure on his fragile frontier community. The British did make some attempt to regulate the situation however; the 1835 Cape of Good Hope Punishment Act made provisions for the punishment of British subjects who committed crimes against the indigenous peoples beyond the colonial frontiers as far north as latitude 25°S. This could only be effective however if the offenders could be arrested and brought into the Colony for trial. It really required the extension of British authority over the whole area, if it was to be put into practice properly.

The expansion of white settlement up to the Stormberg Spruit and the Orange river, and the beginning of settlement in Transorangia did not suffice to remove the pressure of white land hunger in the better-watered areas near the coast. In periods of drought, white farmers in the *zuurveld* drove their cattle into the neutral strip, and some pressed well beyond the frontiers, settling amongst the Xhosa as far as the Kei river.

Without the support of the colonial government, however, their position remained precarious. Pressure of the African population on land resources in the area behind the border had already been considerably increased by the expulsion of Ndlambe from the *zuurveld*. The subsequent establishment of the neutral strip made it worse.

View of Griquatown
from John Campbell's *Travels in South Africa*, 1815

4 *The mass migrations of the mfecane & the Great Trek*

In the late eighteenth century a process of rapid political change began in the area of modern Zululand and Natal. It involved the reversal of the process of fragmentation of chiefdoms and the emergence of powerful kingdoms each of which united numbers of previously independent chiefdoms under a single paramount ruler. It produced a violent upheaval, known as the *mfecane* ('unlimited warfare') which spread, not only over the greater part of southern Africa, but vast areas of central and east Africa as well.

The process had its parallels in other parts of South Africa. Earlier in the eighteenth century the Pedi, a northern Sotho people who were a branch of the Kgatla, built a substantial kingdom in the neighbourhood of the Leolu mountains of the eastern Transvaal. This kingdom brought numerous previously separate communities under the hegemony of the Pedi kings. It succeeded in building up a sense of common loyalty amongst some of them at least, which proved capable of surviving into the twentieth century in spite of repeated disastrous defeats in the nineteenth. A somewhat similar but less long-lasting paramountcy can be seen in the expanded hegemony of the Rolong in the western Transvaal in the mid-eighteenth century. Soon after it reached its height, however, the death of its greatest ruler Tau in about 1760 led to its disintegration. Further attempts at bringing surrounding chiefdoms under permanent domination in expanded political systems were made by other Tswana chiefdoms. These included the Mangwato and the Ngwakatsi who, after the collapse of the Rolong state, built the most powerful political system in the Tswana area. They successfully drove back Jan Bloem's Korana and their Bantu-speaking allies. A rather different approach to the creation of an expanded political system can be seen among the Sotho in the career of a chief, Motlume. He married widely into a number of different chiefdoms and exploited a reputation for wisdom and justice in arbitration. This gave him control over a substantial area. However, this lasted only during his lifetime, and broke up again after his death. At the southern end of the eastern coastal strip near the borders of white settlement, Ndlambe and Ngqika of the Rharhabe and Hintsa of the Gcaleka each at different times attempted to unite the Xhosa chiefdoms in a single kingdom.

It was only in Zululand and Natal, however, that this process assumed revolutionary proportions. A possible explanation of the process is the eighteenth-century expansion of trade, especially in ivory, through Delagoa Bay. Chiefs were able to impose considerable control over this trade. One tusk off each elephant killed (the one lying against the ground when the animal fell) was usually claimed by the chief as lord of the soil. Some rulers among the northern Nguni exercised greater control amounting to a virtual monopoly of the trade. They thus acquired new and scarce goods which they could use to attract more followers. This in turn gave them good reason to expand their political power over other communities and so increase their revenue from trade goods. The expansion of trade at Delagoa Bay seems to have been responsible for the development of expanded state systems among some of the Thonga peoples to the immediate south of the bay. The Pedi kingdom also emerged on a trade route from the bay to the interior plateau. There is evidence to show that in the eighteenth century African traders with links to Delagoa Bay were not only active in the northern Nguni area but penetrated down the coast to the vicinity of the Cape Frontier. There is evidence also that some of the outstanding leaders of the *mfecane* were consciously interested in the development of trade and control of trade routes. In the case of the northern Nguni it has been speculated that the assembly of large bodies of young men to engage in mass hunts for elephant and other game may have initiated the process of military and political reorganisation.

Though it is quite possible that trade may have had some role in sparking off the process, the patterns of expansion followed by rulers who emerged do not suggest a primary concern with trade routes, but rather with grazing lands. The evidence, moreover, does not suggest that trade goods at any time played anything approaching the key role occupied by cattle in the economic, social and political life of the northern Nguni. Along the eastern coastal lands occupied by the Nguni peoples, as in some other parts of southern Africa, the grazing lands available to cattle keepers fell into two main types. On the more exposed higher ground, which attracts most rain, there grew lush grasses which provided abundant good grazing in the period of summer rains. Because of leaching of certain minerals from these soils, however, these grasses could not provide satisfactory cattle food once they became dry. In the winter months cattle had to be taken from this sour veld to the drier river valley areas where the grass was more sparse but of a type (sweet veld) which provided good dry feed. Each chiefdom thus needed to control land of both types and it was particularly important to have enough river-valley sweet veld for the dry winter months. How much would be needed would depend upon the numbers of people and their cattle. It would also depend on the rainfall. The whole of the east coast area was subject to cycles of wet years followed by drought years. Where a series of good years which encouraged population growth and expansion of herds was succeeded by a drought cycle the probability of chiefdoms coming into conflict over grazing lands would be most acute. An attempt to trace past climatic changes by the study of tree rings (thicker in wet years, thinner in drought) suggests that just such a change took place shortly before the outbreak of the *mfecane*. The worst of the drought, and the Mahlatule famine it produced, occurred some years before the *mfecane* reached its height. It may well have initiated a process which soon became self-escalating, however.

At the heart of the revolution in political and military organisation in Zululand was the transformation of the system of initiation-mate groups (*butho*, Nguni plural *ama-butho*) into a system of military organisation. This

*The mass migrations
of the* mfecane
& the Great Trek

was not unique to the northern Nguni. The Pedi, in building up their kingdom, also appear to have made use of age-regiments (*ama-butho*) as military units. It was in Zululand, however, that this was developed to the fullest degree. The traditional circumcision rites and subsequent period of seclusion were abandoned. Possibly this was because they left the youths and the community as a whole too dangerously defenceless at a time when the frequency and violence of warfare was increasing. Instead of the traditional ceremonies, young men of an age to be initiated were simply grouped together in age regiments (*ama-butho*), each with a distinctive name. These were then attached to one or other of the royal households which served as their assembly points (*amakhanda*). They fought as military units, and service in warfare took the place of circumcision and ritual seclusion as the means of initiation into manhood. The abandonment of circumcision meant that membership of a *butho* was no longer tied to participation in a particular initiation school. Young men could be grouped together on the basis of apparent age alone, and young men of conquered chiefdoms could be incorporated in a *butho* together with those of the conquering group. Living and fighting alongside their age-mates they would develop a sense of common identity and common loyalty to their new ruler. It was a powerful means of permanently welding together a series of previously independent kingdoms in an expanded kingdom. The potential of the system as a means of developing common loyalties and a sense of identity were limited at first, however, by the fact that the *ama-butho* only assembled in time of war. Except when they were engaged in actual military operations the members lived at home in their own communities.

The rise of the northern Nguni states

Towards the end of the eighteenth century a number of chiefs in the area were engaged in the attempt to build enlarged paramountcies by bringing neighbouring chiefdoms under their sway. One of the most successful was Zwide of the Ndwandwe, who conquered and subjected many neighbouring chiefdoms to build a powerful, extensive and aggressive paramountcy. Some evidence suggests that the militarisation of the initiation-mate system may have begun among the Ndwandwe. If so it was soon taken up by some of their neighbours. On the other hand it may have been adopted independently by a number of communities in response to the pressures of increasingly frequent warfare.

Zwide's greatest rival was Dingiswayo of the Mthethwa. Because of the subsequent history of the area the traditions of the Mthethwa acquired greatest prominence and were recorded by the first European visitors. They naturally stressed the role of Dingiswayo, who is credited with sole responsibility for ending circumcision and initiating the age-regiment (*butho*) military system. Allowing for their bias, it does seem that Dingiswayo was for a time the most powerful of the ambitious kingdom builders. He brought many chiefdoms under his control. He also made deliberate efforts to increase trade with Delagoa Bay and encouraged his people to copy some of the imported commodities they acquired there. Among other leaders who followed this path the Dlamini chief Sobhuza, who ruled a community which then identified itself as Ngwane and had its base near the upper Pongola river in uncomfortable proximity to the expanding Ndwandwe, was probably the most powerful. In the heart of modern Zululand between the Tugela and Mhlatuse rivers the Qwabe built a substantial paramountcy. Further inland the Nyuswa and the Mkhize also enlarged their followings along the Tugela. On the upper Mzinyathi river the Hlubi, under pressure from the Ndwandwe, aggregated a substantial but weakly centralised community. Conflicts generated by this process produced a chain reaction affecting much of modern Natal. The Thuli, driven across the Tugela by the Qwabe, created a significant paramountcy near modern Durban and in doing so displaced others, spreading the chain of disturbance as far south as the Umzimkulu river, provoking the Pondo to start enlarging their chiefdom in defensive reaction.

During the first fifteen years of the nineteenth century the pace of conflict quickened. This was possibly the result of change in the pattern of trade at Delagoa Bay, although a recent suggestion that it was a response to dramatic expansion of the slave trade there has proved unsustainable. Documentary evidence makes it clear that the slave trade at Delagoa Bay only assumed large proportions after these upheavals were under way. Perhaps competition between the various aggressively expanding chiefdoms of itself escalated the intensity and scale of conflict. As the heightened competition for power and territory developed, Sobhuza was defeated by Zwide's Ndwandwe forces in a conflict over garden lands along the Pongola river.

Sobhuza fled with his people into the area of modern Swaziland. There he began the process of conquering the numerous small chiefdoms, some Sotho and some Nguni-speaking, which he encountered there and uniting them in an enlarged kingdom. During his lifetime the process was incomplete and the loose paramountcy he created remained precariously exposed to disintegration in face of repeated Zulu attacks. After his death, and especially in the reign of his most famous successor Mswati, the military and political organisation of the kingdom was greatly strengthened and extensive conquests undertaken. It is thus from this later ruler that the people take their modern name Swazi.

When Sobhuza began conquering the small chiefdoms in Swaziland he left them under the administration of their own ruling families, insisting only on allegiance to himself as overlord. Consolidation of the kingdom involved incorporation of their young men in the king's *ama-butho*, thus expanding his forces and simultaneously building a sense of loyalty to the kingdom as a whole. Initially the Swazi age-regiments assembled only in times of war, but later ambitious youths from all sections of the community were encouraged to come to the royal homesteads where they remained on continuous service until their *butho* was dissolved. The king thus came to possess a substantial standing army which could be expanded in the event of a major war by calling up the rest of the young men from their villages to join with their fellows already on active service. Through this system, together with the development of a highly complex political system, the chiefdoms of Swaziland were permanently united in a single political community which today constitutes an independent African nation.

In addition to driving Sobhuza into Swaziland, Zwide's Ndwandwe also attacked the expanding Ngwane chiefdom of Matiwane who were driven to migrate to the neighbourhood of the upper Mzinyathi river where they

*The mass migrations
of the* mfecane
& the Great Trek

encountered the Hlubi paramountcy, then greatly weakened by internal rivalries. The Hlubi confederacy disintegrated in face of the Ngwane attack, some joining Matiwane while others remained in the neighbourhood of their original home. A substantial segment, led by Mpangazita, fled across the Drakensberg onto the highveld, thus initiating the spread of the *mfecane* to Transorangia.

Shaka: the military leader

As the lesser rivals were driven from the immediate area, Dingiswayo and Zwide found themselves face to face. After a number of initial victories, Dingiswayo (probably in 1817) led all his forces against his rival. On mounting a hill to look down on the battlefield, however, he was seized in an Ndwandwe ambush and later put to death. Having lost their leader, his forces broke up and the Mthethwa kingdom rapidly dissolved. Its collapse, however, opened the way for an ambitious client ruler of Dingiswayo named Shaka.

Shaka was a junior son of Senzangakona, ruler of a small chiefdom known as the Zulu. His mother, Nande, had been driven from his father's court on account of her uncontrollable temper, and Shaka grew up amongst strangers. He developed a strong determination to assert himself and an unquenchable thirst for absolute power. As a young man he served in Dingiswayo's forces, attracting the attention of the king by reckless deeds of bravery. On the death of Senzangakona, Dingiswayo lent his young follower the military support necessary to oust and kill a senior brother and make himself chief of the Zulu.

Once in power Shaka began reorganising the forces of his people in accordance with ideas he had developed while serving Dingiswayo. He had seen that the most commonly used type of spear, a long-handled *assegai* thrown at a distance, was inappropriate for the ordered combat in close formation now made possible by the expansion and improvement of military organisation. A group which retained its spears instead of throwing them and advanced right up to the enemy behind the protection of an ordered line of shields would have its opponents at its mercy and be able to achieve a total victory. Shaka thus armed his forces with short-handled stabbing spears, training them to move up to the enemy in close formation with their body-length cowhide shields forming an almost solid barrier to anything thrown at them. The formation most generally used was crescent-shaped and known as the 'cows' horns'. A number of *butho* drawn up several ranks deep formed a dense body known as the chest (*isifuba*), while one *butho* moving forward on each side formed the horns. As the horns curved inward around the enemy the main body would begin its advance, massacring all who could not break through the surrounding lines.

Shaka was certainly not alone in adopting these tactics. The evidence shows that the Ndwandwe and Matiwane's Ngwane also employed the stabbing spear, long a part of the traditional armoury, as the main battle weapon at about the same time. It seems probable that the new tactics came into general use in reaction to the increase in scale and intensity of battles rather than being invented by a single individual. Shaka appears however to have adopted them more rigidly and systematically than his contemporaries and this led him to a further major innovation of his own. The use of the new weapons and tactics required much drilling and Shaka kept his forces on continuous military service. They were accommodated at

Shaka, king of the Zulus from Nathaniel Isaacs, *Travels and Adventures in Eastern Africa*, 1836

*The mass migrations
of the* mfecane
& the Great Trek

his royal homesteads, which thus became substantial military towns, and remained there until they were formally dissolved and were allowed to adopt the insignia of manhood and marry.

When Dingiswayo fought his last campaign, Shaka did not reach the scene of battle until after his overlord's capture. He thus retained his forces intact, and as the Mthethwa state collapsed he immediately began conquering surrounding chiefdoms himself, adding their forces to his own and building up a new kingdom. A crucial victory over the Qwabe brought their substantial forces under his control at this critical time. Zwide soon became aware of what was happening and resolved to crush his new rival. After a first expedition had been defeated by the Zulu he sent his entire forces into Zulu territory. Shaka wore out the invaders by retreating before them, destroying the crops and removing the cattle from their line of march; then, as they were retreating in exhaustion, he attacked and routed them in a decisive battle on the Mhlatuse river.

The defeat catalysed tensions within Zwide's composite paramountcy which broke up into a number of sections. Part of the Ndwandwe force under Soshangane, together with the Jere under Zwengendaba, the Maseko under Ngwane and the Msene led by Nxaba, fled northwards by separate routes to the area of southern Mozambique. The core of the Ndwandwe force, however, remained loyal to Zwide who re-established his kingdom on the upper Pongola river. Its forces remained a formidable threat to the emerging Zulu kingdom and Shaka had to maintain a largely defensive stance towards it. In 1826, however, full-scale war broke out between the Zulu and the Ndwandwe, then under Zwide's successor, Sikhunyane. This time they were totally defeated. The majority then submitted to Shaka, while others fled to join the followings of other Nguni military leaders.

In southern Mozambique the refugee groups that had fled north after the defeat of Ndwandwe on the Mhlatuse river, using tactics similar to those of the Zulu, conquered many local communities, absorbing their young men into their fighting forces. Conflict between them left Soshangane the victor in southern Mozambique where he built the Gaza kingdom. His *ama-butho* expanded by the incorporation of large numbers of young men from the conquered communities in southern Mozambique, mustered in case of war at a series of royal household settlements established in the core area of his kingdom. This force enabled Soshangane to enforce his paramountcy and extract tribute from chiefdoms over an extensive area. The small Portuguese settlements in southern Mozambique also bought peace at the price of tribute to him.

Zwangendaba's following and the Maseko driven from Mozambique passed through modern Zimbabwe, raiding and looting cattle from many Shona chiefdoms and critically weakening the Rozwi kingdom in western Zimbabwe. The two conquering groups, both coming to be known as the Ngoni, then crossed the Zambezi at different points and moved by different routes through modern Malawi.

Zwangendaba's Ngoni moved northward in a series of long stages, keeping to the west of Lake Malawi. Passing the head of the lake they settled for a while in the Fipa country in modern Tanzania. There, at a settlement named Mapupa ('dreams'), Zwangendaba died. His following, swollen to many times its original size by the absorption of captives of many different

Northward migrations: foundation of the Gaza and Ngoni kingdoms

Zulu warrior in full regalia

*The mass migrations
of the* mfecane
& the Great Trek

ethnic origins, was torn apart by a prolonged and complex succession dispute. Zwangendaba's following and the Maseko Ngoni eventually created seven substantial Ngoni kingdoms in Tanzania, Zambia and Malawi and made a very significant impact on the history of most of the peoples of this vast area. Nxaba and the Msene, after participating in the devastation of the Rozwi empire, moved up the Zambezi to Barotseland where Nxaba was killed and his following broken up.

Shaka: the consolidation of power

After the battle on the Mhlatuse river, Shaka was able to expand and consolidate his kingdom by bringing more neighbouring chiefdoms under his authority while others moved to escape falling under his hegemony or that of his client chiefdoms. When a chiefdom was conquered or submitted, he left local administrative authority in the hands of the reigning chief or another member of the traditional ruling family appointed by himself. Except in the case of the most powerful or especially favoured chiefs, their young men were enrolled alongside others from all sections of the kingdom in Shaka's *ama-butho*. Each of these had its own name and was permanently accommodated at one of a series of royal households which thus became military settlements as well as retaining their traditional character. Each settlement contained a section of the royal women and was headed by a queen. Shaka, however, had a horror of producing a legitimate heir: he never married and women found pregnant by him were put to death. His households were thus not headed by wives but by senior women of the royal family. In the absence of the king, administrative authority was exercised jointly by the queen of the settlement and by an appointed *induna*. Each military settlement had a herd of royal cattle attached to it, from which the young men were supplied with meat. The hides of the cattle were used to provide the shields for the warriors and an attempt was made to select cattle of a particular distinctive skin colouring for each of the *butho*.

In addition to the young men, a large number of the young women of the kingdom were assembled at the military settlements. Officially wards of the king, they were organised in female equivalents of the male *butho* and engaged in ceremonial dancing and displays. When one of the *ama-butho* was dissolved its female equivalent would also be broken up and the women given out as brides to the warriors. Until such time, however, sexual relations between members of the male and female *butho* were forbidden and punished by death.

The development of the military system under Shaka produced a sense of common identity amongst the young men of many originally independent communities who were brought together in the *ama-butho* and thus in the kingdom as a whole. However, the traditional rulers of the subject chiefdoms still held local administrative authority, they had the fighting strength of the adult men under their command, and on the dissolution of the *butho* the young men would return to live in their community of origin. This meant that the sense of identity of these previously separate polities was not entirely lost but remained an important element in the later politics of the Zulu kingdom. Moreover, some of the more powerful chiefdoms which, as in the case of the Qwabe, had been incorporated in the early stages of Shaka's career, retained their own *ama-butho*. This meant that the rulers of the subordinate chiefdoms remained among the great men of the realm and a potential threat to the position of the king. When Shaka was uncertain of the loyalties of a subjected community he often stationed a trusted friend or relative with a group of followers in the neighbourhood to keep an eye on the behaviour of the chief concerned.

In addition, the military *indunas* as trusted favourites of the king received many cattle from him and were able to build up large personal followings. These developments resulted in later reigns in the emergence of powerful figures with strong local power bases which they had been able to develop as a result of royal appointments and favours. Though the *indunas* were generally commoners, the need for them to command respect meant that they were usually chosen from among the heads of substantial households. They frequently married daughters of chiefs and as their position enabled them to build up large households and many personal clients they sometimes established new hereditary chiefdoms.

The development of the military system involved major economic and social changes. The concentration of so much of the youth of the kingdom in the royal barracks meant a massive transfer of economic potential from private households to the state. The loss suffered by the households, however, was probably balanced by the fact that the energies of the young men were used more fully and effectively for amassing, guarding and herding cattle through the *butho* system. Thus the cattle wealth of the whole community was greatly increased. Even though a much larger proportion of the total herds was now owned by the king and his chiefs and *indunas*, all shared in the benefits to some extent. All members of the kingdom also shared in the pride evoked by the magnificence of the royal herds as well as the consciousness of unrivalled military power.

The new system offered particular benefits to the administrative class of the kingdom, the sub-chiefs and *indunas* who shared most directly in this public wealth. Though sub-chiefs might have lost independence, they gained greater security from incorporation in the kingdom. So long as they had the king's favour, no local rival could challenge them and their subjects could no longer evade paying their dues by deserting to another ruler. The young men also found some attractions in the system to balance the hardships and restraints it imposed on them. Service in the *butho* not only offered excitement and adventure but the possibility for even a lad from a poor home to achieve fame, wealth and power within the political system of the kingdom.

The Zulu kingdom, however, was born in a situation of crisis and extreme danger. To strengthen his forces against the more numerous Ndwandwe, Shaka initially adopted a variety of expedients allowing a substantial degree of autonomy to be retained by some chiefdoms like the Qwabe who even had their own *ama-butho*. Though centralisation increased as the kingdom consolidated its position, Shaka's reign was too short and turbulent for him to be able to impose a rigid logical uniformity on his extensive, diverse, and hastily assembled following. In the aftermath of his victory over Zwide he faced a continuing threat of renewed attack from the Ndwandwe now based on the upper Pongola. The core of his kingdom lay near the white Umfolozi river and a number of military settlements were built along the Black Umfolozi and the Mkuze to guard against attack from the north.

The extension of his influence to the south as far as the Tugela and the area immediately beyond it was entrusted to three semi-autonomous subordinate chiefs, Jobe of the Sithole, Zihlandlo of the Mkhize, and Magaye of the Cele, whose forces were buttressed by a Zulu *butho* known as the izi

Yendane. These three succeeded in conquering and subordinating a number of the chiefdoms which had been expanding in that area. Others migrated south through Natal to avoid this fate. The powerful Ngwane chiefdom however remained independent, dominating the upper Tugela.

During the early twenties internal tensions within his kingdom, the continuing threat from the north and possibly ecological considerations arising from the concentration of men and cattle at the military settlements, led Shaka to shift his main settlements southward nearer to the Tugela and close to the Qwabe. He began consolidating his dominance along the Tugela and as far south as the Umzimkulu more directly than before. The Ngwane were defeated and a large part of their community led by Matiwane fled across the Drakensberg in the wake of their old enemies, the Hlubi. Zulu forces advancing southwards through Natal also encountered and broke up the substantial Chunu chiefdom of Macingwane which had recently re-established itself in southern Natal after moving south from the Tugela to avoid subjection by the Zulu client chiefdom of the Mkhize. Most of its people migrated back north and submitted to Shaka. He established regular control only over a narrow strip south of the Tugela but his dominance was maintained as far as the Umzimkulu by periodic raiding forays.

In 1824 a Zulu army crossed the Umzimkulu, invaded the Pondo chiefdom and returned with many cattle. As this force was returning through Natal a number of English traders were establishing themselves near modern Durban, then known as Port Natal. They made contact with Shaka, and provided him with an alternative to the Portuguese at Delagoa Bay as customers for ivory and a source of European manufactured goods. Their firearms also made them potentially useful military auxiliaries. In 1826 the Ndwandwe, then under Zwide's son Sikhunyane, launched an all-out invasion of the Zulu kingdom. Two of the traders were present and may have contributed to the decisive defeat of the Ndwandwe, the majority of whom subsequently accepted Zulu overrule. They subsequently helped Shaka in other campaigns. He allowed their leaders to establish their authority over the remaining population in the neighbourhood of their settlement so that they became, in effect, chiefs of a series of client chiefdoms.

The end of Shaka's reign

The elimination of the Ndwandwe threat allowed Shaka to rule in a more authoritarian manner. Royal prestige was emphasised in the drastic manner in which mourning rights for his grandmother and, still more, for his mother Nande were enforced. Many people were killed for failing to display adequate grief or for breach of the mourning taboos. There was now no major obstacle to further expansion of his kingdom. After the mourning period for his mother in 1828, Shaka decided to launch a major campaign against the chiefdoms along the eastern coastal area between Natal and the Cape Colony. The evidence suggests that this was more than a cattle-raiding expedition and that Shaka had in mind the opening of direct communication and regular trade between his kingdom and the colony. To prepare the way for the campaign, Shaka first sent some of his senior *indunas* to the Cape in the company of one of the English traders, Lieutenant King, as an embassy to the Governor. His own forces passed through Pondoland but stopped before attacking the Tembu and Xhosa. The embassy had not returned from Cape Town and another trader, Henry Fynn, persuaded the Zulu king that the chiefdoms near the frontier were under British protection.

Shaka therefore turned his army about and directed it instead to the north of his kingdom, to attack the kingdom that Soshangane was building in southern Mozambique. As he did so however, Shaka left a message that the people should fatten up their cattle because he would return to collect them the next year and would not rest until he had opened a road to talk to his English friends in the colony.

Shaka himself remained behind while the majority of the fighting men were away on this new campaign in the north. Two of his brothers, Dingane and Mhlangane, took advantage of the growing discontent at the rigours of his rule and the never-ending wars to conspire against him with an *induna*, Mbopha. They found their opportunity to strike when Shaka was standing in the cattle enclosure, interviewing an embassy from a Sotho chiefdom that had brought him a tribute of cranes' feathers. As Mhlangane crept up behind him concealed by the enclosure fence, Mbopha distracted the king's attention by abusing the embassy for their late arrival and driving them out of the enclosure. Mhlangane stabbed him from behind, Dingane joined in and between them they killed him. Later Dingane succeeded in getting rid of his brother and fellow conspirator, Mhlangane, and succeeded to the Zulu kingship himself.

The settled life of the numerous chiefdoms between the Tugela and Umzimkhulu rivers in modern Natal began to be seriously disrupted by the intrusion of those groups from further north which pushed into the area as a result of the rise and expansion of the Ndwandwe and Mthethwa. Still more serious disruption followed with the establishment and expansion of the three Zulu client chiefdoms beyond the Tugela and then again as a result of the raids of Shaka's armies themselves and their destruction of the recently established Chunu chiefdom of Macingwane. As a result of these multiple migrations the previous settlement pattern in much of modern Natal was for a time substantially changed. Large numbers belonging to the many different chiefdoms of this area which were broken up or suffered severe defeat and loss of cattle migrated north across the Tugela and placed themselves under the authority of Shaka, the ruler who seemed most capable of guaranteeing protection.

In the extreme south of Natal and northern Transkei a whole series of refugee chiefdoms crowded together in the near neighbourhood of the Pondo under Faku, who had been stimulated to strengthen and expand his chiefdom by the impact of the first group of migrants from the north during the period of Ndwandwe and Mthethwa rivalry. A complex series of conflicts ensued involving these chiefdoms and the Pondo but also the Thembu and Xhosa. From this maelstrom Faku emerged as the most powerful, while much of the following of the various chiefdoms from further north was incorporated in the composite following of the Baca chief Ncapaai. Soon after the death of Shaka, the powerful Qwabe chiefdom broke away from his successor Dingane and, under the leadership of Nqeto, migrated south through Natal into this area. They threatened to force their way into the heart of the Transkei but were totally defeated in a desperate battle by Faku's Mpondo. As he fled from the victorious Pondo, Nqeto was killed by Ncapaai, his cattle were seized and his following broken up. As a result of the multiple conflicts, insecurity and overcrowding in this area, significant numbers of refugees fled further south and, along with the remnants of Matiwane's composite following, accepted

Dingane
from Gardiner, *Narrative of a Journey to the Zoolu Country*, 1836

*The mass migrations
of the* mfecane
& the Great Trek

client status under Thembu and Xhosa chiefs constituting part of the group known as Mfengu. Their settlement in the neighbourhood of the colonial frontier added to pressure on land resources and increased pressure in other ways: they soon came to resent their subordination, and began to look to white missionaries and, subsequently, the colonial authorities for help in extricating themselves from it. In spite of some southward migration, however, the neighbourhood of Pondoland remained crowded with people many of whom looked forward to returning to their homes and garden lands in Natal as soon as the security situation improved.

While population was thus concentrated in the Zulu kingdom and around the Pondo area, it was temporarily reduced in much of the intervening areas of Natal except in the vicinity of Port Natal where the English traders commanded considerable followings. The population which did remain in these areas tended to keep itself concealed in areas of heavy bush, thus giving passing European travellers an impression of a far greater degree of depopulation than actually existed.

The difaqane: *the* mfecane *on the Transorangian highveld*

The pattern of intensified conflict which accompanied the process of enlarged state building in the Zululand area began to affect the eastern regions of the highveld between the Orange and Vaal rivers as a consequence of the break up of the Hlubi paramountcy by the Ngwane on their initial migration to avoid subjection to Zwide.

The intrusion of the Hlubi on to the Transorangian highveld began a long series of wars and migrations often called the *difaqane*, the Sotho version of *mfecane*.

One of the first major Sotho groups encountered by the Nguni invaders was the Tlokwa, then ruled by a queen, Mma Nthatisi, who was acting as regent for her son Sekonyela. Driven from their homes, the Tlokwa wandered widely over much of modern Lesotho and eastern Orange Free State, plundering and destroying weaker groups. They finally established themselves on the mountains of Kooaneng and Yoalaboholo near the north-eastern border of modern Lesotho, where under the rule of Sekonyela they attempted to build up a kingdom in rivalry with Moshoeshoe.

The arrival of Matiwane and his Ngwane, after their defeat by the Zulu, added further to the devastation in the Transorangian highveld. In addition to raiding the settled Sotho chiefdoms, and conflicting with the migrating Tlokwa, the two predatory Nguni-speaking groups fought a series of bitter battles with one another. Matiwane's Ngwane eventually defeated their Hlubi rivals, absorbing most of the survivors into their own forces and becoming for a time the dominant group in the area. In 1828, however, after being attacked by the Ndebele of Mzilikazi and by the Zulu, and having failed to defeat Moshoeshoe, they abandoned the highveld for the coast, re-crossed the Drakensberg and invaded the territory of the Thembu.

There they were met by colonial forces who had crossed the frontier to protect the Xhosa and Thembu chiefdoms from an anticipated Zulu attack. Mistaken for a Zulu force, the Ngwane were attacked and broken up. The majority then settled as clients known as Mfengu among the Xhosa and Thembu, while a few fled with Matiwane to take refuge for a time with Moshoeshoe. Though Moshoeshoe advised against it, Matiwane finally returned to offer his submission to Dingane but was seized and put to death on a flat-topped hill that became known as Matiwane's Kop.

Moshoeshoe, 1833
from Casalis, *Les Bassoutos*, 1859

Sotho-Tswana
upheavals

*The mass migrations
of the* mfecane
& the Great Trek

The dislocation caused by these wandering bands complemented the disruptions produced by the raiding activities of mounted gun-bearing bands of Korana and rebellious sections of the Griqua. The activities of these bandits were initially confined to the western areas of Transorangia and south-western Transvaal. However, encouraged by the expanding market in the Cape for raided cattle and captive African 'apprentices' and by the breakdown of ordered political life in the aftermath of the passage of the various marauding bands, they spread eastward as far as the Caledon valley. After the departure of Matiwane these Griqua raiders became the major cause of continuing devastation throughout the Transorangian highveld.

The combined impact of two sets of marauders produced appalling conditions in the Transorangian highveld. Much of the area gave the appearance of being deserted as survivors took refuge in mountainous country or hid in heavily bush-clad valleys, keeping out of the way of passing travellers and traders. Starvation was widespread and some were forced into cannibalism. Sotho refugees poured into the Cape Colony where they provided a much-needed labour supply for the white farmers of the eastern districts.

Driven from their homes in the course of the upheaval, a number of Sotho groups fled across the Vaal river and formed wandering armed bands, raiding the Tswana chiefdoms. In June 1823 three such groups, the Fokeng led by Sebetwane, the Hlakoane and the Phuting, converged on the Tlhaping settlement of Dithakong. The missionary Robert Moffat sought aid from the Griqua and with the aid of their guns the invaders were beaten off. The Hlakoane and the Phuting returned eastwards to the Vaal.

The Fokeng of Sebetwane, who subsequently became known as the Kololo, retreated to the north of Dithakong and associated for a time with another wandering group, the Taung led by Moletsane. After an attack by Mzilikazi's Ndebele, the two groups separated and the Kololo moved on northwards, attacking and plundering the Tswana chiefdoms of modern Botswana. After wandering in the Kalahari they moved north to the Zambezi, then up the river to enter the flood plain of Barotseland just as the Lozi kingdom there was weakened by a succession dispute. Sebetwane was able to conquer the Lozi kingdom and establish a temporary Kololo empire in the area.

In 1851 Sebetwane was visited by David Livingstone, who made the Kololo kingdom the base for his expeditions to Angola and down the Zambezi. Some of the porters from the kingdom who accompanied Livingstone on this journey settled in the Shire valley of modern Malawi. There they succeeded in establishing leadership over the Manganja peoples who were being harassed by Yao and Portuguese slave raiders and Ngoni attacks. They built a series of Kololo chiefdoms in the valley, saving the population from threatened extermination and playing an important part in the early stages of the establishment of British control over Nyasaland (modern Malawi).

After the Griqua defeat of the groups threatening Dithakong, and the departure of Sebetwane and the Kololo, the Taung of Moletsane remained for a time the most powerful group in the southern Tswana area. They harassed the Seleka-Rolong, forcing the abandonment of the Wesleyan mission station at Maquassie. A new station was founded at Platberg where three Rolong chiefdoms came together with a number of Griqua under Barend-Barends and a Kora community led by Gert Taaibosh. In 1834, faced with danger of Ndebele attack, the missionaries led this mixed group

David Livingstone from *Last Journals of David Livingstone in Central Africa*, 1880

Moshoeshoe and the establishment of the Lesotho kingdom

The devastated conditions in the area of Lesotho created by the invasions of the Hlubi and the subsequent wars and migrations gave Moshoeshoe the opportunity to gather the broken southern Sotho peoples into an expanded kingdom. The son of an insignificant sub-chief of the Mokoteli, Moshoeshoe established himself with a group of age-mates at an early age in a strong position on a flat-topped mountain called Butha-Buthe in what is now north-eastern Lesotho. Successful cattle raiding had already enabled him to attract a substantial following when the Hlubi invasion threw the area into confusion.

His mountain stronghold enabled Moshoeshoe to beat off a first attack by the Tlokwa of Mma Nthatisi and Sekonyela; but when Sekonyela attacked Butha-Buthe a second time, Moshoeshoe's following was reduced to the verge of starvation and he was saved by the intervention of an Nguni group who drove the Tlokwa away. It was after this that the Sekonyela and the Tlokwa settled at Kooaneng and Yoalaboholo.

It was clear that Butha-Buthe offered poor protection in face of a determined siege, so Moshoeshoe led his people on a dangerous migration to the large and stronger position provided by another flat-topped mountain, Thaba Bosiu. This stronghold proved impregnable to all attackers and during the rest of Moshoeshoe's reign provided the fixed point around which he was able to build up and preserve the kingdom of Lesotho. Successful raids against the Thembu soon after his settlement on Thaba Bosiu gave Moshoeshoe substantial herds of cattle. By providing cattle on loan to destitute groups on the basis of the traditional *mafisa* system, he secured their loyalty.

As he gathered the broken remnants of Sotho chiefdoms under his protection, Moshoeshoe placed them under the authority of his brothers and sons whom he established in a series of settlements throughout his kingdom. Larger and more coherent groups, however, were allowed to remain under the authority of their own rulers. Moshoeshoe's kingdom thus remained a patchwork of different groups, some with a continuing strong sense of identity of their own. It was held together by common danger, the practice of continuous consultation, and respect for the outstanding ability and personality of the king.

After establishing himself on Thaba Bosiu, Moshoeshoe at first paid tribute to Matiwane and the Ngwane but as they became increasingly demanding he offered tribute to Dingane instead and persuaded him to send an expedition against Matiwane. The Ngwane lost many of their cattle in this attack and also suffered a defeat at the hands of an Ndebele expedition. When they attempted to make good their losses by a direct attack on Moshoeshoe, they were forced back by the strong defence of Thaba Bosiu. This defeat brought about their movement out of Transorangia into the Thembu country where they were broken up by colonial forces in 1828.

After the withdrawal of the Ngwane, Moshoeshoe's kingdom was subjected to repeated raids by Kora and Griqua bandits. In return, the Sotho resorted to night ambushes, seizing their attackers' horses and guns. Within a few years the Sotho adopted the tactics of the white and mixed blood frontiersmen, breeding their own variety of horse, the Basuto pony, and turning themselves into a nation of mounted gunmen.

As the worst of the turmoil in Transorangia died down, Sotho who had

Sekonyela
from *Diary of Andrew Smith*, 1834

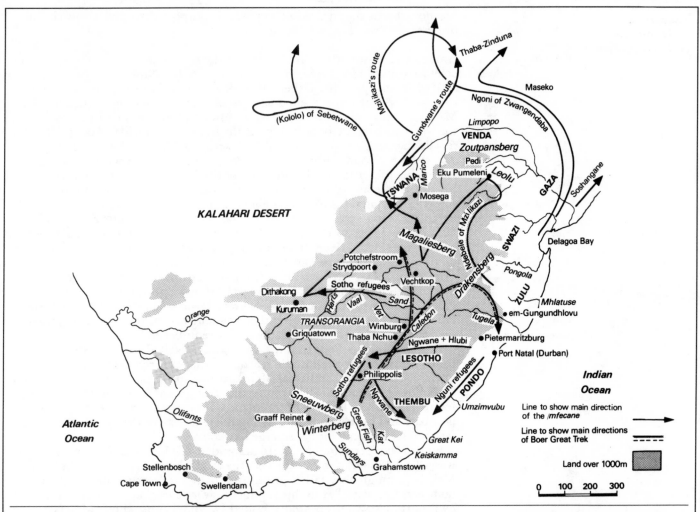

taken refuge in the Cape returned to the area. They were often accompanied by the cattle they had earned while in the service of the whites. Many of them placed themselves under the protection of Moshoeshoe who settled them on the fertile lands between the Orange and Caledon rivers, where they increased his following. In 1833 after repeated efforts, Moshoeshoe succeeded in attracting a party of missionaries belonging to the Paris Evangelical Society to his kingdom. They soon established a number of mission stations and proved useful as diplomatic advisers and allies of the king in his subsequent conflicts with white groups.

The expansion of Moshoeshoe's kingdom brought him into competition and conflict with his old enemy, Sekonyela, and in 1834 the position was further complicated by the arrival on his frontiers of the Rolong, Griqua and Kora accompanied by the Wesleyan missionaries. Neither the Rolong nor the Wesleyan missionaries were prepared to submit to the authority of Moshoeshoe and his Paris Evangelical Mission Society advisers. In the absence of any of the French missionaries the Wesleyans persuaded

4.1 Approximate directions of major movements during the *mfecane* in southern Africa and the main directions of movement of the Boer Great Trek

65

*The mass migrations
of the* mfecane
& the Great Trek

Moshoeshoe to sign a deed of sale which purported to give them absolute
ownership of the Thaba Nchu area.

*Mzilikazi and the
Ndebele*

Among the most outstanding leaders of the *mfecane* period was the Khumalo
chief Mzilikazi. His chiefdom had been part of the Ndwandwe paramountcy
of Zwide who had his father, Mashobane, put to death on suspicion of
treachery. According to some accounts, after succeeding to the chiefdom
Mzilikazi broke away from the Ndwandwe and joined Shaka shortly before
the decisive conflict between the Zulu leader and Zwide. About 1821 he
rebelled against his overlord and fled with his Ndebele followers on to the
Transvaal highveld. Other accounts deny his association with the Zulu and
ascribe his migration to the break-up of the Ndwandwe paramountcy which
led to the northward migrations of the Ngoni and others. At all events, he
subsequently used his royal households as military settlements on lines similar to the Zulu system, and was the object of an enduring Zulu vendetta.
He migrated first to the north-eastern Transvaal, and settled briefly on the
middle Steelpoort river. It is probably to this area that Mzilikazi and his
followers gave the name eku-Pumeleni (the resting place).

In about 1822, Mzilikazi invaded and overthrew the Pedi kingdom. One
heir to the kingdom, Sekwati, however, did make good his escape. When the
Ndebele departed in about 1823, Sekwati returned to rebuild the Pedi state.
He succeeded in re-establishing the kingdom which, with its strongholds in
the Leolu mountains, finally reappeared, strengthened from the ordeal.

Abandoning the Pedi country, Mzilikazi travelled south-west and established himself near the middle reaches of the Vaal river. During his period
in the north-eastern Transvaal Mzilikazi had incorporated many conquered
Sotho into his regiments. His following had grown far larger than the original band he had led out of Zululand. This process was continued at his
new base and his expanded following made necessary the establishment of a
series of settlements for his enlarged *ama-butho*.

From these settlements Mzilikazi raided a wide area, especially to the
west. In 1825 his forces attacked the Ngwaketse and killed their ruler,
Makaba, though they failed to capture many cattle or to subdue the chiefdom permanently. While his regiments were away on this expedition, his
own outposts were repeatedly raided by the Taung chief, Moletsane, in
alliance with a number of Kora and Griqua. However, an Ndebele force
fought back and temporarily drove Moletsane south of the Vaal.

Under pressure from the Griqua raiders Mzilikazi abandoned the Vaal river
area in 1827 and established a series of new settlements in the area between
the Apies and Elands rivers. The Ndebele failed to find security in their new
position, however. During 1828 Jan Bloem and his armed Kora horsemen
combined with Moletsane's Taung and raided the Ndebele while the greater
part of Mzilikazi's forces were away on a campaign against the Ngwaketse.
As the raiders retreated with a large haul of cattle, however, pursuing
Ndebele forces surprised them in a night attack and recaptured the cattle.

The following year Mzilikazi despatched the punitive expedition which
smashed Moletsane's following and forced him to take refuge at
Philippolis. In 1829 Mzilikazi was visited by two white traders, William
McLuckie and Robert Schoon, and by two missionaries, James Archbell of
the Wesleyan Missionary Society and Robert Moffat from the LMS station
at Kuruman. Moffat won the close friendship of the Ndebele king and visited

him on a number of subsequent occasions at his different settlements.

From the central Transvaal, Mzilikazi's regiments continued to raid the Tswana, and in 1830 or 1831 an expedition south of the Vaal attacked Moshoeshoe's stronghold on Thaba Bosiu but was driven back. In 1831 Barend-Barends organised a large commando made up of about three hundred mounted Griqua and Kora armed with guns, and numerous Tswana allies. He planned to undertake a full-scale conquest of the Ndebele kingdom and to break its power permanently. The commando initially met with complete success. As it returned with the huge captured herds, however, it suffered a similar fate to Jan Bloem's earlier expedition. Surprised in a night attack by the Ndebele, the captured cattle were lost and a large proportion of the commando were killed. The Griqua and Kora were thus seriously weakened, though they still had enough strength to harass Mzilikazi's settlements.

Soon after the Barend-Barends commando, news of the succession of Dingane to the Zulu throne aroused Mzilikazi's fears of a Zulu attack. He prepared to move his settlement further to the west, launching a series of devastating attacks on a number of Tswana communities. Before his plans were complete, however, the Ndebele were surprised by a Zulu army which overran a number of their settlements and looted many cattle. After a full-scale battle which ended indecisively but with heavy losses on both sides, the Zulu withdrew.

Immediately after the battle with the Zulu in August 1832, Mzilikazi launched expeditions against the Rolong of Tawana, the Kwena of Kgama and the Ngwaketse, the last of whom alone offered serious resistance. They were drastically crushed, however, and their long period of influence in the southern Tswana area was finally destroyed. The Ndebele then moved their settlements to the Marico valley. Many Tswana were incorporated into the Ndebele community and enrolled in their *butho*. Others, however, lived as separate dependent communities scattered among the Ndebele settlements and on the edge of the kingdom's core area.

The migration from the central to the western Transvaal still did not give Mzilikazi the security he was seeking. In 1834 he was attacked once again by a Kora-Griqua party supported by a section of the Hurutshe and led by Jan Bloem II. Once again the victorious raiding party was ambushed as it retired with the loot and Jan Bloem only narrowly escaped. The Griqua, however, continued to boast that they would soon renew their attacks, and Mzilikazi maintained regular patrols to the south-east to ward off any new expeditions. As a further protection against the Kora and Griqua raiders, Mzilikazi sought to build on his friendship with Moffat at Kuruman. He thus permitted two American missionaries, Daniel Lindley and Henry Venable, to begin work among his people. In 1835 he entered into a treaty with the government of the Cape Colony in the hope that the Governor would control his 'children'.

Thaba Bosiu
from Casalis, *Les Bassoutos*, 1859

The effects of the mfecane

The *mfecane* was primarily a process of change towards larger and more strongly centralised states. The migrations and wars associated with it spread the process and led to the establishment of such states over a vast area. The Zulu kingdom itself, though not the origin of the *mfecane* but just one of its products, was the prime example of this revolutionary development.

The mass migrations
of the mfecane
& the Great Trek

It brought about within a very short time a sense of common identity amongst peoples of many different origins and it also concentrated immense power in the hands of the king. Other states founded at this time by Nguni-speaking peoples, including the Swazi, Gaza and Ndebele kingdoms together with the Ngoni kingdoms in what are now Malawi, Zambia and Tanzania, also made use of the *butho* system of military organisation in a variety of ways as the basis of their political organisation. Lesotho was built on different lines but also owed its origin to the impact of the *mfecane*. The creation of the short-lived Kololo empire on the flood plain of the Zambezi, the strengthening of the Pedi kingdom and the expansion of a number of chiefdoms (like the Mangwato in Botswana or the Bhaca in the Pondoland area) by the incorporation of other groups were further consequences of the upheaval.

At the same time, some previously established kingdoms were weakened or destroyed like the Rozwi kingdom which was replaced by the Ndebele in south-western Zimbabwe. The loose hegemony of the Cewa king Undi over wide areas of modern Mozambique, Zambia and Malawi was similarly shattered by the Ngoni invaders. Within South Africa settled life was temporarily gravely disrupted in large areas. There was significant population displacement as frightened communities temporarily abandoned their lands in the open country of the modern Orange Free State and the Transvaal to find safety under Moshoeshoe in mountainous Lesotho, with the Pedi in the Leolu mountains, in the fastnesses of the Zoutpansberg or in broken country near the Kalahari. As those who remained in less easily defensible country took care to hide themselves in valleys, patches of bush and rocky areas, a much greater impression of population displacement was created than actually existed. Natal was also very seriously affected and though a significant population no doubt remained concealed within the area, European travellers gained the impression of wide areas of fertile land lying empty.

The disruptions of the *mfecane*, moreover, meant that the peoples who remained in areas outside the powerful kingdoms were more likely to welcome the arrival of whites as possible allies against their African enemies than to offer any sustained resistance. Large areas in the Orange Free State, the Transvaal and Natal thus appeared to offer ideal opportunities for white settlement just at a time when land hunger and dissatisfaction with the British government at the Cape were combining to urge the Dutch-speaking white farmers of the eastern frontier areas towards a mass breakaway from the Colony.

European observations

News of the situation in the interior soon reached the Cape where it was fairly widely discussed, thus helping to make the idea of migration and settlement in the interior appear a practicable answer to the white frontiersmen's problems. The situation in Natal, the most desirable area for settlement, was particularly well known from the English traders at Port Natal who maintained regular contact with the Colony both by sea and by a land route up the coastal strip beyond the Cape's eastern frontier. In 1835, Captain Allen Gardiner arrived in Natal to start missionary work. He persuaded Dingane to admit missionaries to the Zulu kingdom itself and in 1836 three Americans and the English missionary Francis Owen started work there. Soon after the establishment of the English traders at Port Natal they began pressing for the area to be made a colony. In 1832 the governor at the Cape appointed Dr Andrew Smith to lead an expedition to Natal to examine the prospects for such a development. The expedition members, who included a young Afrikaner, were enthusiastic when they saw the fertile, well-watered land lying vacant. On the return of the expedition, a group of Cape merchants formed an association to promote the colonisation of the area, and its attractions became widely known to Afrikaner farmers as well. So far as the highveld of Transorangia and the Transvaal was concerned, the area was known to travelling traders like McLuckie and Schoon, the first whites to visit Mzilikazi, and to the missionaries Moffat and Archbell. From 1825, moreover, Afrikaner farmers from the north-eastern districts of the colony were moving across the Orange in increasing numbers.

By early 1834 the idea of a mass migration out of the Colony to establish a new society beyond the frontiers began to be seriously considered. Two prominent men, Gert Maritz, a wealthy wagon-maker from Graaff-Reinet, and Piet Retief, a widely respected farmer and contractor who held the office of commandant in the Winterberg area, travelled widely in the eastern districts, secretly spreading the idea of a mass trek. To prepare the way, reconnaissance parties (*commissie trekke*) were organised to investigate the situation in the interior and the availability of suitable land for settlement.

The reconnaissance parties returned to report in 1835. One, which had travelled to the dry lands of what is now Namibia, reported that there were no prospects in that direction. The second, however, passed through Transorangia into the Transvaal reaching as far as the Zoutpansberg where it met some of Coenraad de Buy's descendants. The third party, led by Piet Uys, attracted the greatest attention. It travelled up the east coast strip and was warmly welcomed by the English at Port Natal. Its members were enchanted by the beauty and natural richness of the land which appeared to them to be almost entirely deserted. By the time the reconnaissance parties returned, however, thoughts of secession were temporarily laid aside because the frontier areas were involved in another war with the Xhosa.

The sixth Xhosa war of resistance

The origin of renewed conflict between Europeans and the Xhosa lay in the overcrowding and land hunger among the Xhosa immediately beyond the frontier. This was the result of the way that they had been robbed of their lands and driven from the *zuurveld*. They had also lost a large part of the area between the Fish and Keiskamma rivers (the neutral strip by now known as the ceded territory) which had been the original home of Ngqika and his followers. While white settlers had been established in some of this land and a substantial area had been taken for the Khoi Kat river settlement, Ngqika's chief heir, Macomo, and his relative, Tyali, had been allowed to reoccupy other parts of it. This permission, however, was subject to their 'good behaviour' in the eyes of the colonial authorities and by 1834 Macomo and his people had already been forced to abandon their homes, gardens and grazing lands on three occasions.

When Governor D'Urban arrived in 1834, charged with the main task of ending slavery, he also brought with him instructions to find a better way of regulating relations with the frontier chiefdoms. Soon after his arrival he asked Dr John Philip to visit the frontier chiefs to inform them of his intention to adopt a more just system of frontier regulation and to prepare the way for his

Crossing Cradock's Pass
by C.C. Michell

*The mass migrations
of the* mfecane
& the Great Trek

own visit. Philip met a warm response from the Xhosa chiefs he visited and relations on the border much improved, but D'Urban, caught up in endless paper work over slave emancipation, kept delaying his visit to the frontier.

The border districts were suffering a severe drought which threatened the livelihood of black and white pastoralists alike, and once more raised tension over grazing lands. As the Governor delayed, the chiefs became convinced that Philip's visit had been planned to keep them quiet while the colonial authorities prepared their forces to drive them from their homes. The sight of white farmers openly driving their cattle beyond the frontier heightened this suspicion and it only needed some over enthusiastic patrolling by the military to start conflict. In December 1834, the Xhosa invaded the colony on a broad front from the Winterberg to the sea. The frontier districts were devastated before British reinforcements could come up. The colonial forces struck back and, after invading the lands of the Ngqika and Ndlambe, spread the war to the Gcaleka chiefdom of Hintsa around the Kei river.

Accused of providing safe refuge for cattle stolen from the Colony Hintsa was invited to an interview with the commander of the colonial forces, Harry Smith. Seized and held as a hostage, he subsequently broke free, tried to escape and was killed. His head was cut off as a trophy. The capture and murder of Hintsa involved the colonial forces in outright conflict with the Gcaleka. Their Mfengu clients took advantage of the upheavals to rebel. They flocked to the mission stations bringing the cattle that had been entrusted to their care. The missionaries pleaded hard for a people who had responded so well to their teaching, and Governor D'Urban, seeing the possibility of using them to good purpose, granted them British protection in May 1835. Guarded by the colonial troops, they migrated with their cattle to be resettled on land taken from the Xhosa around Fort Peddie in the Ceded Territory. Here the Mfengu were to constitute a defensive buffer settlement to protect the Colony.

As the colonial forces fought the Gcaleka, Smith became convinced that the Boer community which, under the leadership of Louis Trichardt, was settled on Hintsa's lands, was guilty of treason. Trichardt's arrest was ordered; to avoid this fate in 1835 he and the members of his community trekked out of the area to the north. Together with another party under Janse van Rensburg which left the north-eastern districts of the Cape at about the same time, they were the advance guard of the Great Trek which was soon to follow.

Sir Benjamin D'Urban
by E. Hareman

Queen Adelaide Province   When D'Urban at last reached the frontier, he was so outraged by the destruction that he condemned the Xhosa as 'irredeemable savages'. The whole area between the colonial frontier and the Kei river was annexed as Queen Adelaide Province. The land was all to be granted to white farmers and the Xhosa were to be driven out of it for ever. The frontier farmers were delighted. At last they had a governor who shared their view of the frontier situation and supported their interests. With the prospect of rich new farms in the new province, thoughts of migration out of the colony were once more set aside. But such dreams were soon shattered by Xhosa courage and determination. Fighting on in desperation, they not only resisted all attempts by the colonial forces to drive them out of the area between the Fish and Kei rivers but even launched a number of daring raids into the Colony itself.

D'Urban was forced to adopt a new policy. The Xhosa were persuaded to make peace in return for retaining possession of most of their lands in the new province, but they were to become British subjects under direct British rule. Large areas were still to be available for white settlement, but the prospects were now far less attractive when compared with those put forward in the earlier reconnaissance party reports. D'Urban's original idea of driving out the Xhosa for ever had aroused strong protest from missionaries and humanitarians in Britain. After querying the wisdom of the frontier policy and calling in vain for a full explanation of the Governor's plans, the British Secretary of State for the Colonies, Lord Glenelg, told D'Urban to prepare the public mind for the abandonment of Queen Adelaide Province and appointed the liberal ex-*landdrost*, Stockenstroom, as Lieutenant-Governor of the eastern districts. His duty would be to set up a new system of relations with the African peoples there.

The loss of Queen Adelaide Province was the final insult as far as frontier farmers were concerned. In reaction to the rumours surrounding Glenelg's criticisms and instructions, the first major party of the Great Trek set out, led by Andries Hendrik Potgieter and Sarel Cilliers. Then, as the future of the area became more certain with Stockenstroom's appointment, Gert Maritz, accompanied by a large body from Graaff-Reinet, crossed the Orange. Finally D'Urban, annoyed by Stockenstroom's appointment, denied him any chance of controlling the movement by withdrawing martial law from the eastern districts and publicly announcing the abandonment of Queen Adelaide Province. The Great Trek then got fully under way.

The Great Trek

The Great Trek was in some respects simply a speeded-up continuation of the expansion which had already led to the occupation of vast areas. At that very time the process was still continuing, with increasing migration of cattle farmers from the north-eastern districts across the Orange to settle in Transorangia. In its scale and organisation, however, the Great Trek was very different from that continuing process of expansion undertaken by individuals or small groups seeking new land beyond the frontier. Unlike the continuous expansion of the *trek boer*, the Great Trek was a conscious political movement. Those who had been and still were moving across the Orange in search of new lands maintained contact with the Colony, paid taxes within the Colony and hoped to persuade the colonial authorities to extend the frontiers to cover their area of settlement. In contrast, those who left on the Great Trek deliberately rejected the authority of the British government at the Cape and set out to establish an independent community in the interior, free of British rule.

Their grievances were many and various. The anglicisation of the Colony, and of legal proceedings in particular, not only created considerable difficulty for those with little command of English, but struck at their self-esteem and emphasised the fact that they were living under foreign domination. The abolition of the traditional urban councils (*heemraaden*) and all means of direct representation not only meant that they had no obvious means of getting the ear of government but also deprived the more ambitious of avenues of political leadership. This was probably important in the motivation of some of the outstanding leaders of the trek, who were men of considerable wealth and education.

71

Above all other reasons, however, it was the British government's attitude towards the two closely linked questions of race relations within the Colony and on the frontier which drove the frontiersmen to mass secession. To them it seemed that the British authorities had failed to advance the eastern frontier for many years, thus denying the growing sons of Afrikaner farmers the opportunity to acquire the new farms on which their position as a pastoralist aristocracy depended. The government did not even seem prepared to afford them the security which was essential if they were to maintain themselves on the land they did occupy. The authorities seemed not to sympathise with or understand the white farmers' points of view but rather to be swayed by the arguments of missionaries and reformers and to favour the interests of blacks rather than whites. The emancipation of slaves and the unsatisfactory provisions for compensation to their owners meant heavy financial losses for some. Coming on top of Ordinance no. 50 and the overruling of Wade's vagrancy ordinance, it promised to worsen farmers' labour problems still further. Worst of all, to the Boer settler the pattern of this legislation as a whole appeared to threaten the entire system of colour distinction. Most frontiersmen believed this to be divinely ordained. They also felt that their control over their Khoi and African slaves and servants, their security, self-esteem and entire way of life depended on it.

These various grievances operated on different individuals in different ways. For some the land issue was paramount and the opportunity to find new farms the key attraction, for others the appeal of political ambition and a sense of adventure was paramount. As the Trek extended over several years, the motivations of those who went later often differed from those of the first to depart. It may have been to join the bulk of their relatives who had already left, to go to the rescue of kinsfolk in peril or to take advantage of victories won over African peoples.

Taking the movement as a whole, however, it was undoubtedly a revolt against the racial policies of the British government at the Cape. In a wider sense it was a revolt against the new ideas of equal rights and opportunities and free competition between individuals which had developed with the growth of commerce and capitalism in Europe and expressed itself in different ways in the eighteenth-century enlightenment, and in the anti-slavery and humanitarian movements. In this respect, it was another in the series of revolts which had disturbed the eastern frontier since the initial rising against Maynier in the last days of the Dutch East India Company. Memory of the Slachter's Nek uprising and its consequences also helped to ensure that this political move would take the form of secession rather than rebellion. The Trek expressed rejection of the egalitarian principles of the Ordinance no. 50. Its key aim was the establishment of an independent political society in which the traditional pattern of frontier farmer society could be sustained by the strict maintenance of colour distinction and of 'proper relations' between master and servant. In setting out on this journey, most of the travellers believed that it had divine blessing. They believed that the Trek was God's will, like the flight of the Israelites from Egypt recorded in the Bible.

In yet another sense, however, the Trek was a response to the courageous resistance of the Xhosa on the east coast and the opportunities offered by the wars and migrations of the *mfecane*. The Afrikaner frontiersmen contemplated and began to plan their Trek when they were barred by the Xhosa from continuing their advance along the natural route of greatest rainfall, and learnt of the rich grazing lands available in the interior. Then, when a combination of Xhosa determination and humanitarian pressures finally dashed their hopes of Queen Adelaide Province, they poured out of the Colony to the north. Outflanking the dense concentration of African peoples in Lesotho and along the east coast strip they moved into and settled the three areas in Transorangia, Natal and the Transvaal that the wars of the *mfecane* had particularly devastated.

As they moved into the interior, the Boers were organised in trekking parties. Each of these was headed by a recognised leader, generally accompanied by a number of families of relatives, relatives by marriage and neighbours. The larger treks could involve a hundred or more wagons and huge numbers of cattle and sheep.

The progress of the Trek

 Though all the trekkers thought of themselves as constituting a single company (*maatschappij*) and aimed to create a united society in the interior, each trekking party was very much an autonomous unit. Each of the larger treks contained, moreover, smaller, potentially separate, trekking parties which had been attracted to join the leader and his core followers. Even within groups of relatives, each head of family with his wagons, horses, flocks and herds, his sons of gun-bearing age, his slaves and his Khoi and Bantu-speaking servants, headed a small political unit capable of a considerable degree of self-sufficiency. This pattern of organisation and the distribution of power which it created lay behind many of the quarrels between the leaders of the Trek and the difficulties the trekkers found in establishing a workable political constitution. It helps to explain the conflicts between the principle of executive leadership and the sovereignty of an elected council (*volksraad*) on the one hand, and between the authority of such a council and the direct voice of the people in open assembly on the other.

W.H. Coetzer's picture of Louis Trichardt's party bringing waggons down a mountain

The trekkers had certain vital advantages over the African peoples with whom they were to come into conflict. Their guns gave them the capacity

Military tactics

to kill at a distance, their horses a degree of mobility with which none of their African enemies could at first compete. The commando system and the experience of fighting on the eastern frontier had led to the development of tactics which made the very best of their advantages. When travelling with their wagons and threatened by attack they would form the wagons into a circle or a square, filling the spaces beneath the wheels with thorn trees to create a defensive stronghold known as a *laager*. From this shelter they could pour deadly gunfire into the ranks of their attackers. When on commando without their wagons or when moving out from such a *laager* they made use of the speed of their horses and the range of their guns. They would ride to within gunshot of their enemies, fire a deadly volley from horseback, and then wheel their horses and ride away, keeping well out of spear-throw while reloading; then they would turn and fire again. The very changes in fighting methods that had made the Zulu and the Ndebele so successful in conflict with African enemies were to be disastrously disadvantageous in their conflicts with the trekkers. Advancing in closely packed masses, they were exposed to devastating losses from the Boers' guns. By relying on set battles involving large masses they played right into the hands of their enemies.

Though the Boers had the enormous advantage of guns, which enabled them to win dramatic victories in mass encounters, they did not have the resources to sustain prolonged conflict. The need for grazing for their flocks and herds made it very difficult for them to remain in *laager* for long periods. They could not even remain loosely congregated close to each other for very long, but had to scatter in small groups over a wide area if their cattle were not to starve. They lacked the financial resources to police and administer on a regular basis the wide areas they conquered or to purchase the gunpowder, bullets and other necessities required to sustain frequent commandos. The further they moved away from the markets for meat and animal products the weaker the economic basis of their survival became.

As they moved into the interior, especially in the Transvaal, there were great opportunities for elephant hunting and ivory trading. The high value of ivory in relation to its bulk made it possible to cover transport costs over long distances and maintain a level of profit at a distance from the market which would be quite impossible on the basis of cattle products. Elephants were soon shot out, however, and the ivory frontier receded in advance of the farmers' frontier. While the trekkers were able to win victories and conquer large areas, they consequently had much greater difficulty in effectively occupying them or maintaining the degree of regular control over the African population necessary to ensure adequate labour supplies as well as their own security.

Early trekker groups   Louis Trichardt's party and that of Janse van Rensburg crossed the Orange at the end of 1835 or the beginning of 1836. Encountering one another they travelled together through the Transvaal, then after a quarrel separated at a place they named Strydpoort (*stryd* meaning 'conflict'). The van Rensburg party moved on to the Zoutpansberg and then eastwards in the hope of reaching the Portuguese at Delagoa Bay. When the route in that direction appeared too difficult, they changed their destination to Inhambane. Towards the end of July 1836 they became involved in a conflict with one of Soshangane's military settlements and their entire party was wiped out. Trichardt meanwhile also reached the Zoutpansberg and settled for some time near the subsequent Transvaal settlement of Schoemansdal.

The first major party of the full-scale emigration was led by Andries Hendrik Potgieter, a farmer from the Tarka district. A very forceful and authoritarian personality, who could not easily accept the leadership of another or any restraint on his own, Potgieter belonged to the strictly conservative and rigid section of the Dutch Reformed Congregation which even objected to the singing of hymns in church. They were known as the Doppers.

A number of other family and neighbourhood groups joined his original following *en route* and after crossing the Orange he was joined by another substantial trek led by Sarel Cilliers. Amongst its members were three Kruger families in one of which was a boy, Paul, then 10 years old, who was to be the future President of the Transvaal. The Potgieter trek passed through Transorangia to halt for a while at Thaba Nchu where they were made welcome by the Rolong chief, Moroka, and the missionary Archbell. They then pushed on to the Vet river where Potgieter encountered a Taung chiefdom under Makwana. Anxious to place a bulwark between himself and the Ndebele, Makwana appeared to grant Potgieter possession of almost the entire area between the Vet and Vaal rivers in return for forty-nine head of cattle. Leaving most of their party to spread out over this huge area, Potgieter and Cilliers rode on, following the wagon trail of the Trichardt trek to the Zoutpansberg. After visiting Trichardt they then rode back to the Vaal. Trichardt stayed on in the Zoutpansberg until August 1837 when the entire party set out to try to reach Delagoa Bay. After an epic journey they succeeded but the majority died of malaria. In July 1839 the twenty-five survivors were brought by ship to join the Boer Republic of Natal.

When Potgieter reached the Sand river on his return from Drakensberg, he found that his party had suffered severe losses from an Ndebele attack. During his absence a number of small parties in his following had crossed the Vaal and begun grazing the lands beyond its banks. At the same time, a hunting party of members of the Erasmus family from the eastern Cape also crossed the river and without asking permission of Mzilikazi pressed on as far as the Magaliesberg mountains. News of their movements was picked up by the patrols which Mzilikazi maintained in the area. Taking the Boer immigration to be another hostile invasion like that of Jan Bloem or Barend-Barends, the Ndebele swooped on the intruders. A number of the Erasmus party were killed and a party of Liebenbergs was almost wiped out, though another group under Johannes Botha and Hermans Steyn formed a *laager* and drove the attackers off. Two days later, Potgieter arrived and gathering all the groups that had crossed the Vaal he led them back across the river to form a strong *laager* at Vechtkop. Here they were attacked by a large Ndebele force on 15 October 1836. The Ndebele were beaten off with heavy losses but took all the trekkers' cattle as they retired. Potgieter's stranded party was then helped by Moroka, and other trekkers who had arrived at Thaba Nchu, to fall back there. By this time the second large-scale party of the Great Trek had arrived at the Rolong settlement. Led by Gert Maritz from Graaff-Reinet, one of the first advocates of the emigration, it was made up of over a hundred wagons.

Trekker government

At Thaba Nchu the first attempt at establishing a government for trekker society was made at a meeting on 2 December 1836. Potgieter was elected commandant and chairman of the council of war (*krygsraad*), Maritz was made president of the *volksraad*, an elected council of seven members. He

*The mass migrations
of the* mfecane
& the Great Trek

was also to be the magistrate (*landdrost*) and in his judicial capacity would be assisted by the same seven elected members serving as *heemraaden*.

The first task of the new government was to organise a punitive commando against the Ndebele. Soon after the New Year, just over a hundred Boers accompanied by forty Griqua and Kora, and sixty Rolong set out. Mzilikazi's settlement of Mosega was stormed and the Ndebele regiment stationed there was routed. The commando took their lost wagons and more than 7000 cattle and also the American missionaries, who chose to retire with the trekkers from the ruined settlement. Already Mzilikazi was contemplating a move further north, primarily to avoid another conflict with the Zulu. After the Boer raid, he speeded up his plans; most of the Ndebele population moved out of the Mosega basin and gathered along the lower Marico.

Before they could move on much further, however, the Zulu attacked again. Hearing the news of the successful Boer commando, Dingane despatched a major expedition against Mzilikazi in May 1836. It reached his settlements on the Marico probably in late June. Though the Zulu once again failed to win a decisive battle and destroy the Ndebele state, they inflicted heavy losses and retired with many cattle. Hardly had the Zulu withdrawn than another Griqua and Kora party led by Jan Isaacs and Jan Bloem, with Hurutshe and Tlhaping allies, fell upon the Ndebele's westernmost cattle posts and successfully made off with several herds of cattle.

Soon after the return of the commando, tension between Potgieter and Maritz and the problems of grazing for the flocks and herds of the two parties led to their separation. Potgieter and his followers moved into the area he claimed to have purchased between the Vet and Vaal rivers and there began building the town of Winburg.

Leaders of the Trek

At the end of 1836, when D'Urban cancelled the creation of Queen Adelaide Province and withdrew military law, Piet Retief, one of the most respected figures among the Afrikaners of the eastern frontier and one of the earliest advocates of the Trek, finally made up his mind to go. After publishing a manifesto in the *Grahamstown Journal* in which he recited a number of the Boers' grievances and made clear their intention of establishing an independent state in the interior, he headed for the Orange. He was joined there by many other smaller parties and met by representatives of both the Maritz and Potgieter Treks who invited him to take over the leadership of the whole *maatschappij*. In April, a huge congregation of over a thousand wagons assembled near Winburg. In a general meeting, Piet Retief was elected both governor and commandant-general while Maritz remained *landdrost* and president of the *volksraad*. After much argument, Erasmus Smit, the Dutch Reformed Church ex-missionary and brother-in-law of Gert Maritz, was formally accepted as *predikant* (preacher) to the Trek. With the growth of the community, provision for local officers was also necessary and Retief installed local commandants and *veldkornets*.

The choice of Retief to combine the military and civil leadership of the community did not bring an end to wrangling. Potgieter was given no post in the new government and did not accept the new order. Division over leadership was also combined with disagreement over the destination of the Trek. Retief and the majority decided on Natal as the home for their new republic, but Potgieter had his eyes fixed on the Transvaal highveld and believed that the extension of the English settlement at Port Natal implied a severe risk that the British would seek to extend their authority over that area. Potgieter's position was strengthened with the arrival of another large party led by Piet Uys. As the leader of the *commissie* trek to Natal, he regarded that area as personal territory. He was determined to settle there, but not under the authority of the Retief/Maritz government which he made his followers formally reject. Though not interested in permanent settlement on the highveld he temporarily allied with Potgieter.

In October 1837, Retief set off with a party to visit Natal and seek Dingane's permission for the trekkers to settle there. While he was away, Potgieter, Uys and Maritz completed arrangements for a second commando against Mzilikazi. As Maritz was ill, the commando was led by Potgieter and Uys and it was accompanied by Andries Pretorius, who was on a brief exploratory visit to the trekkers' encampments and asked to be taken along as an observer. On 4 November the commando of about three hundred and sixty Boers and a number of Rolong auxiliaries encountered the first Ndebele resistance about eighty kilometres north-east of Mosega. In the following nine days of running fighting they drove the Ndebele from all their main settlements and seized a huge number of cattle. As the commando retired, some of the cattle were recovered from the Rolong herders by an Ndebele pursuit party.

This second Boer commando, coming on top of the Zulu and Griqua attacks, finally set into motion Mzilikazi's withdrawal to the north. Immediately after the battle the Ndebele population streamed out of the Marico valley in confusion. Many captive Sotho-Tswana, notably Hurutshe and Kwena, now took the opportunity to break away and gradually began to resettle their old homelands. The majority of the Ndebele crossed the Limpopo and assembled near the Tswapong hills in Ngwato territory in modern Botswana. There they divided into two companies; one, under the leadership of an *induna*, Gundwane Ndiweni, was accompanied by many of Mzilikazi's wives and children, including his senior heir, Nkulumane (so named in honour of Moffat's mission station). This party travelled north-east to the Gwanda district of modern Zimbabwe and then north to settle about mid-1838 near the Malungwane hills to the east of the Matopos mountains. This was the core area of the recently disrupted Rozwi kingdom. The other party under Mzilikazi himself took a more westerly route through north-eastern Botswana as far as the Nata river and then south-east again to the Bembezi river where he established a temporary settlement. There he learnt the position of the other party and finally joined them in about mid-1839.

During Mzilikazi's absence, the *indunas* had despaired of finding their king and had installed Nkulumane in his place. Mzilikazi had Gundwane and the other *indunas* of the party put to death on a hill which was thereafter named Intaba Yezinduna. Nkulumane was almost certainly also killed at this time though rumours that he survived in exile in the colony were subsequently to play an important part in the politics of the Ndebele kingdom. In his new home, Mzilikazi rebuilt his kingdom, incorporating large numbers of Shona in his regiments, while others were attached to the kingdom as tribute-paying client communities who still retained their separate identities.

Organised around a series of military settlements which developed into permanent divisions of the kingdom, the Ndebele community in Zimbabwe developed three distinct status groups. At the top was the relatively small nucleus of Nguni descent known as the Zansi; beneath them and almost twice as numerous were the Enhla, made up of Sotho-Tswana incorporated in the Transvaal and their descendants; finally, most numerous of all, were those of Shona origin known as Holi. From the core area of their kingdom which corresponded fairly closely to the earlier Rozwi kingdom the Ndebele raiding parties harassed wide areas inhabited by the Shona peoples. The main Shona chiefdoms, however, successfully resisted Ndebele attacks and maintained their independence.

In his new home Mzilikazi was visited by Moffat on three occasions, 1854, 1857 and 1860. In spite of the suspicions raised by the behaviour of the American missionaries at Mosega, he allowed a new mission to be established in his kingdom. In 1847, he was attacked again by a commando led by Potgieter from the Transvaal but as it returned it lost most of the cattle it had taken to an Ndebele pursuing force. In 1852 a treaty was made under which Boer hunters gained access to the kingdom. In his last years white traders and hunters were frequent visitors at Mzilikazi's court, and after gold was discovered at Tati in 1867 the number of whites in the kingdom rose dramatically. The old king finally passed away in 1868.

After the victory over the Ndebele, Potgieter laid claim to vast areas in the Transvaal by right of conquest. His followers were however too few to occupy more than a small fraction of this at first. While the greater part remained settled around Winburg and the extensive area of northern Transorangia between the Vet and Vaal rivers, some began settling the lands immediately north of the Vaal that the Ndebele regiments had previously largely cleared of population. There on the Mooi river they built the settlement of Potchefstroom.

Dingane and Retief

In the meantime, after a warm welcome from the English at Port Natal, Retief had visited Dingane and received a promise that if he would recover some Zulu cattle stolen by Sekonyela he would be given Natal for his people. Dingane was thoroughly alarmed by Retief's visit. He already had difficulties with the English at Natal who tended to undermine his authority by giving protection to fugitives from his judgement. He was uncomfortably

The great dance at Mbelebele in 1836 from a drawing on stone by T.M. Baynes in Gardiner, *Narrative of a Journey to the Zoolu Country*, 1836

aware of the power of firearms and remembered Xhosa warnings that the white men coming first in ones and twos would eventually come with an army and eat up all the land. To avoid conflict he sent Retief against Sekonyela, probably hoping that he would be destroyed in the fighting. Subsequent developments further increased the king's alarm. Retief made things worse by writing a threatening letter pointing to the Boers' first defeat of the Ndebele as a warning to the king to be loyal to his agreements and suggested that he consult the missionaries about the fate of wicked kings. Then, even before Retief had returned from his mission, let alone carried out his promise to the Zulu king, his impatient followers hearing of Dingane's promise began pouring down into Natal and spreading out in small groups around the tributaries of the upper Tugela river.

Dingane's fears, already keenly aroused, were much increased when he received another letter from Retief telling of the Boers' second victory over Mzilikazi and how they had driven him from his land. Retief's conduct towards Sekonyela was still more alarming. He rode in to see the chief, dangled a pair of bright handcuffs before him, persuaded him to try them on, then locked them on his wrists and held him to ransom until his people surrendered over seven hundred cattle and all his horses and guns.

The Zulu who accompanied the expedition undoubtedly informed Dingane of Retief's contempt for the dignity of chiefs, his treachery and his awesome powers of witchcraft. Dingane resolved to attempt to save his kingdom and his people by a massive counter-move. Taking the Boers unprepared, he planned to wipe them out before they could strengthen their position. As Retief and a strong deputation rode in to claim the promised cession of Natal, Dingane concentrated his regiments at his household of em-Gungundhlovu. When Retief arrived he was well received. Dingane put his mark to a document granting the Boers the entire area from the Tugela to the Umzimvubu. The Zulu gave displays of dances, and the Boers gave a performance of manoeuvres on horseback firing their guns in the air. Then on 6 February 1838 Retief and his company were invited to attend a final farewell dance. They left their guns outside the royal enclosure and took their place among the densely packed throng. Suddenly as the dance reached its climax the king shouted 'Seize the wizards'. They were caught, dragged away and put to death on Matiwane's Kop. At once Dingane despatched his regiments to wipe out the Boer encampments near the upper Tugela.

On the night of 16 February, the Zulu fell on the Boer encampments. A whole series of parties around the Moordspruit and Blaauwkrantz rivers were taken unawares and completely massacred. Others, however, received the alarm in time and were able to put themselves in a state of defence. Fighting lasted until the afternoon of the following day when the Zulu, who had suffered very heavy losses, were finally driven off. Though the Boers had lost nearly six hundred killed, including the members of Retief's party, and the retiring Zulu had driven off most of their cattle and sheep, Dingane's coup had failed.

Continued conflict

The position of the trekkers remained very precarious, despite the reinforcements Uys and Potgieter soon brought down from the highveld. A punitive commando was organised but as neither Uys nor Potgieter would serve under the other, it was placed under their joint command. The result was

*The mass migrations
of the* mfecane
& the Great Trek

disaster. Uys, rejecting Potgieter's advice, led his section of the commando into a trap. Piet Uys, his son Dirk and eight other men were killed and the commando ended in panic flight. The commando became known as the *vlug kommando* (flight commando) and Potgieter was subjected to such criticism that he rode off back to the highveld with all who would follow him.

Meanwhile the English at Port Natal had been planning an attack of their own on Dingane to co-ordinate with the Boer punitive expedition. An expedition under Robert Biggar in early April dispersed after seizing the cattle of one of Dingane's outermost settlements but Biggar then organised a second force with about seventeen Englishmen and twenty Khoi with guns and about fifteen hundred Africans from around Port Natal. On 17 April they fought a major battle with a Zulu army near the Tugela river. At the critical moment, further Zulu forces, fresh from their victory over the Boers, came up. The English-led force was overwhelmed, and thirteen of the English and most of their African followers were killed. The survivors fled back to Port Natal and the remaining English took temporary refuge on the *Comet*, a ship which happened to be in the harbour. The Zulu forces withdrew after devastating the settlement, and a few of the traders returned.

After this disaster the trekkers formally annexed Port Natal to the United Laagers and appointed a *landdrost* and *veldkornet*. Their situation was extremely difficult and uncertain, however, because they were forced to remain grouped together far too closely for the welfare of their remaining stock while they awaited a renewed Zulu attack. Foot-and-mouth disease broke out among the cattle, and a measles epidemic spread among the people. Nevertheless, when the Zulu attacked again in August they found the trekkers well prepared. In skirmishing around one of the two main *laagers* at Gatsrand they suffered serious losses and withdrew, taking much of the trekkers' remaining stock but without venturing an all-out attack. In September, Gert Maritz died and the trekkers' fortunes reached their lowest point. Dingane's struggle to save his kingdom had come very near to success, but in November Andries Pretorius, with a strong, well-armed following from the Cape, arrived at the Tugela *laagers*. He was at once elected head commandant and at the end of the month led a strong commando of over four hundred men accompanied by sixty-four wagons and two cannon towards em-Gungundhlovu. On Sunday 9 December, when the men assembled for divine service, Cilliers led them in taking a solemn vow that if God would give them victory over their enemies they would observe the day as an anniversary ever after and build a church to worship Him as soon as possible. This was the Day of the Covenant which has subsequently played such an important part in the rituals and beliefs of Afrikaner nationalism.

A.W.J. Pretorius

The battle of Blood river

On 15 December the commando built the *laager* in a strong position alongside Blood river. The following day the Zulu made an all-out attack. With extreme bravery they repeatedly charged the *laager* in the face of devastating fire. But courage was no substitute for gunfire. The Boer guns took a fearful toll and every shot of the cannon mowed the Zulu down in heaps. Finally the Boers sallied out on horseback from the laager, turning the victory into a rout, so many Zulu throwing themselves into the river that it ran red with blood. After this crucial victory, the commando (now named the *wenkommando*) pushed on to em-Gungundhlovu. They found it in flames and Dingane fled, but on Matiwane's Kop they found the remains of

Retief and his comrades and the vital document ceding Natal.

By this time a small British force had arrived at Port Natal. It had been despatched by Governor Napier (who replaced D'Urban in January 1838) to prevent conflict between the emigrant British subjects and the indigenous peoples. Arriving while the commando was away there was little the commander could do in the light of the Boer victory except encourage both sides to make peace. Captain Jervis did, indeed, succeed in arranging a peace conference at the port. Dingane agreed to pay huge reparations in cattle and – in a clause kept secret from the British commander – he also agreed to a further massive cession of land. The whole area between the Tugela river and St Lucia Bay, almost half the core area of the Zulu kingdom, was to be added to Natal.

After the Blood river victory the trekkers were able to start building the capital for their republic at Pietermaritzburg and to disperse themselves over a wide area of Natal. The Zulu kingdom was still far from broken, however, and the Boers' position remained insecure on that account. At the same time the continued presence of the British force at Port Natal threatened that British authority might be extended to the area.

After the agreement with the Boers, Dingane launched a series of raids against Sobhuza to prepare the way for the removal of his people to the north-east. He also instructed his people to withdraw from the lands near the Tugela and settle beyond the Umfolozi river, the boundary agreed in the secret clause of the peace agreement. This demand, coming after the shock of defeat, placed Zulu loyalties to their king under too great a strain. His surviving brother, Mpande, saw his opportunity, rebelled against the king, fled with his followers across the Tugela and pleaded for protection from the Boers. An alliance was soon concluded under which the trekkers were to assist Mpande to win the Zulu kingship. In December Napier, denied permission to annex Natal, ordered the British troops home. They left on Christmas Eve. Then, in February, a commando of 400 men set off, advancing in parallel though at a considerable distance from Mpande's army, led by his *induna* Nongalaza. The commando never saw any fighting. On 29 February, Nongalaza's forces encountered Dingane's army led by Ndlela. The fate of a fiercely fought battle was determined by further desertions to Mpande and an alarm that the Boers were coming. Dingane fled into Swaziland where he was killed by a local sub-chief.

The Zulu kingdom had temporarily destroyed its own military capacity, to the advantage of the Boers. Capitalising on their chance to establish a measure of authority over Mpande, Pretorius formally proclaimed him king but insisted that he should never make war without the *volksraad*'s permission. The grateful Mpande surrendered a huge herd of cattle; 36,000 were taken back to Natal and a further 15,000 were demanded later. The commando thus gained the name of Cattle Commando (*Beestekommando*). So the trekkers settled their Promised Land and began to build their ideal republic.

The death of Dingane

5 *Boer republics, African states & the British*

Developments after the Great Trek

The Great trek involved more than the migration of several thousand Boer families with their servants and stock to settle in Natal, northern Transorangia and the western Transvaal. It also established in these areas the white-dominated social and economic system which had developed in the Cape. Each area of Boer settlement in the interior was also certain to become a centre for future expansion. The circumstances under which the new lands were taken by the trekkers increased the pressure for expansion. As the victories over the Zulu and the Ndebele gave them access to vast new areas of land, each member of the initial trekker communities was entitled to lay claim to two 6000 acre farms and many established claims to considerably more than this.

Many of the initial land claims soon fell into the hands of wealthier and politically better-placed members of the trekker community who used this opportunity to build up large holdings for speculation. In the longer term, claims to vast areas fell into the hands of absentee landlords and land companies. As huge areas of land were locked up in this way, the pressure for further expansion increased. At the same time, the fact that so much of the land formally owned by whites was neither effectively occupied nor directly farmed by them meant that large numbers of Africans were able to continue living on or to resettle their traditional lands. Whether they were aware of it or not, however, they had become tenants on white-owned land without security of tenure, and subject to such demands for labour, or rent in cash or kind, as their landlords felt capable of enforcing. In some areas trekker communities were established where there were large African populations and powerful African states which put up resistance to the seizure of their land and demands for labour. The Great Trek thus meant that the conditions of continuous tension previously typical of the Cape's eastern frontier had spread to huge areas of the interior.

In conflicts, the trekkers were by no means always at an advantage. Far from the markets at the Cape, they could only conduct very limited trade and they lacked the money to maintain regular administration or to fight lengthy wars against their African neighbours. In contrast, some of the African states, strengthened politically after the wars of the *mfecane*, were now able, through trade, to acquire significant quantities of arms and ammunition. As their populations increased they were often able to effectively resist further trekker expansion, or even to drive them back from lands they had previously occupied. Trekker control of many of the areas

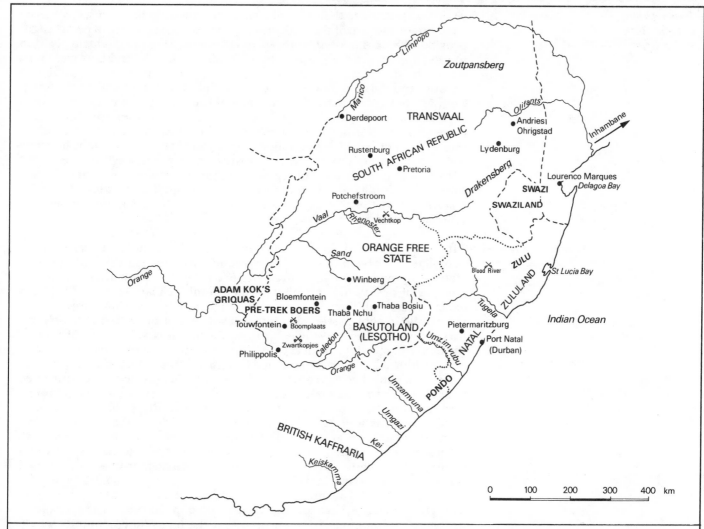

they occupied thus remained very uncertain and initial expansion was sometimes followed by retreat.

The Great Trek and the settlement of the trekkers in the interior presented problems for British policy in South Africa. The trekkers were British subjects and the British government had a clear moral responsibility to protect the indigenous peoples of the interior from losing their lands. This responsibility had been clearly recognised in the passing in 1835 of the Cape of Good Hope Punishment Act (see Chapter 3). Yet once it had become clear that the trekkers could not be persuaded to return to the Colony, the only way that the law could be enforced was to extend British control over the areas where they were settled. This, however, would involve heavy costs for administration and defence of areas of little commercial value and might involve the indefinite extension of British responsibility if the trekkers should move still further into the interior. However, the alternative – to

British legislation over trekker lands

leave the trekkers to their own devices – posed serious problems, apart from concern for the fate of the indigenous peoples. The trekkers in Natal might provide a base for a foreign power, thus undermining the strategic position of the Cape on the sea route to India. Additionally, the trekkers were now settled to the north-east and west of a great bloc of African peoples in Lesotho and the adjoining eastern coastal belt which bordered on the Cape. Conflicts between the trekkers and any of these peoples would be likely to send shock waves through the bloc and result in further conflict on the Cape's eastern frontier. To ignore the trekkers thus threatened to produce the very expense which the policy was intended to avoid. Caught between these conflicting considerations British policy wavered between the extremes of directly controlling the trekkers on the one hand and, on the other, abandoning all attempts to control them. These swings of policy resulted from the developing situation in South Africa and changes in political opinion in Britain.

The republic of Natalia
After the defeat and death of Dingane, the trekkers in Natal were able to complete the organisation of their republic. Following their Blood river victory, a government structure had been established involving an elected *volksraad* of twenty-four members, which combined legislative, judicial and executive powers, but which was to be subject to the overriding authority of the people in public assembly. Between sessions of the *volksraad*, a *kommissie raad* of five members was to deal with public business, subject to approval at the next full meeting. To deal with military matters a war council (*krygsraad*) was established. Pretorius remained Commandant-General but his post was later to be abolished except in times of war. In fact, however, he continued to act in many ways as a head of state. Local administration was based on the traditional system of *landdrosts* and *veldkornets*. Pretorius entered into negotiations with Potgieter with a view to uniting the white trekker community in Natal and the highveld in a single republic. In October 1840 agreement was reached, under which Potgieter accepted the post of Chief Commandant while Pretorius remained Commandant-General. Elected representatives of the highveld community were also to sit on the *volksraad* at Pietermaritzburg. The unity thus achieved, however, was extremely fragile. The great distance between the centres of population and the resulting problems of communication ensured that the highveld community would continue to go its own way with little reference to the Pietermaritzburg *volksraad*.

In Natal itself, the new republic was faced with mounting problems. In the scramble for land, those with influence in the community succeeded in accumulating numerous claims and soon the whole available area was parcelled out, leaving many legitimate claimants unsatisfied. The return of the cattle commando with its huge haul of cattle was likewise followed by hasty and ill-organised division in which the strong were able to gain possession of such numbers that many burghers were left without. The *volksraad* now began to make further demands on Mpande. Then in December 1840, a punitive expedition was launched to the south of the republic against the Bhaca Chief Ncapayi. The commando returned with a loot of 3000 cattle and a number of apprentices. At the same time, the *volksraad* was grappling with an even more serious problem. The defeat of the Zulu and the return of peaceful conditions to Natal opened the way for many of its previous inhabitants who had been in hiding, had taken refuge to the south or had been unwillingly incorporated in the Zulu kingdom, to return to their traditional homes. They poured back into Natal in thousands, settling on lands now claimed by the trekkers though for the most part unoccupied. The *volksraad* could not control this process, and developed a scheme to remove a large part of the African population *en masse* and settle them on land claimed by the Pondo Chief Faku, between the Umtamvuna and Umzimvubu rivers.

The raid against Ncapayi aroused strong missionary protest which met a warm response from humanitarian circles in Britain already disturbed at accounts of the huge herds stolen from the Zulu by the 'cattle commando'. It also aroused official concern at the Cape which was alarmed by the *volksraad*'s plan to expel its 'surplus' African population to the south. Though the scheme was far beyond the capacity of the republic's forces, it seemed likely to start a chain reaction of conflict and population movement down the east coast, with grave dangers for the peace of the Cape's eastern frontier. In the light of the raid against Ncapayi, a British force was despatched to the Umgazi river to protect Faku against possible Boer aggression. Then, as the *volksraad*'s plans to expel its unwanted African population to the south became known, Governor Napier gave orders for the force to march on to Port Natal.

HMS *Southampton* covering the landing of the British troops at Port Natal, 1842 by T.W. Bowler

British annexation of Natal

The small British force soon met with resistance and was besieged at Port Natal, but Dick King, in an epic ride, made his way right down the coast to Grahamstown to give the alarm. Reinforcements were brought up and the trekkers were repelled. Negotiations then took place with a very divided *volksraad*. Many burghers now felt that the republic lacked the resources to maintain adequate security in face of the continuing influx of Africans returning to their homes and were prepared to welcome the establishment of British authority. A compromise was reached; in return for recognising British rule, the republican authorities would continue to administer the interior of Natal from Pietermaritzburg. Plagued by disagreements, however, and too weak to maintain authority, the republican institutions steadily disintegrated over the next few years and in August 1845, Natal was finally annexed as a detached district of the Cape.

Land and settlement schemes in Natal

With the collapse of the Republic of Natal many of the trekkers left at once in disgust and crossed the Drakensberg to join their fellows on the highveld. Dissatisfied with the British approach to their land claims and to the problem of the returned African population, most of the rest followed. The Boer population of the ex-republic was eventually reduced to a handful. The British administration thus inherited a territory that was rapidly emptying of white inhabitants but increasingly heavily populated by Africans. Even before the collapse of the republic, moveover, some individuals had succeeded in buying up and accumulating claims, thus building up huge, speculative landholdings. As the republic collapsed and the trekkers departed across the Drakensberg, Cape speculators with connections in London rapidly collected claims and established a number of land companies with immense holdings. These were later sometimes further supplemented by grants of Crown Land made in return for undertakings to introduce British settlers.

To handle the re-established African population as well as relations with the Zulu, authority was entrusted to Theophilus Shepstone, son of a missionary. He succeeded in establishing excellent relations with Mpande and preserved peace with the Zulu for a prolonged period. Within Natal itself he developed a variant of the trekker policy of mass segregation. A commission appointed in 1846 demarcated a number of substantial reserves within the confines of the Colony and Shepstone persuaded a large proportion of the Natal African population to move on to them. Thousands more, however, remained as tenants on land owned by the land companies or by lesser speculators. Others lived on Crown Land or on land attached to mission stations.

Between 1849 and 1852 a number of schemes were developed by the land companies to bring English settlers to Natal and settle them on small landholdings. The companies hoped that the settlers would rapidly develop commercial farming and seek to buy more land, thus raising the value of the companies' huge holdings. In fact, however, the circumstances were most unfavourable for settled farming, and very few established themselves permanently on the land. Most sold back their holdings very cheaply to the companies or individual speculators. The price of land remained very low and the great bulk of agricultural production in Natal stayed in the hands of the African population.

Indian cane-cutters in the sugar cane fields, Natal

The few new settlers who did remain on the land, however, experimented with a wide range of commercial crops of which maize, fruit, timber and wattle cultivation and sugar planting on the warm coastal lands were to prove the most profitable. By the mid-1850s a number of Natal farmers were beginning to embark on commercial production of these commodities. Africans in Natal, however, had opportunities for maintaining themselves and paying their taxes as independent pastoralists and agriculturalists on the reserves or Crown Land or as tenants on the vast estates of absentee landlords and land companies. White commercial farmers thus faced a continuing acute shortage of labour. It was for this reason that in 1859 the decision was taken to import indentured Indian labour. Between 1860 and 1866 about six thousand Indians were brought to Natal. There was then a break until 1872 when importation was resumed. The indenture system was only finally ended in 1911. After completing their period of indentured service the Indian workers had the right to settle permanently in the Colony. Many decided to do so and a permanent Indian population grew up. It was joined by other Indian immigrants who came independently. By the 1890s it outnumbered the Natal white population. At first most Indians who left the sugar estates took up small-scale market gardening around Durban. Later, increasing numbers were to take to trade and extend their commercial activities out of Natal to the Transvaal and the Cape.

Conflicts of interest in
the Vaal/Orange rivers area

While Natal illustrates the first step towards the establishment of British authority over the areas settled by the trekkers, tensions developing in the area between the Orange and Vaal rivers were soon to lead to a second. Boers who had moved into the southern part of this area before the Trek intermingled with more recently established trekkers who had their main centre in the north at Winburg. Members of these Boer communities had encroached on land claimed by the Sotho chief Moshoeshoe and his African neighbours in the east and on those claimed by the Griqua leader Adam Kok

III in the south-west. Divided amongst themselves, the Boer communities were nevertheless united in rejecting the authority of the chiefs on whose lands they settled and whom the British regarded as the only legitimate authorities in the area. Governor Napier made a first attempt to bring order to the chaotic situation in Transorangia. He made treaties with Moshoeshoe and Adam Kok, recognising their authority and requiring them to maintain peace and return white offenders for trial at the Cape under the 1835 Cape of Good Hope Punishment Act in return for annual subsidies. These arrangements soon broke down, however. When Adam Kok III attempted to exert his powers under the treaty by arresting a Boer named Jan Krynauw, the Boers flew to arms and threatened to attack him. A British force, accompanied by a number of Griquas, dispersed the Boer force at Zwartkopjes in May 1845 but the futility of leaving the African chiefs to exercise authority over the trekkers without support was now evident.

Governor Maitland, who succeeded Napier as Governor in Cape Town, attempted a new solution. At a meeting with the chiefs held at Touwfontein in June 1845, it was agreed that each chief should divide his lands into an 'alienable' and an 'inalienable' area. The chiefs would retain complete authority over the 'inalienable' areas and no whites would be allowed to settle there. Authority over whites in the 'alienable' area, however, would be delegated to a British Resident. Major Warden was appointed Resident under this new arrangement and established himself at Bloemfontein. Warden lacked the force to exercise firm administrative control over the white community, one section of which bitterly resented being placed under British authority anyway. Neither was he in a position to resolve the conflicting land claims of the trekkers, the Griquas and the African chiefs. In the absence of firm and effective authority, the tension between the various communities continued, with the danger of further outbursts of violence, which were likely to endanger the peace of the Cape as well.

Adam Kok III

British Kaffraria

It was indeed the outbreak of further conflict on the Cape's eastern frontier that finally brought about a more definite forward move. As a result of the war of 1834–5, a further attempt was made to bring peace to the frontier, this time by entering into treaties with the frontier chiefs who would be made responsible for maintaining order and returning stolen stock. A number of government agents were appointed to assist the chiefs in this task. Unfortunately the colonial authorities lacked the resources to police the colonial side of the border at all adequately. In the circumstances it was impossible to distinguish genuine trans-frontier thefts from those taking place within the Colony. Frontier officials demanded more from the chiefs than the treaties provided for and put them in an increasingly impossible situation in relation to their own people. Settlers blamed all losses on the chiefs and, with their eyes on possible new lands beyond the frontier, insistently called for stronger action and for the Xhosa to be driven back.

In March 1846 an escort accompanying a prisoner arrested for the theft of an axe was attacked and killed on Cape Colony soil. The chiefs refused to surrender the culprits and the 'War of the Axe' began. The Xhosa mounted a desperate resistance campaign, initially overcoming colonial troops and invading the Colony. By late 1847, however, Xhosa resistance had been broken and the chiefs were prepared to submit. Responsibility for the post-war settlement fell on a newly appointed Governor, Sir Harry Smith, who also held the title of High Commissioner for the affairs of the interior. He decided to adopt a version of the policy long advocated by Dr John Philip of extending British rule over the frontier chiefdoms while guaranteeing them the possession of land. He first annexed the old 'ceded territory' as a new district (Victoria East) of the Cape, allowing loyal Mfengu to settle in part of it and giving out much of the rest in farms. Then the entire area between the Keiskamma and the Kei was annexed as the new colony of British Kaffraria. The chiefs were guaranteed fixed locations within it, provided they agreed to become British subjects and accept the final authority of British magistrates. A limited amount of land was offered to white settlers around the forts and mission stations.

The Orange River Sovereignty

Having initiated a new experiment in extending British rule over African peoples on their land on the eastern Cape frontier, Harry Smith set off rapidly through Transorangia to Natal where he hoped to reconcile the remaining trekkers to British authority. He rapidly formed the opinion that the extension of British authority to Transorangia was the only means of bringing an end to the chaotic situation there. It was the only way of preventing the exploitation of the indigenous peoples at the hands of the settlers, making peaceful development and progress possible and preventing serious upheavals which must endanger the peace of the Cape. He held a hastily summoned conference at Bloemfontein attended by Moshoeshoe and some of the Boer leaders and gained the impression that all parties approved of his plans. Shortly after arriving in Natal he proclaimed the annexation as the Orange River Sovereignty of the entire area between the Orange and the Vaal rivers, including the lands of Adam Kok and the kingdom of Lesotho.

The reversal of British policy

In Britain, the free trade group, which regarded all colonial possessions as a useless encumbrance, was growing in influence and news of Governor Smith's new annexation was received very critically by Colonial Office officials. It was only finally accepted on the understanding that it was not to involve any additional expense, a provision which doomed whatever chance of success it might have had. Major Warden, who was appointed to administer the new possession, was thus denied the support which was needed to impose his authority impartially on white and African inhabitants and to resolve the conflicts of interest between the various groups in the area. Almost at once he was faced with an uprising by the trekker section of the white population. Harry Smith rushed up a force and dispersed the Boers at Boomplaats but Warden was still left dependent on the support of the white population in the area, many of whom were now deeply alienated. Under such circumstances conflicting land claims between the Boers and the Sotho of Moshoeshoe and his neighbours were to a greater or lesser extent biased in favour of the whites.

With the annexation of the Orange River Sovereignty the only trekkers still beyond the scope of British rule were the scattered white communities in the Transvaal. The principle of accepting responsibility for the behaviour of emigrant British subjects in the interior required that they too should be brought under British authority. Such a move was contemplated but

Sir Harry Smith
by W. Melville, 1842

Xhosa ambushing a British patrol

nothing was done before the collapse of Harry Smith's policies in the Orange River Sovereignty and on the eastern frontier led to a complete reversal of British policy.

In the new colony of British Kaffraria the subjection of the Xhosa to colonial law meant they could no longer practise the detection and execution of witches. The custom of *lobola* by which marriages were celebrated was also outlawed and thus the colonial law suppressed an essential social institution on which the fabric of Xhosa society depended. The understaffed administration lacked the resources to interpret and apply the law with an understanding and appreciation of African customs. Deprived of much of their land, bitter at their recent defeat, the Xhosa found hope in a new prophet, Mlangeni, who, like Makana in the past, promised supernatural aid to assist in the overthrow of their oppressors. In December 1850 British Kaffraria erupted in a massive uprising which was only finally suppressed late in 1852.

In the Orange River Sovereignty, Warden addressed himself to the basic task of defining the limits of white and African settlement. Dependent upon the support of the whites, he defined a border between them and the Sotho of Moshoeshoe which secured the whites in the great majority of their claims, but cut off large numbers of Sotho from their kingdom. Moshoeshoe was reluctant to accept the 'Warden line', so Warden exerted pressure by playing on his differences with his neighbours. The Rolong and the Kora who had settled in the borderlands of the Lesotho kingdom under missionary guidance (but who subsequently repudiated Moshoeshoe's authority) and his old enemies, the Tlokwa of Sekonyela, were therefore given borders which cut off much territory that Moshoeshoe claimed for his people.

Moshoeshoe was in an even more difficult position than Warden. He appreciated that the greatest danger to the kingdom he had built up from the remnants of many shattered chiefdoms during the *mfecane* lay in the

Moshoeshoe, 1845

expansive tendencies of his Boer neighbours. His best protection against this lay, he believed, in placing himself under the protection of the strongest power in South Africa, the British government. For this reason he had warmly welcomed the extension of British rule to the Orange River Sovereignty. Warden's demands for territorial concessions, however, placed him in an intolerable situation. The concessions he could make in the pursuit of peace were limited by the need to maintain the loyalty of the many diverse groups in his loosely organised kingdom. If, for the sake of long-term interests, he attempted to enforce agreements contrary to the vital interests of sections of his following, the bonds of loyalty might snap and his composite kingdom disintegrate. Thus, while sincere in his desire for peace, he was unable in practice to prevent his people from retaliating against and harassing their hostile neighbours whom Warden was supporting.

As conflict between Moshoeshoe, together with his subordinate ally Molestane, and Warden's new protegés increased, Warden determined to assert his authority by force. At the head of a very inadequate force supported by Rolong auxiliaries, he launched an attack. At the first encounter on Viervoet hill, however, the Rolong were routed and Warden had to fall back in defeat on Thaba Nchu. Reinforcements could not be brought up from the Cape where all available troops were committed to the war on the eastern frontier. The Sovereignty lapsed into chaos. Moshoeshoe, aware of the weakness of his situation in the long term, deliberately avoided taking full advantage of his victory. Warden's Rolong allies were raided and some white farmers who had joined his expedition suffered reprisals, but in general whites in the Sovereignty suffered little, though British authority had been gravely compromised.

Abandonment of the Sovereignty

The collapse of Harry Smith's experiments in the extension of British rule over African peoples on the eastern frontier and in Transorangia greatly strengthened the hands of those in Britain who believed that colonial possessions were a needless expense. The missionary and humanitarian movement was in decline. Concern for the fate of indigenous peoples seemed to many British people to be misguided and futile. Rather than spending vast sums on the administration and defence of areas which had little commercial value they felt it would be better to leave the whites to conduct their own affairs and deal with the indigenous population in their own way. In such an atmosphere the final abandonment of the Sovereignty was accepted in principle by the British government and a two-man commission was despatched to investigate the situation.

The commission's first move was to seek to put an end to interference in the Sovereignty by the Boers in the Transvaal. In January 1852 a meeting was held on the Sand river and a convention was drawn up with Pretorius and other members of the Transvaal delegation. Under this Sand River Convention, Britain renounced all claims to authority beyond the Vaal river and the Transvaalers were left free to deal with their African neighbours as they pleased. The British authorities even undertook to give the Transvaalers free access to the Cape gunpowder market, while denying this to the African chiefdoms.

In the Sovereignty, where Moshoeshoe continued to practise restraint, a relatively peaceful situation was restored. The British government was, however, still only prepared to retain the territory if this could be done without substantial expense. It soon became evident that this was impracticable. Governor Cathcart, who replaced Harry Smith in July 1852, visited the Sovereignty in October and formed the impression that abandonment was inevitable. Before implementing a decision, however, he felt that Moshoeshoe must be humbled and forced to pay compensation to the Boers who had suffered for giving their support to Warden. Moshoeshoe was faced with a demand for 10 000 head of cattle and 1000 horses to be surrendered in three days. When Moshoeshoe was unable to meet this in the time allowed, Cathcart led a strong force towards Thaba Bosiu. After an inconclusive battle on the Berea mountain where the British troops captured large herds of cattle but were then forced to draw back, Moshoeshoe sent a diplomatic message acknowledging defeat and urging that the captured cattle be taken as adequate recompense. Cathcart, anxious to avoid involvement in a prolonged campaign, agreed. Moshoeshoe was left with his kingdom intact.

Thereafter Sir George Clark was appointed to wind up the affairs of the Sovereignty. Brushing aside the protests of many whites who did not want the withdrawal of British protection, he managed to find a group who were prepared to take on the responsibilities of government. In February 1854, the Bloemfontein Convention was signed. It renounced all British authority north of the Orange river and any treaties with indigenous rulers north of the river, except for Adam Kok. Faced with the tangled problem of the border between Moshoeshoe and the whites, Clark simply left the whole matter in the air, and the status of the Warden line remained quite unclear. In the same way, Adam Kok was simply left to make whatever arrangements with the new republican authorities he could manage.

Changes in British policy

The Sand River Convention and the Bloemfontein Convention marked a great change in the direction of British policy in South Africa. Britain formally renounced the responsibility it had previously always maintained for the conduct of emigrant British subjects in the interior and at the same time the commitment to protect the indigenous peoples from being exploited was abandoned. The policy of withdrawal was a response to the disillusionment felt in Britain as a result of the renewed violence on the eastern frontier and in the Sovereignty. It was also a consequence of the swing in influential British opinion against the expense of maintaining colonies and in favour of handing over authority to white settler communities throughout the British empire. It was undertaken in the light of the economic and strategic situation in South Africa. Isolated in the interior, the Boer communities in Transorangia and the Free State offered no real threat to Britain's strategic position at the Cape. As the attempts made by the Transvaalers to establish links with the Portuguese ports in Mozambique failed, they were to remain wholly dependent on trade through British ports in the Cape and Natal. Such commercial value as they had could be adequately tapped without the administrative expenses necessary for the control of the interior.

At the time that the Convention policy was being adopted towards the trekker communities in the hinterland there was also a major advance in the constitutional position of the Cape. This development was partly brought about by the swing in British opinion described earlier. It also reflected the changed economic situation in the Cape where the spread of wool farming had provided greatly increased export earnings and enough revenue to make representative institutions economically viable. It involved a reaction to the existing system of government in the Cape which had fallen into such disrepute that concessions to colonial opinion were inevitable.

Almost from the beginning of British rule there had been agitation for representative institutions in the Cape; after 1826 one or another group of citizens was almost constantly petitioning for a legislative assembly. But though elected town councils were established in 1837, the grant of a central assembly continued to be delayed. In 1828 some concessions to public opinion were made when two nominated colonists were added to the Governor's Advisory Council. In 1834 further changes were made when a legislative council was established. Its powers were limited, however, and it commanded little respect. In 1849 the despatch of a convict ship to the Cape provoked a brief constitutional crisis when some of the nominated members of the legislative council resigned under pressure of public opinion, leaving the body without a legal quorum. By this time, the need for a representative body was widely recognised.

Controversy centred, however, on the nature of the franchise or voting system. The British government insisted from the beginning that no formal colour bar would be permitted. A high economic franchise would have had much the same results by making it impossible for any large number of Coloured voters to qualify. Such a franchise would also disqualify a large part of the Dutch-speaking population and leave the government to be completely dominated by the wealthier English-speaking merchants. Dutch-speakers therefore joined in a strange alliance with humanitarian and progressive groups supporting the interests of the Coloured population. They all had reason to press for a low property qualification. As a result the so-called Cape 'colour-blind' franchise was adopted in which the economic qualifications were set sufficiently low to allow a significant number of Coloured (and subsequently African) voters to qualify.

However, though it did provide for the enfranchisement of some non-white voters, any economic qualification at all was bound to discriminate against Coloureds and Africans who made up the poorest section of the population. The system ensured that white voters formed the great majority of the electorate. The creation of the Cape Parliament in 1853 thus marked one important stage in the transfer of authority over the whole population to representatives of the whites. Though the Governor and his officials still had a great deal of control, they were subject to increased pressure from settler opinion through the new legislature.

Sir George Grey:
the eastern frontier and the interior

The Convention policy, though reflecting the economic and strategic realities of the South African situation, left the peace of the Cape and Natal at the mercy of upheavals which might arise from conflicts between Boers and their African neighbours in the hinterland. This point was quickly appreciated by the new Governor, Sir George Grey, who came to the Cape from the governorship of New Zealand in 1854. He turned first to the problem of the eastern frontier. His policy there was to introduce further white settlement interspersed with the African population in British Kaffraria. He felt that through mixed settlement, together with considerably increased opportunities for African education, Africans would learn the values of Western civilisation, develop improved agricultural methods or be drawn into white employment. From a dangerous menace to the Colony they would be converted into one of its greatest assets.

The Xhosa, however, were soon driven to desperate action by the threatened loss of still more of their land. A prophetess, Nonqause, proclaimed that if the people would slaughter their cattle and destroy their food stocks before an appointed day, the sun would rise in the west. Subsequently, fat new cattle and abundant grain would be miraculously provided. In a mood of mass hysteria born from despair at repeated military defeat and growing poverty, the Xhosa widely obeyed the message. A violent upheaval seemed imminent, but when on the appointed day the sun rose in its normal place, excitement gave way to bitter disillusionment. Thousands died of starvation and still greater numbers poured into the Colony to seek white employment. The widespread cattle killing prevented another war on the eastern frontier, and Grey quickly took the opportunity to take more land for his mixed settlement scheme. He also sent large numbers of Xhosa to work on farms in the Western Cape.

The whole incident on the eastern frontier, and the fact that Moshoeshoe was rumoured to have played a role in inciting the cattle killing, drew Grey's attention to the interior and led him to broader conclusions. He soon formed the opinion that so long as the white communities in South Africa remained weak and politically divided they would be unable to provide for their own educational, social and economic stability or progress, or to deal with their African neighbours, except by the customary reprisal raids and attacks. Caught in a cycle of violence, South Africa was drifting, he believed, into chaos and barbarism. The solution he recommended was a federation of the white communities which would then be able to provide stable administration and adopt a rational and enlightened policy towards the African peoples. The opportunity to launch this policy was offered by developments in the Orange Free State. Grey urged the Colonial Office to support his recommendation.

Sir George Grey

The Orange Free State

Formation and early history

With the departure of British authority after the signing of the Bloemfontein Convention, the white settlers in Transorangia drew up a republican constitution based in part on their reading of the American Constitution. It provided for an elected president and legislative body (*volksraad*). The unity of the new state, however, remained extremely fragile. Though the acceptance of the two Conventions had made the Vaal river a legal boundary, many of those settled south of the river continued to think of themselves as belonging with their fellows to the north. They wanted the union of all the Boer communities north of the Orange in the single *maatschappij* which had been the ideal of the Great Trek and which had seemed so close to fulfilment in the Republic of Natalia. The dream of overall unity of the Boer communities beyond the British frontier was shared by many living beyond the Vaal.

After the death of Andries Pretorius in 1853, the dream was championed by his son, Martinus Wessels Pretorius who inherited much of his father's following in the south-western Transvaal. One theme in the early history of the Orange Free State therefore consisted of repeated but ultimately

93

M.W. Pretorius

unsuccessful attempts to unite it with the Transvaal. Indeed, Josiah Hoffman had hardly been elected first President of the new Orange Free State, when Pretorius rode into Winberg from across the Vaal and attempted to unseat him. His plans were ill-prepared, however, and as Hoffman stood firm Pretorius retired back across the Vaal.

A still more serious problem for the new state, however, was its relations with the kingdom of Moshoeshoe. The failure of the British to resolve the border problem left continuing misunderstanding and conflict. As Moshoeshoe's following was growing with the return of many Sotho refugees, pressure on the borders of settlement was soon to become intense. Hoffman, who was a personal friend of Moshoeshoe, attempted to maintain good relations by personal contact, inviting Moshoeshoe to Bloemfontein and himself visiting Thaba Bosiu. The gift of a keg of gunpowder to recompense Moshoeshoe for that which had been fired in salute on the President's visit, however, raised such popular hostility in the Free State that Hoffman was turned out of office in February 1855. His successor Jacobus Boshoff appealed to Sir George Grey to resolve the border issue with the Sotho, and in October 1855 Grey persuaded the parties to agree to the Smithfield Treaty which, in effect, restored the Warden Line.

In 1857 Pretorius made another attempt to gain control of the Orange Free State. After a failed attempt to raise a general uprising by riding into the Republic with a few supporters, he assembled a commando and advanced to meet Boshoff at the Rhenoster river. Pretorius's enemies in the Transvaal, however, raised a commando against him in the Zoutpansberg and, faced with this threat from behind, he agreed to recognise the Free State's independence.

Increasing instability

The following year the survival of the Republic was even more seriously threatened. Continuing tension along the border with Moshoeshoe's kingdom led the Free State to declare war and advance on Thaba Bosiu. The Free State commando proved unable, however, to storm Moshoeshoe's mountain stronghold. In the meantime, mounted Sotho groups penetrated deep into the Free State and raided a wide area. Alarmed at the news, the Free State commando broke up and returned home. Boshoff, in defeat, appealed both to Pretorius and to the Cape. Pretorius offered to come to the Free State's support if it would unite with the Transvaal. Sir George Grey, however, was determined not to lose the opportunity to extend his wider schemes of federation. He warned that in the event of such a union Britain would no longer be bound by the terms of the Conventions. Pretorius then drew back. The Free State accepted Grey's mediation and, in the first Treaty of Aliwal North, Moshoeshoe reluctantly agreed to a border settlement which largely confirmed the Warden Line once more, but gave the Sotho a small extension of territory.

The question of federation

Grey now encouraged the Orange Free State to consider the possibility of federation with the Cape. The *volksraad* agreed to a positive proposal along these lines. Grey then took advantage of a query from the British Colonial Office concerning the possibilities of federating the Cape and Natal to allow the Cape Assembly to discuss the *volksraad*'s proposal. He had been accustomed to a wide measure of freedom of action in his period in New Zealand and was insensitive to the more critical attitude towards colonial matters that accompanied the growing influence of the free trade school in Britain. In encouraging local debate on federation, Grey had seriously overstepped his authority. He was promptly recalled and, though with a change of government in Britain he was sent back a year later, it was only on condition that his federation proposals were dropped.

Consolidation in the Transvaal

Meanwhile the scattered Boer communities in the Transvaal were drawing together. In 1845, as the population in the neighbourhood of Potchefstroom increased with trekkers from Natal, Potgieter led a number of his followers to the north-east to establish a new settlement at Andries-Ohrigstad on land he had acquired from the Pedi Chief Sekwati. His object was to withdraw from any further possible extension of British authority and to establish direct contact with the Portuguese at Delagoa Bay. The new settlement was intended to be the political capital for all the trekkers settled beyond the Vaal. A *volksraad* was established there and a *landdrost* was left to manage the affairs of the original settlement. Andries-Ohrigstad proved a disappointment, however, and the hope of establishing regular trading relations with Delagoa Bay failed. The settlement was badly hit by malaria and this, together with pressure from the surrounding African population, led to its abandonment and relocation at Lydenburg in 1849–50. In the meantime, the politics of Andries-Ohrigstad were disturbed by conflict between a *volksraad* party led by an ex-Natalian, Jacobus Burger (ex-secretary of the Natal *volksraad*), and Potgieter as commandant-general. The *volksraad* party tried to deny Potgieter any executive authority except in times of war.

As Ohrigstad declined, Potgieter then led his followers to found yet another new settlement in the Zoutpansberg from where he hoped it might be possible to trade with the Portuguese at Inhambane. In the long run the Zoutpansberg settlement also proved unworkable. It lacked the resources to control the large surrounding African population and in 1867 it was finally abandoned. Initially, however, it proved a profitable centre for ivory hunting and trading and enjoyed a brief period of considerable prosperity.

Unification of the South African Republic

The trekkers in the Transvaal had thus established three main centres of settlement: the initial settlement in the south-west around Potchefstroom which soon gave rise to further settlements along the Magaliesberg range and in the Marico valley; the eastern settlement at Lydenburg; and Zoutpansberg in the extreme north. They were all on the edge of the Transvaal and also near to substantial African populations whose labour they could hope to exploit. It was only gradually that the much less populated areas of the central Transvaal were occupied by white farmers.

The geographical dispersal of the trekker communities in the Transvaal brought with it problems of political fragmentation. At Derdepoort in 1849, a meeting was held to discuss this problem, and a decision was taken that all the communities should form a single state with a central *volksraad*. In practice, however, the problems of communication were so great and the rivalries between leaders so strong that the different areas very much went their own way. In 1855, Martinus Pretorius persuaded a *volksraad* meeting at Pienaar's river, from which the Lydenburgers were absent, to establish a committee to draw up a single constitution for the Transvaal which was to be known as the South African Republic. The constitution, which for the first time provided for a single leader in the form of an elected president, was finally adopted in December 1856. Pretoria was to be the capital and Pretorius was elected first President of the Republic. The new constitution aroused strong disagreement from the Lydenburgers, who already had their differences with the south-western settlements. By 1860, however, the difficulties between the different communities had been resolved, the new constitution was universally accepted and all the communities were united in the South African Republic.

Final separation between the
Orange Free State and the
South African Republic

Hardly had this degree of unity been achieved, however, before it was endangered by a further attempt from Pretorius to bring the Free State and the Transvaal together. With the collapse of Grey's federation proposals, opinion in the Orange Free State swung back in favour of some association with the Transvaal. President Boshoff, who had supported the initiative for association with the Cape, resigned. Pretorius stood for election in the Free State and was elected. He planned to avoid the danger to the status of the Conventions involved in a formal union of the two republics; he believed he could do this by bringing them into a personal unity through his own presidency of both. His opponents in the Transvaal, however, fearful that this move might provoke British intervention, got the *volksraad* to insist that he must choose between the two presidencies. He then formally resigned from the presidency of the Transvaal where he was replaced by W.C.J. van Rensburg. Pretorius, however, continued to involve himself in the affairs of the Transvaal. His supporters there rejected the authority of the *volksraad* and declared him still to be their president. Conflict between the official authorities and the rebellious supporters of Pretorius continued to divide the Transvaal.

In the Orange Free State, Pretorius's presidency was not a great success. One problem was resolved in 1861 when the Griqua of Adam Kok II, fearing for their own independence, accepted a suggestion made by Sir George Grey that they move to settle between the Sotho of Moshoeshoe and the coastal chiefdoms in the strip of land previously known as No man's land. Trekking across the Drakensberg, they established themselves in their new home where they made a determined effort to build up an independent republican state.

In 1864 Pretorius, who had failed to resolve the problems of relations between the Orange Free State and the Sotho of Moshoeshoe, resigned his Free State presidency and returned to the Transvaal. New elections were held and he was duly elected. The idea of uniting all the trekker communities in one republic was now dead and the two states remained separate. In the Orange Free State, Pretorius's place was taken by J.H. Brand, son of the Speaker of the Cape House of Assembly. Under him, close links with the Cape were maintained, strengthened by growing trade as wool farming brought a measure of prosperity and an expanding white population.

Economic weaknesses in the
South African Republic

The Transvaal, though politically united, remained economically very weak. It lacked the resources to obtain and control labour from the large African population within its boundaries and on its borders or even to defend its most outlying settlements. The abandonment of the Zoutpansberg settlement in 1867 is a case in point. To provide the most limited measure of administration and to purchase the arms and ammunition needed for defence, it had often to pay its officials in land or to pledge land against loans. *Veldkornets* and other officials accumulated large landholdings in this way, and by buying up the farms of their poorer neighbours. A class of 'notables' possessing large landholdings began to emerge, while huge areas also fell into the hands of foreign-owned land companies. At the same time, growing numbers of whites in the Transvaal were unable to obtain land and become client tenants (*bywoner*) on the land of their wealthier fellows or the land companies. Though the areas formally set aside for African occupation were very small, vast areas of land formally owned by the state, the wealthier citizens, missions or the land companies were in fact occupied by Africans. Where owners were in a position to require it, the African tenants paid a small rent in cash or kind or undertook limited labour service. The weakness of the state, however, meant that the state could not collect any substantial revenue from taxes on Africans to sustain its expenses. Landowners could only acquire labour if they could offer adequate land to substantial numbers of labour tenants. To an even greater extent than in Natal, therefore, Africans in the Transvaal were able to retain their economic independence, conducting their agricultural activities on their own account and meeting their obligations with the surplus of their produce, participating to only a very limited degree in work for whites.

War between the Orange Free State and the kingdom of Lesotho

In the Orange Free State, problems of relations with the Sotho of Moshoeshoe had grown steadily worse since the First Treaty of Aliwal North in 1858. As the Sotho population increased, it overflowed on to lands claimed by the Free State which lacked the administrative organisation to keep such areas under regular control. Moshoeshoe used all his diplomatic skills to prevent conflict. He could not, however, restrain his people completely without risking the loss of their loyalty and the break-up of the kingdom. The Sotho had never seen the loss of their lands under Warden's arrangements as anything but unjust. As Moshoeshoe pointed out, his people were confined to a narrow strip of land while a tiny number of whites claimed vast areas of what had been Sotho territory.

In 1865 war finally broke out. In response to the Orange Free State's accusations, Moshoeshoe made a powerful bid for British sympathy by publishing a well-argued declaration of war. He maintained that he was fighting 'only to protect my people from the aggression of the Free State Government', and concluded, 'all persons know that my great sin is that I possess a good and fertile country'.

*King Moshoeshoe urges
British intervention*

The Free State was, however, much stronger now, while in Lesotho Moshoeshoe was old and his sons already divided in rivalry for the succession. Though the Free State commandos could not capture Thaba Bosiu, they devastated Sotho crops and food stores, reducing the population to the edge of starvation. In 1866 Moshoeshoe, hoping to buy time, agreed to the treaty of Thabu Bosiu, handing over almost all the cultivable land of his state to the Free State. Once the commandos had withdrawn, however, the Sotho returned to cultivate these lands and when Free State citizens attempted to take up farms there they were forcefully resisted. The war thus began again. Once again, the Sotho food stocks were destroyed and the people brought to the brink of collapse but Moshoeshoe hung on grimly at Thaba Bosiu, repeatedly pleading for British protection.

Moshoeshoe's cause was eloquently supported by the French missionaries expelled by the Boers, while at the Cape Governor Wodehouse regarded with growing alarm the possibility of the break-up of the Lesotho kingdom spreading anarchy to the frontier areas of the Cape. He therefore encouraged Moshoeshoe to hold on while he sought permission from Britain to intervene. However, as the military situation grew worse and Wodehouse was not able to respond, Moshoeshoe approached the Lieutenant-Governor of Natal with the suggestion that Natal take possession or annex his kingdom in some way. Moshoeshoe knew that Natal was as greedy for his lands as the Free State but felt that British protection was essential at any price. He gambled on the hope that if he secured protection in this way he might be able to get free of the Natal connection later.

5.2 White encroachment on Basutoland (Lesotho)

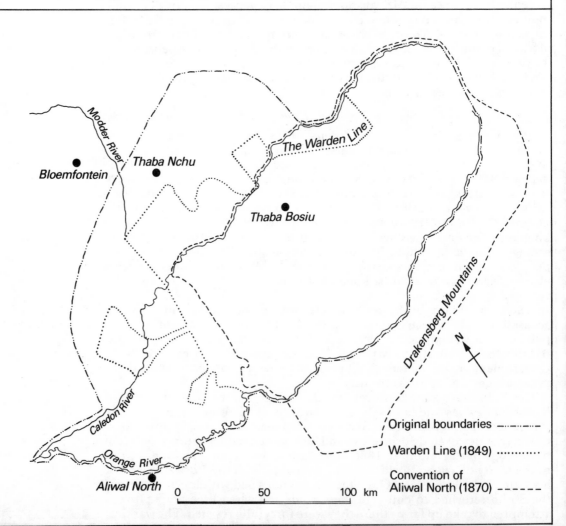

Original boundaries ⎯·⎯·⎯

Warden Line (1849) ⋯⋯⋯⋯

Convention of
Aliwal North (1870) ⎯⎯⎯

At the very last moment, things worked out as Moshoeshoe had hoped. Wodehouse received qualified permission to extend British protection to Lesotho on the assumption that it would be annexed to Natal. Natal had shown willingness to take over the country and this way it would not cost the British government anything. Wodehouse, however, did not trust Natal to administer Lesotho fairly. Accordingly he took advantage of the qualified permission he had received, but exceeded his instructions by announcing the annexation of the kingdom without qualification in March 1868. Thus Moshoeshoe was able to insist that annexation to Natal was unacceptable to himself and his people. Wodehouse supported him by pointing out that geographical difficulties also stood in the way of such an arrangement. Basutoland (as the Lesotho kingdom was then called) thus became a direct dependency of the British crown. The boundaries were finally settled in the Second Treaty of Aliwal North. The Sotho retained sufficient territory for the coherence of the kingdom to be preserved but lost a good deal of the fertile land they had held before the outbreak of war in 1865. With a growing population, it would not be long before the Sotho would be forced to supplement the returns of agriculture by migrating to South Africa to work for whites. Lesotho was thus doomed to provide a labour reservoir for white South Africa in due course. In 1871 responsibility for Lesotho's administration was handed over by the Crown to the government of the Cape in spite of strong Sotho protests. Throughout the period of Cape government, however, the Lesotho kingdom remained a separate entity and, after returning to direct British rule in 1884, eventually became an independent African state in 1966. Moshoeshoe had thus achieved his life's ambition and earned the reputation as one of the greatest statesmen in southern African history. He had saved the kingdom which he had built from being broken up and dispersed. The modern nation is his legacy.

At the time, however, the annexation of Lesotho had another significance for the future. It represented a major step in the establishment of white control and administration over African communities on the land as opposed to the practice of seizing African land and granting it to white settlers. It also represented a first significant step towards the reversal of the policy laid down in the Conventions and the reassertion of British authority north of the Orange river. It came just as the white economy of South Africa was about to be transformed: mineral discoveries were shortly to create greatly increased pressure for further advance.

The start of the Kimberley Mine, 1871

Diamonds & the first British attempt to unify South Africa

I n April 1867 a solitary diamond was found near Hopetown in the Cape Colony. A few months later Carl Mauch proclaimed the existence of gold at Tati in the borderlands between the Ngwato and the Ndebele and also at Hartley Hills and other areas of the Shona country in modern Zimbabwe. The first diamond discovery was soon followed by the unearthing of substantial diamond deposits on the north bank of the Vaal river near its junction with the Harts. In 1870, still richer deposits were discovered further south at the so-called 'dry diggings' which thereafter became the main centre of diamond mining. Whites flocked to the diamond fields from many parts of South Africa, along with still larger numbers of African workers. By 1871 it was estimated that the white population of the diamond fields had reached 20 000–25 000 and the African and Coloured population was between 40 000 and 50 000.

The significance of the diamond fields

The development of the diamond fields began to transform the South African economy. This process was to be carried forward and accelerated by the exploitation of gold at the Witwatersrand. The economy lost its essentially agricultural and pastoral nature and became based on mining and industry. The development of the diamond fields for the first time made South Africa a fruitful field for large-scale capital investment and opened the way to the establishment of modern industrial capitalism in the country. The new wealth won from the diamond fields and the urgent need for improved communications with the ports led to massive investment in railway building which had been undertaken on only a very limited scale before the diamond discoveries. Now lines from Cape Town, Port Elizabeth and East London were rapidly extended towards the fields.

The development of the diamond fields and the building of new means of communication intensified economic activity all over South Africa. The white states and the remaining independent African states were drawn into closer association with one another. Expanded markets for agricultural produce were created, providing new opportunities for white commercial farmers but also for African peasants, who greatly expanded their commercial production and continued to resist being drawn wholly into wage employment. At the same time, the development of diamond mining, railway building and expanded economic activity generally produced

Increased competition

The diamond fields, 1872

enormously increased demands for African labour. In relation to the labour supply not only were the white states in competition with one another, but within them the interests of different sections of the white population conflicted with each other. Farmers were in competition for labour with the diamond mines, railways and other public works. Other groups had interests opposed to those who wished to squeeze Africans off the land on to the labour market; these included missionaries, absentee landlords and land companies who obtained rents from African tenants; merchants whose livelihood came from trade with African peasants; and farmers who practised share cropping or provided themselves with labour by maintaining large numbers of labour tenants on their properties.

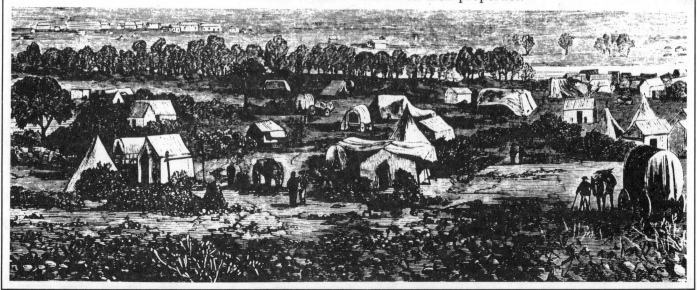

The greatly increased need for African labour could not be met from within the areas of white occupation and control alone. They had to be drawn very largely from areas of African occupation and the still independent African states within South Africa, Mozambique and Zimbabwe. Workers from these communities came as labour migrants, leaving their families behind them and intending to return home after acquiring the money to meet tax, rent or other obligations and to purchase highly prized commodities. The pattern of reliance on migrant labour on a large scale thus became established as an essential feature of the economic and social life of southern Africa.

As they migrated to and from the diamond fields and other major centres of employment, the African workers traversed the territory of the white states that lay across their routes. This not only created a concern for security but also opportunities for the states through which they passed to divert labour supplies to their own use. From the proceeds of their earnings at the diamond fields many Africans purchased guns, thus contributing to a process of African rearmament which was seen as a threat to white supremacy. The fact that Africans from many different areas were now being drawn together as workers at the diamond fields led the whites to develop exaggerated fears of a general African uprising.

Rival claims to the diamond deposits

The area of the diamond discoveries was disputed between a number of claimants. The Transvaal claimed the area of the river diggings and a broad sweep of territory further north (through which ran the road opened by missionaries Moffat and Livingstone, giving access to the Tati gold fields, the kingdom of the Ndebele and the Lozi and the trade of central Africa). The area of the dry diggings was claimed by the Orange Free State. The Transvaal's claims were disputed by Tswana chiefs, and David Arnot, a Coloured lawyer, succeeded in advancing plausible claims on behalf of the Griqua Chief Waterboer to rights over virtually the whole diamond area.

With the rapid growth of population at the diggings there was an obvious and urgent need for the establishment of an effective and stable government over the area. When Pretorius attempted to assert Transvaal claims to the river diggings and unwisely granted exclusive rights of diamond mining to three Transvaal burghers, the diggers at Klipdrift rejected the South African Republic's authority and declared themselves an independent republic with Stafford Parker, an ex-sailor, as President.

Sir Henry Barkly, who took up his appointment as Governor and High Commissioner in December 1870, urged on by his imperialistic Colonial Secretary, Robert Southey, was determined to establish British authority over the diamond fields. He persuaded the British government that to allow them to fall to the republics would alter the balance of power in South Africa and threaten British dominance there. He also urged the humanitarian case against allowing the Boers of the republics to dominate the Griquas and neighbouring African peoples. He received qualified permission to annex the diggings to protect the interests of Chief Waterboer, provided that the Cape was prepared to take over the administration of the area.

When it proved impossible to reconcile the claims of the Tswana chiefs,

Diamonds &
the first British attempt
to unify South Africa

The beginnings of
migrant labour

The sorting table at the diamond diggings, 1872

The Keate awards:
Britain takes the diamond fields

103

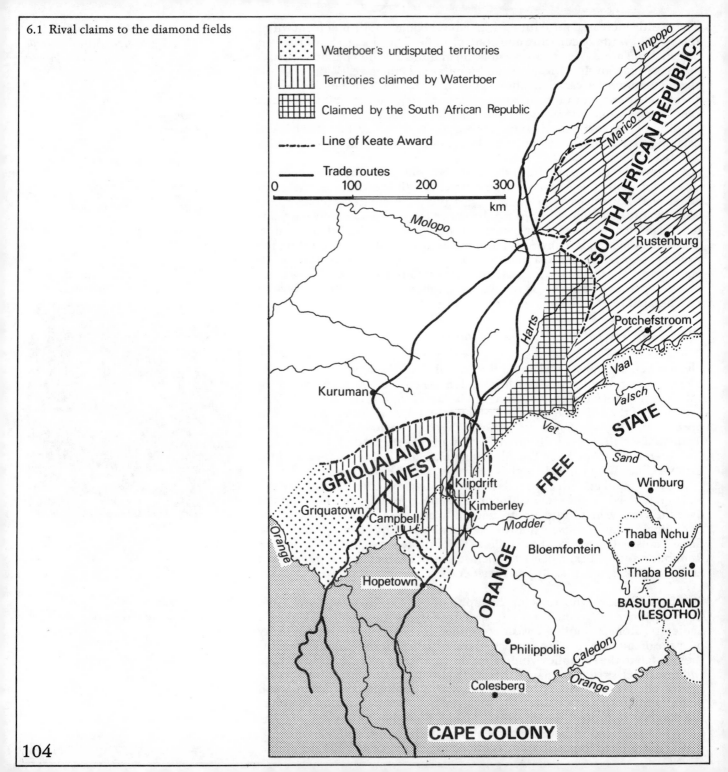

6.1 Rival claims to the diamond fields

Waterboer's undisputed territories
Territories claimed by Waterboer
Claimed by the South African Republic
Line of Keate Award
Trade routes

0   100   200   300
km

Limpopo
Marico
SOUTH AFRICAN REPUBLIC
Rustenburg
Potchefstroom
Molopo
Vaal
Valsch
Kuruman
STATE
Harts
Vet
FREE
Sand
Winburg
GRIQUALAND WEST
Klipdrift
Kimberley
Griquatown
Campbell
Modder
Thaba Nchu
ORANGE
Bloemfontein
Orange
Thaba Bosiu
Hopetown
BASUTOLAND (LESOTHO)
Philippolis
Caledon
Colesberg
Orange

CAPE COLONY

Diamonds &
the first British attempt
to unify South Africa

Waterboer, the Transvaal and Orange Free State governments, Barkly gained Pretorius's consent to a referral of the question to the judgement of Lieutenant-Governor Keate of Natal. Basing his argument on the historical evidence of past treaties between the British and the Griquas, the Transvaal and the Tswana chiefdoms, Keate defined boundaries for Waterboer which included the greater part of the diamond area, and to the north held the Transvaal boundary well back from the missionary road.

In 1871 Barkly declared British authority over the lands ascribed to Waterboer and published the Keate award defining the Transvaal's western border, thus preserving a corridor between the Transvaal and the Kalahari for British trade to central Africa and labour migration to the diamond fields. Barkly, however, had failed to obtain the required undertaking from the Cape Parliament before annexing the diamond fields.

The annexation and the Keate award on the Transvaal boundary aroused a storm of protest in both republics. The Orange Free State *volksraad* protested strongly. In the Transvaal, Pretorius was forced to resign and was succeeded by D.F. Burgers, a well-educated liberal Cape *predikant* who the Transvaal burghers hoped would make a better match for slippery lawyers in the future. In the Cape there was widespread sympathy for the republics among the Dutch-speaking population; the Cape Parliament refused to accept responsibility for the new annexation.

Responsible government status for the Cape

Griqualand West, as the diamond fields area was now called, thus became a new, unwanted and, as it soon proved, troublesome dependency of the British Crown. This new imperial possession in South Africa came just as the government in Britain was making a determined effort to get the Cape to take over much of the burden of its own defence under the status of 'responsible government'. It was also pressed to take over the administration of Lesotho (then known as Basutoland). Some of the Lesotho chiefs objected to the proposals and argued that if they were to be subjected to laws made by the Cape Parliament they should be entitled to vote for representatives in that Assembly. Their protests went unheeded, however, and the territory was handed over to the Cape.

Demands for responsible government at the Cape were long resisted by representatives of eastern areas who pursued a long-drawn-out struggle to achieve separation from the west. In 1872, however, the supporters of responsible government, led by J.C. Molteno, were able to win a majority and the Cape assumed its new self-governing status.

The nature of
responsible government

The introduction of responsible government marked a further increase in the power of the settler minority over the Coloured and African majority. Executive as well as legislative and financial power now lay in the hands of a parliament overwhelmingly dominated by the representatives of the whites. Molteno, who became Prime Minister of the new government, saw the strengthening of the unity of the Colony and the destruction of eastern separation as his most immediate task. He introduced new electoral arrangements to do away with the sharp distinction between east and west.

Once the annexation of the diamond fields had taken place, a federation

*Diamonds &
the first British attempt
to unify South Africa*

of white states seemed a good way of disposing of the unwanted administrative burdens of Griqualand West. At this stage, however, the British government was determined that the initiative should come from the Cape which should be prepared to carry the administrative and financial responsibility for such a change. Cool relations with the two republics at the time offered little hope of progress in the immediate future, and when Molteno indicated that the time was not right for such a scheme the matter was allowed to drop.

It was soon raised again as the result of a general election in Britain which brought a Conservative government headed by Disraeli into office in 1874. Lord Carnarvon, the Secretary of State for the Colonies in this government, had played an important role in helping to bring about the Canadian federation in 1867. It is therefore not surprising that he looked for a similar solution to the problems of South Africa. His conclusion was that the answer lay in a federation of the white South African states under British auspices and the extension of white political control over all the African peoples of

Colesberg Kopje before the discovery of Kimberley Mine

Colesberg Kopje 12 months after the start of the mine

southern Africa, possibly as far as the Zambezi. This would make it possible to exploit African labour to the full and avoid the dangers of African rearmament. At the same time it would create a strong British dominion in southern Africa which would be a vital strategic bastion for the British empire. The problems of two areas within South Africa, Griqualand West and Natal, moreover, emphasised the need for some overall political scheme. To inform himself of the situation Carnarvon persuaded his friend, the historian J.A. Froude, to visit South Africa. He also pressed British claims to the port at Delagoa Bay on the grounds that the Portuguese were not in effective control of the area. Britain and Portugal agreed to submit the matter to the arbitration of the President of France, Marshal MacMahon.

Within the new Colony social tensions mounted as the nature and economics of diamond mining there evolved and changed. In the early stages diamond digging had been undertaken by individuals with little capital, working single claims with the aid of a few African workers. As the excavations deepened, however, this became increasingly impractical. The walls of earth between claims tended to fall in, sometimes burying the miners. Water seeped into the pits and pumping it out was expensive. The massive output of diamonds and the unrestricted competition between producers resulted in a dramatic fall in diamond prices. Many small operators were forced out of business while others held on grimly.

The answer to these problems lay in the amalgamation of holdings into highly capitalised units but there was strong resistance on the part of the small operators. The Colony's first Lieutenant Governor, Robert Southey, tried to protect the small-scale miners by limiting the number of claims an individual could hold to ten. As the economic situation for the small miners became increasingly desperate, however, they turned their anger against the government. Their opposition was intensified by Southey's attempt to preserve the principles of formal equality before the law for persons of different race, a characteristic of the Cape. Coloureds and Africans could, therefore, legally own and operate diamond claims at the diggings and some Coloureds did so. White miners claimed, however, that this added to the difficulties of preventing diamond theft and demanded that mining and dealing in diamonds be restricted to whites.

In conditions of growing unrest at the diggings, an Irish adventurer, Alfred Aylward, established a Mutual Protection Society, later renamed the Defence Association, which built up a substantial armed following. In June 1875, prompted perhaps by Southey's investigation of land claims, miners at Kimberley broke into open revolt, imperial troops occupied the Colony and Southey was relieved of his duties. With his removal, the colour bar was established in the diamond mining industry. The limitation on the ownership of claims was also soon abolished, and the way was then open to large mining interests.

An advertisement in the Kimberley *Diamond News*, 8 January 1876

The Langalibalele affair

In 1873, white fears of a general African uprising expressed themselves in panic reaction to a minor incident. All Africans in Natal were required to have their guns registered. But Langalibalele, Chief of the Hlubi, had

Diamonds &
the first British attempt
to unify South Africa

difficulty in persuading some of his followers to travel to the magistrate's office for this purpose. He was summoned to appear before Theophilus Shepstone, the Secretary for Native Affairs in Pietermaritzburg, but failed to respond because he feared that he might be led into a trap. After he had ignored the summons three times a large force of British troops, white volunteers and African auxiliaries with two cannon moved in on the Hlubi.

Langalibalele fled to take refuge with the Sotho Chief Molopo who handed him over to the Cape Mounted Police. Some of the troops pursuing Langalibalele, however, were fired upon and three whites were killed, including the son of Natal's Colonial Secretary. These deaths raised the feelings of whites in Natal to the level of hysteria; and the Hlubi were repressed with great brutality. Their chiefdom was broken up, and their land and all their cattle and horses were confiscated. Their women and children were sent by force to the south of the colony and indentured to serve as servants to whites for three years. After a mockery of a trial, Langalibalele himself was banished for life and with the agreement of the Cape authorities was imprisoned on Robben Island.

The Langalibalele affair roused white fears all over South Africa and prompted offers of assistance to the Natal forces from volunteers in all the white states. The incidents made whites conscious of the need to adopt a common policy towards the African peoples but also aroused an outbreak of humanitarian protest and demonstrated Natal's unfitness to exercise control over its own African population. The British Secretary of State for the Colonies, Lord Carnarvon, saw the need to change the Natal constitution to give the British government effective control over the Colony's native policy. This was essentially an interim measure, however. The long-term solution for the problems of native policy in Natal, like the administrative problems of Griqualand West, would be to hand responsibility for it to a South African federation.

Early in 1875 Lord Carnarvon therefore despatched Sir Garnet Wolseley as Lieutenant-Governor to Natal with secret instructions to achieve the desired reform of the Colony's constitution. He duly succeeded in persuading the Natal legislature to agree to an increase in its official membership which almost made officials a majority.

The issue of confederation

Having openly referred in the British Parliament to the desirability of a federal approach to the problems of South Africa, Carnarvon prepared a despatch which he sent off in May 1875 to High Commissioner Barkly and copied to Wolseley in Natal. It suggested that a conference of delegates of all the white communities should be held to discuss a common policy towards Africans which might give rise to a consideration of confederation. Not only did the despatch propose the idea of the conference, however, it also went on to suggest much of the membership. In particular, it was suggested that the Cape should be represented by Molteno and also by John Paterson, the leader of the eastern separatist opposition.

Carnarvon's suggestion ran into an immediate obstacle from the Molteno ministry at the Cape. The Cape Assembly, having so recently assumed responsible government, resented the imperial government taking the initiative in the affair. The Cape's resources, moreover, were heavily committed to railway-building and the Colony was little inclined to share its customs revenues with the poverty-striken Boer republics or to take on the heavy burden of defending Natal against the Zulu. Above all, Molteno feared that the confederation scheme would revive the eastern separation issue that he had struggled so hard to suppress. The Cape government thus pressured Barkly into withholding publication of the despatch while they studied it, then sent it to the Cape Assembly accompanied by an angry minute rejecting any action on the despatch and deploring the attempt to revive the eastern separatist issue. Carnarvon's initiative had been brought to a full stop.

In the meantime, on 13 June 1875, the MacMahon award was published, giving Delagoa Bay to Portugal. A crucial lever had been removed from Carnarvon's hands since the Transvaal was now assured of the possibility of utilising a port free from British control. Carnarvon did, however, succeed in getting the Portuguese government to agree to give Britain a formal right of pre-emption over the port. The danger of its falling into the hands of another major European power had thus been averted and the chances of its ultimately coming into British hands appeared good.

Carnarvon, moreover, gained the impression that President Burgers of the Transvaal was favourably disposed to the idea of federation. In fact, however, the President was visiting Europe with a view to borrowing the money necessary to build a railway to Delagoa Bay which would free the Transvaal from dependence on British ports. In the Cape an agitation led by Carnarvon's friend, Froude, roused white public opinion in favour of confederation to such an extent that Molteno was almost forced to agree to participate in the proposed conference. At the last moment, however, Carnarvon sent a despatch suggesting shifting the conference to London. This altered the psychological atmosphere and allowed Molteno to avoid making any commitment.

Sir John Charles Molteno, 1872

Carnarvon, still hopeful of getting the confederation policy under way, made plans to bring leaders of the South African states together in London. He invited J.H. Brand, President of the Orange Free State, and Molteno to discuss settlement of the diamond fields issue, confident that with this out of the way they could be persuaded to move on to consider confederation. President Burgers of the Transvaal was also invited.

The London confederation conference

When Brand arrived in England in May 1876, his hand was strengthened by the decision of Judge Stockenstroom in the Griqualand West Land Court that the territorial claims of Waterboer were largely invalid. The President obstinately refused to enter into any deal over the diamond fields issue. He simply demanded his republic's rights in the matter. In the end he agreed to accept £90 000 in settlement of Free State claims on the diamond fields with a promise of £15 000 more if the republic connected itself by rail to the Cape or Natal within five years. In return, Brand made no commitment on the confederation issue.

When Molteno arrived in England in July he protested that the diamond fields issue had been settled without him. He then refused to attend the conference on the grounds that the Cape Assembly had not authorised him to do so. The Transvaal was also unrepresented as Burgers, having finally succeeded in his European business (raising a railway loan in Holland, and

109

Diamonds &
the first British attempt
to unify South Africa

obtaining a commercial agreement with Portugal), had returned home. The conference assembled on 3 August 1876. It was attended by President Brand, by Froude representing Griqualand West, and by Theophilus Shepstone and two other delegates from Natal. Confederation was not even discussed.

Alternative means of
achieving confederation:
the Transvaal

Carnarvon now looked for some other way of breaking the deadlock. He found this in the situation in the Transvaal. The project of President Burgers for the construction of a railway line from Delagoa Bay soon collapsed, leaving the republic heavily in debt. It was also troubled by conflict which broke out between the republican authorities and the Pedi ruler, Sekhukhuni. In 1876 the Transvaal commando failed to storm the mountain stronghold of the Pedi kingdom and dispersed in defeat. The republic lapsed into bankruptcy and Zulu regiments were widely rumoured to be on the point of invading the crippled state. Carnarvon determined to take advantage of the situation to get hold of the Transvaal if he could. Theophilus Shepstone was thus sent to the Transvaal in January 1877 with instructions to declare the republic annexed if he could win the consent of a sufficient number of the white inhabitants or the *volksraad*.

To carry the confederation programme through to what he believed was its imminent conclusion, Carnarvon appointed a new High Commissioner, Sir Bartle Frere. Frere was well acquainted with the problems of African labour in South Africa. In a previous post as consul in Zanzibar, where he had been concerned with fighting the slave trade, he had taken part in the export of emancipated slaves as 'indentured workers' to Natal. In his eyes the unification of the white states and the extension of white control over African communities were two sides of a single policy. Combined with the disarmament of Africans and the introduction of taxes and other measures to make them work for whites it would make possible the full exploitation of the resources of the country. In this way civilisation would be advanced and a strong British dominion created.

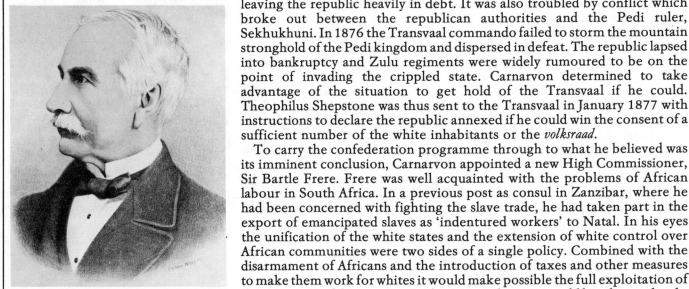

Sir Bartle Frere

Annexation of the Transvaal

Meanwhile, Shepstone rode into the Transvaal, enthusiastically greeted by the English trading community. He met with little encouragement from the *volksraad*. When that body refused even to consider confederation as a way out of the republic's difficulties, Shepstone ignored protests and on 12 April 1877 hoisted the British flag. The annexation of the Transvaal soon proved to be a mistake. The Orange Free State would have nothing to do with the federation scheme until the elected representatives of the Transvaal *volksraad* had agreed to the annexation. In the Cape, Molteno's opposition was still further hardened. All over south Africa, Afrikaner sentiment was roused by the treatment of the Boer republic. In the Cape, Stephanus du Toit, the fiery editor of the Afrikaans language newspaper, *Die Patriot*, bitterly denounced the annexation.

In the Transvaal itself Shepstone's action was accepted without open resistance. So desperate was the situation of the republic, indeed, that had the *volksraad* been permitted to continue functioning it might well have been persuaded to accept the extension of British rule. However, fearful that an elected assembly might condemn the annexation, the new British authorities made no immediate provision for an elected assembly. The longer the right to a representative assembly was withheld, the more confirmed became the

Diamonds &
the first British attempt
to unify South Africa

Transvaal burghers' rejection of the annexation. Anger and bitterness towards the new regime was increased by the fact that while the British government adopted a generous attitude towards the settlement of the republic's existing debts, it was not prepared to provide a continuing subsidy to sustain the Transvaal's administration. To establish the elements of an orderly administration, however, would involve raising revenue on a scale considerably in excess of anything raised by the republican authorities in the past. Taxes would have to be imposed and collected which, in a society where so little money circulated, might force many burghers to part with their land and reduce them to the growing ranks of *bywoner* tenants. The new administration hoped to tax the African population much more effectively than the republican authorities. This would not only bring in revenue but make African labour more readily available. It was not possible, however, to squeeze enough from the African population to shield the Transvaal burghers from tax burdens. Pedi resistance to tax payment had in fact been strengthened by their recent triumph over the republican authorities. The British authorities therefore decided to attack the Pedi kingdom. With the use of imperial troops, supported by a substantial force of Swazi made available by the Swazi king, the Pedi were finally crushed in September 1879. It was a costly campaign, however, and victory came too late to rescue the popularity of the British regime.

Xhosa war on the eastern frontier

While the confederation issue remained unresolved, war broke out once again on the Cape's eastern frontier. After the Xhosa cattle-killing tragedy, Governor Grey had taken the opportunity to redistribute land between communities beyond the colonial frontier in the Transkei as well as within the colonial boundaries. The Mfengu, who had been granted additional land after every war since 1835, were then given a substantial area in the Transkei (subsequently known as Fingoland). The Thembu were also allocated additional land (subsequently known as Emigrant Tembuland). The Griquas were encouraged to trek from the Free State and settle in the valley between the Drakensberg and the coastal strip previously known as No man's land and subsequently as Griqualand East.

The main sufferers in this redistribution were the two main branches of the Xhosa. The Gcaleka were left with a greatly reduced reserve in the Transkei, while the Ngqika retained a very inadequate reserve in the colony. As the human and cattle population gradually recovered from the effects of the cattle killing in the 1850s, tension rose between different groups in the border area. Feeling between the Xhosa and the Mfengu was naturally particularly bitter. With the increased pace of economic life that followed the diamond discoveries, the frontier areas had been increasingly drawn into the market economy. African peasants throughout the western districts of the Transkei, as well as the Ciskei, became actively involved in production for the market and white traders opened up stores on a much larger scale than in the past. Following on from this economic penetration, Cape administration was informally extended through the appointment of magistrates to reside with and advise the chiefs in Griqualand East and the lands occupied by the Thembu. In August 1877, a fight at a drinking party between Xhosa and Mfengu escalated into serious conflict. Cape frontier

*Diamonds &
the first British attempt
to unify South Africa*

police crossed the Kei to protect the Mfengu. Kreli, the Gcaleka chief, refused to answer a summons to present himself before Frere who was visiting the eastern frontier on his way to the Transvaal. War began with the Gcaleka. The Ngqika in the colony rose to join them. Colonial troops with the support of Mfengu and Thembu auxiliaries had to be supplemented by imperial forces. Disagreement over the conduct of the war brought Frere and Molteno into open conflict. Aware that the ministry by then had very slender support in the Cape Parliament, Frere took a major constitutional gamble and dismissed the Prime Minister. His move was successful, for Gordon Sprigg was prepared to take over the role and succeeded in getting parliamentary endorsement for a new ministry.

The escalation of conflict

With the dismissal of Molteno, a major obstacle to the confederation policy had been removed. Sprigg could be counted on to co-operate with the British imperial initiative. War on the eastern frontier continued, however, and expanded in scope in February 1878 when Griquas and Pondos in Griqualand East rose in rebellion against an administration which appeared to be giving unfair favour to the traders. In Griqualand East, traders were skilful in exploiting their complex role as money lenders. They were also the only purchasers of African produce and the sole source of imported commodities, and as a result of these advantages they were gaining increasing control of Griqua and African land.

Pondo warriors

While the eastern frontier conflicts were still in progress, the Griqua of Griqualand West also rose in desperate resistance to the loss of their lands and their forced reduction to unskilled labourers. The Griqualand West rebellion spread across the northern frontier of the Cape. It was not over in Griqualand West until November 1878 and continued a little longer south of the Orange. On the eastern frontier fighting had ended in June 1878. Afterwards the Cape government, with Frere's active support, prepared to annex the western districts of the Transkei, establish regular white administration and disarm the African population. To this end, the Sprigg government passed a Peace Preservation Act providing for the disarmament of Africans under Cape authority. Only Griqualand East and Emigrant Tembuland had in fact been annexed, however, before the Zulu War and the 'War of the Guns' between the Cape and the Sotho brought the whole process of white expansion to a temporary halt.

The Zulu War

Imperial desires

While progress towards the federation of the white communities still hung fire, Frere sought for other opportunities to advance the grand design. The Zulu kingdom appeared to him to be the key piece in the southern African jigsaw. If the Zulu military system could be destroyed and the Zulu brought under British control, substantial reserves of the labour which it locked up would be made available to white employers. The most formidable African military power, the natural rallying point for any general resistance to white authority, would also have been removed. The destruction of Zulu power, moreover, would greatly ease the way towards white federation. Anxieties in the Cape about the burden of defending Natal would be eased. Transvaal Boers would be gratified by the grant of the disputed Blood River territory. Imperial prestige would be raised and an atmosphere of goodwill created in which confederation could be smoothly fulfilled.

During the reign of Mpande, the Zulu kingdom recovered from the disastrous defeat at Blood river and the subsequent civil war. The military system was retained and young men continued to be enrolled in the *butho* even though no campaigns were undertaken. The prolonged peace led to considerable tensions, however, as large bodies of young men were kept at the military towns training for combat which never took place.

Under these strains, while Mpande failed to keep a tight hand on the day-to-day administration of his kingdom, factions began to form around several of his sons. The question of the succession was complicated by the fact that Mpande never married a 'Great Wife'. There was thus no obvious heir apparent. The two who appeared to have the greatest claims were Cetshwayo and Mbulazi. Cetshwayo was the king's first son by his first wife. Mbulazi's mother had been married later and was of lower rank than Cetshwayo's, but she was Mpande's favourite and he also seemed to favour Mbulazi as his heir. Two powerful factions grew up around the two princes although other sons of Mpande also had smaller followings. Cetshwayo's faction took the nickname u-Suthu and Mbulazi's called itself izi-Gqoza. Conflict broke into the open in 1856 when Cetshwayo was nearly thirty. Outnumbered, the izi-Gqoza retreated to the Tugela river. They were then encountered by the u-Suthu forces at Ndondakasuka and decisively beaten. Cetshwayo established himself as heir apparent and for the rest of his father's reign exercised much of the power in the kingdom. So long as Mpande was still alive, however, Cetshwayo's position was still not absolutely certain. A number of other possible rivals existed and the old king allowed them considerable independence and influence.

Cetshwayo thus had to deal with several rivals and much intrigue. (It was in this period that negotiations were held with some Transvaal Boer leaders which they subsequently construed as giving them rights to the Blood River Territory.) To strengthen his hand, Cetshwayo also sought white support and gladly accepted Shepstone's offer to proclaim him heir apparent. To help him maintain the support and understanding of Natal, Cetshwayo relied on the help and advice of an English trader and adventurer, John Dunn. He was allowed to rule a large area as a Zulu sub-chief and built up a substantial personal following.

In 1872 Mpande died after a peaceful reign of thirty-two years. To consolidate his position, Cetshwayo invited Shepstone to participate in the formal inauguration of his reign. In a colourful ceremony on 1 September 1873, Shepstone placed a crown on Cetshwayo's head and proclaimed him king of the Zulu nation in the name of Queen Victoria. Shepstone tried to use the occasion (as Boers of the Republic of Natal had done when they crowned Mpande) to establish a permanent paramountcy over the Zulu king. He thus read out a list of principles of government which the king was to abide by in future.

Once established on the throne, Cetshwayo did everything in his power to retain good relations with the Colony while at the same time insisting on his independent sovereignty. For fifteen years he maintained peace with all his neighbours. In face of disagreement with the Transvaal over the Blood River Territory he repeatedly appealed for British arbitration. It was certainly through no fault of his that the destruction of his kingdom was to come to

Diamonds &
the first British attempt
to unify South Africa

appear to Frere as an essential step towards the fulfilment of British policy in South Africa.

Frere seeks war

To achieve this aim Frere looked for a way to start a conflict with the Zulu. He took up the disputed issue of the Blood River Territory and submitted it to an arbitration court appointed by the Natal government. He anticipated that the court would find in favour of the Transvaal and that Cetshwayo would be forced to fight rather than suffer the loss of popularity that surrendering land would entail. Frere's expectations were shattered when the court found the Transvaal's claims unsubstantiated and gave the Zulu even more than Cetshwayo had asked for.

Frere was determined to extricate himself from his difficult position and force the Zulu kingdom to war by any means. He found an excuse in a minor incident of frontier violation. In July 1878 two wives of a Zulu sub-chief, Sihayo, were detected in adultery and fled with their lovers to Natal. They were pursued by a party including the chief's brother and a number of his sons, led by his eldest son Mehlokazulu. The party found the women just across the Natal border and took them back to Zululand where they were killed. Mehlokazulu was not aware that this was an offence against British sovereignty. Natal forces never hesitated to cross into Zululand to apprehend fugitives from justice.

Frere treated the case as a major one and used it as the justification for an ultimatum to the Zulu king. In this Frere demanded not only the surrender of Sihayo's brother and sons together with a substantial fine, but the demobilisation of the Zulu army and the permanent abandonment of the military system. Cetshwayo had also to agree to accept a British diplomatic resident who would see that these demands were carried out in full. Frere was well aware that it would be virtually impossible for Cetshwayo to agree to these demands. They meant the destruction of the political system of his kingdom and the surrender of its independent sovereignty. In spite of repeated warnings from London not to provoke war with the Zulu, Frere was determined to do so. In November, Cetshwayo was asked to send representatives to a meeting near the Tugela river where the decision of the Boundary Commission would be announced. On 12 December, the Zulu *indunas* and John Dunn listened to the report and were about to depart in a mood of great goodwill when they were summoned to a further meeting. There they listened in shock and amazement as Shepstone laid out Frere's demands. Frere set a deadline of twenty days for the first three of his demands and thirty days for the rest.

Crossing a drift in the Zulu War

The British invasion of Zululand

When Cetshwayo heard of the ultimatum, he held a meeting of his Great Council at which it was decided to seek peace by agreeing to the demands which did not involve surrender of independence. A message was sent offering the surrender of the men and the cattle demanded as a fine. He begged that no action should be taken if the twenty days ran out before the fine was collected, because of the difficulties of communication in his kingdom where the rivers were in flood. Cetshwayo's peaceable response was brushed aside and, as the ultimatum expired, British forces entered Zululand in three separate columns. The British invasion happened to coincide with the annual first fruits ceremony in the Zulu kingdom. The whole Zulu army was thus assembled at Ulundi and Cetshwayo determined to despatch its full force against the British centre column. His purpose was entirely defensive and his hope was that if he could check that column, the British could be persuaded to negotiate peace. Thus his regiments were given strict instructions not to cross the borders into Natal. They were also instructed not to attack British civilians but only soldiers who could be recognised by their red uniforms. Subsequently, several British personnel were saved by the fact that they were wearing uniforms of other colours.

The British centre column moved slowly forward after crossing the Tugela at Rorke's Drift and camped on the side of a hill called Isandhlwana. The Zulu army, made up of twelve *butho*, loosely grouped in three corps, moved by easy stages. Taking advantage of the broken nature of the country, it was not detected by the British scouts, and came upon the British camp with little warning on the morning of 22 January 1879. The force at the camp had been considerably weakened as the commander-in-chief had advanced some miles further with a strong contingent, hoping to meet up with the Zulu forces. The remaining troops still constituted a very powerful force, however. Relying on their strength, the commander had not made a defensive *laager* with the wagons. Then, when he became aware of the impending Zulu attack, instead of concentrating his forces in a dense mass, he spread them out over a long front of nearly two miles. Approaching at the run, the Zulu regiments fell into the horns-of-the-cow formation enveloping the British force on both flanks. As they advanced, they were met by a murderous hail of fire, which cut many men to the ground. With extreme courage, however, they held their position and even continued their advance, crawling on hands and knees to lessen the chances of being hit. Faced with this, the British forces had to maintain a rate of fire which used up their ammunition faster than it could be replenished from the wagons. Then, as the firing slowed, the *butho* found new heart. Raising their battle cry 'u-Suthu' they made a desperate charge. At the critical moment, the race prejudices of the white troops proved their undoing. A section of the line was held by African troops under white officers. They were very poorly supplied with guns, let alone ammunition. Thus, as the Zulu charged, they found themselves unarmed and helpless. As they broke and fled, the Zulu poured through the gap. The British troops were quickly overwhelmed and with the exception of a few fugitives the entire force was destroyed.

The battle of Isandhlwana

British troops attacking a Zulu stronghold

Two *butho* had not been involved in the battle. Disappointed at being left out of the action they crossed into Natal and attacked the border post of Rorke's Drift. The defenders, firing from behind a hastily built wall and the shelter of the mission hospital building, succeeded in preventing themselves from being completely overwhelmed in the night. In the morning the *butho*, satisfied that they had proved their manhood, and aware that they were acting in defiance of Cetshwayo's orders, withdrew leaving the defenders to believe that they had staved off a massive invasion of Natal.

The significance of the Zulu victory

The battle of Isandhlwana was the most outstanding victory ever won by an African army in sub-Saharan Africa against white forces. Sheer courage, discipline and determination for once overcame the advantages of gunfire. The Zulu victory at Isandhlwana, moreover, had a major impact on the course of South African history. The disaster shocked British opinion and shook the government's confidence in its whole South African policy. Frere

*Diamonds &
the first British attempt
to unify South Africa*

was censured for provoking the Zulu war. Though he was not recalled, his authority in South Africa was undermined by the creation of a separate High Commission for south-east Africa covering Natal and the Transvaal. Wolseley was appointed to this new position and soon proved unwilling to co-operate closely with Frere. With such divided leadership it would now be difficult to push the confederation scheme ahead.

The Zulu victory had shaken the prestige of British troops and encouraged the opponents of British rule in the Transvaal. The victory did not, however, save the Zulu kingdom. The British authorities felt that military honour must be retrieved at all costs. Reinforcements were brought up and the advance on Ulundi was resumed. Cetshwayo was fully aware that winning a battle did not mean winning the war. He was appalled at the heavy Zulu losses. He repeatedly despatched messengers seeking a negotiated peace but to no avail. The Zulu regiments fought on bravely and won some minor engagements. The British forces, however, did not expose themselves again in such a vulnerable position and the Zulu suffered drastic casualties in a number of battles.

The end of the war

The final battle was fought near Ulundi. As the regiments charged the British troops drawn up in square formation, they were mercilessly slaughtered by volleys of rifle fire and hails of lead from the rapid-firing Gatling guns.

After Ulundi, the Zulu army was decisively crushed and its capacity to face the invaders in a full-scale battle was destroyed. The Zulu, however, were still capable of offering very serious resistance by reverting to guerrilla tactics, small-scale attacks and ambushes. Wolseley took over the command immediately after the battle of Ulundi. He realised that the systematic conquest necessary for direct British rule would cost far more than the British government could afford to expend on an unpopular war. He therefore decided to buy peace by offering the Zulu a considerable measure of autonomy in return for their acceptance of the break-up of the kingdom and its military machine. British military prestige might have been restored, but the drive behind British policy had lost its force. The defeated Zulu kingdom was not annexed but an attempt was made to render it harmless by dividing it up into thirteen separate chiefdoms under chiefs who included descendants of Zwide and Dingiswayo; Hamu, a cousin of Cetshwayo; and Zibhebhu, descended from a brother of Shaka's father, Senzanghakona. One chiefdom was to be ruled by John Dunn. A British Resident was appointed to judge disputes between the chiefs who were to undertake not to create armies of their own. Cetshwayo was hunted down and taken prisoner to Cape Town.

Sotho resistance: The 'Gun War'

While the British imperial part of the drive to extend and tighten white control over the African peoples was blunted by the resistance of the Zulu, the Cape-led part of the movement was halted by the resistance of the Sotho.

Zulu attack at Intombi Drift, 1879

*The Phuthi are driven
to rebellion*

After the annexation of Lesotho, Moorosi, Chief of the Phuthi in the Quthing district of Lesotho, found his position with his own people undermined by the local white magistrate's interference in matters of

British forces using the laager method of defence during the Zulu war

traditional law. In 1878 confrontation between them reached such a point that the Cape authorities had to call on the Sotho paramount Chief Letsie to exert pressure on Moorosi to accept the magistrate's authority. Aware that rebellion against the Cape authorities could result in seizure of further Sotho land, Letsie co-operated. A substantial Sotho force was despatched to support the magistrate. A *pitso* was held and Moorosi accepted the imposition of a fine.

Though the magistrate whose brash conduct had enflamed this affair was removed, he was succeeded by another who was even more determined to demonstrate his superior authority over the chief in unmistakable terms. Moorosi's son Lehana was charged with stealing horses on very flimsy grounds. He was tried and given the very severe sentence of four years' imprisonment to be spent in hard labour on the Cape Town breakwater. Fearing that their chief's son was to be taken away from them for ever, some of his people broke open the jail and helped him escape. When Moorosi was ordered to surrender his son he knew that to do so would discredit him with his people completely. He refused and this was taken as an act of rebellion.

As forces from the Cape assembled to attack the chief, Letsie was summoned to give military aid to the authorities. Many of his senior chiefs sympathised with Moorosi. The Sotho paramount, however, feared the consequences of

Moorosi besieged

117

Diamonds &
the first British attempt
to unify South Africa

rebellion. He and his people had also been given to understand that, if they proved loyal, the disarmament policy that had already been announced would not be applied to Lesotho. A substantial Sotho force thus took part on the side of the Cape forces in the attack on Moorosi. The chief and his people took refuge on a fortified mountain-top where they made good use of the guns in their possession to resist an eight month-long siege. Two full-dress attempts to storm the mountain were repelled. Finally, on the night of 19 November 1879, the mountain-top was scaled and Moorosi and many of his closest followers were killed. The Cape troops cut off his head and mutilated his body. After the campaign, vast herds of cattle were taken, and the Phuthi community was broken up and forcibly distributed to Cape farmers as farm workers.

Sotho disarmament Even though Letsie had demonstrated his loyalty so strikingly, the Moorosi campaign simply increased the determination of Sprigg and Frere to disarm the Sotho without exception. In spite of protests at the injustice and unfairness of the measure, the warnings of the French missionaries and the advice of the Cape's own administrator, Colonel Griffith, the proclamation calling for the surrender of guns was issued in April 1820. The Sotho were well aware that without guns they would already have been completely dispossessed by the whites. Guns were crucial symbols of personal prestige within Sotho society and they enabled the Sotho to preserve a sense of pride and dignity in relations with whites. The proclamation thus produced a greater sense of unity in Lesotho than had existed since the death of Moshoeshoe. Though Jonathan, one of the rivals to the succession to Molapo, was prepared to betray the cause of the kingdom and gave support to the colonial forces, the other senior chiefs offered united resistance.

In the 'Gun War', the Sotho conducted a skilful guerrilla struggle and, after an initial attempt to take the Maseru garrison by frontal assault which proved a costly failure, they avoided full-scale battles. They relied on a chain of fortified hilltops and on the speed of their horses. When colonial forces adequate to storm a stronghold were assembled, the Sotho would allow them to take it with relatively little resistance, moving their cattle and stores to another position. As the colonial troops moved on, they would re-occupy the abandoned stronghold. Wherever the colonial forces moved, groups of Sotho horsemen shadowed them, firing from time to time and always waiting for the opportunity to cut off stragglers or isolated detachments. Through these tactics the Sotho exhausted the Cape's troops. Still more important, they ensured that the expenses of the campaign would outrun the Colony's capacity and willingness to pay. The conflict also spilled out of Lesotho and provoked the Mpomdomise and some of the Thembu and Griqua as well as Sotho communities resident in the Transkei to rise in rebellion.

Parallel resistance to confederation

*Diamonds &
the first British attempt
to unify South Africa*

African resistance to being brought under closer white control was accompanied by increasing Afrikaner resistance to the British imperial policy of confederating the white communities. The news that Frere had been reprimanded and his authority divided excited Transvaal Boers' hopes of breaking away from British rule. The Free State *volksraad* voted its sympathy with the Transvaal and in the Cape Jan Hofmeyr, political leader of the Dutch wine farmers, organised a protest against the annexation. Meanwhile, S.J. du Toit had founded the Afrikaner Bond, the first organised expression of Afrikaner nationalism, in a bitterly anti-British mood.

In the Transvaal itself, opposition to the annexation greatly increased over the two years before 1879. In January 1879 as the imperial troops began their advance into Zululand, the Transvaal Boers met at a mass congress at Wonderfontein and made a solemn vow to regain their independence. News of Isandhlwana greatly strengthened their confidence. Soon after this, Frere's authority in the area was taken over by Wolseley who further angered the Transvaalers by establishing a legislative assembly with no elected members. In December 1879, the Boers assembled again at Wonderfontein, hoisted the republican flag, the Vierkleur (Fourcolours) and agreed to summon their old *volksraad* to meet in April.

In April too, the Liberal party, led by William Gladstone, won the British general election. This naturally raised Transvaal hopes that their independence would be peacefully restored. Once in office, however, Gladstone found the problems of the Transvaal more complicated than they had seemed when he was in opposition. Not only was Queen Victoria strongly opposed to abandoning British territory but humanitarians in the party were against leaving the African population open to Boer oppression. Frere was accordingly encouraged to make a new attempt to get the confederation policy moving. He persuaded Sprigg to submit a federal motion to the Cape House of Assembly in June.

Kruger and his fellow Boer leader P.J. Joubert were visiting the Cape at the time to arouse feeling against the Transvaal annexation. They met with Dutch-speaking members of parliament at Hofmeyr's house, and Sprigg's motion was defeated without even being put to the vote. All immediate hope of pushing confederation through was now abandoned and Gladstone recalled Frere on 4 August.

British authority over the Transvaal was still maintained, however, until Boer resentment and frustration was finally sparked off in December: Potchefstroom officials ordered the seizure of a wagon belonging to a farmer named Bezuidenhout over a tax question. The wagon was rescued by 300 armed burghers and the Transvaal rose in open rebellion. British troops were severely mauled at Bronkhorst Spruit and the Transvaal garrison was then besieged in Pretoria, Potchefstroom and other fortified villages. Reinforcements were rushed up from Natal but they were severely beaten back at Laing's Nek on 26 January 1880 and again soon after at Ingongo. The Liberal administration, uneasy from the outset about the annexation of the Transvaal, was not prepared to face a war to retain it. Even before the Laing's Nek encounter, an offer of negotiations had been despatched to the Boer leaders. In face of the initial defeats it was proposed to establish a Royal

*Diamonds &
the first British attempt
to unify South Africa*

Commission with wide powers, but before an armistice could be arranged, British forces were heavily defeated in a battle at Majuba Hill.

British policy on withdrawal

After Majuba Hill, Kruger agreed to negotiations. Gladstone's government was now fully prepared to abandon the Transvaal but as parliament had legislated for the colony, it could not do so without another Act of Parliament. As opposition to abandoning the Transvaal was still strong in the Liberal Party, however, a compromise was suggested which proposed that the Transvaalers should be restored to full internal independence with Britain as suzerain. This meant that Britain was to have control over the republic's relations with foreign European powers, frontier questions and issues concerning the rights of the African peoples. This last responsibility was to be discharged by a British Resident in Pretoria. These terms were reluctantly accepted by the Boer leaders and embodied in the Pretoria Convention which was signed in August 1881. With the Transvaal free of direct British control, Kruger was elected president of the restored republic. Britain had thus once again returned to a policy of withdrawal and limitation of responsibility in South Africa.

The Cape for its part also retreated from its recent forward policy. Though its forces succeeded in suppressing the revolts in East Griqualand and the Transkei, the Sotho successfully held out. In April 1881 the conflict was submitted to the arbitration of the new High Commissioner, Hercules Robinson. He ruled that the Sotho might keep their guns so long as they were registered and payment for damage was made. The Sotho had won but they were deeply divided. The Cape's administration had been discredited and, in the absence of alternative arrangements, the kingdom seemed likely to slide into anarchy. The Cape's defeat in the Gun War, coming on top of the heavy expenses of warfare in the Transkei, ensured the defeat of Sprigg's administration. It was succeeded by a new ministry led by Thomas Scanlen in May 1881. The new ministry sought to withdraw as far as possible from responsibilities for the administration and control of African peoples on its borders.

In an attempt to bring order to Lesotho, administrative authority was briefly entrusted to General Gordon noted for his role in suppressing the Tai-Ping rebellion in China. Gordon, however, was not prepared to use force in support of government authority against obstinate chiefs and abruptly resigned his position. The Scanlen government then appealed to the British government to resume responsibility for the Sotho kingdom. As most of the chiefs expressed a strong desire for this solution as well, British rule was restored in 1884 and Basutoland was thereafter to remain a British protectorate in South Africa. The Scanlen government even tried to persuade the imperial authorities to take over responsibility for the Transkei. This was refused, however, and in 1885 the Cape consolidated its administration there by annexing all the territories south of the Mthatha river.

The new policy of withdrawal in southern Africa was not to be long-lived. The development of the diamond fields was leading to the establishment of large-scale capitalist industry and drawing international capitalist finance into southern Africa. The development of the diamond fields and the

Prospecting for gold
by Thomas Baines

modest gold discoveries at Tati and near Lydenburg in the Transvaal suggested the possibility of further rich mineral discoveries. The international scramble for territory in Africa was about to commence. The breaking away of the Transvaal was thus to ensure that, when Britain returned to the task of attempting to unite the white communities of South Africa under the imperial flag, it would require a major war.

New era: industrial revolution in the diamond fields

The transformation of diamond mining in South Africa from an activity conducted by large numbers of independent diggers to the operation of a single, giant capitalist concern was to be brought about by the son of an English country parson, Cecil Rhodes. He first arrived in South Africa in 1870 when, as a youth of seventeen, he came to assist his brother, Herbert, who was trying to establish himself as a farmer in Natal. Soon after his arrival, Herbert moved to the newly discovered diamond fields and Cecil left the farm to join him. Rhodes was one of those who saw at an early stage that success in diamond mining required expansion of the scale of operations. One of his early ventures, the purchase and importation of a small steam engine which could be employed on contract to pump out waterlogged digging, yielded enough profit to enable him to start buying up multiple claims. Soon he was making enough money to be able to afford to travel between South Africa and England in order to study for a degree at Oxford.

The effect which competition between companies had on the world price of diamonds made a number of people believe that the answer lay in an amalgamation of the South African diamond mining industry into a single

Amalgamation of the diamond fields

Cecil Rhodes and Alfred Beit, 1901
photograph by E.H. Mills

giant monopoly which could then regulate the entire world market. In the struggle to dominate the diamond fields, Rhodes had a powerful rival in Barney Barnato, a Londoner who had arrived at the diamond fields with nothing but a load of cigars and, like Rhodes, had made his fortune by buying up claims and bringing them together in a more economically viable enterprise. While Rhodes dominated the diamond digging on the farm once owned by De Beers and hence known as the De Beers Mine, Barnato controlled the greater part of the richer Kimberley mine. Rhodes, however, had as his ally Alfred Beit, a diamond buyer of German descent, who had built up the largest diamond-buying business on the fields and was a convinced believer in the need for amalgamation. Through Beit, Rhodes gained access to Lord Rothschild and the immense financial resources of the Rothschild family. With this backing, he was able to get the upper hand in a massive takeover battle. Barnato was forced into amalgamating his holding with that of Rhodes in the giant De Beers Consolidated which, after it had bought up the only remaining significant diamond-producing companies in South Africa, virtually monopolised South African diamond production and dominated the world market for the stones. Barnato became a life director of the new company but Rhodes had the effective executive power.

Increased control of
African working conditions

The amalgamation of the diamond mines not only allowed control of the world market in the interests of the diamond producers, it also brought about an extreme form of control and discipline over African labour. In the early days of the diggings, African workers had built huts for themselves near their work places. Living conditions were squalid and extremely unhealthy, and mine employers found it was very difficult to prevent African workers from deserting when they found their working conditions so unsatisfactory.

*Diamonds &
the first British attempt
to unify South Africa*

It was also extremely difficult to prevent the theft and illegal sale of diamonds and to stop African workers finding relief from the tedium and hardship of their work in heavy drinking, which resulted in subsequent absenteeism or poor work performance. As the regime of the individual digger gave way to that of the highly capitalised mining company, so the living conditions of workers were regulated. Eventually, all African labour at the diamond fields was housed in closed compounds with no uncontrolled outlet except through a shaft to the mine. Apart from permitting extreme labour discipline and a fuller exploitation of the miners' physical powers, this system of virtual imprisonment made it difficult for the African miners to organise themselves and fight for improved wages and conditions. The compound system developed at the diamond mines was later to provide a model for the system of labour exploitation and discipline on the gold mines.

By 1888, when Rhodes achieved the amalgamation of his and Barnato's mining concerns in De Beers Consolidated Mines Ltd, he had already acquired a substantial stake in gold mining on the Rand. His company, the Consolidated Gold Fields of South Africa Ltd, was constituted in 1887. He had also entered upon a political career in the Cape parliament. He was first elected as a member in 1880 for Barkley West, a predominantly Dutch-speaking electorate, not long before the Transvaal rebellion and the final collapse of the British confederation scheme. He held the loyalty of his voters in every subsequent election until his death.

Rhodes was not interested in money purely for its own sake but rather as one source of the power to fulfil his own extreme vision. He envisaged the whole of Africa united under the British flag, knit together by a Cape-to-Cairo railway and telegraph system. This vast African dominion would then form part of an imperial federation which, in alliance with the United States of America and Germany, would dominate the world in the interests of peace, progress and the good of humanity. He himself was destined to play a key role, he believed, in the extension of the British empire through Africa and in the introduction of this new world order. The Cape was to be the southern base for the imperial push through Africa. The northward drive was to be achieved by the energies of the white South African peoples rather than by the direct action of the British government. He saw his role as linking the financial resources of modern capitalism to the expansive energies of the two white South African peoples (two branches of the Teutonic race which he believed was destined to rule the world) and lead them in a great northward push through the continent. To enable him to use the vast resources of his diamond and gold mining enterprises for this territorial expansion, he inserted clauses in the constitutions both of Consolidated Gold Fields and De Beers Consolidated permitting these concerns to 'acquire any tract or tracts of country in Africa or elsewhere'. One of Rhodes's first major political concerns was to be the preservation of the missionary road to the north as a channel for British expansion beyond the Zambezi.

After the withdrawal of British authority, the Transvaal settlers began expanding vigorously both to the west and to the east. To the west of the Transvaal, white mercenaries offered military aid to Tswana and Korana chiefs in their conflicts with one another. In return for their services they

*The many ambitions of
Cecil Rhodes*

Punch shows Rhodes as a colossus
straddling the African continent

New states, new boundaries

123

Diamonds &
the first British attempt
to unify South Africa

demanded massive land grants on which they erected two small republics, Stellaland and Goshen. These new white mini-states straddled the missionary road to the north. If, as seemed most probable, they were absorbed by the South African Republic, British trade and influence might be denied access to central Africa.

In 1883 the strategic situation in southern Africa was transformed when the German flag was hoisted at Angra Pequena Bay. The following year, Britain was forced to recognise a German protectorate over South West Africa (now Namibia). The British government was thus prepared to make concessions to the Transvaal if the South African Republic would clearly recognise a limit to its expansion to the west and renounce the incorporation of the two mini-republics. In the London Convention of 1884, the Transvaal was given a little more territory on the west but held well back from the missionary road. In return, Britain dropped the word suzerainty from the Convention and abandoned control over the Transvaal's native policy. Although the London Convention formally excluded the possibility of the Transvaal annexing Stellaland and Goshen, it did nothing to establish an alternative order in the area.

Though Rhodes agitated in the Cape parliament for the Colony to take control of what he described as 'the Suez Canal to the interior', the Cape administration was cautious about taking on the financial burden that this would involve. The British government appointed the missionary, John Mackenzie, as deputy commissioner for the area but with ill-defined powers and inadequate resources to enable him to impose order. Gey van Pittius, the leader of Goshen, rejected Mackenzie's authority which was also undermined by Rhodes who was determined to see Cape rather than British imperial authority established in the area. Later, Rhodes was himself appointed deputy commissioner but he also failed to win over the Goshenites.

Then, in September 1884 President Kruger proclaimed the extension of Transvaal protection to the mini-republic, despite the restrictions imposed by the London Convention. In face of this and the threat of expanded German influence from South West Africa, a substantial British force under General Warren moved into the area. The people of Stellaland and Goshen submitted without bloodshed, the Tswana chiefs accepted British protection, and the area south of the Molopo river was annexed as the Crown Colony of British Bechuanaland in 1885. In 1895 it was incorporated in the Cape Colony.

Further north along the missionary road, the three most important Tswana chiefs, Sechele of the Kwena, Kgama of the Ngwato, and Gaseitswe of the Ngwaketse, were also prepared to receive British protection as a defence against the Transvaalers to the east and the Ndebele to the northeast. These territories were thus annexed as the Bechuanaland Protectorate (now Botswana). In the 1890s this was further extended northward and took in the lands of the Tawana around Lake Ngami.

Wolseley's settlement in Zululand weakened the kingdom as a military force but initiated a period of chaotic struggle. White adventurers and gun traders contributed to the growing anarchy. The restoration of Cetshwayo soon appeared desirable as a means of re-establishing order. His case was strongly advocated by Bishop Colenso in Natal and supported by several British newspapers. In 1882 he was allowed to visit England and was received

Cetshwayo
from a photograph taken
at Cape Town by J.E. Bruton

Diamonds &
the first British attempt
to unify South Africa

by Queen Victoria, and in 1883 he was restored to the Zulu throne.

While the Zulu king had been in exile, vested interests in the changed order had developed and these were threatened by Cetshwayo's restoration. The opposition found leadership from Zibhebu and, after a brief civil war, Cetshwayo was forced to flee the kingdom. He died the following year in exile in Eshowe Reserve. He left as his senior heir Dinizulu, then a boy of fifteen. Taking advantage of the conflict in Zululand, a group of Transvaal burghers led by Lukas Mayer offered military aid to Dinizulu. With their help he regained the Zulu throne, but had to surrender a large part of what remained of the territory of his kingdom to his mercenary allies. On this land they proclaimed the New Republic. The frontiers of this new state extended to include St Lucia Bay. Spurred by rumours that this was about to be sold to German interests, the British government annexed the Bay in 1884. In 1886 the New Republic, deprived of access to the sea, was recognised and forthwith joined the Transvaal. In 1887 the remainder of Zululand was annexed and placed under Natal. Only Swaziland and a strip of coast occupied by the Tsonga peoples remained independent of white control in this area.

By 1884 the Cape government had also resumed the extension of its authority up the east coast. Gcalekaland and Thembuland were annexed. In 1886 the Xesibe chiefdoms of the Mount Ayliff district were added to the colony which extended its authority over Port St Johns also .The two sections into which the original Pondo chiefdom of Faku had divided after his death were left independent for a while longer, however, although a British protectorate was declared over the coast.

By 1884–5, then, the policy of withdrawal that followed the setbacks of the Zulu war and the Transvaal rebellion was being replaced by a new forward movement of British authority in South Africa. It even looked briefly as if the ideal of the union of the white states in some form of association within the British empire might be achieved without further conflict. The withdrawal of British political authority from the Transvaal did not reduce its economic dependence on the ports of the British colonies. A new attempt to build a railway from Delagoa Bay was making very slow progress. Kruger twice asked for a customs union with the Cape and for the extension of the railway line from Kimberley into the South African Republic. The Cape ministry was, however, hard pressed to meet its own commitments and refused to share its customs revenues. Its refusal came the year before the chance was lost altogether, for in 1886 the Struben brothers announced the discovery of gold-bearing areas on the Witwatersrand and the entire economic balance of power in South Africa was radically transformed.

7 Gold & the unification of South Africa

I n 1886 a gold-bearing reef was discovered on the Witwatersrand by Frederick and Henry William Struben. This discovery was a major turning point in the history of South Africa. In the long run, gold production was to prove far more significant than diamonds in transforming the economy. It was to change the social and economic pattern of South Africa from a patchwork of agricultural and pastoral communities to a predominantly industrial urban society.

In the short run, the development of gold mining in the Transvaal was to bring about a major war between Britain and the Boer republics. In turn, this opened the way for the political unification of South Africa. When unification did come, in spite of British victory in the South African War and the extinction of the independent Boer republics, it was to be brought about under Afrikaner leadership.

Initial changes caused by gold mining

The development of gold mining in the Transvaal generated internal tensions. These developed between the mixed European but predominantly British and British South African immigrant mining community known as *uitlander* (foreigners) and the Boer government and community at large. Underlying the tension was a conflict between the essential economic interests of some of the most important mining magnates and the interests, policies and very nature of the Boer state.

The sudden wealth in the Transvaal, which resulted from the gold discoveries, also drastically altered the balance of economic power within the system of white South African states, and appeared to threaten British control in southern Africa. Thereby it seemed to threaten the strategic integrity of the entire British empire at a time when competition between European powers for territorial possessions in Africa was at its height. This apparent threat to Britain's position in South Africa also came at a time when gold, because of its greater availability, was becoming more and more important in the world economy. These two factors, reinforced by the attitude of a number of British men of influence, led to the outbreak of the South African War.

Reactions in the Transvaal volksraad

Kruger and the leading Boer 'notables' who dominated the Transvaal *volksraad* were determined to preserve the political independence of their state which they had so recently regained. They were equally determined to maintain the character of their society which was dominated politically by its established Afrikaner citizens or burghers. They were naturally afraid of granting political rights to the hordes of *uitlander* who poured into the country in the trail of the gold discoveries and threatened to swamp the existing Boer population. It was feared that these European immigrants with little fixed stake in the republic might well use any vote granted them as a means of bringing the republic back under British control.

Kruger's response was to raise the residential requirements for the right to vote in *volksraad* and presidential elections from five to fourteen years. To balance this restriction he created a second *volksraad* with local government powers covering the area around Johannesburg for which *uitlander* could vote after only three years. As the second *volksraad* lacked final political authority, however, few *uitlander* were satisfied with or even interested in obtaining the right to vote for this.

Kruger and the members of his *volksraad* were conscious of the need to develop the mining sector of the economy and enacted relatively generous mining laws. Nevertheless, they naturally hoped to make use of the wealth generated to increase the economic independence of their state. Schemes for promoting this included the provision of a rail link to the coast independent of a British port and the development of industries within the Transvaal. Among these was the production of explosive dynamite, essential for blasting operations on the gold mines. At the same time they sought to serve the interests of their own class and to improve the lot of increasing numbers of poorer burghers. These included *bywoner* (client tenants) and the altogether landless. In order to achieve these ends they granted monopoly rights to individuals or companies to provide services or manufacture commodities. The two most politically important of these were those given to the Netherlands South African Railway Company to build the railway from Delagoa Bay and operate the main lines within the republic, and the dynamite monopoly.

The very nature of the Boer state, however, meant that it was inherently inefficient as a modern industrial state. Apart from an injection of overseas expertise in the form of a number of officials imported from the Netherlands, it relied for the most part on a bureaucracy of relatively uneducated burgher officials.

The nature of the Rand deposits

The gold discovered on the Witwatersrand consisted of small particles embedded in quartz material. Its extraction therefore required crushing of the rock and the separation of the gold from the rest of the material. Though the richness of the gold ore varied from place to place very considerably, really rich ore was found only in very limited pockets. On average the ore was of lower grade than would have been considered worth commercial exploitation in most other gold-producing countries. What made the Transvaal potentially worthwhile were the immense quantities of ore that were available.

The sheet of gold-bearing ore or 'banket' which crops out along the Witwatersrand reef tilts downwards to the south of the line of the reef. At first mining was confined to the line along which the banket approaches the surface. Only in 1893 was it finally established that it was possible to mine the ore successfully by driving shafts further to the south and striking the

President Kruger
from a painting by E. Rinaldi

Battery and tramways on a Witwatersrand goldfield, 1889

sheet at much deeper levels. Only when this was known did it become clear that gold mining around Johannesburg had a long-term future.

The nature of the Witwatersrand gold deposits meant that gold production would require considerable capital investment from the outset. Much of this capital came originally from individuals and companies already involved in diamond production. Among those joining the rush to establish gold mining concerns was Rhodes's closest associate, Otto Beit, who with Julius Wernher established Wernher, Beit and Co., economically the strongest group on the Witwatersrand. Rhodes at first regarded prospects of gold mining in the Transvaal with some caution. As it became clear that the gold deposits were real and extensive, however, his agent began buying up claims to mining ground and established Consolidated Gold Fields of South Africa Ltd which was to become one of the most powerful mining groups in the Transvaal.

Though starting very often on the basis of capital transferred from the diamond mines, gold mining on the Rand subsequently drew in massive additional investment from abroad. In the case of the deep-level mines, huge investments had to be made over a long period before any profitable ore could be brought to the surface.

Effects of boom on the industry

Not surprisingly, therefore, after the first speculative boom led to the establishment of a large number of companies (over 139), the number remaining in business was soon much reduced; these were brought together in a small number of groups each consisting of a central holding company owning a majority shareholding in a series of mining companies. These groups in turn began to come together for the purpose of regulating their common interests in such matters as labour recruitment and wage levels in the Johannesburg Chamber of Mines. This association was only fully united after the South African War, however, and before that time political differences between the mining groups prevented it from functioning fully.

In marketing their product the gold mining companies were in a different position from the diamond mines. For many years gold was sold in London at a fixed price, regardless of the amount produced. This helps explain why the amalgamation of gold mining companies stopped short at the stage of the groups and their association in the Chamber of Mines instead of proceeding to the stage of a single giant monopoly like De Beers Consolidated on the diamond fields.

The nature of gold mining on the Rand, and of deep-level mining in particular, meant that mining companies needed to use large quantities of equipment, supplies of explosives and other commodities. Large quantities of coal were needed to generate the power required to operate winding gear, and pumps to keep the mines dry. Because of the immense initial investment, the continuing high overhead costs and the relatively low grade of the ore when finally brought to the surface, the prices of such equipment and commodities were highly significant. But most of all the mines required massive inputs of labour, most of which could be unskilled. As the skilled labour needed had to be imported from outside the Transvaal and in most cases from overseas, it had to be relatively highly paid. This made it all the more important to the mines to have access to massive supplies of unskilled African labour at very cheap rates.

The nature of the Transvaal state and the policies of President Kruger and his *volksraad*, however, worked against the interests of the mining companies. The concessions policy tended to raise the price of transport, thus raising the cost of all equipment and supplies, while the dynamite monopoly, in particular, directly increased the cost of that essential mining input. The Transvaal bureaucracy was also unable, or unwilling, to suppress the sale of liquor to the African work force on the mines. This had serious consequences for labour discipline and productivity. The Transvaal authorities, moreover, did not do as much as the mining magnates felt necessary to assist with the recruitment of labour or to enforce a pass system to prevent desertion and make strict labour discipline possible.

This conflict made some of the mining magnates feel that it was essential to replace the Boer republican state with one more in tune with their interests and expectations. Broadly speaking, it was those with a commitment to long-term investment and development of the gold mines who felt this way and worked for the overthrow of Kruger's republic. Others who still looked primarily to the possibility of short-term speculative profits feared the consequences to mining which any political upheaval might bring; such people gave their support to the republican authorities.

Crown Deep Gold Mine, Witwatersrand, 1898. A high-capital mine

The rush to build rail links

The development of the Witwatersrand gold mines, like the previous development of the diamond fields, constituted a tremendous spur to railway building. The Cape and Natal vied with each other to build lines to the rich market of Johannesburg. Kruger, however, was determined to use the opportunity to fulfil his republic's long-standing ambition to develop an outlet to the sea independent of British control through the construction of a railway line from Delagoa Bay.

This idea was revived in 1882 when an American, E. McMurdo, obtained a concession from the Portuguese government to construct a railway from Lourenço Marques to the Transvaal. With the discovery of the Transvaal goldfields the scheme became a genuinely viable commercial proposition. The concession for the construction of the line from the Transvaal border to Johannesburg was given to the Netherlands South African Railway Company. The resources which McMurdo could mobilise proved inadequate for the construction of the Mozambique section of the line and this was ultimately completed by the Portuguese government.

In the meantime the Transvaal and the Orange Free State kept the Cape and Natal lines out of their territory. The Cape, however, built lines from Cape Town to Fourteen Streams, from Port Elizabeth to Colesberg and from East London to Aliwal North, all on the borders of the Orange Free State, in the hope that republican resistance would eventually give way. The Natal government similarly built a line from Durban to Charlestown.

In 1888 the Cape succeeded in breaking through the Free State's resistance to the extension of the Colesberg line on to its territory. The Transvaal, however, continued to keep the railways of both British colonies out as the building of the Delagoa Bay line crept on. In 1890, however, the Netherlands South African Railway Company ran into serious financial difficulties, and the Kruger government was under strong pressure from mining interests to allow at least some line to reach the Rand and thus reduce transport costs for imported supplies.

129

By this time Rhodes was Prime Minister of the Cape. His government entered into an agreement with the Transvaal, under which it would advance a loan to the Netherlands South African Railway Company to enable it to complete the Delagoa Bay line. It did so on the understanding that the Company would first construct a stretch of line from Johannesburg to the Orange Free State frontier to link up with the Port Elizabeth line that had entered the Free State via Colesberg. Forced to admit the Cape line, Kruger decided to admit the Natal line also so that Transvaal would be able to play the two British colonies off against each other. The Cape line was completed in 1892 but enjoyed a monopoly for two years only. The Delagoa Bay line was finally completed in 1894 and the Natal line reached the Rand in 1895. The Transvaal then had three alternative lines at its disposal and by varying the allocation of traffic on the different lines could vitally affect the economic well-being of the two British colonies.

The potential conflict in this situation was dramatically demonstrated as soon as the Delagoa Bay line was completed in 1894. The Cape, in an attempt to outdo competition on the shorter route from Delagoa Bay, drastically reduced freight charges along its section of the line from the Cape to the Transvaal border. In response, the Netherlands South African Railway Company raised tariffs along the section of the line from the Free State border to Johannesburg so that the Delagoa line would still have an overall advantage. To beat this, the Cape had goods transported along its own line transferred to wagons at the Transvaal border and so taken on to Johannesburg at a total charge cheaper than that of transport from Delagoa Bay. Reacting to this, Kruger brought about a political crisis by closing the drifts (fords) over the Vaal river. This drastic act provoked a stern British ultimatum, but Kruger then drew back from the brink of war. The drifts were re-opened and an agreement on tariffs was reached between the Cape and the Netherlands syndicate. Not only did the Transvaal frustrate the railway construction plans of the Cape and Natal, until it could be assured of having its own line independent of British control, but with its new-found prosperity it resisted repeated attempts by the Cape to draw it into the customs union which was established between the Colony and the Orange Free State. Instead it imposed tariffs on Cape-produced goods to the

Lobengula and his sister at the great military dance

advantage of its own farmers. The Transvaal had once been economically dependent on the Cape and, to a lesser extent, Natal. Now the situation was reversed and the Transvaal seemed likely to break free from the slender ties of British political control, possibly drawing the Cape after it.

The politics of capitalism: Cecil Rhodes

The conflicts between the mining companies and the Boer state and those created for Britain by the Transvaal's sudden rise to economic importance in South Africa had a direct influence on the interests and ambitions of Cecil Rhodes. Through Consolidated Gold Fields of South Africa he was involved in massive investment in the Witwatersrand gold mines, investments which could be put severely at risk if the Transvaal government failed to provide the right economic climate for developing the deep-level mines.

For a solution to these problems, Rhodes looked to the north, seeing the occupation of what are now Zimbabwe, Zambia and Malawi (along with, as he hoped and intended, a good deal of Mozambique) as the first step in the great push from the Cape to Egypt. Most crucial to his plans was the area of modern Zimbabwe. Ever since Carl Mauch had announced his discovery of gold in the area and published his description of the Zimbabwe ruins, the belief had grown that fabulous gold resources were to be found there, far exceeding those of the Rand. The development of a new British settlement with such huge gold resources to the north of the Transvaal would swing the balance of economic power in southern Africa against the Transvaal and ensure that it would eventually be drawn into association with the British colonies.

The first step towards the achievement of this scheme lay in obtaining a suitable concession from the Ndebele king, Lobengula, who Rhodes calculated could be plausibly portrayed as enjoying sovereign rights over the whole of modern Zimbabwe by right of conquest. Even before the death of Mzilikazi, Robert Moffat's last visit to the Ndebele king in 1860 and the establishment of missionaries in the kingdom had opened the way for treaty and concession hunters. Lobengula's succession to the throne had involved

Mining concessions from
Lobengula

Lobengula reviewing a dance before
missionaries

Lobengula, king of the Ndebele

a bitter struggle in which white interests had been involved. Mzilikazi's senior heir, Nkulumane, had been executed along with the *indunas* who had prematurely installed the young man in his father's place. Many Ndebele, however, believed that the young man had been sent away to the south. Theophilus Shepstone encouraged the rumour that his groom was, in fact, the missing Nkulumane, though Ndebele *indunas* sent to speak with the lad in Natal denied that he could be the missing heir.

Lobengula only finally secured the throne after a bloody fight. Even after this, political opposition remained and seemed most often to centre on the myth of Nkulumane's continued existence. Lobengula was thus in a far from secure internal position and was fearful of antagonising the British, who could use the pretended Nkulumane against him. He also felt threatened by possible Portuguese expansion from Mozambique, while the Boers of the Transvaal had long had their eyes on his country.

In 1887 Piet Grobler, an agent of the Transvaal government, succeeded in persuading Lobengula to agree to a treaty allowing the Transvaal to establish a consul in his kingdom with rights of jurisdiction in matters involving Transvaal citizens. On returning from a visit to the Transvaal, however, Grobler was killed while passing through the territory of the Ngwato.

Rhodes then made his move; he got John Smith Moffat (son of Robert Moffat, Mzilikazi's friend) to persuade Lobengula to sign a treaty in which he agreed not to cede or abandon any part of his kingdom without prior British approval. Rhodes's agents, Charles Rudd and Rochfort Maguire, then sought a concession from the king granting sole rights to the exploitation of minerals in the Shona-occupied eastern areas of Zimbabwe (Mashonaland).

Lobengula was well aware of the superiority of white military power and the danger that his kingdom would be 'eaten up' by the whites. Observing how a chameleon stalks a fly then shoots out its tongue and swallows it, he once remarked, 'Britain is that chameleon and I am the fly.' He was terrified of being cheated into signing away more than he intended, but was afraid of antagonising the British, and anxious for their support against other political enemies. Finally, deliberately deceived by Rhodes's agents, he put his mark to the fateful Rudd concession granting the right to exploit the minerals of the Shona territory and to do everything necessary to this end.

Armed with this concession, Rhodes then set about establishing a company to exploit it. He persuaded the British government to grant the company a charter conveying the right to exercise administrative authority in the territories he hoped to occupy. His agents, while reassuring Lobengula that the Rudd concession granted no more than the right of white men to come and dig holes for minerals in the Shona country, cabled London that Lobengula had conceded the right to occupy the country.

Rhodes's scheme was very attractive to the British government. It offered the chance to bring a potentially rich area under British authority and to hold the door open for further northward expansion of British trade while at the same time providing a solution to the problem of the Transvaal's growing economic influence in southern Africa, all without any direct British government expenditure. The prospect of rich profits from the supposed mineral resources of the area attracted numerous rich and influential backers. Rhodes's British South Africa Company was granted its royal charter in 1889. In the meantime another of Rhodes's agents, Frank

Lochner, with the moral support of the French evangelical missionary, François Coillard, persuaded the Lozi king, Lewanika, to sign a treaty bringing his kingdom under the authority of the Company; in this, Lewanika was deliberately deceived into believing that he was placing his kingdom under the direct authority and protection of the British Crown. This treaty was interpreted to give the Company rights of control over much of the western half of Zambia, well outside the effective limits of Lozi rule. Other agents secured treaties establishing the Company's claim to eastern Zambia. Rhodes's agents failed, however, to reach the Yeke ruler Msiri in Katanga before his kingdom was snapped up by an agent of King Leopold of Belgium for his Congo Free State.

Rhodes also entered into an agreement with and provided funds for Harry Johnston, the imperialist-minded British consul in Mozambique, to help him establish British authority in modern Malawi. In return Johnston was to watch over the British South Africa Company's interests in the area of modern Zambia. Later Rhodes and Johnston were to quarrel over the consideration to be given to African land rights. This quarrel and the strength of the missionary influence in the area was to result in Malawi coming directly under the British Crown as Nyasaland instead of becoming part of the Company's territory as Rhodes had hoped.

Rhodes's 'pioneer column'

By early 1890, Rhodes was in a position to start his 'pioneer column' on the way to Mashonaland. There was a danger, however, of a direct confrontation with the Transvaal, for many Transvaal burghers thought of what is now Zimbabwe as the natural extension of their republic and believed that their right to expand into it had been established by the history of their struggle with Mzilikazi and subsequent diplomatic relations with him and Lobengula. The continuing problem of poor and landless burghers meant that there were strong pressures for an expansion across the Limpopo. As Rhodes prepared to move, Louis P. Bowler, a burgher of British origin, announced the intention of leading a trek from the Transvaal into the area. Kruger, however, was more anxious to expand eastward through Swaziland to Kosi Bay, thus gaining an outlet to the sea which would remain directly under Transvaal control.

The Swazi kingdom established by Sobhuza, employing its own version of the age-regiment, had been able to conquer and absorb many Sotho-speaking chiefdoms and integrate them successfully with the Nguni-speaking nucleus of the kingdom. Under Sobhuza's successor, Mswati, the kingdom expanded vigorously and reached the peak of its military power; it is after him that the kingdom and its people have come to be known as Swazi. Successive Swazi rulers were careful to avoid conflict with their more powerful neighbours. In this way they avoided being destroyed by the Zulu.

After the fall of Dingane, Swazi rulers were careful to avoid military conflict with whites. This, however, left the kingdom exposed to pressure from white concession hunters. Boers from the Transvaal sought and gained grazing rights over large areas of the kingdom, while a host of British individuals and companies pressed for mining, commercial and industrial concessions. To protect himself from being cheated and his people despoiled, King Mbandine employed Theophilus Shepstone's son (also Theophilus and known as Offy) as official adviser, but as Offy was often in

The Pioneer Corps on the way to Mashonaland, 1890

league with the concession hunters he was of little use. By the time Mbandine died in 1889, he had granted concessions covering all the land of the kingdom several times over.

Anticipating that he would be given the right to take over the Swazi kingdoms and the neighbouring coastal chiefdoms of the Tsonga, Kruger agreed to abandon the Transvaal's claims to expansion into modern Zimbabwe and stopped the proposed trek from the republic. In a meeting held in March 1890 at Blignaut's Pont, however, the British High Commissioner, Sir Henry Loch, refused to offer Kruger more than joint Transvaal-British sovereignty over Swaziland. A railway strip to Kosi Bay was also promised but only on the understanding that the Transvaal would enter a customs union with the Cape, a condition which the *volksraad* was eventually to reject.

The Transvaal was finally permitted to assume authority over the kingdom in 1899. By this time, however, British authority had been established along the relevant sections of the coast, thus ensuring that the republic would be denied direct access to the sea.

With Transvaal attention diverted by the false promise of expansion to the sea through Swaziland, Rhodes's column set out at the end of June 1890. In accordance with Rhodes's idea of uniting the two white races in northward expansion through Africa, a number of Afrikaans-speakers accompanied the British majority. The column also contained a number of high-born and wealthy young Englishmen whose influence in Britain might subsequently be useful to the Company. The column made its way into Mashonaland without meeting any resistance. Forts were built along the route at Tuli, Victoria and Charter, and the flag was hoisted over Fort Salisbury in September 1890.

Political tactics in the Cape

While preparing to despatch his pioneer column to Zimbabwe, Rhodes consolidated his political position in the Cape. First elected to the Cape parliament in 1880, he had cultivated an alliance with the Afrikaner Bond. This movement was boosted by the upsurge of Afrikaner pride and emotion which followed the successful independence struggle in the Transvaal. It blossomed briefly as a South Africa-wide Afrikaner nationalist movement. It soon withered away in the northern republics, however. In the Transvaal where the founder, Stephanus du Toit, held the post of Superintendent of Education for a while, the movement became too closely associated with Piet Joubert, Kruger's main political rival for the presidency. In the Cape, the Bond had joined forces at an early stage with a movement of the Dutch-speaking Cape farmers founded by Jan Hofmeyr and aimed at obtaining tariff policies more favourable to the wine-producing and grain-farming interests. Hofmeyr's Boeren Beschermings Vereniging (Farmers' Protection Association) also fought for improved status for the Dutch language. With such a union, the Bond acquired an organised body of supporters at the Cape, sufficient to ensure its political survival. As du Toit left for the Transvaal, the Bond in the Cape came under Hofmeyr's leadership and developed as a political party, content to operate within the Cape's political system. It pushed farmers' interests and Dutch-language rights but, though it retained the ideal of contributing to the creation of a united South African state, it was prepared to contemplate this taking place within the British empire. The Bond usually held enough seats in the Cape parliament to make its support essential to any government, though not enough to make an absolute majority. Under Hofmeyr, who shied away from assuming direct political responsibility, the Bond gave its support to a series of English-speaking leaders rather than attempting to form a government of its own.

Rhodes won popularity with the Bond by giving his support to measures serving the interests of Cape farmers and by a strong stand for the limitation and reduction of non-white voting rights. He also won support for his ideas for a union of the two white peoples of South Africa. Hofmeyr was at first suspicious of Rhodes's northward expansion plans, regarding them as harmful to the interests of the Transvaal. However as the republic continued to pursue economic policies which directly harmed the Cape farmers, Hofmeyr was won round to support Rhodes's plans for an Anglo-Dutch partnership in a great northward drive. Bond members' loyalty to the alliance was considerably strengthened by a favourable distribution of shares in Rhodes's companies. As his column moved into Mashonaland in July 1890, therefore, Bond support made Rhodes Prime Minister of the Cape. Once in power in the Colony he strengthened his alliance with the Bond by favouring the removal of legal disabilities affecting Dutch-speakers and by a whole series of measures directed to the interests of Cape farmers. Under his administration a ministry of agriculture was created and, for the first time, scientific expertise was made available to the farming community. Tariff systems favoured the farmer and railway policies were geared to their interests.

Rhodes further strengthened his political support by introducing a Franchise and Ballot Bill in 1892 which increased the income qualifications for the vote and also introduced an educational qualification. The growth of African peasant farming and of economic activity generally in the eastern-most districts of the Cape had led to a considerable increase in the number of Africans who were qualified to vote. In a number of constituencies in this area, Africans formed a clear, or near, majority of the registered voters. When Rhodes's bill was enacted, however, large numbers were struck off the rolls and white feelings were satisfied.

In 1894, this action against the African voter was followed by Rhodes's most important legislation in relation to Africans, the Glen Grey Act. This was mainly designed to make African labour more readily available to the mines and the white farmers, while also serving to restrict African access to the vote. The Act was introduced to deal in the first instance with the problem of overcrowding in the African reserves district of Glen Grey but was intended as a model for all the Cape's African reserves. It was, in fact, extended to a number of districts in the Transkei as well. Each landholder was to be restricted to a single ten-acre lot. This would ensure that there could be no relatively wealthy African peasants capable of providing for themselves and their families without turning to paid employment: in short, Africans who could compete effectively with white farmers. Land held under the scheme, moreover, was not to count towards the qualifications for the vote for the Cape parliament. Instead Africans were to have representation on local councils with purely local powers. So, by abolishing communal land ownership and restricting individual access to land, the Act was intended to force an increasing proportion of the growing population to look to wage labour for its support.

Head of De Beers and of Consolidated Goldfields, Prime Minister of the Cape and uncrowned king of the new settlement of Rhodesia, Rhodes was at the peak of his fortunes. Immense though his personal empire might have been, however, much of it rested on very shaky foundations. Not only was the investment in deep-level gold mining on the Rand a risky venture with huge capital sums at stake, but the British South Africa Company's move into Rhodesia was another great gamble. It was not long, indeed, before this showed signs of proving a disappointment.

Changes in Rhodes's fortunes

In the first place, Rhodes failed in his attempts to seize a Portuguese port in Mozambique to serve his new settlement. More seriously, the expected new Rand did not materialise in Mashonaland. Faced with potential economic disaster, the British South Africa Company's eyes turned naturally to the Ndebele country. The expected gold reef was now rumoured to run through Lobengula's settlement at Bulawayo while the large herds and wide grazing lands of the Ndebele kingdom offered the opportunity for the Company to recoup some of its heavy expenditure.

In 1893 a minor Ndebele raid near Fort Victoria was exploited as a pretext to force war on the Ndebele. A Company force, largely made up of volunteers, attracted by the offer of farms and a share of the loot of Ndebele cattle, moved towards Bulawayo. The massed Ndebele regiments were helpless in the face of Maxim guns. Lobengula fled from his capital and died while trying to reach the Ngoni kingdom of Mpezeni. The Company took over the Ndebele country and now rested its claims to Rhodesia (Zimbabwe) on 'right of conquest' rather than the flimsy foundations of the Rudd concession.

The conquest of Matabeland resulted in an immediate boom in the chartered company's shares. The railway line could now be pushed through Bechuanaland to Bulawayo, then across the Zambezi into modern Zambia. The anticipated gold reef was still not found, however, and there was now no prospect that the new settlement would outshine the Transvaal and draw it into a British association of African states. There was also no prospect that rich profits from royalties on Rhodesian gold mining could be used to pay for development work on the Rand gold mines or to offset losses on mining operations there. Both from the economic point of view and in the interests of his wider political ambitions, Rhodes felt the need for immediate political change in the Transvaal.

The lever Rhodes planned to use to overturn the Kruger regime and bring the Transvaal within a British federation of southern African states was the discontent of the *uitlander* population of the Transvaal. The *uitlander* were out of sympathy with the conservative values of the pastoral society of the Transvaal Boers and irritated by their contacts with the burgher bureaucracy. They resented the insistence on Dutch as the official language of the state and the lack of government support for English-language education. They also resented the fact that they were denied the vote although the mines where they worked provided by far the greatest part of the republic's wealth.

Organised opposition in the Transvaal

The *uitlander* had begun to organise agitation to bring pressure on the republican authorities as early as 1887. In 1892 they formed the Transvaal

National Union. The folowing year it at last became clear that mining at the deep levels was worthwhile. Soon after this some of the most powerful mining magnates put their weight behind the *uitlander* agitation and it became a strong and potentially revolutionary force. The British High Commissioner, Loch, who visited the Transvaal in 1893, was encouraged by the weakness of the republican government and the warm welcome he received from the *uitlander* population. He developed a plan to use a British force based in Bechuanaland to back up an *uitlander* rising on the Rand which would bring the Transvaal into a British federation. The scheme was rejected by the British government of the time but was taken up in modified form by Rhodes.

Rhodes first discussed his plans with the British Secretary of State for the Colonies and gained his general approval. Soon afterwards, High Commissioner Loch, who was a firm believer in direct British control of colonial ventures, was replaced by Hercules Robinson, a friend of Rhodes and a wealthy shareholder in Rhodes's companies. Little progress was made, however, before the British Liberal government fell in June 1895. Under the succeeding Conservative government of Lord Salisbury with the strongly imperialist Joseph Chamberlain as Secretary of State for the Colonies, the project was fully developed.

The plan was to prepare an armed uprising by the *uitlander* population on the Rand. At the same time a force of the British South Africa Police was to be assembled in Bechuanaland. Rhodes had hoped to acquire control of the whole of this territory for his Company but humanitarian pressures evoked by a diplomatic visit to England by the two Christian chiefs, Sechele of the Kwena and Khama of the Ngwato, forced Chamberlain to retain direct imperial control. The Company was, however, granted a strip of land along which to build its railway to Rhodesia. The assembly of the police force was to be covered by the pretext that it was required to protect the railhead from attack by the 'ferocious Bechuana'. Once the rising was under way in Johannesburg, the column would move into the Transvaal, thus preventing the republic from concentrating its forces on the Rand and so ensuring the success of the rebellion. To justify this invasion of Transvaal territory, a letter from the *uitlander* leaders calling on Dr Jameson, commander of the column, to come to the assistance of women and children in Johannesburg where lives were in danger, was pre-prepared. Arrangements were made with the colonial editor of *The Times* newspaper to publish the letter at the appropriate moment to justify Dr Jameson's march.

In the meantime a train was to be kept ready in Cape Town station. Once the rebels had seized effective control of the Rand, the High Commissioner, Sir Hercules Robinson, was to offer to mediate in the dispute, and board the train to Johannesburg. There he would declare that as representative of the imperial power it was his duty to take action for the preservation of peace; he would then summon a constitutional assembly for the republic, to be elected by all adult male residents and to have powers to determine the future status and constitution of the country.

The date was finally fixed for midnight on 28 December. Rhodes had smuggled arms to the Rand, and the British South Africa Police column was ready. *Uitlander* determination was lacking, however. The mining magnates were also divided. Some who had initially given support to the scheme were no more than unscrupulous speculators hoping to cause a scare which would produce a brief fall in the price of Rand mining shares. This would enable them to buy shares cheaply and then resell at a profit when the scare subsided.

The Jameson raid

In December, *uitlander* leaders informed Jameson and Rhodes that the uprising must be postponed. Jameson, however, convinced that the *uitlander* population would never rise on its own, made up his mind to go in uninvited and thus force a rising. Cutting the telegraph wires to prevent Rhodes cabling him to stop, he set out for the Rand. As his column advanced, the conspirators in Johannesburg were forced into some sort of revolutionary action. Organised in a Reform Committee, they established a measure of control over the city, but they did not openly reject the authority of the republican government. Instead they entered into negotiations with Kruger over demands for reform. Meanwhile they took no military action, leaving the republic's armed forces free to deal with Jameson's column.

When Rhodes heard of Jameson's move he was amazed. He had reason to hope, however, that Jameson's action might yet succeed. He therefore took no action to stop Jameson until it was clearly too late to do so. It was not long, however, before Jameson's expedition ended in disaster. It failed to get through to Johannesburg, was surrounded by Transvaal troops and, after some loss of life, surrendered unconditionally.

As a result of this humiliation, Rhodes was forced to resign as Prime Minister of the Cape. Sir Hercules Robinson did, indeed, go to the Transvaal but under very different circumstances from those the plotters had planned. The British government still hoped that the High Commissioner could push Kruger into accepting electoral reforms that would in any case achieve the aims of the plot. The High Commissioner, however, knowing that Jameson's men were in Kruger's hands and judging the temper of the republic in its hour of victory, contented himself with persuading Kruger to exercise mercy while convincing the members of the Reform Committee in Johannesburg that they should submit unconditionally. Kruger, for his part, acted with great wisdom and generosity. In spite of high feeling in his *volksraad*, the lives of the captured raiders were spared and they were handed over to the British for punishment. The members of the Reform Committee were arrested and tried and some were condemned to death for treason. The sentences were, however, commuted and all were eventually released after relatively short periods of imprisonment.

The raid left Rhodes, Chamberlain, and the Conservative British government in a weak position. Chamberlain denounced Rhodes's actions and denied all responsibility for the plot. He was forced, however, to agree to the establishment of a Parliamentary Committee of Inquiry which might well reveal his involvement in the affair. With Rhodes's disgrace, the question of his Company's charter was also bound to be raised.

At the critical moment, however, the German Kaiser cabled Kruger to congratulate him on the defeat of the raid. Such action was seen by many as evidence of German interference in the Transvaal. It raised a wave of patriotic feeling which swung British public opinion back in favour of the government. Rhodes himself now appeared an imperial hero to the British, and his unscrupulous methods were conveniently overlooked. Chamberlain was able to delay the opening of the Committee of Inquiry, leaving plenty of

Jameson's men cutting the telegraph wires, 1895

time for favourable evidence to be suitably prepared. Rhodes forced a promise from Chamberlain to protect the British South Africa Company's charter and his own personal honour, by threatening to reveal telegrams that might have established Chamberlain's involvement. In the meantime, events in Rhodesia offered him the opportunity to improve his reputation in Britain still further and to re-establish it to a considerable extent in South Africa.

Ndebele and Shona uprisings

Rhodes's column had occupied Mashonaland on the basis of the myth that the Shona were subject to the Ndebele king, Lobengula. Rhodes knew that this was false and that the Shona paramountcies of Mashonaland were independent of the Ndebele ruler, but probably most of the members of the pioneer column were ignorant of this and acted in the belief that they were liberating the Shona from cruel servitude. As the validity of the Rudd

7.1 The consolidation of white rule and the extinction of African independence in southern Africa: the situation in 1896

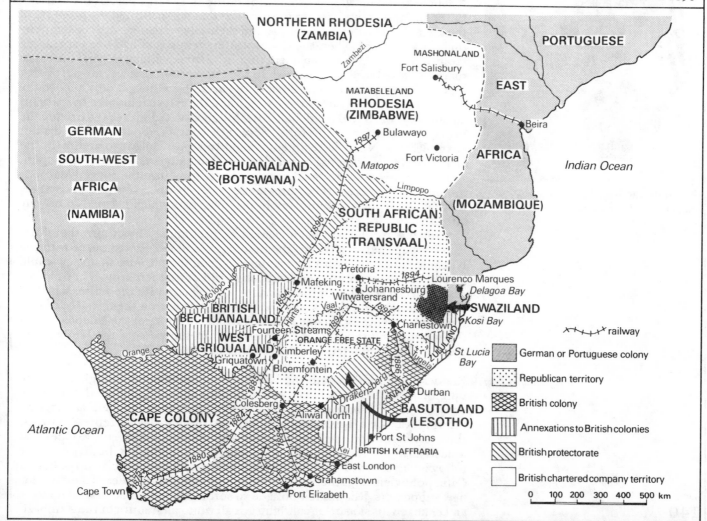

Nehanda and Kagubi mediums in
Salisbury prison awaiting
execution, 1898

concession depended on the myth of Shona subjection to the Ndebele,
Rhodes could not allow it to be called into question by entering into treaties
with the Shona chiefdoms. The opportunity to win the co-operation of these
chiefs and to establish a system of indirect rule by exploiting their authority
over their subjects was thus missed. Attempting to colonise on the cheap,
the Company made quite inadequate provision for the administration of the
African population in the territory it had occupied, and matters were thus
left very much in the hands of individual whites, backed up by punitive raids.
The Shona at first took the column to be simply a much larger trading
caravan than usual. They soon discovered, however, that this new group of
whites intended to stay and regarded themselves as masters of the country.
Not only did they stop the established trade with the Portuguese but they
staked out land for farms, opened up mines and demanded labour from the
chiefs.

After Lobengula had been overthrown, the whole heartland of the
Ndebele kingdom was staked out for farms and a large part of the cattle of
the community was seized on the grounds that it constituted the property of
the king. Proud Ndebele *indunas* found themselves treated with contempt by
their new masters. Then the rinderpest epidemic that had been spreading
rapidly through Africa from north to south arrived, killing most of the cattle
that the white looters had spared. In the circumstances it was not surprising
that this disaster was also credited to the invading whites. It only needed the
news of the defeat of Jameson's column and the arrest of his men to spark off
an uprising. In 1896 the Ndebele rose, killing isolated whites and driving the
rest to the shelter of the forts. A month later the Shona followed their
example. The Ndebele regiments failed to storm Bulawayo and, with the
arrival of British imperial forces that the Company was forced to call upon,
were soon driven on to the defensive. Retreating into the rugged Matopos
mountains, however, they threatened to keep up prolonged resistance,
thereby involving the Company in massive costs which it could in no way
afford.

After the ground had been cleared by preliminary meetings, therefore,
Rhodes went personally into the mountains and negotiated peace with the
Ndebele chiefs. In return for an amnesty, and the promise that they would
be allowed to return to their lands, they laid down their arms. They did not
realise that ownership of their lands was to remain with the whites who had
staked out farming claims, and that the right to live on them free of charge
was a purely temporary concession. With the majority of the Ndebele out of
the war the military forces concentrated on suppressing the Shona, who
were finally completely subjugated by the end of 1897.

*Rhodes profits from
peace talks*

Rhodes's negotiation with the Ndebele chiefs appealed strongly to public
opinion in South Africa as well as Britain. Strengthening his hand further, he
bought off the discontent of many white settlers in Ndebele country by
offering seats on a legislative council to two of their elected representatives,
thus setting out on the road towards settler self-government. Rhodes had
indeed lost the leadership of the Cape government but built up a new
following in the form of the Progressives, a group largely made up of liberal
Cape politicians together with personal followers of Rhodes. To satisfy his
new supporters, Rhodes felt obliged to soften his position on racial matters
and changed his slogan 'equal rights for all white men south of the Zambezi'

to 'equal rights for all civilised men', a formula acceptable to the vote-holding Coloured and African elite at the Cape. The Afrikaner Bond and a number of English politicians at the Cape stood out against him, however. In 1898, after a bitterly fought election, Rhodes's Progressives were narrowly beaten, and a Bond-backed ministry led by W.P. Schreiner was formed.

The South African War

Continuation of conflict
in the Transvaal

The Jameson raid had done nothing to remove the sources of conflict in the Transvaal. Kruger was more determined than ever to maintain and strengthen the independence of his state and the influence of its leading burghers. The Jameson raid and its suppression had greatly increased his personal popularity within the republic as well as arousing sympathy for the Transvaal among Afrikaners throughout South Africa. Chamberlain remained convinced that the interests of the British empire required the incorporation of the republic in a British federation or at least the full establishment of British paramountcy. Moreover, the long-term interests of the mining magnates remained in conflict with the nature and policies of the burgher republic.

In reaction to the crisis of the Jameson raid a pro-British imperialist organisation, the South African League, was founded by English-speaking South Africans in the Cape and branches were soon established in the Transvaal and Natal. Rhodes put his resources behind this organisation, which took over the role of the National Union in leading and co-ordinating *uitlander* agitation on the Rand. An affiliated body of the League was established in London, also to act as a pressure group in favour of British intervention in the republic.

Kruger consolidates his
position in the Transvaal

In the period immediately after the raid, Chamberlain hoped to gain Kruger's acceptance of British control and the need for reform in the Transvaal by negotiation and the president was invited to talks in London. At first he considered accepting the offer, hoping that Chamberlain might now be prepared to change the clauses in the London Convention which gave the British government a right to overrule treaties between the republic and foreign powers. As it became clear that once again Chamberlain was not prepared to change the original Convention, Kruger abandoned the idea of a visit to Britain, and the invitation was eventually withdrawn.

Chamberlain then adopted more threatening methods. In April 1897 he presented Kruger with two despatches protesting at the republic's conduct over two issues where it could be claimed to have been in breach of the London Convention. One was the republic's pursuit of extradition treaties with Portugal and the Netherlands without reference to Britain, the other the adoption by the *volksraad* of immigration and aliens expulsion legislation which affected the rights of British subjects. The despatches were backed by a naval demonstration at Delagoa Bay and the sending of British troop reinforcements to South Africa. Faced with these threats the Transvaal *volksraad* repealed the immigration law and modified the aliens expulsion law.

In other ways, however, Kruger succeeded in strengthening his position. In the period after the raid he began rearming the republican forces with modern weapons, largely imported from Germany. Relations between the

Transvaal and the Orange Free State were strengthened, and in 1897 Kruger and President Steyn renewed their existing treaty of mutual assistance. An advisory council was established to prepare proposals on a federal association of the two republics. In that year also the *volksraad*, rejecting proposals from the mining magnates, renewed the dynamite monopoly, thus heightening confrontation between the mine owners and the state. In 1898 Kruger won an overwhelming majority in the republic's presidential election. He further strengthened his position and that of the *volksraad* by defeating a constitutional challenge from the judiciary.

Milner and the Transvaal

In mid-1897 a new High Commissioner was appointed to succeed Hercules Robinson at the Cape. Sir Alfred Milner, the man chosen by Chamberlain for the task, was a man of wide influence. He had been under-secretary to the Egyptian Ministry of Finance, and Chairman of the British Board of Inland Revenue; he had also published a widely read book on England and Egypt.

Milner shared Chamberlain's dedication to the strengthening of the British empire. In addition he was a convinced believer in the racial myths current at the time, believing that the cultural qualities and achievements of particular societies were the expression of the inborn characteristics of different races. It followed that the only true bonds capable of holding people together were those of race. The British, he believed, constituted a race with its own unique characteristics destined to spread itself all over the world creating an empire. Like Chamberlain, he believed this empire should be formed into an imperial federation. He had even once described himself as a 'British Race Patriot'.

At the same time, his experience in the Egyptian Ministry of Finance and the British Board of Inland Revenue made him fully conscious of the importance of economic power. Milner's race mythology made him deeply distrustful of the motives of all Afrikaners in the South African situation. As members of the Boer race he felt they must desire to be united in a single Boer state. He thus came to believe in a wholly fictitious Afrikaner conspiracy. He believed that they aimed at uniting the Cape with the Orange Free State and Transvaal, thus completely reversing the British imperial position in southern Africa. His distrust of Cape Afrikaners extended not only to the political leaders of the Afrikaner Bond but even to such notably loyal figures as the Chief Justice, Sir Henry de Villiers. With his appointment as High Commissioner, Milner was to take much of the initiative in South African affairs from Chamberlain's hands and to play a key role in pushing the Secretary of State to a showdown with the Transvaal republic.

On arrival in South Africa, Milner adopted a patient attitude towards the republic, hoping that if Afrikaner nationalist feelings were allowed to settle, internal opposition to Kruger in the Transvaal would be strong enough to ensure reform. Kruger's election victory and his success in eliminating the challenge from the judiciary, however, made Milner lose all hope of reform from within. Thereafter he was convinced that a showdown backed by open force was essential to the preservation of the imperial position in South Africa. He therefore used all his influence and energies to bring this about.

Sir Alfred Milner

In November 1898 Milner left South Africa to hold consultations with Chamberlain in England and persuade him of the necessity of bringing matters to a head without delay. While he was away, the Transvaal government declared its intention of again renewing the dynamite monopoly. The mining magnates, prompted by the British agent in Pretoria acting on Milner's cabled advice, made a public protest which was backed up by the publication of a despatch from Chamberlain declaring the concession contrary to the London Convention. The magnates offered a substantial loan to the republic if it would abandon the monopoly but by a narrow majority the *volksraad* decided to renew it once more. Kruger now realised that it was important to buy off the magnates' hostility. He began negotiations with them and offered reforms to compensate for the renewal of the monopoly. On the crucial issue of the vote he offered to give the franchise to the *uitlander* population after five years. In reply the magnates called for the five years to be made retrospective and Kruger agreed to consider this. Milner and Chamberlain, however, while hoping to use the talks to find out how much Kruger would be prepared to concede, realised that an agreement between the republican government and the magnates could mean the end of *uitlander* agitation and deny them the opportunity of forcing a showdown and the firm and final establishment of British control. They therefore persuaded a member of the mining magnates' team at the talks to leak information to the press, thereby making it politically impossible for Kruger to proceed with negotiations.

Agitation for a show of force

On his return, Milner pressed matters to a crisis. He sent despatch after despatch, raking up every possible complaint against the Kruger regime. To prepare British public opinion for a showdown he despatched a telegram in May 1899 in which he wrote of 'thousands of British subjects kept permanently in the position of helots' (quoted in Warwick, ed., 1980; p.53), arguing that this was undermining the respect for Britain throughout the empire, and calling for intervention.

As the confrontation became more menacing, moderate Cape politicians persuaded Kruger to meet Milner at Bloemfontein. Milner, however, adopted a totally uncompromising attitude. He refused to offer the republic any concessions in return for modification of the franchise, rejected the president's franchise proposals out of hand, and broke off the talks. A book containing an indictment of the republic, including the 'helot' telegram, was then published in London. This was clearly seen as the preliminary to war, and friends of the republic in the Cape, making another attempt at conciliation, persuaded the *volksraad* to offer a seven-year retrospective franchise.

Moderates attempt negotiation

Once again, however, Milner rejected the proposal and persuaded Chamberlain to demand a joint British-Transvaal enquiry into the franchise issue. This Kruger rejected on the grounds that it implied a surrender of the Transvaal's right to run its own internal affairs. Instead, the republic made one last offer. Jan Smuts, the Transvaal State Attorney, conveyed this to the British agent in Pretoria. The Transvaal agreed to the five-year retrospective franchise and undertook to create ten new *volksraad* constituencies on the Rand. In return, however, the British government was to undertake 'that no further interference in the internal affairs of the Transvaal will take place'. It was also to agree to drop the assertion of supremacy over the Transvaal.

Matters in dispute would in future be submitted to arbitration (though this would be from within South Africa).

Though the offer met the demands which Milner had made on behalf of the *uitlander* population it meant abandoning the underlying principle of British supremacy which he believed essential. He therefore persuaded Chamberlain to accept the franchise offer but reject the accompanying conditions. The Transvaal then withdrew its offer and fell back on the earlier proposal for a seven-year retrospective franchise. The British government now reinforced its troops in South Africa, moved units near to the borders between the British colonies and the republics and prepared an ultimatum. Convinced that Britain would be satisfied with nothing less than the surrender of the Transvaal's independence the republics determined to fight. Anxious to take advantage of the fact that their troops considerably outnumbered British forces in South Africa (before British reinforcements changed the balance), they narrowly beat the British timetable and

7.2 The South African War, 1899–1902

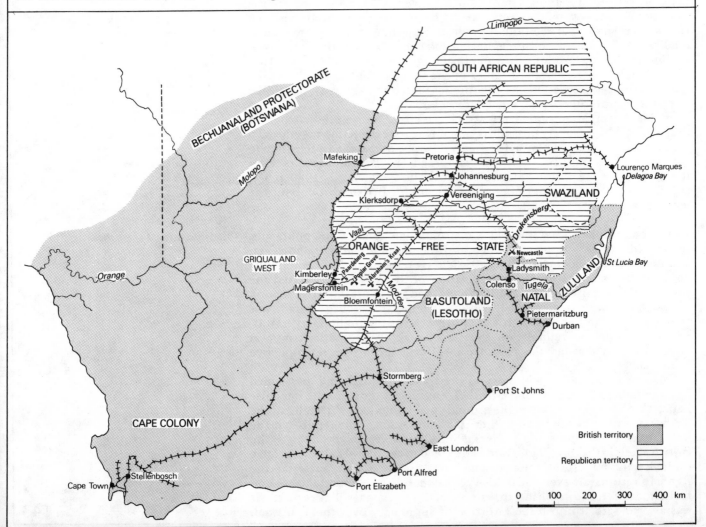

submitted their own ultimatum first. When this was rejected war began on 12 October 1899.

The course of the war

In the first phase of the war, Boer forces took the offensive, invading Natal, the Cape Midlands (where many colonial Afrikaners rose in rebellion and joined them), Griqualand West and British Bechuanaland. British garrisons were penned up in Kimberley and Mafeking. In December 1899, British attempts to drive them out of these areas were defeated in a series of battles at Colenso, Stormberg and Magersfontein. Boer forces, however, did not take full advantage of their initial successes. Instead of advancing deep into Natal and the Cape they occupied themselves in besieging British positions at Ladysmith, Kimberley and Mafeking. In the face of these setbacks massive British reinforcements were brought in. General Roberts was appointed in overall command with Kitchener as his chief of staff, and early in 1900 the British push began. The main force under Roberts moved into the eastern Orange Free State. Kimberley was relieved and on 27 February Cronje and 4000 men were forced to surrender at Paardeberg. Free Staters were now forced to abandon the districts of the Cape they had occupied while others rode home from the siege of Ladysmith to defend their own republic. British forces in Natal under General Buller were thus able to fight their way across the Tugela and Ladysmith was relieved. Boer forces in the Orange Free State were defeated at Poplar Grove and Abrahams Kraal and British forces entered Bloemfontein. Then in May a general attack was mounted all along the line. Mafeking was relieved and the rebellion in Griqualand West suppressed. Buller in Natal pressed his advance as far as Newcastle, Roberts in the centre annexed the Orange Free State and marched to Johannesburg and Pretoria which he entered on 5 June. The Kruger government retreated down the Delagoa Bay line and in August Kruger left for Europe. The Transvaal was annexed and Roberts then declared the war at an end.

Boer commandos, however, continued to hold the field and mounted a highly effective guerrilla war, even invading the Cape. Faced with a situation in which a Boer might be fighting one day and the next sitting peacefully on his *stoep*, Kitchener responded with drastic measures. Whenever guerrilla attacks took place, farm houses in the vicinity were burned and the women and children gathered in concentration camps. At the same time lines of barbed wire were strung out along the railway lines cutting up the country

General C.R. de Wet addressing his commando by John Beer

Boer women being taken to a
concentration camp

and reducing the commandos' mobility. The policy of burning farms and
establishing concentration camps roused humanitarian outrage in Britain. It
also deepened the Afrikaner bitterness which was to be a legacy of the war. In
the camps Boer families were crowded together in squalor and unhygienic
conditions made worse by the fact that they were unaccustomed to life in
large communities; the camps were swept by epidemics of dysentery,
measles and enteric fever and about 25 000 women and children died.

As the war dragged on, mines in Johannesburg were brought back into
operation, Boers who surrendered voluntarily were re-established on their
farms, and some who felt that the war was a hopeless struggle were enrolled
as National Scouts to assist in maintaining law and order. The capacity of the
Boer leaders to maintain their armies in the field was gradually worn down
while, at the same time, the British became increasingly weary of the war and
anxious to arrive at a negotiated settlement. An initial attempt was made at a
conference at Middleburg in February–March 1901. The British proposals
were rejected, however, as they required the surrender of republican
independence. The following year the republican governments met at
Klerksdorp and submitted their own proposals which involved continuing
independence with an *uitlander* vote and a commercial union with the British
colonies.

The Vereeniging peace terms

The British government, however, strengthened by a massive vote in the
recent British General Election, was not prepared to go back on the
annexations. Finally, in May 1902, a conference at Vereeniging agreed on
terms of peace. The republics had to surrender their independence but in
return, apart from the release of Boer prisoners-of-war, the British
government promised massive assistance with reconstruction. Most

important of all for the long-term future, the British authorities, anxious to win peace and aware of Boer feelings on the matter, agreed to a clause in which Britain promised that the question of an African franchise would not be raised until after responsible government had been restored to the ex-republics. In agreeing to this clause the British authorities threw away their best chance ever to exercise their moral reponsibilities towards the great majority of South Africa's population. From then on it would never again be possible for the British government to impose a policy which might have opened the way to the eliminations of colour barriers.

Betrayal of African interests

The betrayal of Africans' rights and interests was all the more callous in view of the fact that the great majority of Africans in South Africa had strongly supported the British in the war. Africans in Lesotho offered military support to the British side. Zulu, Xhosa and some of the Tswana offered to serve in arms against the Boers. These offers were rejected on the grounds that this was a 'white man's war'. Both sides, however, did in practice make very considerable use of Africans in a whole variety of non-combatant but often highly dangerous roles. As the British had the loyalty of the great majority, however, they were able to make use of Africans on a much larger scale than the Boers. The Boer war diary of Solomon Plaatje, an educated African who assisted on the British side in Mafeking when it was under siege by the Boer forces, makes it clear that Africans were very directly involved in the fighting and gave considerable support to the British side. Not only were Africans directly involved in the war but they also suffered very severely from the disruptions which it produced. When Afrikaner farms were burnt and their owners taken to concentration camps their African servants were herded into separate camps. Deaths from disease were just as high in the African camps as those for the Boers but they never received a fraction of the attention, concern, and medical and nursing aid that was eventually provided for the Boer families.

Probably the most crucial way in which Africans were involved in the war lay in their own spontaneous actions. In the Transvaal, Africans living on white-owned land frequently took over the whole farm. In Swaziland, Afrikaners were denied provisions. In Zululand, a party of Afrikaner troops was attacked and killed. When they finally surrendered, the Boer leaders made it clear that such incidents, together with the fear that they would lose

'Camp for undesirables'

control over the African population, played an important part in persuading them to give up the struggle. Africans thus made an important contribution to the British victory in the war. They anticipated that with the Boer defeat they would get their land and liberty back again.

African attitudes, moreover, provided an opportunity to consolidate British authority over the ex-republics as Milner wished. If they had been given the vote in significant numbers there can have been little doubt that they would have used it in support of continuing British rule. To have made concessions to Africans on the land or by freeing them from pass laws or, above all, by giving them political rights, however, would have undermined the possibility of exploiting them to the full as ultra-cheap labour. One of the main causes of the war had been the mine owners' need for a political administrative system which would allow them to exploit African labour more fully. Thus, when British troops first entered Johannesburg in 1900 and African mineworkers demonstrated joyfully and burnt their passbooks, the British authorities punished them severely for breaking the republican laws and forced them to work on road and railway building at extremely low wages. Once the British occupied Johannesburg, moreover, the mine owners reduced African wages on the mines from over fifty shillings to thirty shillings a month.

Similar policies were applied in agriculture. When peace was agreed with the Boer leaders the British helped Afrikaner farmers to re-establish control over Africans on the land. Moreover, while many Afrikaner soldiers were allowed to keep their guns, the British police force disarmed Africans who had acquired firearms.

Post-war reconstruction

With the annexation of the Transvaal and the Orange River colonies Milner was made High Commissioner for the two new colonies and moved the seat of his authority to Johannesburg. Anxious to bring about a federation of all South Africa without delay, he tried to get the Cape Constitution suspended but this Chamberlain refused. Milner had to be content with uniting the railways of the two ex-republics in the Central South African Railways, establishing an inter-colonial council to deal with their joint problems and creating a customs union uniting all the British colonies in southern Africa. To prepare the way for fuller unification, a commission was established to look into the central issue of southern African society and economy, the treatment of the African peoples and the exploitation of African labour. The South African Native Affairs Commission (1903–5) extended its hearings to Rhodesia as well as to Swaziland, Basutoland and Bechuanaland. Its conclusions were to form much of the basis of social development in South Africa after the achievement of Union.

Though he did not succeed in obtaining unlimited authority over the whole of South Africa, Milner's powers, like the work of reconstruction which awaited him, were immense. To assist with this tremendous task he recruited a group of young Oxford graduate administrators who became known as Milner's 'kindergarten'. Milner's policy in the ex-republics was directed to the supreme end of ensuring that they, and the Transvaal in particular, would be irreversibly integrated into the British empire. To achieve this he planned to settle substantial numbers of British settlers on the land in the Transvaal.

A further key measure in Milner's policy was the attempt to anglicise the next generation of Afrikaners through public education. Towards the end of the war schools had been opened for children in the concentration camps. With the war over, a massive programme of public education was launched, for whites, in the ex-republics. The language of instruction in all state schools, however, was to be English, and Dutch was only allowed to be used as a medium of instruction for a maximum of five hours a week.

Milner's policy, however, depended on creating an economic climate favourable to English settlement. This meant getting the gold mines – the only source of surplus for investment in other areas – back into full operation as quickly as possible. Mining operations were hampered, however, by a serious shortage of African labour. A major cause was the substantial wage reduction implemented by the mine owners. In the immediate post-war period, moreover, there were plenty of opportunities for Africans to find employment above ground on the numerous and varied reconstruction works. African peasants were also in a good position to meet their cash needs by the sale of their produce, while white farming was still crippled by the consequences of the war.

In 1901 Milner negotiated an agreement with the Portuguese under which the Rand mines would be entitled to recruit labour in Mozambique through the Witwatersrand Native Labour Association on payment of a fee for each African recruited. In return, the Delagoa Bay line was to enjoy the same proportion of the Johannesburg rail traffic that it had before the war. In spite of this agreement, however, a massive shortfall of labour persisted. Many mines worked at less than their full capacity and at a level well below the requirements of profitability.

The shortage of African labour on the mines coincided with the development of a serious problem of white unemployment and poverty on the Rand and elsewhere. The problem of landless burghers and of burghers owning farms too small to be economically viable had its roots in the very early days of settlement after the Great Trek, and had grown as land holdings accumulated in the hands of the burgher 'notables', foreign individuals and land companies.

Many of the landless whites had lived as *bywoner* tenants on the land of their wealthier neighbours. The early days of the Rand had offered many of them opportunities as transport drivers. The movement of Rhodes's pioneer column into Rhodesia and the subsequent construction of the railway to and across the Zambezi had provided further opportunities of this sort. After the completion of the main lines to Johannesburg, however, the numbers of poverty-stricken burghers increased further as a result of the devastating rinderpest epidemic which reduced many smaller-scale farmers to bankruptcy.

In the aftermath of the South African War, as the 'notables' struggled to re-establish themselves and take advantage of the opportunities for the sale of agricultural produce, they found it was better to retain African tenants who were more accustomed to intensive crop cultivation and open to exploitation as labour tenants than to allow white *bywoners* back on their land. Driven from the land, poverty-stricken whites thus flocked to the Rand and to a lesser extent other urban centres.

In these circumstances, the idea of replacing black with white labour on the gold mines was enthusiastically advocated by Frederick Creswell, manager of the Village Deep mine. He conducted an experiment to show that with a re-arrangement of work white labour need not be very expensive. He argued that this was the only way that the white man could preserve white civilisation in the country. Creswell's views gained wide popularity among South African whites, but the mine owners recognised their weaknesses. The expectations of white families were much greater than those of Africans. The landless whites would, moreover, have been entirely dependent on their wages for the support of their families, while migrant African workers' families were largely sustained by the proceeds of agricultural work in their home villages. Whites were not subject to pass laws or other discriminatory labour legislation. They could not be submitted to the rigorous labour discipline which could be imposed on Africans or prevented from forming associations for collective action to improve their pay and conditions. Above all, they had the vote, which they could exploit to secure their rights. Creswell's policy thus had little appeal to the mine owners. They pointed out that on the figures of costs per shift attained in his experiment a substantial number of mines would be put out of business. In contrast to arguments often heard about the laziness of black labour justifying low pay, they argued that whites were incapable of arduous physical toil which blacks could survive. Rejecting the idea of employing white labour they pressed for the importation of Chinese workers to meet the shortage of unskilled labour.

Importation of Chinese mine labour

Milner gave his support to the mine owners' arguments and the importation of Chinese workers was undertaken. To lessen the bitter opposition of white workers on the Rand, however, it was agreed that Chinese workers would be limited to unskilled work. When the Chinese eventually left, these restrictions were applied to Africans. Chinese labour helped to bring the mines back into full production without the increase in wage rates which the employment of whites would have entailed. Opposition to Chinese labour, however, supplied a rallying point for English-speaking as well as Afrikaner critics of the Milner regime in the Transvaal, while in England the conditions under which the Chinese were employed was the subject of widespread humanitarian protest.

White opposition to Milner's policies

Milner's anglicisation policy threatened Afrikaners with cultural extinction. They drew together in an educational and cultural movement aimed at the establishment of schools based on the principles of Christelike Nasionale Onderwys (Christian-National Education) which would offer Dutch-medium instruction. As they lacked the resources to recruit and employ qualified teachers, the Christian-National schools were not a great success. The movement aroused a great deal of Afrikaner nationalist feeling, however, and prepared the way for the development of Afrikaner political movements.

In the Transvaal, Milner's regime was unpopular with a section of English-speaking opinion. There was considerable English-speaking hostility to the importation of the Chinese. In addition, diamond mining interests and some gold mining interests were injured by some of the measures which were taken in the interest of the majority of the gold-mining magnates.

Returning from the gold mines

Political developments

Alfred Lyttelton, who replaced Chamberlain as the British Secretary of State for the Colonies in September 1903, felt that some immediate move towards the restoration of responsible government was essential. A constitution for the Transvaal was accordingly drawn up, providing for an elected legislative assembly but retaining official control of active authority. To ease the way for this change, Milner left South Africa in April 1905 and was replaced by Lord Selbourne. Meanwhile, in the expectation of political change, the Transvaal 'notables' drew together to defend their threatened interests and under the leadership of Louis Botha and Jan Smuts formed the Het Volk (The People) party. In the Orange Free State, ex-President Steyn and J.B.M. Hertzog took the lead in the establishment of another Afrikaner party known as Orangia Unie (United Orangia).

On assuming office as Governor of the ex-republics and High Commissioner, Selbourne reversed Milner's approach to the republican burgher 'notables'. Instead of attempts to undermine their influence he sought to conciliate them by supporting their economic interests. He thus put forward the idea of the establishment of a land bank with capital supplied by the state which would offer low-interest loans to landowners with substantial holdings to enable them to restock or to develop their properties for commercial agriculture. This scheme, which was brought to fruition under the subsequent Het Volk government in the Transvaal, showed the wealthier Afrikaner farmers how resources could be creamed off from the mines to their benefit. It made them aware, therefore, that their own prosperity and that of the mining industry were interdependent. The Het Volk party thus rapidly lost its anti-imperialist character and showed itself willing to work closely with capitalist interests within the framework of the British empire.

While the rural Afrikaners in the Transvaal under the leadership of the 'notables' gave their support to the Het Volk party, the majority of the

151

English voters, led by the main Johannesburg magnates, formed the Progressive Party. A substantial minority, however, who had opposed the Milner regime, formed a Responsible Government party to campaign, as did Het Volk, for the restoration of self-government to the ex-republic. Finally, white workers, who supported Creswell's white labour policy, formed a Labour Party to fight for its adoption.

Elections

The anticipated elections were not to take place under the Lyttelton constitution, however, for this never came into force. In December 1905 the Conservative government in Britain fell and in the subsequent British General Election the Liberals, who made extensive use of the issue of Chinese labour conditions on the Rand, won a massive majority. The new Campbell-Bannerman administration in Britain was uneasy in conscience over the whole question of the South African War and the concentration camps. It sought to win back Boer goodwill by a generous policy, and so agreed to an immediate restoration of responsible government in the Transvaal. This was implemented in 1906 and Het Volk, in alliance with the Transvaal Responsible Government Association (now renamed the Nationalist Party) won the February 1907 Transvaal elections. Louis Botha formed a coalition government. Smuts, as his second-in-command, became Colonial Secretary. Once in office they followed a policy of reconciling the two white peoples and working harmoniously with the mining interests. The pledge to remove Chinese labour was fulfilled, but the exercise was carried out gradually, with groups of Chinese being sent home as their contracts expired. By this time African labour was becoming more readily available and the magnates were able to replace the Chinese without having to raise wage rates or resort to the employment of whites as unskilled labour. The increasingly close alignment of Het Volk with the mining interests was seen most clearly in 1907 when white trade unionists on the Rand went on strike and the government called in British troops to maintain law and order.

In June 1907, the Orange Free State also received responsible government. There the Orangia Unie Party won the elections with very little opposition except in Bloemfontein itself where there was a substantial English-speaking population. The two ex-republics had thus returned to Boer rule within five years of the war.

In the Cape, the first post-war election held in 1904 was affected by the disfranchisement of colonial rebels. The imperialistic Progressive Party thus at last won power and Dr Jameson, Rhodes's chief henchman and leader of the notorious raid, became prime minister. In the changed atmosphere which accompanied the restoration of self-government to the ex-republics, and faced with declining popularity as the Cape felt the effects of post-war slump, he abandoned his earlier extremist imperialist views and showed himself willing to work with Afrikaner leaders for a united South Africa. They were not, however, prepared to accept him as a full partner in this.

Economic developments

Increased pressures on Africans in Natal

In Natal, as in the Cape, the increased economic activity which followed the discovery of gold in the Transvaal had finally swung the economic balance against African peasant farming and in favour of more-highly capitalised white commercial farming. It now became more profitable for the land companies and other landlords to sell their land to white would-be commercial farmers than to rent it to African tenants. Measures to squeeze Africans off the land altogether and into the labour market now no longer met opposition from powerful interests. With the grant of responsible government to the colony in 1896, African peasants were placed under increasing pressure. The growing numbers who were evicted as land companies sold their lands found little Crown Land available as an alternative. In 1903, steps were taken to prevent Africans purchasing more land. Higher taxes were imposed on squatter tenants on Crown Land or private land. Finally a poll tax was imposed on all African males. Driven to desperation by this chain of measures aimed at destroying their economic independence, many openly refused to pay the new tax. Then the rash behaviour of a police patrol led to a disturbance in which two white policemen were killed. This incident aroused the deep-seated fear of whites in Natal that Africans were planning a united mass uprising. They were determined to crush all resistance before it could spread. Martial law was declared and all signs of opposition to the tax were ruthlessly dealt with. Those involved in the killing of the policemen belonged to an independent Christian sect. They were hunted down, then two of them were shot out of hand. Twelve more were convicted in hasty court martial trials and publicly executed. Several others were sentenced to twenty years' imprisonment with hard labour and lashes.

Bambatha's rebellion

This ferocious conduct of the authorities was largely responsible for provoking a wider rebellion. Chief Bambatha of the Zondi in Natal was unable to persuade all of his people to pay the hated tax. When he was summoned by the magistrate he held back for fear of arrest. A force of police and troops was sent to arrest him and he fled to take refuge for a while with the Zulu king, Dinizulu. On his return he found that the Natal authorities had deposed him in favour of an uncle. He captured the government-appointed chief and so placed himself in a position of open rebellion towards the colonial authorities. He successfully ambushed a party of police, then retreated to the difficult, forested, mountain country of the Nkandla just across the Tugela in Zululand. There he attempted to build up a large force by claiming that he had authority from Dinizulu. He also claimed that Dinizulu had given him a charm that would turn bullets into water.

Bambatha succeeded in attracting men from a number of different chiefdoms. He was also joined by Mehlokazulu, the chief whose conduct had been used as the excuse for the British war against Cetshwayo. The most powerful chief to join Bambatha was Sigananda, chief of the Cube. He was a very old man and as a boy had served as a mat carrier in Shaka's army.

After a number of engagements, the decisive battle was fought on 10 June at Mome Gorge. The two sections under Siganande and Bambatha allowed themselves to be attacked separately. They were crushed with very heavy losses. Bambatha and Mehlokazulu were killed. Sigananda surrendered soon after, but died before he could be executed.

Just as the Natal government forces seemed to have finally crushed the rebellion, a new outbreak took place in the Mapumelo district of Natal. Angered by the brutal conduct of the troops stationed in the area, several chiefs joined the uprising, but with the defeat of Bambatha the whole of the Natal force was available to crush the new rebels and by mid-July resistance in the Mapumelo district had also been repressed. The suppression of the rebellion was accompanied by widespread burning of African settlements and seizure of cattle as well as other extreme forms of punishment. Apart from the 3000–4000 Africans killed, about 7000 were gaoled and over 4000 subjected to lashing. Though Dinizulu had tried his best to keep out of the affair and even offered military help for the Natal authorities, he was arrested, tried by a special court and sentenced to four years' imprisonment.

The failure of this last major attempt at armed resistance of the traditional type in South Africa marked the defeat of African efforts to maintain their economic independence from the demands of the white-dominated capitalist economy. After the defeat of the rebellion the numbers of Africans from Natal and Zululand working in the Transvaal increased by 59 per cent. By 1909 it was estimated that 80 per cent of the adult males in Zululand were away as migrant workers. The rebellion also alerted white opinion in South Africa generally, and more particularly in Natal, to the need for white political unity to maintain control over the African population.

White political unity

The need for a closer union Apart from the events in Natal, other developments also indicated the need for union. With the restoration of self-government to the Transvaal, there was a real danger that the conflicts of interest between the ex-republic and the other colonies would re-assert themselves, leading perhaps to open strife. The Transvaal, anxious to reduce mining costs, would benefit from a low external tariff, while Cape revenues depended on a high tariff. It would be in the interest of Transvaal farmers for the colony to impose a tariff on agricultural produce from the other colonies. It was also in the interest of the Transvaal to import as much as possible along the Delagoa Bay line, thus reducing the traffic available to the Cape and Natal. In the first place, total transport costs along the Delagoa Bay line were less than for the alternatives. In the second place, a higher proportion of the total length of the Delagoa Bay line lay within the boundaries of the Transvaal than was the case with the Cape or Natal lines. The Transvaal thus received a higher proportion of the rail charges for goods brought via Delagoa Bay than by any other route.

It was members of Milner's 'kindergarten' who had remained as administrators in the Transvaal who first drew attention to the need for political unity to resolve these problems. They formed a discussion group to consider the possibilities of closer union, and early in 1907 assisted the High Commissioner in drafting a memorandum openly raising the issue of political unity. The Selbourne memorandum pointed to the incompatibility of the railway and customs interests of the different colonies. So long as the colonies remained politically separate these matters could only be regulated by periodic conferences. At these conferences agreement between the governments was virtually impossible as each had to support the interests of its own community. The High Commissioner had therefore to be called upon to arbitrate. Decisions, once arrived at in such inter-colonial conferences, could not be subject to genuine review by the elected colonial parliaments without risking economic chaos. Only closer union, therefore, could avoid the danger of open conflict and allow white South Africans to exercise effective control over matters vital to their welfare and prosperity.

The memorandum also drew attention to the need for a common approach to the problems of relations with the African and Indian population.

The draft constitution

The Selbourne memorandum was favourably received by the Afrikaner Bond in the Cape parliament. Jameson also gave it his support and gained a majority for a proposal calling for steps to be taken towards closer union. Afrikaner leaders were not prepared, however, to work with Jameson and the Bond succeeded in bringing about the defeat of his government. In the subsequent elections the South Africa Party, led by John Merriman with Bond support, won an overall majority and in February 1908 Merriman was able to form a Bond-Moderate government. Smuts promptly opened a correspondence with Merriman with a view to preparing for unification. In an exchange of letters the two statesmen arrived at a common understanding over several of the most crucial issues. Then in May 1908, on the occasion of an inter-colonial railway and customs conference, Smuts moved six resolutions proposing procedures to be adopted towards the achievement of the immediate political union of the South African colonies.

The four parliaments agreed to send delegates to a National Convention to draft a constitution for a United South Africa. The National Convention met first in Durban and then transferred its sessions to Cape Town. One of the first issues to confront it was the nature of the state – unitary or federal – that was to be formed. In most previous thinking on the subject the federal model had been assumed but now that unification was taking place under predominantly Afrikaner rather than imperial influence the leaders of the two ex-republics, like Merriman, favoured a unitary system. As W.P. Schreiner, the most eloquent advocate of a federal approach, was absent defending Dinizulu against charges arising from the Bambatha rebellion, it was left to the Natal delegates alone to support it. They interpreted the advantages of federation almost exclusively in the light of the special interests in Natal, which did little to impress the other delegates, and the proposal went through virtually unopposed. South Africa was to be a unitary state with a single central government and parliament, the existing colonies were to be reduced to provinces with purely local government powers. For the structure of central government the Convention proposed an executive consisting of a governor-general representing the British Crown and ten ministers headed by a prime minister all of whom were obliged to find seats in parliament within three months of appointment. The ministers would be responsible to a two-house parliament. The upper house or senate was to have eight members for each province. These were to be elected by the provincial councillors and lower-house parliamentary representatives of the province concerned.

The Cape franchise

Most crucial for the whole structure and balance of power in the new state, however, was the composition of the lower house, known as the house of assembly. A majority of the Cape's representatives at the Convention wanted to see the existing Cape franchise, which allowed the vote to a limited elite of Africans and Coloureds together with almost all white adult males, retained and extended throughout South Africa. Representatives of the Transvaal and Orange Free State, however, wanted no African or Coloured to be able to vote for members of the central parliament anywhere in South Africa. In this they were supported even more decisively by the representatives of Natal. Eventually a compromise was reached under which only whites would be eligible for election to the Union parliament. The Cape franchise would not be extended to the ex-republics. Africans and Coloureds would retain the right to vote in the Cape, however, in accordance with the existing franchise regulations. Further, to satisfy the conscience of Cape members, it was agreed that the existing voting rights of Africans and Coloureds at the Cape, together with the equal status of the Dutch and English languages, should be protected by an 'entrenched clause'. This laid it down that changes involving a reduction of existing African and Coloured rights at the Cape would need to be passed by a two-thirds majority of both houses sitting together.

These arrangements meant that the existing political rights of Africans and Coloureds in the Cape were to be very much reduced in the Union. Whites would have a virtual monopoly of political power and non-Europeans would be denied much effective representation, while the development of the mining industry led South Africa along the path towards industrial revolution and massive urbanisation.

Not only did the franchise proposals leave the interests of the majority of the population at the mercy of the white minority, they also favoured the farmers as against the townspeople. As a general rule, the number of voters required to make up a constituency and elect a member to parliament was to be determined by dividing the number of seats allowed to each province by the number of its voters. In thinly populated rural areas, however, a constituency could be made up of voters numbering as much as 15 per cent less than this provincial quota. To balance this out, densely populated urban areas would need up to 15 per cent more voters than the provincial quota to be entitled to a member of parliament. A disproportionate weight was thus given to farming interests, enabling them to cream off much of the surplus produced by the mining industry. It also gave an advantage to the Afrikaans-speaking section of the population which dominated most of the rural areas, as against the more fully urbanised English-speakers.

After the draft constitution had been submitted to the parliaments of the four colonies, a final session of the National Convention was held in Bloemfontein in May 1909 to consider proposed amendments. These were speedily dealt with and the draft constitution was accepted by the colonial parliaments of the Cape, Orange River and Transvaal colonies and by a referendum in Natal. A delegation then accompanied the draft to London to see it through the British parliament.

Attitudes to the constitution

The adoption of the draft constitution and, in particular, the franchise clauses aroused politically conscious Africans and Coloureds. They quickly became aware that their political rights were gravely threatened. An African Native National Conference brought politically aware Africans from all the provinces together for the first time. They agreed to send John T. Jabavu and Walter Rubusana to England to oppose the acceptance of the draft constitution and campaign for the extension of the Cape franchise to the other provinces. The African People's Organisation, the mouthpiece of politically conscious Coloured people, under the leadership of Dr A. Abdurahman, also sent a delegate to press for the extension of the Cape vote. The Liberal white leader, W.P. Schreiner, prepared an 'Appeal to the parliament of Great Britain' and gained the support of many influential signatories for his argument that only a loose federal constitution could preserve the Cape's franchise system and that the protection offered by the 'entrenched clause' was inadequate.

The protest delegations achieved nothing, however. The franchise clauses of the draft constitution did, indeed, arouse concern in the British parliament but the Liberal majority was anxious not to miss the opportunity of seeing South Africa united within the British empire in a mood of goodwill. They were convinced that any attempt to impose a more equitable system from the outside would not improve matters. They allowed themselves to be convinced, in the face of all the contrary evidence, that the inherent advantages of the Cape's franchise system would lead to its being adopted before long by the other provinces. The Bill passed with no more than formal amendments after the British prime minister had closed the government's case with a solemn appeal to the South African parliament 'that they, in the exercise of their undoubted and unfettered freedom, should find it possible sooner or later, and sooner rather than later, to modify the provision'. Thus the British parliament finally washed its hands of British moral obligations in South Africa. It abandoned any attempt to establish the political foundations on which a racially just society could have been built, and brought into existence a South African state so structured that the majority of its people were left politically helpless and unprotected against social discrimination and economic exploitation by the privileged white minority.

The fact that the British government did not agree to the immediate incorporation of Swaziland, Basutoland and Bechuanaland in the newly formed Union did little to offset their general attitude at the time. Though, like African-occupied areas such as the Transkei within the boundaries of South Africa, they were to be economically little more than labour reserves for white South African mines, industry and farms, they enjoyed a distinctly different political and social regime as High Commission Territories, until finally achieving independence as Swaziland, Lesotho and Botswana in the 1960s.

8

From Union to apartheid: the politics of segregation

A changing society

The constitution under which the four South African colonies came together in 1910 to form the Union of South Africa gave the white minority very nearly a monopoly of political representation. Within the white group the farmers were given a disproportionately powerful voice by the favourable provisions for representation in rural constituencies. This political power structure was to have vitally important effects on society as the economy changed from being mainly agricultural and pastoral to being urbanised and industrial under the influence of the mining industry.

The gold-mining (and, to a lesser extent, diamond-mining) industry created the money with which to build and maintain the transport systems and to provide the many and varied subsidies, loans and scientific services which the white farmers were to enjoy. Later the mining industries made possible the development of manufacturing industry on a large scale. The health of the mining industry was therefore of great importance. The social and economic policies which succeeding governments were to follow had to preserve the profitability of the industry. Social and economic policies since the union of South Africa have thus very much reflected the interests of white farmers and mine owners in what has been called 'the alliance of gold and maize'. In addition to these main interest groups, white workers and the poorer whites generally also possessed votes. Their demands for expanded employment opportunities and a continuing position of privilege in the job system were to have an important impact on the development of social and economic policy.

Overlapping the divisions between classes in white society were those between English-speakers and Afrikaans-speakers. The Afrikaners made up the majority of the farming population except in the Eastern Cape and Natal, a growing proportion of the white workers and a substantial majority of the poorer whites generally. The mines and most substantial businesses, on the other hand, were owned by English-speakers who also formed most of the professional classes. As the economy changed a complex pattern resulted from the interweaving of rivalries between the two white language groups and the conflicts of interest between the different classes in white society. This goes a long way towards explaining the course of political development in South Africa from the Union to the present.

The interests of the main groups in white society, while often in conflict, coincided in one very important respect. All of them required non-European labour to be available at very cheap rates. On this depended the profitability of the mines and their capacity to subsidise white farming. Without cheap labour, white farming, even with substantial subsidies, would be unprofitable. Only if the non-European workers were paid exceptionally low rates could white workers enjoy the much higher rates they regarded as their right. Only if the mines made large profits would it be possible to utilise part of these to start other industries and increase white job opportunities. This common interest also necessitated the maintenance and strengthening of measures which weakened non-European bargaining power in the job market.

To ensure that enough African labour should be available, measures were needed to prevent Africans supporting themselves by independent agricultural activity. One solution might have been to break up the reserves and encourage wholesale urbanisation of th African population. It was aeready clear, however, that while the employment of permanently urbanised Africans was suitable and perhaps essential in some forms of employment, reliance on temporary labour migrants had many advantages in other areas and particularly in the gold mines. As labour migrants left their dependents in the reserves (or, in the case of Africans recruited from outside South Africa, in their home countries) it was possible to pay them at rates appropriate for single men. These would have been inadequate if they had been accompanied by their families. The system of migrant labour, moreover, enabled white society to avoid the burden of caring for the workers in times of unemployment, prolonged sickness or old age. Limiting the rate of growth of the fully urbanised African population reduced the political danger which this posed for white society. Instead of a policy of breaking up the reserves, therefore, the interests of the most influential sectors of white society could be best served by a policy of territorial segregation which would limit African land ownership to areas specifically set aside as reserves, preserve and expand the system of migrant labour, and restrict the growth of the permanently urbanised African population. From the establishment of Union, therefore, successive governments continuously pursued segregationist policies.

The first Union governments

On the formation of Union, the coalition of the Het Volk and National parties in the Transvaal amalgamated with the Orangia Unie Party of the Orange Free State and the South Africa Party in the Cape to form the South African National Party. This party, led by Botha with Smuts as his deputy, won a majority in the first Union elections and formed the first Union government. The party brought English and Afrikaners together in a common political organisation and represented a wide range of white interests, though mainly those of white farmers and the professional classes. Opposition was provided by the remnants of the Progressive parties in the ex-colonies who now formed themselves into a Unionist Party very much associated with capitalist interests, a small Labour Party representing the interests of white workers, and a number of Independents, mainly from Natal.

General Louis Botha

The South African National Party soon developed serious internal tensions. Botha and Smuts were strongly committed to achieving the complete reconciliation of English and Afrikaners and the creation of a united white nation in South Africa. They fully accepted and ascribed a positive value to South Africa remaining within the British empire though they were determined to maintain and develop South Africa's political independence within the loose imperial framework. At the Imperial Conference of 1911 at which Botha represented South Africa, he allied with Sir Wilfred Laurier of Canada to smash proposals advanced by Sir Joseph Ward of New Zealand for the creation of a federal imperial parliament, attacking the idea as an infringement on self-governing rights.

J.B. Hertzog, who was Minister of Justice, however, while wishing to see complete equality between English and Afrikaners, feared that a policy of fusing the two white groups would inevitably lead to the swamping of the Afrikaner language and culture by English. He and his supporters also remained resentful of the loss of republican independence and felt that Botha and Smuts took too positive an attitude to imperial links.

Matters came to a head in 1912 when Hertzog declared that he supported membership of the British empire only so long as it was good for South Africa. He insisted that the two white groups should develop as two separate streams and that South Africa should be ruled by true Afrikaners. Though Hertzog included in his definition of true Afrikaners those English-speakers whose first loyalty was to South Africa, this was not fully understood by English South Africans.

As these speeches were made while Botha was campaigning in English-speaking areas, they were a serious embarrassment to him. He called on Hertzog to resign. When he refused, Botha resigned himself and then formed a new government without Hertzog. In 1914 Hertzog and his supporters formed the National Party while the rest of the South African National Party came to be known simply as the South Africa Party.

J.B. Hertzog

With the formation of the National Party, Afrikaner nationalism became for the first time a single nationwide organised political movement. The National Party appealed to the sense of common identity of Afrikaans-speakers, to the historical memories of the Great Trek and British persecution, culminating in the South African War, the horrors of the concentration camps and the destruction of the Afrikaner republics. The party also appealed to the interests of some Afrikaner farmers, unhappy with the implications for their products of the system of imperial preferences, to others who wanted more drastic action against African tenants to help them solve their labour problems, and to Afrikaner white-collar and professional people frustrated by the predominance of English and English-speakers at the higher levels of commerce, administration and the professions. Under Hertzog, however, with his view that the term Afrikaner included English-speakers who put South Africa first, the National Party had no very clear ideology. Its Afrikaner nationalism was not very clearly distinguished from the white South Africanism professed by the South Africa Party.

The development of African nationalism
In the same year that the South Africa Party split and two years before the

first nationwide Afrikaner nationalist party was formed, politically conscious black South Africans established the first – and still surviving – nationwide African nationalist movement in South Africa, the African National Congress (ANC). Those who started this movement belonged to the group of Western-educated Africans which had emerged through the educational efforts of the Christian missions in South Africa and the growth of a class of relatively prosperous land-owning and tenant farmers. In the latter part of the nineteenth century the energies, aspirations and frustrations of many Africans were directed into religious channels. The breakaway from the Wesleyan Mission Church by Nehemiah Tile in 1884 and the formation of an independent Tembu Church marked the beginning of a widespread movement. This 'Ethiopian Movement', which led to the formation of very large numbers of independent African Christian sects, had many aspects. The new religious bodies reflected a rejection of white authority and offered Africans opportunities for personal leadership. They helped sustain African dignity and pride in the face of constant racial humiliation. They provided a sense of community and a system of values to people facing the difficult transition from kinship and chiefdom-based rural society to the more individualistic and technologically complex life of the towns. In some cases they fulfilled economic functions, founding church stores and farms, providing services for their members and opportunities for entrepreneurship for their leaders. They undoubtedly helped many Africans to sustain an inner rejection of the total subservience demanded by white society. Such attitudes, however, were also often maintained by the larger numbers who remained within the white-led mission churches.

Well before the end of the nineteenth century, some of the African educated elite had begun to take a leading part in specifically political activity. In addition to mission education, the new elite was influenced by black activities in America. Booker T. Washington, with his belief that the way to black emancipation lay through education and self-improvement, inspired the Reverend John Dube to found the Ohlange Institute in Natal on the model of Washington's Tuskegee Institute in Alabama. Many other black South Africans were influenced by the ideas of W.E.B. Du Bois and his belief in the need for political organisation. In 1896 the American-based African Methodist Episcopal Church was introduced to South Africa by the Reverend James Dwane. This made it easier for African students to gain access to black colleges in the United States. In 1903 the Church placed twelve students in American colleges. In South Africa itself the South African Native College was established at Fort Hare in 1915. It became a major training ground of a politically conscious African elite throughout South Africa.

Nineteenth-century African political activity was particularly strong in the Cape where 'civilised Africans' could participate in political life. Sometimes they received support from white liberals who needed the African vote. The first African political association, Imbumba Yama Afrika, was founded there in 1882. In 1884 a Native Electoral Association was formed and helped secure the election of a liberal white lawyer, James Rose Innes. The same year whites supporting Rose Innes gave financial support to John Tengo Jabavu, enabling him to establish the first African newspaper in the Cape, *Imvo Zabantsundu*. It soon became a forum for the discussion of

161

From Union to apartheid:
the politics of
segregation

African interests in the Cape. In 1889 John L. Dube, founder of the Ohlange Institute, launched his own paper, *Ilanga lase Natal* (the Natal Sun). In 1901 a Natal Native Congress was established.

The clause concerning the African franchise in the Vereeniging Agreement ending the South African War bitterly disappointed politically conscious Africans. Two new political organisations, a Native Vigilance Association and the South African Native Congress, appeared in the Cape in 1902. African associations were also formed in the two ex-republics. In the Orange River Colony there was the Orange River Colony Congress and in the Transvaal the Transvaal Congress as well as a Bapedi Union and a Basuto Association. In 1903 the Coloured leader, Dr A. Abdurahman, founded the African People's Organisation (APO) which became the vehicle for Coloured political aspirations. In March 1909, in response to the threat posed by the franchise proposals of the National Convention, members of a number of African associations assembled in Bloemfontein in the South African Native Convention. They sent John Tengo Jabavu and Walter Rubusana on what turned out to be a futile mission to London.

With the failure of the delegation and the establishment of the Union of South Africa, African organisations went back to their earlier fragmented pattern. In 1912, however, Pixley Ka Izaka Seme, who had taken a BA in the United States and had been called to the Bar in England, called a conference at Bloemfontein to found a national African organisation. The conference brought together chiefs and Westernised leaders of African political organisations from all over the country. It agreed to the establishment of the South African Native National Congress, later re-named the African National Congress (ANC). The constitution of the new body left a great deal of autonomy to the branches in the provinces. At the centre provision was made for a separate House of Chiefs but this never functioned successfully.

Leadership of the Congress came very predominantly from members of the Western-educated elite. They were respectable middle-class men strongly attached to the life style and values of white society and the humane Christian principles expounded by the mission churches to which they owed their education. They had no desire or intention to overthrow white society or white supremacy in South Africa. They simply wished to be accepted by white society on the basis of the civilised values on which it claimed to be based. Thus they did not seek the vote for all Africans but only the extension of the qualified franchise from the Cape to the rest of the country. Rhodes's slogan 'Equal rights for all civilised men' summed up their ideals and they repeated it endlessly. At the same time the discrimination to which they were subjected on grounds of colour reinforced their identification with the wider African population. In seeking social acceptance for themselves and the redress of grievances affecting Africans in general, their preferred approach was that of reasoned argument expressed in petitions and deputations. They constantly appealed to the liberal, humane, Christian values for which white society claimed to stand. Through repeated disappointments they clung desperately to the faith that if only they presented their case sufficiently clearly and rationally it would carry conviction. The year after the formation of the Congress, however, they faced a major piece of legislation which threatened to destroy their most deeply cherished hopes.

The establishment of the
African National Congress (ANC)

THE SOUTH AFRICAN

NATIVE NATIONAL CONGRESS.

SPECIAL CONFERENCE

HELD IN THE

St. JOHN'S HALL, KIMBERLEY,

FEBRUARY 27th to MARCH 2nd, 1914,

IN CONNECTION WITH THE NATIVE LANDS ACT, 1913.

President: REV. J. L. DUBE.

Sr. Vice-President: MR. S. M. MAKGATHO.

Treasurer: MR. P. KA I. SEME, B.A.

Junior Treasurer: MR. T. M. MAPIKELA.

Hon. Secretary: MR. SOL. T. PLAATJE.

Organising Committee of Protest against the Lands Act:

W. F. JEMSANA (Chairman).	B. G. PHOOKO.
ELKA M. CELE (Treasurer).	D. D. TYWAKADI.
D. S. LETANKA.	D. MOELETSI.
R. W. MSIMANG.	M. D. NDABEZITA.
H. D. MKIZE.	H. SELBY MSIMANG (Hon. Sec.)

S. MSANE, Organiser.

Native National Congress
Special Conference programme,
March 1914

Ever since the mineral discoveries had begun to transform the South African economy, growing pressure had been applied to prevent Africans from maintaining themselves on the land without working for whites. In spite of these pressures, however, some Africans succeeded in buying land outside the reserves. Many more still maintained their economic independence by farming white-owned private land, or Crown Land, as sharecropping or rent-paying tenants. Milner's Native Affairs Commission of 1903–5 had recommended steps to end this. Future land purchases by Africans should be limited to the reserves and the practice of allowing African tenants to live on white-owned farms was condemned. Within the first Union government Hertzog had begun preparing legislation along these lines. When he was forced out of the Cabinet, the government felt it must proceed with the measure to keep the loyalty of Afrikaner farmers. The 1913 Land Act made it illegal for Africans to purchase or lease land from Europeans anywhere in South Africa outside the reserves. It also specifically prohibited the practice of farming 'on the halves' in the Orange Free State. It was recognised that the areas of the African reserves would need to be more clearly defined and somewhat enlarged. A commission was established for this purpose. The recommendations of the Beaumont Commission, however, raised so many objections from white farmers that no action was taken. It was only in 1936 – over twenty years later – that parliament was finally to define the additional areas within which African land purchase was to be permitted.

The application of the 1913 Land Act to the Cape was later legally invalidated since its operation would affect African franchise rights protected by the entrenched clause in the Constitution. Its application elswhere, and particularly in the Orange Free State, caused great hardship. African sharecroppers were faced with accepting unfavourable labour-tenancy arrangements or were simply turned off the land with their stock with nowhere to go. The legislation marked the permanent division of South Africa into areas of exclusive white or black land ownership and the total rejection of the ideal of a common society as the final goal of social development in South Africa. Politically conscious Africans recognised the passage of the 1913 Land Act as a major tragedy. As Solomon Plaatje put it in his book *Native Life in South Africa*, 'South Africa has by law ceased to be the home of any of her native children whose skins are dyed with a pigment that does not conform with the regulation hue.' The African National Congress condemned the bill at its annual conference and sent a deputation to Cape Town to lobby for its withdrawal. They then petitioned the Governor-General to withhold his assent. When that failed they sent a deputation to Britain in 1914 only to be informed that the Act concerned only the government and the parliament of South Africa.

The 1913 Land Act

South African Native National Congress delegation to England, June 1914. Sol Plaatje is sitting on the right

Indian protest: the origins of Satyagraha in South Africa

Organised protest by Indians against discriminatory laws in South Africa dates back to 1893. It was started by Mahatma Gandhi, then a young lawyer who was visiting South Africa on the way back to India after legal studies in Britain. He led protests against a Natal franchise bill aimed at denying the vote to Indians. For this purpose he founded the Natal Indian Congress in 1894. Though Indians had grievances against their treatment in Natal, discrimination against them in the Boer republics was worse. Indians were debarred from entry into the Orange Free State altogether and those few living there were subject to legislation barring them from all occupations except the most menial. In the Transvaal, where many Indians had been attracted by the opportunities for trade and employment created by the development of the gold mines, they were barred by republican regulations from citizenship. They could not own land and were forced to register in a procedure which involved giving their fingerprints as well as paying a £3 sterling registration fee.

The British government repeatedly protested to the government of the South African Republic against this discriminatory treatment of British Indians. After the South African War, however, Milner's government in the Transvaal retained the republic's discriminatory legislation and in 1906 tightened it further through an Asiatic Law Amendment Ordinance under which every Indian was required to re-register. Thereafter they would have to carry their certificates of registration whereever they went and be prepared to show them on demand to any policeman or official. To fight this, Gandhi developed the practice of non-violent resistance aimed at winning over the oppressor by 'the force of truth and love', *Satyagraha*. In January 1908 he and over a hundred other *Satyagrahis* were sent to prison for defying the law.

After the creation of the Union of South Africa the struggle continued. In 1912 Indians were faced with further humiliation when the Supreme Court denied the validity of Indian marriages. Thousands of Indian coalminers in Natal went on strike and marched into the Transvaal forcing the authorities to arrest them. By mid-December 5000 Indians were courting arrest by defying the law. Smuts then entered into personal negotiations with Gandhi. In July 1914 the Indian Relief Act established the validity of Indian marriages. Gandhi called off the *Satyagraha* campaign and left for India where his methods were to have a much wider impact. Though Indian mass non-violent protest had achieved some significant concessions it had done little to change the basic pattern of discrimination against them. It had, however, demonstrated a form of mass action which was to influence African nationalist leaders in the future.

White labour unrest

The year of the 1913 Land Act was also marked by conflict between government and employers on the one hand and white workers on the other as these sought to establish trade union organisations to protect and enhance their interests. A dispute between some white miners and a mine manager at New Klipfontein caused a widespread strike by white miners in support of demands for the recognition of their unions. The strike led to riots in Johannesburg and the government, which so soon after Union still lacked an effective national security force, called on the services of British imperial troops to prevent the white mine workers holding a mass meeting. This sparked off further rioting and, though the troops opened fire, shooting was stopped before the rioters had been crushed. Johannesburg passed effectively into the hands of the strikers. Botha and Smuts then entered the city and in negotiations with the white workers undertook that if they would go back to work a judicial committee would be set up to investigate their grievances, and that the government would secure the

From Union to apartheid:
the politics of
segregation

Police charging white strikers, 1913

recognition of their unions and the re-employment of those sacked in the course of the dispute. After the judicial committee reported, a number of measures aimed at the improvement of conditions for white miners were prepared.

The white workers, however, had lost patience with the slow progress of constitutional procedures. In January 1914 strikes began in the Natal coal mines, spread to the railways and the gold mines, and culminated in a national strike. By this time, however, the government had created a national army, the Union Defence Force, and prepared to use it to smash the white workers' movement. On 10 January troops were called to action stations and on 14 January martial law was proclaimed. As army cannons were trained on the Johannesburg Trades Hall the strike collapsed. Smuts then took advantage of the atmosphere of crisis and the white workers' sense of defeat. Exceeding his legal powers and without reference to the courts or parliament he had nine of the mine workers' leaders summarily deported. In the bitter parliamentary debate which followed he successfully defended his action in the name of public security in a time of crisis. The political repercussions which might well have followed from this first major open clash between government and white workers, however, were largely overtaken by the First World War.

The First World War

When war broke out in 1914, the Union government agreed to participate in an assault on German South West Africa (modern Namibia). Volunteers were enlisted and the first troops were despatched in September and October for a seaborne operation in co-operation with the British navy. This was to lead to the capture of Luderitz Bay and Swakopmund.

Many nationalist-minded Afrikaners were outraged at being asked to take arms on the side of the British empire, which as they saw it had so recently unjustly destroyed the independence of their republics. In parliament,

Afrikaner opposition

165

Jan Smuts, 1922

Hertzog called for neutrality. In the armed forces the commander-in-chief, General C.F. Beyers, and two other important officers, Colonel S.G. Maritz and General Jan Kemp, expressed strong dislike of the idea of the South West Africa campaign. J.H. de la Rey, one of the best known of the Boer generals in the South African War, believed that the British empire would collapse in any case and that the republics would re-emerge. On 15 September de la Rey and Beyers set out at night for the western Transvaal, apparently with the intention of rousing public opinion against the South West Africa campaign. De la Rey, however, refused to stop at a road block which had been set up to prevent the escape of some dangerous criminals, and was killed by a shot fired at the car.

The death of de la Rey, though accidental, further deepened feeling against the government. Maritz went over to the Germans with the majority of the men under his command. C.R. de Wet, another South African War general, raised a commando in the Orange Free State, as did Beyers in the western Transvaal. Attempts made to persuade these leaders to lay down their arms ended in failure and Botha had to crush the rebellion by force. It was soon over, and the leaders were either arrested or killed in action. About 5000 rebels were captured and another 400 surrendered. The captured rebels were treated with considerable leniency. All the rank and file were set free by the end of 1915 while most of the leaders were subjected to fines and short periods of imprisonment. Only one officer, Jopie Fourie, was tried and shot. The rebellion nevertheless inspired Afrikaner poets to link the tragic heroism of the South African War and the martyrs of 1914. A voluntary organisation (Helpmekaar: 'Help one another') which was set up to collect money for the defence of the rebels greatly exceeded its targets. The surplus provided the basis for the establishment of the first significant Afrikaner finance company (Santam) in the Cape. In 1915 the government fought a general election on the war issue. The South Africa Party (SAP) came out as easily the biggest and with a collapse of the Labour vote the Unionists massively increased their strength. In the country districts of the Transvaal, Orange Free State and the Cape, however, the National Party substantially increased its vote at the South Africa Party's expense.

The conquest of German South West Africa

With the suppression of the rebellion, South African forces were free to concentrate on the invasion of South West Africa. Botha assumed overall command in person and on 9 July 1915 the last of the German forces surrendered. After completing the conquest of German South West Africa, South African forces took a major part in the campaign in East Africa against the Germans led by the brilliant General P.E. von Lettow-Vorbeck. In this campaign Smuts assumed overall command of the British forces. South African forces subsequently served in Europe also. In addition to both English and Afrikaner white South Africans many Africans and Coloureds from South Africa took part in the war. The racial attitudes and fear of white South Africans, however, meant that non-whites were not permitted to bear firearms and were restricted to non-combatant, though often equally dangerous, roles.

Smuts and the League of Nations Mandate system

During the First World War Smuts made a great impression in Britain and was asked to participate not only in the Imperial War Cabinet but in the British War Cabinet itself. Towards the end of the war he became a keen supporter of the idea of forming a League of Nations. In particular, he put forward the idea of a League of Nations Mandate system for colonial possessions conquered from Germany and its allies. He did not, however, intend this to apply to territories in Africa and indeed he and Botha hoped to absorb German South West Africa fully into South Africa. They were unable to get the Peace Conference to approve this, however. Very reluctantly they had to accept that South Africa should only have the right to administer the territories as a League of Nations Mandate under the system Smuts himself had devised.

Post-war political developments

In August 1919, soon after Botha and Smuts had returned from the Paris Peace Conference, Botha fell ill, had a heart attack and died. Smuts was left to lead the South Africa Party alone. In the election which Smuts called for 10 March 1920, the National Party greatly extended its hold over the Afrikaner electorate, gaining three more seats than the South Africa Party, though Smuts was able to continue governing with the support of the Unionists and Independents on votes of confidence. After the failure of further attempts at reuniting the National Party and the South Africa Party, Smuts entered into agreement with the Unionists under which they became completely absorbed in the South Africa Party. In new elections in February 1921 his enlarged South Africa Party won an absolute majority but it had become very much the expression of English and capitalist interests. Its gains had been mainly in urban seats, while the National Party had further strengthened its hold on the rural Afrikaner electorate.

The end of the war also saw the birth of a new Afrikaner nationalist organisation. Appalled by what they saw as the desperate plight of Afrikaners in a society dominated by English-speaking capitalists, civil servants and professionals, a group of young Afrikaner teachers and white-collar workers founded a society first called Jong Suid Africa (Young South Africa). This later developed into a secret society renamed the Broederbond (Brotherhood), the purpose of which was the preservation of the Afrikaner language and culture and rescuing Afrikaners from a condition of relative deprivation in their own country.

The plight of many of the less fortunate whites on the Rand was undoubtedly serious and that of the unemployed, predominantly Afrikaner poor whites, truly desperate. Yet white wages were far in advance of those paid to Africans and in some areas the gap had increased substantially during the war. African workers, whose capacity for effective industrial action was weakened by their lack of political rights and by discriminatory laws, felt a deep sense of grievance. Following a successful strike by white municipal workers in Johannesburg in May 1918, African municipal workers also went on strike. Over a hundred were arrested, but this sparked off a wider movement. On 19 June the Transvaal branch of the ANC held a mass meeting at which the call was made for an increase of a shilling a day for all African workers by 1 July. If this was not forthcoming a general strike would be called. A further mass meeting followed and violence flared up on 29 June when at a meeting of about a thousand the Union Jack was torn up and the crowd attempted to stop trams and motor cars, stoning them as they passed. When Botha agreed to meet a Congress deputation, however, they called off the strike. The deputation met him in July and a commission of inquiry was appointed. Groups of Africans, however, did continue to go on strike during July. The Moffat Commission reported in September 1918 but did not recommend any increase in wages. The ANC, which was now engaged in preparing to send a delegation to the Peace Conference in Europe, abandoned further involvement in the strike action over the wage issue.

Early in 1919, however, Transvaal ANC leaders decided to launch a protest against the pass system. Meetings were held at which a call for passive resistance was made. On a particular day passes would be destroyed or handed in. The idea received enthusiastic support as African workers clearly recognised the relationship between the pass laws, the failure of strike action and the low wages they endured. As an ANC circular declared, 'We came to the conclusion that passes prevent money.' After delegations to government had failed to secure any promise of change the passive resistance campaign was duly launched. Meetings were held to demand higher wages and hand in passes. Alarmed at the spread of the movement, the Chamber of Mines, with government support, introduced a number of chiefs to the mining compounds to speak against the anti-pass agitation. They were temporarily successful in cutting off the mine workers from the movement by means of this propaganda. Outside the mine compounds, however, the movement attracted a massive response. At one meeting alone it was reported that more than two thousand passes were handed in. The police, however, took action against the leaders. In response the police were stoned in one incident at Vrededorp and at Fordsburg an inter-racial riot broke out. ANC meetings in April were frequently attacked and broken up by white civilians. Over two hundred Africans were put on trial and when an African crowd gathered outside the courthouse in Johannesburg singing *Inkosi Sikelele Afrika* they were charged by mounted police. Many were injured and further arrests were made.

At the end of 1919 agitation over low wages flared up again. The Transvaal ANC had made a study of the cost of living and argued that an unmarried man could not live on less than £2 per week or a family on less than £4. As African wages averaged about £3 it was decided to press for a general increase. A delegation of African workers was invited to meet with representatives of employers and it was finally agreed that some increases would be recommended for those Africans who had to provide their own food and lodging. This, however, left out the mine workers who were to receive no increase. As the real value of their wages had been held almost constant throughout the war while the value of white wages had increased by about 40 per cent, this was the last straw. Between 17 and 19 February 1920, 71 000 African mineworkers on twenty-one mines went on strike. It was a most impressive example of disciplined industrial action. As the President of the Chamber of Mines put it, African workers had previously expressed their grievance in 'something in the nature of a riot', but now 'there was for the first time, a native strike in the true sense of the word . . . an absolutely peaceful cessation of work'. The response of the authorities was far from peaceful, however. The Chamber of Mines argued that if the strikers' demands were met the entire mining industry would become unprofitable. The government then decided to break the strike by force. Troops were

*From Union to apartheid:
the politics of
segregation*

introduced into the compounds, strike leaders were arrested, and strikers were generally given the alternative of returning to work or being arrested. The different compounds were isolated from one another and strikers in one compound were told that those in another had already gone back to work. At the Village Deep mine, African workers offered resistance and some were shot as troops forced their way into the compound and drove the strikers back to work.

The involvement of the ANC in the wages and pass agitation in the Transvaal in 1919 represented a high point in the organisation's activity. It was, however, uncharacteristic of its approach and after this brief involvement in mass action it returned to its more usual pattern of petitions, deputations and submissions of evidence to government commissions. After 1920 African discontent in the industrial field began to be expressed through a new organisation, the Industrial and Commercial Workers' Union. Far from acting to increase the rights of African urban dwellers and workers, however, the Smuts government legislated to restrict them.

The legal foundations of urban segregation and influx control: the 1923 Urban Areas Act

The increase in economic activity through the war years in South Africa had led to a considerable rise in the urban African population, which often lived in appalling shantytown conditions. In 1918–19 the spread of the devastating world-wide influenza epidemic took a heavy toll of South Africans of all races (though the African population, as the poorest section, naturally suffered most severely). It also drew attention to the poor conditions of African urban accommodation, and the dangers which this held for the health of their neighbouring whites. The problem of African urban settlement and accommodation was considered by two committees, the 1921 Native Affairs Commission and the 1922 Transvaal Local Government Commission (the Stallard Commission). On the basis of their reports, legislation was proposed which rested on the principle that the towns were the preserve of the white man, that Africans should only be permitted to live in the towns so long as they served the needs of the white man and that they should be removed from the towns when they ceased so to serve. The Natives (Urban Areas) Act of 1923 laid down the principle of residential segregation in urban areas and reinforced the doctrine that Africans had no permanent rights in the towns and no justification in being there unless needed by the whites as units of labour. Though implementing these measures fully was to take many years, the basis had been laid for the exercise of rigid control over African urban populations. Indeed in adopting this legislation, together with the 1913 Land Act, the South Africa Party government had established two of the key pillars of segregation.

The Bulhoek Israelites and the Bondelswarts

The repressive approach of the Smuts government towards Africans was not confined to legislation or the suppression of the strikers on the Rand. In 1920 a religious sect known as the Israelites camped at Bulhoek Common near Queenstown in the Cape to celebrate the Passover. After the ceremony, however, they stayed on and settled down to live. When approached by the

*From Union to apartheid:
the politics of
segregation*

authorities they stated that they had been commanded by Jehovah to stay there and await the end of the world. In May 1921 a large force of police supported by army units was brought up. Called on to leave, the Israelites refused and charged the police and soldiers with makeshift spears and swords. The soldiers waited until they were a few yards away and then opened fire with machine guns and rifles; 160 Israelites were killed and 129 were wounded.

An even more dramatic example of forceful repression occurred the following year when the Bondelswarts, a Khoi community in South West Africa, refused to pay a heavy tax imposed on the owners of dogs. The tax was intended to make it difficult for them to support themselves by hunting and so to force them to work for whites. In May 1922 they were suppressed by a force of 400 men with 4 machine guns and assisted by bombing planes. Over a hundred were killed and many more wounded.

Race relations in the Rand mining work force

From the beginning of mining operations on the Rand the labour force had been divided into a small, skilled and semi-skilled group of white workers and a very much larger force of unskilled African workers. As many of the white workers came from outside South Africa, their rates of pay had to be relatively high by world standards. African workers, on the other hand, were paid at very low rates. This was made possible by discriminatory laws. Breach of contract on their part was a criminal offence. Desertion was checked by the fact that they were forced to carry passes whenever they left the mining properties. On the mines they were housed in enclosed prison-like compounds. The mines themselves had eliminated competition in the search for African labour and the Witwatersrand Native Labour Association was responsible for recruiting all African mine labour from outside South Africa while after 1912 the Native Recruiting Corporation handled all recruiting within the country. Finally, African mine workers were labour migrants (many recruited from outside South Africa, Mozambique being the

Rand gold miners

main area of recruitment). As they left their families at home they could be paid at rates appropriate for single men.

Ever since the departure of Chinese labour, the mines had been able to stabilise African wages at very low rates in spite of increases in the cost of living. Because of the low grade of the ore on the Rand and the high cost of its extraction, this was the only reason the mines could operate profitably. In the early days of gold mining the division of the work force along racial lines had been inevitable as no Africans possessed the skills involved in modern deep-level mining. In course of time, however, Africans began to acquire these skills and the composition of the white work-force also underwent some change.

With the increased opportunities for commercial farming opened up by the development of the mining industry, landlords sought to make more profitable use of their land and this often meant getting rid of their white *bywoner* tenants. Farming also became more highly capitalised and competitive with the result that those less able to compete were driven from the land. Finally, as fixed boundaries had been established throughout southern Africa it was no longer possible to acquire land by trekking new areas, and as Boer farmers continued to have large families, increasing numbers found themselves landless and had to join the trek to the towns.

The whites who flocked to the towns were in a weak position. They lacked skills necessary for mining or other forms of urban employment, and unskilled work was undertaken by Africans at rates well below what was generally regarded as the minimum necessary to sustain a white family. The majority of these poor whites were Afrikaans-speakers who found themselves further handicapped in urban environments dominated by English-speakers. Their experiences eventually bred a fierce spirit of Afrikaner nationalism and a determination to use political means to improve their conditions.

During the First World War a substantial proportion of the white labour force left the mines for active military service. In their absence considerable numbers of Afrikaner urban migrants were employed in semi-skilled and supervisory roles although their levels of skill were often very low. At the same time, the mining companies, taking advantage of the shortage of white labour, were able to employ a number of African and Coloured men in semi-skilled roles usually reserved for whites. In September 1918, however, the white mine workers succeeded in persuading the Chamber of Mines to agree that no position filled by a white worker should be given to an African or Coloured worker.

Soon after the end of the war mining profits were severely squeezed by the rising cost of stores and materials and the increased wages won by white workers. The reduction of premium prices for gold faced many companies with the prospect of losses. The crisis could only be overcome by lowering labour costs, by making fuller use of cheap African labour in semi-skilled roles and re-organising work to economise on expensive white supervisory workers.

The Chamber of Mines thus gave notice of its intention to abandon the agreement of September 1918. In response, the white workers launched a prolonged strike in January 1922. In March the strike turned into open revolution and the white workers, led by the semi-skilled Afrikaner workers

Pauperisation of rural Afrikaners: the poor-white problem

Poor whites

The Rand rebellion

Troops clearing the Johannesburg streets during the 1922 strike

who were organised in commandos, seized control of the greater part of the Rand. Smuts rushed in troops supported by artillery, machine guns and tanks, however, and in two days of fighting from 12 to 14 March the white workers were overwhelmed. They were then forced to accept the mine owners' terms unconditionally. The subsequent re-organisation of the work force resulted in restored profits for the mining companies. A further blow to white workers followed when the courts invalidated regulations under the Mines and Works Act of 1911 that reserved many of the more highly skilled jobs (then generally occupied by English-speaking workers) for whites.

The Labour–National Party alliance

Beaten on the military front, the white workers turned to political action. The Labour Party, which represented them, entered into an alliance with Hertzog's National Party representing Afrikaner farmers. This was a natural alliance of interests. White workers and Afrikaner farmers were equally suspicious of Johannesburg capitalism. Afrikaner farmers, moreover, wished to keep African labour on the land and were naturally opposed to any modification of the race/class hierarchy in the towns which might undermine their authority over their African workers on the farms. The National Party also shared with the Labour Party a concern for the white unemployed, so many of whom were Afrikaners. In 1924 the Labour–Nationalist alliance won the elections and formed a government. It was to follow a policy of increasing employment opportunities for whites and introduce a programme of African segregation

Increased labour discrimination

To increase employment opportunities, the new government actively pursued a policy of industrial development. A government-owned Iron and Steel Corporation (ISCOR) was established in 1928 and a wide range of secondary industries was encouraged behind a protective tariff wall. At the same time the government adopted a 'civilised labour' policy. In state-controlled enterprises, particularly the railways, non-white workers were simply displaced to provide jobs for whites. Private industry was persuaded to employ a high proportion of whites, since tariff protection was dependent on the industry following satisfactory labour policies. To legalise the reservation of skilled jobs for whites on the mines, a Mines and Works Amendment Act was passed in 1926 which specifically prohibited the employment of Africans or Asians in skilled work.

In pursuit of greater segregation of whites and Africans Hertzog succeeded in passing an Immorality Act in 1927 which made sexual intercourse outside marriage between whites and Africans a criminal offence. A Native Administration Act (1927) placed all Africans outside the Cape under the unlimited authority of the government without the need to refer to parliament. The core of Hertzog's segregation programme, however, was contained in four closely related pieces of legislation introduced in 1926. The key measure was contained in the Representation of Natives Bill which aimed at destroying the African franchise in the Cape. This was accompanied by a Bill to establish a Native Council, and a Native Land Bill aimed at providing some increase in the land area of the reserves. The last of the four legislative proposals, the Coloured Persons' Rights Bill, reflected Hertzog's view that the Coloured population was naturally affiliated to the white and should eventually enjoy the same political rights. Hertzog was unable to get the two-thirds majority of both houses in parliament as demanded by the constitution for the alteration of the Cape Franchise and temporarily withdrew his four Bills.

South Africa becomes independent

Although frustrated over his segregation legislation, Hertzog achieved greater success in relation to another main object of National Party policy, the clear establishment of South Africa's position as an independent nation.

At the 1926 Imperial Conference in London, Hertzog put forward proposals very similar to those which Smuts had elaborated at the same Conference five years earlier. The mood of the Conference was now much more favourable and resulted in the Balfour Declaration, which proclaimed the principles of full autonomy and equality of status with Britain for the Dominions. Now it only remained for these principles to be given final, legal form, which was completed in 1931 with the Statute of Westminster. On returning from the Imperial Conference, Hertzog maintained that the aims of the National Party had been fully achieved and went on to give South Africa's independence symbolic expression in proposing the replacement of the Union Jack with a new national flag.

Hertzog's attitude to the Balfour Declaration and subsequently to the Statute of Westminster was very unsettling to many Afrikaner nationalists who believed that Afrikaner aspirations could only be completely fulfilled if South Africa freed herself completely from the British empire and became a republic. It seemed to them that Hertzog, like Smuts before him, was selling out the Afrikaner to British interests. The Broederbond, which up to that time had been a relatively small movement concerned with Afrikaner language and culture, decided to take an active part in all aspects of the life of the community. It soon succeeded in establishing secret cells in many of

The response of the Broederbond and Afrikaner nationalists

The founding committee of the Broederbond

173

From Union to apartheid:
the politics of
segregation

the major organisational and administrative institutions of the country. In December 1929 the Broederbond established the Federasie van Afrikaanse Kultuurverenigings (FAK, Federation of Afrikaans Cultural Associations). The new organisation, which had the same executive committee members as the Broederbond, was designed to give direction to Afrikaner cultural organisations and act as a public front for the Broederbond. Apart from fighting for an equal place for Afrikaans on national radio programmes, collecting Afrikaans folk songs and arranging exhibitions of Afrikaans art and books, the FAK held large-scale public festivals called 'Culture Days'. By 1937 about three hundred cultural bodies were affiliated to it. It also organised large-scale peoples' congresses (Volkskongres) at which ideas developed within the Broederbond could be publicly debated and receive mass endorsement. The movement for the formation of Afrikaner associations was very widespread. In 1929 the Voortrekker Movement was established to take the place of the Boy Scouts for Afrikaner boys. In 1933 the Afrikaanse Nasionale Studentebond (Afrikaner National Student Union) was formed as a result of a breakaway by Afrikaner students from the National Union of South African Students over the admission of African students to the union. In its manifesto it promised to stand on guard in the struggle for a separate Afrikaner nation.

The 'Black Peril' election

In 1929, Hertzog went to the country in a general election in which he made the preservation of white South Africa the main campaign issue. Smuts was accused of a policy of doing nothing and, worse still, of advocating equality between the races. In a speech at Ermelo in Natal on 17 January 1929, Smuts looked forward to the extension of South African influence and its pattern of race relations northward to East Africa, and held out the prospect of a British Confederation of African States: 'a great African Dominion stretching unbroken throughout Africa'. Hertzog, Tielman Roos and Dr D.F. Malan, as leaders of the National Party in the Orange Free State, seized on this and denounced Smuts in what came to be known as the 'Black Manifesto'. They claimed that Smuts was preparing to swamp South Africa in a 'Black Kaffir state . . . extending from the Cape to Egypt'. In this so-called 'Black Peril' election the National Party emerged with an overall majority. The Labour Party had split, with some members abandoning the white labour policy in favour of a broader socialist approach which regarded Africans as fellow workers. As a result it lost most of its seats.

Though victorious in the election, Hertzog was still a long way from obtaining the majority needed to secure the removal of the Cape African franchise. He drastically reduced its significance, however, by granting the vote to all adult European women, and by removing all economic qualifications for European men.

In order to push residential segregation still further, control over African entry to urban areas was now imposed by a Natives (Urban Areas) Amendment Act (1930) and further measures against African tenants on white-owned land were embodied in the Native Service Contract Act (1932). To complement these measures Africans in the Transkei were given improved local representation through the establishment of the United Transkeian Territories General Council (the Bunga).

The National Party victory in the 'Black Peril' election had been closely followed by the 1929 Wall Street Crash in America and the onset of worldwide economic depression. The economic situation in South Africa was made worse by the fact that the government insisted on maintaining the equivalence between the South African pound note and a gold sovereign when most other countries had abandoned the gold standard. The result was that imports became very cheap while profits from exports were drastically reduced. Farmers were badly hit and many were forced off the land. Manufacturing also suffered severely and the profits of the gold mines were slashed. The number of whites (predominantly Afrikaners) reduced to dire poverty reached its highest level. As the depression deepened in South Africa, the popularity of the government fell. Then in March 1933, after a dramatic appeal by Tielman Roos, the gold standard was abandoned. Hertzog and Smuts came together and agreed to form a coalition government and in an election in May 1933 the alliance won a resounding victory. In 1934 the National Party and the South Africa Party joined together formally as the United Party. Once the gold standard was abandoned the higher price for gold restored the prosperity of the mines, money became more readily available and the economy moved into a phase of rapid growth.

The fusion of the two main parties enabled Hertzog to destroy the African franchise in the Cape. Under the Native Representation Act passed in 1936 Africans in the Cape lost the right to the common-roll franchise. In its place they were entitled to vote for three white members of parliament and two in the Cape provincial council. Africans in the country at large were to have the right to vote for four white senators. A Natives' Representative Council made up of twelve elected and four nominated Africans sitting with five officials and the Secretary for Native Affairs as chairman was set up, but it was a purely advisory body with no constitutional powers. Parallel with the removal of the Cape African franchise, provision was made through the Natives' Trust and Land Act for the purchase of additional land for the reserves which would bring them up to about 13.5 per cent total land area of the Union. Land purchase proceeded very slowly, however.

In 1937 control of Africans in urban areas was further increased by a Native Laws Amendment Act which gave the government power to require towns to enforce segregation measures. It also gave magistrates and native commissioners the right to give or refuse permission to Africans in rural areas or reserves who wished to go to the towns to seek work. Municipal authorities were given powers to exclude Africans from any town where their labour was not needed and powers were also provided under which unemployed Africans in urban areas could be deported to the reserves.

Afrikaner nationalism

Though the fusion of the South Africa Party and Hertzog's National Party as the United Party received widespread support from white South Africans including most Afrikaners, some English-speakers founded a Dominion Party which gained limited support in Natal. Much more important was the fact that 'fusion' was rejected by a small group of more extreme Afrikaner National Party members in parliament. They regarded association with English-speakers in the same party as a compromise of the principles of

*From Union to apartheid:
the politics of
segregation*

Afrikaner nationalism, and broke away under the leadership of Dr D.F. Malan to found the Purified National Party.

Malan's followers were a small group in parliament and had only a precarious power base in the country. Their strongest base was in the Cape where almost the whole of Hertzog's National Party organisation went over to the new movement. In the Cape the Purified National Party could count on the financial support of many wine farmers and of the Santam and Sanlam finance and insurance companies which sustained the Afrikaner nationalist press in the Cape. The new party was much weaker in the Transvaal province where most maize farmers had suffered severely from the problems caused by South Africa holding to the gold standard. They overwhelmingly supported fusion with the South Africa Party in the new United Party. Malan's National Party had only one member in the whole province. It did, however, have the support of the Broederbond.

The Broederbond had come to be led predominantly by Afrikaner theologians and other academics and had elaborated an ideology for Afrikaner nationalism which was to provide the theoretical basis for apartheid. This was the belief that the nation rather than the individual or the family is the basic unit of moral and cultural life. Each nation has been created by God to fulfil a unique destiny and must be allowed to develop separately from others along its own lines to make its intended contribution to God's plan for the world. According to this doctrine the Afrikaner nation had been specially created by God from members of several different European peoples brought together on the soil of South Africa. It was intended to fulfil a divinely ordained role in the continent.

Through the Dutch Reformed churches and the numerous cultural associations belonging to the Broederbond-controlled FAK, the history of the Afrikaner *volk* (people) was elaborated into what amounted to a civil religion. It had its rituals and ceremonies and its martyrs. The history of the *volk* was portrayed as a divinely guided pilgrimage like that of the people of Israel. Led by the divine hand out of the Cape Colony where they had suffered the unjust persecutions of the British, the *volk* had embarked on the Great Trek. This epic migration was portrayed and accepted as an essential element in the heritage of all Afrikaners although historically only a part of the Afrikaner people actually took part in it. The culture and values of the *voortrekkers* were held up as the ideal to which all Afrikaners should aspire. Within the saga of the Trek, the conflict with the Zulu and the Covenant made with God before the battle of Blood river has particular emotional significance. The annual celebration of the Day of the Covenant became perhaps the most important ritual of Afrikaner nationalism. In the period after the Great Trek, Afrikaner nationalists dwelt on the renewed oppression of the *volk* by British imperialism culminating in the destruction of the Afrikaner republics, the deaths in the concentration camps and the evils of Milnerism. Then, after the formation of Union, the Afrikaner, as the nationalists believed, had been betrayed into the hands of British imperialism once more and the heroism of the rebellion led to the martyrdom of Jopie Fourie.

The ideological strength and organisational machinery of the Broederbond and the financial resources and skills of the Cape Purified Party organisation and the businessmen of the Santam and Sanlam groups complemented one another very well. They soon got together. The Cape leaders became members of the Broederbond and an alliance was forged. The aspiring Afrikaner businessmen associated with Malan's National Party in the Cape had experience of the possibility of obtaining capital from farmers and others by appealing to Afrikaner national feeling to create significant capitalist businesses; this was how Santam had first been established in 1918. Now, they saw the possibility of achieving this on a much larger scale by mobilising Afrikaner feeling to the organisations directed by the Broederbond. Their membership of the organisation led to the formulation of a new strategy. This involved using Afrikaner language and culture and the emotional appeal of history to strengthen the hands of the Afrikaner community and to channel the savings of Afrikaner farmers, professionals and workers into the creation of Afrikaner banks, finance companies and other businesses. This would enable Afrikaners to break the monopoly of English-speaking capitalists and by creating employment for Afrikaners help to save the Afrikaner poor white from his desperate plight.

The strategy involved not only appealing to Afrikaners to invest in Afrikaner businesses but also to shop in Afrikaner shops. It also involved the attempt to make Afrikaner workers think of themselves as members of the *volk* first rather than as workers. They were to be persuaded to break away from their English-speaking fellow workers and join specifically Afrikaner unions. The strategy aimed not only at advancing the interests of Afrikaner businesses by channelling Afrikaner savings into them but also at capturing the machinery of state for the pure Afrikaner. Afrikaners would then be able to create their ideal republic which Afrikaner nationalist ideologists believed to be the essential framework within which the Afrikaner nation could develop to the full. State patronage would also ensure the success of Afrikaner business in combating the dominance of English-speaking capitalists.

In 1938 the centenary of the *voortrekkers'* victory over the Zulu offered the perfect opportunity for the Broederbond to launch its new strategy. The FAK organised a symbolic ox-wagon trek to celebrate the event. The idea captured the Afrikaner imagination very powerfully and provoked a tremendous, often almost hysterical upsurge of nationalist emotion. Starting at Cape Town and proceeding by a number of routes to take in virtually every town in South Africa, the ox-wagons proceeded either to Pretoria or to the site of the battle of Blood river. Simultaneous torchlit memorial ceremonies were held at these two sites on 6 December, the centenary of the Day of the Covenant.

The voortrekker *centenary*

The 1938 centenary ox waggon trek

At the Day of the Covenant celebration at Blood river, Malan proclaimed that the Afrikaner was engaged in a new Great Trek to the towns where he faced a new Blood river in competition for employment with Africans. There, and at Pretoria, fervent appeals were made for Afrikaners to contribute funds as a salvation deed to save the nation. The fund that was started was known as the *reddingsdaadbond* (salvation-deed fund). It was subsequently used to assist many Afrikaner enterprises. In addition to the *reddingsdaadbond*, the enthusiasm generated by the ox-wagon trek led to the foundation of a para-military organisation called the *Ossewabrandwag* (Ox-Wagon Sentinel) dedicated to the preservation of the spirit of the Great Trek and the unity of all Afrikaners.

The *voortrekker* memorial celebrations provided the preliminary to the

From Union to apartheid:
the politics of
segregation

summoning of an Ekonomiese Volkskongres (Peoples' Economic Assembly) early in 1940. At this the economic strategy developed by the Broederbond was expounded, debated and endorsed. By this time, however, South Africa was already involved in the Second World War on the side of the Allies and the Afrikaner unity (*volkseenheid*) which the Broederbond struggled to create came under great strain.

African political activity between the wars

The Industrial and
Commercial Workers' Union

The harsh economic conditions which reduced so many whites to dire poverty in the period between the wars resulted in much greater suffering for the black and brown peoples of South Africa. Not only were they overwhelmingly the poorest section of South African society in any circumstances but their lot was made deliberately worse by the measures favouring white workers introduced by the Pact government. As the ANC withdrew from direct involvement from industrial matters after the Rand anti-pass campaigns strikes of 1918–19, African feelings on these as well as general political issues came to find expression at national level in a new organisation. In January 1919 a chance meeting between a Malawian, Clements Kadalie, with a sympathetic European, Mr A.F. Batty, led to the idea of creating an African Industrial Union. At an initial meeting on 7 January the Industrial and Commercial Workers' Union, generally known as the ICU, was founded. In December 1919 it played a part in organising a strike of 400 African dock workers in Cape Town. Though the strike was crushed by the use of white strike-breakers, the ICU soon spread to the seaport towns of Port Elizabeth and East London. Then in 1923 its headquarters were transferred to Johannesburg and the organisation gained an important new recruit in the person of A.W.G. Champion, a Zulu who had previously been secretary to the Native Mine Clerks Association. He was to make Natal the strongest branch of the ICU.

Clements Kadalie

As the ICU grew into a national body with a membership of thousands, the problem of how to use its apparent strength became acute. The members expected something in return for their subscriptions, but after initial dock strikes in Cape Town and Port Elizabeth no further strikes were launched and no mass action was undertaken against the pass laws or other aspects of racial discrimination in South Africa. As a result, while the ICU continued to expand into new areas, subscriptions declined in the areas where it had been long established. The movement became divided between a right-wing group which urged cautious moderation and a radical group made up largely of Communist Party members which called for a militant policy of mass action. The radicals also demanded more effective financial controls and to limit the individual powers of Kadalie and some of the provincial secretaries. Stung by their criticisms and particularly by their determination to establish control over the ICU's finances, Kadalie determined to expel Communists from his organisation. At a stormy council meeting on 16 December 1926, he succeeded in passing a motion making membership of the Communist Party incompatible with membership of the ICU.

In spite of the expulsion of the Communists, the ICU continued to expand throughout 1927 and reached its peak in 1928 but then began to disintegrate rapidly. At the April 1927 conference Kadalie still held the organisation to moderate lines. A call for a general strike in protest against Hertzog's proposed segregation laws was replaced by the decision to hold a day of formal protest. The conference confirmed the expulsion of the Communists. It also decided to send Kadalie to attend the annual International Labour Conference in Geneva. He left in June 1927 and visited London, Paris and Geneva. While in England he met many prominent trade unionists and received a promise that a British trade unionist would be sent to help with the organisation of the ICU. During his absence in Europe, disillusionment with the lack of positive action increased and tensions within the organisation became more acute.

*From Union to apartheid:
the politics of
segregation*

Early in 1928 Kadalie proclaimed that the ICU was to be reformed along proper union lines. He also made an attempt to affiliate with the South African Trades Union Congress. As he applied for affiliation on the basis of his 100 000 members, however, and the Congress could muster a total of only 30 000 it was clear that the ICU would completely dominate the organisation. Not surprisingly, the request for affiliation was turned down.

While Kadalie had been away in Europe, Champion had strengthened his position in the movement and on Kadalie's return it became obvious that Champion was a rival for the leadership. Kadalie succeeded in getting a disciplinary committee to suspend Champion as secretary for Natal, but Champion persuaded the majority of the Natal branches to support him and seceded to form the ICU Yase Natal. This major blow was soon followed by a series of further splits and the ICU began to disintegrate rapidly.

In July 1928, W.G. Ballinger arrived in South Africa, having been sent by a group of British trade unionists to act as the promised advisor to the ICU. Kadalie welcomed him at first, seeing in him his main hope of regaining control of the crumbling organisation. Ballinger's attempts to control and re-organise the ICU, however, soon led him into conflict with Kadalie. In January 1929 Kadalie resigned from the ICU and formed a new organisation, the Independent ICU. This established itself for some time in East London. In the meantime, the original main branch of the ICU soon disintegrated altogether. Only the ICU Yase Natal continued to display significant activity in 1929 when its involvement in a beer hall boycott led to a white mob trying to storm the ICU offices. This provoked a serious riot in which six Africans and two whites were killed. The following year, Champion was banned from Natal for three years.

With the collapse of the ICU in 1928 the ANC once again became the main vehicle of African political activity. In the meantime this organisation and other African groups had continued the policy of seeking to express African opinion through constitutional channels. A new forum for discussion was provided by the Joint Councils of Europeans and Africans established by liberal whites after the visit of the West African educationalist, J.E.K. Aggrey, to South Africa in 1921. In 1929, leaders of the Joint Councils movement set up the South African Institute of Race Relations to undertake research and pursue conciliation to lessen racial tensions.

With the publication of Hertzog's segregation legislation, African opinion concentrated very largely on the franchise issue. Through every forum open to them Africans consistently argued in defence of the Cape African franchise. In 1927, on the initiative of Dr Abdurahman of the African Peoples' Organisation, a non-European conference was summoned, bringing

*Non-whites and the
franchise issue*

From Union to apartheid:
the politics of
segregation

together the ANC, the APO, the Cape Native Voters' Association and the South African Indian Congress. Three more such conferences were held in 1930, 1931 and 1934.

All attempts to build a permanent organisation for the co-ordination of all non-European political activity failed, however, because existing organisations were unwilling to give up their separate independence. In 1930 a group of radical delegates sought to persuade the conference to launch a widespread strategy of passive resistance but this was rejected by the majority, who insisted on maintaining the practice of respectful resolutions and deputations. The conferences thus achieved little, though they did demonstrate the common attitude of different non-European groups to aspects of government policy. The 1931 conference agreed to send a deputation to Britain to oppose Hertzog's attempts to get a voice for South Africa in the determination of British policy throughout southern Africa. D.D.T. Jabavu of the Cape Native Voters' Association was eventually the only delegate and was able to give the British public an account of non-white grievances.

By the late 1920s young members of the ANC were calling for more radical action and in 1927 James Gumede, a representative of the approach which favoured co-operation with the Communist Party, was elected as president. After attending a Communist conference of oppressed nationalities in Brussels he had gone on to visit the Soviet Union, and came back full of enthusiasm. He called on left and right in the African Native Congress to unite in a common front and urged co-operation with the Communist Party in a campaign of mass demonstration. Gumede's association with the Communists, however, raised considerable opposition in the ANC and in 1930 he was defeated for the presidency by Pixly Seme on an anti-communist platform. Thereafter, for five years the ANC became extremely weak and was unable even to hold its annual conferences.

The All-African Convention

The creation of the United Party and the tabling in 1935 of Hertzog's Representation of Natives Bill and Natives Trust and Land Bill faced politically consious Africans with a renewed challenge. They responded by summoning an All-African Convention jointly called by Pixly Seme and D.D.T. Jabavu. It brought together 400 delegates drawn from the African National Congress, the Cape Native Voters' Association, the Communist Party, and the remnants of the ICU. Though the Convention uncompromisingly condemned the direction of government policy, it confined itself once more very much to traditional constitutional forms of action. It appealed to the House of Assembly and to the four senators appointed for their 'thorough acquaintance with the reasonable wants and wishes of the coloured races'. It emphasised the importance of appealing to the Governor-General and the King of Britain, urged government to make use of the consultative machinery available under the 1920 Native Affairs Act, despatched a deputation to meet Hertzog and called for a national day of conciliation and intercession. It did, indeed, accept a proposal that mass protest meetings be held throughout South Africa, but these were never organised. Finally, it agreed that the Convention should remain in existence.

After the passage of the Representation of Natives Act in 1936, the All-African Convention was faced with the need to define its attitude to the segregated forms of representation established under the Act: the Natives' Representative Council, the seats in parliament for representatives of the 'natives' and the Cape Provincial Council. While a vocal minority called for outright boycott, the majority led by Jabavu rejected this and adopted a policy of using the channels provided without accepting the principle on which they were based. When elections to the Natives' Representative Council were held in June 1937 many Africans associated with the Convention competed for the twelve indirectly elected seats. Six of these were obtained by members of the Convention's executive committee. Prominent Convention members also took an active part on behalf of various white candidates for the 'native' representatives' seats in the Assembly and the Cape Provincial Council. The Convention thus came to accept as a major part of its machinery of representation those very institutions which it had in principle opposed. At a December 1939 meeting the decision was also taken to consitute the Convention as a permanent federal organisation. It thus became a new umbrella organisation which seemed likely for a time to render the inactive ANC superfluous.

In 1936, however, Mr James A. Calata of Cradock, the energetic secretary of the Cape African Congress, became national secretary-general of the ANC and set about attempting to resuscitate the organisation. He held a special meeting of members in the Pretoria/Johannesburg area at which it was decided to hold a Silver Jubilee Conference in December 1937. At this conference there were some changes in leadership and the ANC then began to revive slowly. Its activities were nevertheless confined to the holding of annual conferences in 1938 and 1939, and the despatch of a delegation to meet the Minister of Native Affairs and parliamentary natives' representatives in May 1939. The Convention in the meantime was becoming much less active as its conferences were only scheduled for every three years and the next was not held until 1940.

The revival of the ANC

At the outbreak of the Second World War, therefore, African nationalism in South Africa had not yet developed a strong and effective organisation. The ICU, which at one time had seemed capable of leading a genuine mass movement, had collapsed and the ANC and the All-African Convention merely competed for the allegiance of a small elite. This elite was against militant action and wedded to the moderate tactics of respectful submissions, petitions and deputations; but all these methods had long proved ineffectual in challenging policies which reflected only the prejudices and the interests of the white electorate.

South Africa and the Second World War

The outbreak of the Second World War faced the United Party government with an agonising problem. Hertzog and the majority of his supporters from the erstwhile National Party favoured a policy of neutrality. Smuts and his erstwhile South Africa Party following, however, were determined to stand by Britain. The party split when Smuts, with the support of his faction and of members of the Labour and Dominion parties, gained a slim majority in favour of going in on the Allied side.

The Afrikaner nationalist response

In the Second World War as in the First, South Africans of all races served in campaigns in Africa. They took part in the liberation of Ethiopia and the

181

From Union to apartheid:
the politics of
segregation

long desert war in North Africa. Later they saw service in Europe also, mainly in Italy. As in the First World War, black and brown soldiers were prohibited from bearing arms and were confined to auxiliary, though often equally dangerous, roles. Moreover, South Africa's involvement in the Second World War, like her engagement in the First, bitterly divided white society. Not only did the mere fact of South Africa once again fighting for Britain against Germany re-awaken historic Afrikaner resentment dating back to the South African War, but Hitler's Nazi ideology had strong attractions for many Afrikaners.

The National Socialist faith in an Aryan master race (*herrenvolk*) was in tune with the racially stratified structure of South African society which Afrikaner nationalists were determined to preserve. The Nazi emphasis on the unity of the race community and the supremacy of the community over the individual also had much in common with the tenets of Afrikaner nationalism. The Nazi concept of leadership, moveover, appealed to many Afrikaners as more appropriate to their ideal republic than British-style parliamentary democracy with which they were deeply disillusioned. Anti-Jewish prejudice was also strong, especially in some areas where the poorer Afrikaner farmers were heavily in debt to Jewish storekeepers. As early as 1933 Louis Weichardt founded a movement known as the Greyshirts to promote Nazi-style anti-Semitism. The appeal of the Greyshirts proved to be fairly limited but many Afrikaner nationalists were influenced by Nazi views and the leadership of the Ossewabrandwag in particular adopted Nazi ideals of political organisation.

The internal situation in South Africa was thus precarious and, though there was no repeat of open armed rebellion, there was a good deal of planned sabotage. The internal situation, moveover, was directly affected by the changes of fortune in the wider theatre of war. The early disasters, culminating in the collapse of France and the Dunkirk evacuation, strengthened the National Party call for withdrawal from the war since they seemed to indicate that German victory was inevitable. Hitler's invasion of the Soviet Union and the resulting alliance between the Western Allies and the Soviet Union strengthened the conviction of many Afrikaners that Smuts had led the country to support the wrong side. The Allied setback in 1942, the German advance to Stalingrad, Pearl Harbour and the rapid conquest by the Japanese forces once again made the defeat of the Allies seem quite probable. When Japanese submarines were sighted off Madagascar and Smuts declared that in the event of Japanese invasion he would arm the black population, Afrikaner nationalists were horrified. By the end of 1942, however, the tide had turned and, as an ultimate Allied victory became increasingly certain, the idea of militant action against the Smuts government lost its appeal.

The economic impact of the war

The period of the Second World War marked a turning point in the development of the South African economy and society almost as significant as the mineral discoveries of the nineteenth century. The worldwide disruption of transport and the need for large quantities of materials to equip South African troops combined to spur South Africa to produce a wide range of goods for itself. Though the policies of the Pact government and the United Party government had already pointed the way it was the war that provided the necessary push to launch South Africa on its second industrial revolution, which transformed it from a mining economy to a predominantly manufacturing one. Within this general development, progress was particularly rapid and significant in the metal and engineering industries. Before the war, almost all mining and industrial machinery was imported and the South African engineering industry was mainly occupied in service and maintenance work. During the war, however, it was no longer possible to import all the machinery needed and the South African metals and engineering industries responded to the challenge. By the end of the war South African manufacturing industry was not only capable of mass manufacture of a wide range of consumer goods but was also developing the capacity to manufacture the machines with which these goods could be produced. Though still needing technological imports, South African industry had passed the vital point of take-off into self-sustaining growth.

The industrial boom of the war years created a huge demand for industrial labour. It thus greatly accelerated the urbanisation of all races. The African population in the towns grew particularly fast and in 1942 the government facilitated this by temporarily relaxing the operation of the pass laws. This massive migration not only involved large numbers of Africans from the reserves but from white farming areas also. By the end of the war many white farmers, especially in the Transvaal, were suffering a serious labour shortage. Within the towns the massive influx of African workers and their families far outstripped the provision of housing and other facilities. Appalling conditions of overcrowding developed and Africans repeatedly took the initiative in providing their own housing, defying bureaucracy by erecting illegal shantytowns on vacant land. The poor living conditions in these shanty areas with their flimsy dwellings made of sacking or old paraffin tins and the breakdown of ordered planning inevitably encouraged a rapid expansion of crime and violent confrontations between Africans and the police. The new shantytowns and the overcrowded older African locations, moreover, often bordered on areas occupied by the poorest sections of the white population that were also overcrowded, if not so severely as the African areas. In these situations there were repeated instances of racial conflict.

Social changes arising from industrial growth

During the war, moreover, rapid industrial expansion took place at a time when many skilled white workers were absent in the armed forces. This and the fact that the new industries increasingly called for semi-skilled operatives, rather than the traditionally skilled worker, led to a considerable dilution of white labour with black or brown workers. It also led to greatly increased employment of women of all races.

For much of the period of the war the unity among nationalist-minded Afrikaners (*volkseenheid*) which the Broederbond had worked so hard to achieve and which had been launched so successfully by the 1938 Ox Wagon Trek, was gravely disrupted. Unity gave way to bitter struggles between factions which the Afrikaner nationalists called *broedertwis* (brother quarrels). The break-up of the United Party led to a temporary reconciliation between Hertzog and his followers and the Purified National Party led by Malan. At the end of January 1940, they came together to form the Reunited National Party. The reconciliation did not last, however, for Hertzog continued to believe in the need for unity between English and Afrikaner white South

Afrikaner politics in the war period

From Union to apartheid:
the politics of
segregation

Africans. He opposed the idea of pressing for the establishment of a republic while English-speakers were overwhelmingly opposed to it. He also insisted on the principle of equality between English and Afrikaners in any future republic. When the vote went against him on this in a party congress in November 1940 he and a number of his followers walked out. In December 1940, Hertzog resigned from Parliament and the remnant of his following then formed the Afrikaner Party under the leadership of N.C. Havenga. This split was followed by another which involved the followers of Oswald Pirow, previously Minister of Defence in the pre-war United Party government. Pirow formed a movement within the National Party called the New Order. It looked to the fusion of the two white communities of South Africa into a single white master race in a racially structured republic to be organised in accordance with Nazi leadership principles. Pirow was attacked by other leaders of the National Party for his adoption of a foreign ideology and his failure to insist on the separate identity of the Afrikaner nation. He was forced out of the party in January 1942 and thereafter soon lost any significant political influence.

The struggle between the National Party and the Ossewabrandwag

The splits in the National Party were not nearly as serious for Afrikaner nationalism as the bitter divisions which developed between that party and the Ossewabrandwag. The emotional atmosphere created by South Africa's entry into the war on the British side favoured the rapid growth of this Nazi-influenced paramilitary organisation. It actively recruited and trained its version of the Nazi stormtroopers known as *stormjaers* and began a campaign of sabotage against military installations. Under its ambitious leader Dr J.F.J. van Rensburg, the Ossewabrandwag began to openly compete with the National Party for the political leadership of the Afrikaner community. The struggle was much more than a matter of rival personalities. It involved fundamental questions of ideology and tactics. While the National Party placed its faith in constitutional action through the parliamentary system, the Ossewabrandwag rejected representative democracy and placed its faith in extra-parliamentary military action. It hoped to build a Nazi-style republic based on Nazi leadership principles.

Matters first came to a head in July 1941 when the Ossewabrandwag usurped the role of the National Party by distributing copies of a draft republican constitution. After a brief apparent reconciliation, the matter flared up again at the time of Pirow's expulsion from the National Party and Malan determined to smash the Ossewabrandwag as a political force. Early in 1942 Ossewabrandwag members were expelled from the National Party. The party also launched an outright attack on the rival organisation for adopting National Socialist ideology and engaging in sabotage. The quarrel caused a very serious split in the Afrikaner community. The Broederbond itself was very divided and to retain its own unity tried to hold aloof from the struggle. With the change in the fortunes of the war beginning in late 1942, however, the ideals and tactics of the Ossewabrandwag came to appear increasingly unrealistic. The National Party was able effectively to destroy its rival and consolidate its position as the main political mouthpiece of Afrikaner nationalism. This did not, however, make it an immediate political threat to the Smuts government.

By mid-1943 the change in the fortunes of war in favour of the Allies was

*From Union to apartheid:
the politics of
segregation*

very obvious. By May the long campaign in North Africa had ended in complete victory for the Allies. Taking advantage of this, Smuts called a general election for July. His cause was aided by the fact that many farmers (particularly in the Transvaal) were benefiting substantially from the high grain prices which accompanied the wartime industrial boom. The United Party, in coalition with the Labour Party and the Natal Dominion Party, won an overwhelming victory. The National Party, though winning only a small minority of seats, had, however, consolidated its position as the main political expression of Afrikaner nationalism.

With his massive majority in parliament Smuts was able to lead the country through the last two years of the war and into the post-war period. At the international level, he once again played a significant role in planning aspects of the post-war settlement, being asked to make a draft of the Preamble to the Charter for the United Nations Organisation. Ironically, he was thus responsible for setting out the concept of fundamental human rights which was one of the foundations of the position from which South Africa was subsequently to be repeatedly attacked.

Within South Africa, the Smuts government made adjustments to the system of segregation and race discrimination to suit the needs of industry. These changes permitted the employment of many brown and black operatives in positions previously regarded as reserved for whites and facilitated the massive increase in African urbanisation. On the other hand, Smuts's government strenuously maintained those aspects of the system which ensured that African labour would remain cheap and subject to close discipline. The enforcement of pass regulations, waived in 1942, was reimposed during 1943, and in 1942 steps were taken to prevent Africans from taking advantage of the favourable conditions of industrial expansion to push up their wages. War Measure No. 145 made all strikes by Africans illegal in any circumstances.

The determination to keep black wages down was strongest in the gold-mining industry. The abandonment of the gold standard and the consequent raised price of gold in paper currency meant that it would have been possible to let the black mineworkers' wages rise without destroying the profitability of the mines. Because the government was responsible almost entirely to white voters, however, this did not happen. The black mineworkers' wages were kept down and the increased profits were taken through taxation and other methods to subsidise farming and industrial development, thus helping to make the massive industrial expansion of the war period possible. In 1943, in an effort to maintain the hold on African wage rises, a measure was introduced banning all meetings of more than twenty people on the mines.

While the demands of industry led to some limited relaxation of discrimination against Africans the need to retain the support of the Dominion Party in Natal led Smuts to increase restrictions on Indians. In response to white protest that Indians were increasingly buying property in white-occupied areas of Durban, Justice Broome was asked to undertake a one-man commission. In response to his report, submitted in 1942, an Act, generally known as the Pegging Act, was passed restricting such property purchases by Indians for a three-year period. Justice Broome was then asked to head a further commission which included two members of the Natal Indian Congress to make recommendations on future regulations.

From Union to apartheid:
the politics of
segregation

After the Allied victory in 1945 many of the wartime policies were carried over into the first years of the peace. The control of inflation and the balance of payments became the vital concerns. Much of the wartime apparatus of economic control was thus retained. Food prices, in particular, were kept down by price control. While some relaxation of controls over African trade union activities was allowed, the government was as determined as ever not to let black mineworkers' wages be forced up.

African nationalism in the
Second World War:
the recovery of the ANC

The rapid urbanisation of Africans and the relaxation of the job colour bar in response to wartime needs created favourable conditions for African political and trade union activity. In December 1940 Dr Xuma was elected ANC President and launched an energetic overhaul of the organisation. In 1943 the constitution of the movement was revised. The House of Chiefs which had very rarely met was abolished and the whole organisation was made more highly centralised. In 1943, inspired by the Atlantic Charter, the ANC drew up its proposals for a South African Bill of Rights. The document, entitled *African Claims in South Africa*, went considerably further than the ANC had done before in calling for outright universal suffrage. In other respects, however, it restated once again the moderate liberal principles the ANC had always pursued. A copy was sent to Smuts early in 1944 with a request for discussions, but Smuts refused even to meet an ANC delegation, describing the proposals as wildly impractical.

In 1942 a major new development in the ANC had begun with the foundation of a Youth League. This was formally accepted as part of the ANC organisation at the ANC Annual Congress of 1943. The Youth League constituted a politically radical pressure group within the ANC, its members being mostly young African teachers and students of medicine and law. Some of them took a more Africanist approach than the ANC had previously adopted, stressing the need for Africans to act on their own, and some were critical of political co-operation with other race groups. In general, however, they shared the liberal, non-racial ideals traditional to the ANC and pressed for more militant tactics to achieve them. They believed that the ANC should go beyond the method of petitions and delegations and confront discriminatory measures directly with the weapon of mass passive resistance.

The new more militant mood of the ANC was expressed for the first time by its participation in a mass anti-pass campaign first proposed by members of the Communist Party. The campaign reached a climax in 1944 with a protest march of 20 000 in Johannesburg. Thereafter the ANC drew back from more direct confrontation. A scheme for mass pass burning backed by a general strike was abandoned. Instead a campaign was launched to obtain a million signatures to an anti-pass petition. This continued into 1945 when a total of 850 000 had been obtained.

The revival of the ANC soon led to stresses between it and the All-African Convention which had come close to taking over the role of main political mouthpiece for African nationalism. The creation by government of the Coloured Affairs Department in 1943 aroused the alarm of Coloured people who believed that it heralded the imposition of more thoroughgoing segregation measures against them. They formed a new political movement, the Anti-Coloured Affairs Department Movement. In December 1943 this group held a joint conference with the All-Africa Convention and out of this a new political organisation, the Non-European Unity Movement, was founded in 1944. This developed into a predominantly Cape Province-based movement with both Coloured and African membership.

The rapid growth in the numbers of African industrial workers and the continuing labour shortage encouraged African industrial activity. The number of African trade unions on the Witwatersrand rose from 20 with a total membership of 23 000 in 1940 to 50 with a membership of 80 000 in 1945. Trade unions were easier to form and even received official encouragement among semi-skilled black operatives who were permanently urbanised. In spite of the difficulties and official opposition to the unionisation of migrant workers, however, the African Mineworkers' Union had succeeded in establishing a commanding position in the mining compounds at the end of the war. In 1942 a government Wage Board determination for unskilled workers was made. The rise awarded was well short of the poverty datum line for an average African family, however. What is more, the determination did not apply to several categories of worker on the grounds that they were predominantly migrants or worked in the close vicinity of mineworkers whose wages were not to be raised. The result was a series of strikes which led to further increases in a number of cases and prompted the government to issue War Measure No. 145 banning all strikes by Africans.

In the aftermath of the 1942 labour unrest some steps were felt to be needed to appease the mineworkers, whose wages were only about half of the minimum recommended for other industrial workers in the 1942 wage determination. Because of the role of mining profits in the entire economy, however, only very small increases were made. Then a full-scale investigation of mineworkers' wages and conditions was undertaken by the Lansdown Commission. This Commission, influenced by the determination to maintain the mining profits, fell back on the argument that as the families of African workers could be sustained by agriculture in the reserves, African wages were no more than pocket money and need not be raised in line with the cost of living.

The mineworkers, who had awaited the results of the Commission, finally lost patience. In mid-August 1946 the African Mineworkers' Union launched an impressively well-organised strike. It had almost unanimous support and brought the entire Witwatersrand gold-mining industry to a halt. The Smuts government responded with savage repression. The compounds were surrounded by police and isolated from one another and mineworkers were forced back to work at gunpoint. There was resistance at the Village Deep mine and police opened fire, killing some and leaving many injured.

The mood of increased radicalism displayed by the ANC and African trade unionists affected even the most moderate African leaders, members of the Natives' Representative Council. Frustrated at the almost total lack of attention paid to their representations, they felt as Councillor Paul Mosaka put it, 'We have been asked to co-operate with a toy telephone. We have been speaking into an apparatus which cannot transmit sound and at the end of which there is nobody to receive the message. Like children we have taken pleasure at the sound of our own voices.' As the only protest open to them they voted unanimously to adjourn their 1946 session.

The 1948 general election and its background

The United Party approached the 1948 election with the confidence born of its existing massive majority. For this reason it did not see the need to look closely at its current policies from the point of view of their effects on voters' attitudes. The maintenance of much of the wide-ranging system of wartime controls in the post-war period alienated many. Farmers resented price controls which kept their profits down. White workers were unhappy with their wage levels. Almost all whites were irritated by the retention of a wartime measure prohibiting the production of white bread in order to reduce wheat imports. More significant was the fact that the United Party had no clear-cut policies on race issues. By this time many white workers were alarmed at the growing proportion of black and brown operatives being employed in skilled or semi-skilled industrial jobs. White farmers, on the other hand, were finding increasing difficulty in obtaining cheap black labour as Africans living on white farms joined the trek to the towns. Many whites were alarmed at the rapid growth of black numbers in the towns, the mushroom growth of the shantytowns and the accompanying increase in crime and violence.

United Party policy on race matters was based on the report of the Fagan Commission which sat between 1946 and 1948. Its most important recommendation was that the urbanisation of blacks should be facilitated to satisfy the labour needs of industry and that the urban black population should be recognised as a permanent part of the urban population. The proposals had no appeal to white workers afraid of losing their jobs, to white farmers afraid of losing black labour to the towns, or to the many whites frightened at the growing numbers of blacks in the cities. The United Party government, moreover, ran into considerable difficulty and embarrassment in the international sphere.

South Africa had played a significant part in the war, and after it Smuts had continued to command respect as a world statesman and had made a significant contribution to the post-war settlement. He expected South Africa to enjoy an improved status in world affairs. He thus hoped and expected to obtain the approval and support of the United Nations for the full incorporation of South West Africa (now Namibia) into the Union of South Africa. In May 1946 the white Legislative Assembly in Windhoek, the capital of South West Africa, passed a motion calling for this. South African authorities then consulted the opinion of chiefs and on the basis of their replies reported that the great majority of the black and brown peoples of the territory also favoured the move.

The fact that the Second World War in its ideological aspects had been a life-and-death struggle against the Aryan master-race doctrines of the Nazis and the presence in the new international institutions of what would now be called Third World nations meant, however, that open race discrimination such as that practised in South Africa would meet with almost universal condemnation. At the first session of the General Assembly of the United Nations in 1946, South Africa found herself on the defensive as India mounted a bitter attack against the discriminatory treatment of Indians in

*From Union to apartheid:
the politics of
segregation*

the country. One aspect of this that was particularly controversial was the restrictions on the purchase of residential property by Indians in Natal under the 1943 Pegging Act. In April 1944 Smuts had met a delegation from the Natal Indian Congress and reached an agreement under which a mixed Board of whites and Indians would have control over housing in Durban. This was rejected by the Natal Provincial Council, however, with the result that Indian opinion in South Africa and India was further aroused. In 1946 Smuts made another attempt. The Asiatic Land Tenure and Indian Representation Act maintained the restrictions on Indian rights to property ownership but offered them the right to vote for Indian Representatives in parliament on a similar basis to that on which Africans voted for Native Representatives. The Act alienated some Natal white voters who did not want Indians to have any representation. It further increased the anger of Indians, however, who denounced it as the 'Ghetto Act'. They launched a campaign of passive resistance and went to gaol in hundreds. The entire press and all parties in India likewise denounced it. The Indian High Commissioner was withdrawn and an economic boycott of South Africa was undertaken.

In the United Nations South Africa found itself generally condemned. The General Assembly maintained that the treatment of Indians in South Africa should comply with the principles of the UN Charter. In addition to raising the subject of discrimination against Indians in South Africa, India also led the attack on South Africa's request for the incorporation of South West Africa. This opposition was further encouraged by the efforts of the South African ANC President, Dr Xuma, who travelled to New York for the Assembly Session. The South African request was rejected and South Africa was asked to place the territory under the United Nations International Trusteeship. The spectacle of South Africa's humiliation at the United Nations at the hands of a coloured nation together with the defiant attitude of the Native Representative Council added to the impression that Smuts was losing his grip and was unable to keep the race situation under control. By this time Smuts was a very old man who could not be expected to last many more years in office. Moreover his deputy, Hofmeyr, was the leader of the liberal wing of the United Party. His mildly pro-African attitude led to him being bitterly denounced as *Kafir boetie*. The prospect that he might soon take over the reigns of office from Smuts frightened many United Party voters.

With the elimination of the Ossewabrandwag as an effective rival in 1943, the National Party with the support of the Broederbond and its wide network of related associations was able to concentrate on the task of uniting the Afrikaner *volk* under its leadership. The programme of winning over Afrikaner workers was vigorously pressed. In 1944 an apparent disregard of the industrial colour bar in a Germiston clothing factory provided the Afrikaner nationalists with an excellent opportunity. The factory, which employed white women workers, took on some Coloured women as well. Although they were physically isolated from the white women their presence was discovered and some of the white women demanded strike action. The Garment Workers' Union, which was a multiracial union led by a radical socialist, Solly Sachs, refused to support the move. Two of the white women who had demanded the strike eventually

From Union to apartheid:
the politics of
segregation

lost their jobs. Afrikaner nationalists were able to whip up feeling over this to a high level. The Dutch Reformed churches, the National Party and the Afrikaner Cultural Association united to denounce the threat to their wives and mothers who they claimed were in danger of being placed on a level with Coloureds in accordance with communist doctrines of racial equality.

In June 1944 the Broederbond founded a new organisation, the Blanke Werkers Beskermingsbond (White Workers' Protection Society) to fight for greater segregation in industry. In May 1945 the Dutch Reformed churches issued a pamphlet calling on white South Africans to support the white clothing workers and fight for the maintenance of the colour bar and Christianity. Led by Albert Hertzog the Broederbond-inspired drive to wean Afrikaner workers away from multi-cultural trade unionism to Afrikaner nationalist unions gained vital if limited success. On the railways an Afrikaner nationalist-led union (Die Spoorbond) established its predominance. Within the Mineworkers' Union, moreover, an Afrikaner nationalist-inspired reform movement gained massive support, its growth being helped by the continuing discriminatory behaviour of the English-speaking minority towards the Afrikaner majority among the white mineworkers. It was further boosted by the behaviour of the existing leaders of the union who were in close collusion with mine management. The Afrikaner nationalist drive failed, however, to win over workers in a number of industries where whites and members of other races were accustomed to working together, as in the case of clothing workers.

In preparation for the 1948 election the National Party determined to concentrate on the key issue of the future pattern of race relations in South Africa. In this regard it took the doctrine of apartheid and developed it into a definite political policy. The concept of apartheid (separateness) was first put forward by a group of Afrikaner intellectuals in the 1930s. It was further elaborated by Afrikaner thinkers during the war years. Apartheid theory owed much to the theological tradition of the Dutch Reformed churches which had contributed to the ideals of Afrikaner nationalism developed by the Broederbond and its affiliated bodies. It was also influenced by the pseudo-scientific racism which was widespread in the inter-war period and had formed much of the basis of German Nazism.

According to apartheid doctrine each race and nation has its own distinct cultural identity and has been created to fulfil a unique destiny laid down by God. To fulfil its inner potential each nation must be kept pure and allowed to develop freely along its own lines. Excessive contact between races, above all racial interbreeding, would corrupt and destroy the inner potential of both races involved. Fear of racial mixture and white determination to preserve racial purity were of key psychological importance to the appeal of apartheid at this stage. Thus at the 1944 Volkskongres (Peoples' Congress) held by Federasie van Afrikaanse Kultuurverenigings (FAK – Federation of Afrikaans Cultural Organisations) Professor Cronje claimed to have scientific proof that racial mixture led to racial degeneration. The Afrikaner poet, 'Totius' (J.D. du Toit), arguing from the religious point of view, claimed that the separation of races was part of God's plan of creation and racial mixture contrary to God's will. On these assumptions each race and nation in South Africa must have its own separate territory on which to develop along its own unique lines. At the same time social contact between the races must be reduced to the absolute minimum and sexual relations rigorously prevented. This physical and social separation would not only secure the preservation and purity of the white race but also emancipate the black nations. They would be freed from the cultural domination of whites and would enjoy the opportunities for autonomous cultural and political self-expression that Afrikaner nationalists had long struggled to gain for their own people.

The practical effect of the doctrine, however, would depend on the way that the land and resources of South Africa were to be divided between the races. Supporters of apartheid assumed that the territories on which the African communities would fulfil their self-development would be those defined as native reserves in the 1936 Natives Land and Trust Act. These amounted to about 13.5 per cent of the total area of the country and did not include any of the main deposits of mineral wealth or major centres of industrial activity. They were, moreover, conspicuously poorly served by road and railway systems and other infrastructure and clearly could not provide for the support of the great majority of the total population of South Africa. Those living within them would have to earn their living very largely by working in the white-owned areas. Whatever their political development, the reserves could never, in effect be more than labour reserves for the white-controlled economic heartland, reducing the social costs and political dangers for the whites of the exploitation of cheap black labour.

After discussion of the doctrine in the Volkskongres, the National Party set up the Sauer Committee to turn the concept of apartheid into a practical political programme. The Committee recommended that the doctrine should be embodied in a number of definite and interrelated policies. Instead of being eased, African influx to the towns should be regulated by strict controls. Africans should continue to be regarded as no more than temporary visitors and never be allowed to acquire social and political rights equal to those of whites. Africans should not be allowed to form trade unions or engage in strikes. African education should be organised along different lines from that of whites and be directed towards developing their own national characteristics.

In addition, the Natives' Representatives in the House of Assembly should be abolished and the Natives' Representative Council should also be scrapped. In its place local government bodies for the different ethnic groups of the African population should be developed in the reserves. These would consist mainly of the traditional chiefs and would form the institutions through which the African peoples would be able to discover and develop their autonomous political self-expression. It was assumed, however, that this would always take place under ultimate white control. The Sauer Committee also called for the removal of Coloured voters at the Cape from the common voting roll. Instead they should be placed on a separate roll and allowed to vote for three whites in the House of Assembly as Coloured Representatives. The Committee took a particularly hard line with regard to South African Indians. Everything possible should be done to encourage their repatriation. Those that remained should be confined to clearly segregated areas and their rights to live and trade in other areas should be drastically reduced.

The 1948 apartheid election

Apart from an alliance with the Labour Party the United Party did little to organise for election victory. It had few paid organisers and no youth movement. In contrast the National Party, fully supported by the Broederbond and its affiliated associates, was well served by active and energetic committees at all levels. Even so, the National Party had a very long way to go against the United Party's huge lead. In the final vote the United Party still polled substantially more votes than the National Party and the Afrikaner Party combined. The system of electoral weighting which favoured the rural areas, however, worked to the advantage of the Afrikaner nationalists. With the aid of the appeal of apartheid contrasted with the vague indecisiveness of the United Party, by depicting Smuts as the ally of both communism and international capitalism, and by a shrewd political alliance with the Afrikaner Party, the small group of intellectuals and rising businessmen who led the National Party and the Broederbond succeeded in winning enough farmer and white worker votes to win a slender majority of seats. Malan was in a position to form a government. The choice for apartheid had been made.

The first two phases of apartheid

Between 1948 and 1984 the system of apartheid developed through three definable phases. The first phase, which may be called classical or *baaskap* (white supremacy) apartheid, lasted from 1948 to the end of the 1950s. It was the period in which the National Party put its original ideas into legislative form. It may be said to have reached its climax in 1961 with the achievement of the Afrikaner nationalists' most cherished dream, the transformation of South Africa into an Afrikaner-ruled republic.

By this time, however, African nationalist protest within South Africa, the impact of the spread of the decolonisation movement from Asia to Africa, and the changes in the South African economy and its market needs had led to the first major step towards the second phase. This may be called separate development. Separate development continued until 1973–4 when once again the pressure of changes in South Africa, Africa as a whole and the wider world led to new policy departures marking the beginning of a third phase. The main reasons for this were changes in the South African economy; the changed strategic situation following the revolution in Portugal and the liberation of Mozambique and Angola; widespread African strike action on the industrial front; massive violent protest within the African townships; and the beginning of African nationalist guerrilla activity within South Africa on a significant scale.

The third phase, which I have called multiracial co-option, involved considerably greater changes at the political level than the previous two and in 1984 saw the introduction of a new multiracial constitution.

Baaskap *apartheid 1948–61*
Although the National Party and the Afrikaner Party had won only a small majority of five seats in parliament over the other parties, the election victory of 1948 enabled the new government under Dr Malan to launch a major re-organisation of South African society in accordance with Afrikaner nationalist ideals. This involved halting and reversing the trend towards the erosion of segregation which had been evident under the previous government. Instead, segregation was to be systematised as never before and applied rigidly and dogmatically in accordance with the theory of apartheid.

Within the more strictly racially segregated and stratified society to be created by these measures, Afrikaner political control of white South Africa was to be consolidated. The economic situation of poor Afrikaners within white society was to be improved. The Afrikaner share of the business world was to be expanded and Afrikaner language and culture protected and accorded a higher status in national life. Finally, South Africa was to be constitutionally transformed into a republic free of allegiance to the British Crown. The period is referred to as that of classical or *baaskap* (white supremacy) apartheid because in this period the explicit racist assumptions on which apartheid theory was originally based were unchallenged. The innate superiority of the white race was taken for granted by apartheid's architects. Though Africans were to be granted limited political rights in the reserves these were to be expressed predominantly through a re-invigorated system of traditional chiefs and under ultimate white control.

During this period Afrikaner nationalist political control was greatly strengthened. The heightened racial tensions arising from the implementation of apartheid policies as well as the weaknesses of the main white opposition party contributed to this. The period, moreover, was in general one of continuing rapid economic growth. A wide-ranging system of import and exchange controls introduced in 1948 in response to a deteriorating foreign trade balance proved very effective. Major companies unable to export their funds were encouraged to make substantial re-investment within the country. In consequence, the growth of manufacturing industry, which had reached the point of take-off in response to wartime conditions, was further accelerated. In 1949 the devaluation of sterling and related currencies in relation to the United States dollar enhanced the profitability of gold mining and thus boosted the entire economy. The discovery and development of new gold fields in the Orange Free State still further increased the pace of economic expansion. Then, at a time when some gold mines were beginning to reach the end of their useful life, uranium was discovered in the mine tailings and a new major export had been found. Moreover, although the implementation of apartheid created some rigidities in the use of labour disadvantageous to the more progressive capitalist enterprises, the stricter controls imposed on African workers ensured that their labour continued to be available at ultra-cheap rates. The continuing emphasis on migrant labour also kept down the burden of social costs that industry would otherwise have had to bear. In spite of the dogmatism with which apartheid was introduced, moreover, adjustments were made whenever any serious conflict with profitability arose so long as the interests of whites were not directly affected. Thus employers were in practice allowed to employ black and brown workers at higher skill levels in apparent direct conflict with the theory, so long as white workers were not directly replaced.

The first significant advance in the National Party's parliamentary position came with the introduction of legislation in 1949 which provided six seats in the House of Assembly and four in the Senate for the white population of South West Africa. In 1950 the National Party won all these seats and made itself independent of the support of Havenga and his followers. In 1951 the Afrikaner Party finally joined the National Party. In 1953 the National Party won a general election with a significantly increased majority and in 1958 another election victory strengthened its position still further. During this period the National Party government was led by three men. D.F. Malan, who had held the originally small group of 'Purified Nationalists' together and led them to victory in 1948, presided over the initial stages of the intro-

The Nationalist Cabinet, 1948.
J.G . Strydom is seated second from left;
Dr Malan is sitting third from left;
Dr Verwoerd is standing third from right

duction of apartheid. He finally retired in 1954 after leading his party to its second election victory. As his successor the party chose J.G. Strydom, leader of the Transvaal branch, well known for his extreme views and nicknamed the 'Lion of the North'. Strydom died in August 1958 shortly after leading the party in the 1958 general election. Once again the party chose a member of the Transvaal branch, Dr Hendrik Verwoerd. Verwoerd had been born in Holland but had been brought to South Africa by his Dutch parents while still a child. Perhaps because he was to some extent an outsider he identified himself particularly strongly with the Afrikaner people. As a student he rejected the opportunity of a scholarship to study in England and instead went to Germany. He was the most outstanding theoretician of apartheid and the most convinced believer in its racist principles in the National Party government. As Minister of Native Affairs under the previous leaders he had been responsible for framing most of the legislation concerning black South Africans. More than any other individual he deserves to be regarded as the main architect of the system of *baaskap* apartheid.

The ten years after 1948 saw not only the consolidation of National Party control of the South African parliament, but also opened the way for the advancement of Afrikaners and Afrikaner institutions in every aspect of public life. Afrikaners now enjoyed favourable opportunities for promotion in the defence forces and all government departments and corporations. Afrikaner banks, financial institutions and businesses flourished in the favourable climate. Afrikaner cultural organisations enjoyed increased state patronage. These developments opened the way for increasing interlinking of Afrikaner social, cultural, educational, economic and religious organisations. The Broederbond, with its key cluster of relationships with the FAK, numerous affiliated cultural organisations, the Reddingsdaadbond, the Afrikaner press, the Afrikaner universities, the Afrikaner churches and the National Party itself, played an important co-ordinating role. At leadership level there was a high degree of overlapping membership of these different institutions and individuals often moved through a variety of these organisations. Verwoerd, who went from a professorship at the Afrikaans University of Stellenbosch, to editor of the main Transvaal Afrikaans newspaper, to Prime Minister, while also being a leading member of the Broederbond, is just one outstanding example of this pattern. The Afrikaner elite thus became increasingly integrated into a single Afrikaner establishment. At the same time, the favourable economic situation combined with discriminatory measures in favour of whites and Afrikaners in particular, allowed the 'poor-white' problem to be virtually eliminated. This in turn helped to tie the poorer Afrikaner's loyalty more firmly to the Afrikaner elite. The Afrikaner people thus came to be increasingly bound together by a closely inter-locking network of organisations and the National Party came to constitute the single political mouthpiece of united Afrikanerdom rather than just a political party in the ordinary sense.

*The legal framework
of apartheid*

The attempt to re-organise South African society in accordance with the principles of apartheid was embodied in a long series of interrelated laws. These were framed not only in the light of apartheid dogma but also with an eye to the interests of the white population in general and, more specifically, those sections of the white population – Afrikaner farmers, Afrikaner workers and Afrikaner businessmen – from whom the party derived its main political support.

Fundamental to the whole theory of apartheid was a belief in the importance of race purity. Legislation already existed making 'illicit' (extra-marital) sexual relations between whites and Africans criminal. The National Party government took the principle to its logical conclusion by outlawing inter-racial marriage by the 1949 Prohibition of Mixed Marriages Act. In 1950 the Immorality Act was amended to make 'illicit' sex between whites and Coloureds criminal also.

To achieve the racial separation envisaged by the theory it was necessary to divide the whole population into watertight racial compartments. For this purpose the Population Registration Act was passed in 1949. It made provision for every South African to be given a registered race classification. Thereafter they would be required to carry documentation specifying their race category. Because of the considerable overlap between white and Coloured that had developed in the course of South African history, a strictly scientific classification of these two groups proved impossible. The distinction had to be expressed at least partly in social terms. A white person was defined as one who appears to be white, is accepted as white and normally associates with whites. Heartrending anomalies were not slow to appear, even involving some members of the same family being given different racial classifications.

The main aim of apartheid required that existing legislation denying Africans rights of permanent residence and property ownership outside the reserves be reinforced. Above all it required that the influx of Africans into urban areas be brought under closer control and ultimately halted and reversed. Steps in this direction were taken with the 1952 Native Laws Amendment Act which amended previous urban areas legislation so as to define more narrowly those categories of Africans which had a right to permanent residence in the towns. Section 10 of the Act limited this right to those who had been born in a particular town and had subsequently resided there for a continuous period of not less than fifteen years, or who had been employed in the town for a continuous period of fifteen years, or who had resided in the town and been continuously employed by the same employer for a period of not less than ten years.

The rights of those who fell within this category were restricted to the particular town concerned and gave them no right to move and settle in other urban centres. Even so far as that particular town was concerned, moreover, rights of residence could be revoked and an individual denied the right to live outside the reserve areas if their presence was regarded as not conducive to the public good, if they were unemployed for long periods, or because they were judged redundant to the needs of the white population through ill-health or old age. Nevertheless, the 'Section 10 people' were relatively privileged in relation to migrant workers and over the years their relative advantages became more marked.

The main instrument for the control of African urban influx was a tightening of the system of passes. In 1952 an Act which was ironically called the Abolition of Passes and Consolidation of Documents Act was introduced. In place of the many different passes that Africans had previously often had to carry they were now to have a single reference book including a photograph of the holder and full information on his place of origin, employment record, tax payments, and encounters with the police. It was a criminal offence to be unable to produce this document when required by the police. The requirement to carry such documents was extended to African women who had previously successfully resisted the obligation to carry passes. It was also extended to various groups of Africans who had previously been exempt from the pass laws.

This legislation provided a basis for an elaborate system of control over African migrant labour. Under this system no African could leave a rural area for a town without a permit from the authorities in his local area, and on arrival in the town he was obliged to acquire a permit to seek work within seventy-two hours. Assuming that he succeeded in finding work within the time specified and in the sphere of employment stated in the permit, he then had to seek formal permission to take the employment offered. If he was subsequently to lose his job for any reason he was obliged to obtain a new permit to seek work or be 'endorsed out' of the town.

Apart from control over the influx of African workers to the towns, these measures served the interests of white farmers by helping them keep African labour on the land. Large numbers of Africans attempted to evade, or accidentally fell foul of the system and found themselves brought before the courts and jailed. In farming areas near major urban centres, particularly in the Transvaal, where African farm labour was very difficult to obtain at the low rates offered, farm prisons were established and the labour of prisoners (often pass-law offenders) was made available to the farmers.

Within the urban areas, existing legislation already provided for the segregation of blacks in separate locations. Because of the rapid expansion of some towns, however, particularly Johannesburg, some areas originally set aside as African locations had come to be surrounded by white suburbs. In some cases, moreover, Africans had been able to acquire freehold title to land in these areas and could not be simply required to move. In the war years, new squatter settlements had grown up, often in close proximity to white working-class areas. The National Party government launched a massive scheme to rehouse Africans in fully segregated townships well away from white residential areas and to facilitate this the Native Resettlement Act was passed in 1956. This allowed existing property rights to be extinguished. A number of long-established African settlements in Johannesburg were then destroyed and their inhabitants were forcibly shifted to new

The demolition of District Six,
Cape Town

government-built townships which came to form part of the huge complex to the south-west of Johannesburg, known today as Soweto (from the initials of South Western Townships). Though the standard of housing was on the whole rather better than in the slums and shantytowns that were destroyed, the new settlements were soulless agglomerations of standard housing units set out in rigid geometrical patterns. Their occupants, moreover, were forced to travel much greater distances to work than before and had no security of tenure of their homes.

Though the segregation of residential areas for blacks in the towns had long been customary and was legally enforceable under earlier urban legislation, the situation with regard to Coloured and Indian housing was far less clear cut. Many Indian traders owned shops in white city business areas and often lived over their premises. Whites and Coloureds often lived alongside one another, particularly in the western Cape. In 1950, to abolish this situation and provide stricter racial segregation for all race groups, the government brought in one of its most far-reaching segregationist measures, the Group Areas Act. Under this legislation the government could lay down that any area of the country should be reserved for a particular race group. Members of any other race group who lived or owned businesses in an area so proclaimed would then have to dispose of their property and move to an area prescribed for their own race group. The legislation enabled the authorities to force Indian businesses out of central city areas to the advantage of white traders. Indians were therefore sometimes faced with having to sell their homes and businesses and move to segregated areas well away from the main shopping areas. The most devastating impact was probably felt in Cape Town where the main area of Coloured settlement, District Six, was rezoned for whites. The entire Coloured population of this long-established area was eventually forced to move. Its homes were bulldozed, leaving only churches and mosques standing among the rubble and empty desolation of the once colourful and lively community. Inhabitants were forced to move to much more distant suburbs and this involved the break-up of family networks as well as the burden of much heavier transport costs to get to work in the city; one result was very serious demoralisation and rampant juvenile crime.

Restrictions on industrial action by Africans were also strengthened by legislation. In 1953 the Native Labour (Settlement of Disputes) Act prohibited any strike action by Africans under any circumstances. In 1956 the Industrial Conciliation Act further reinforced race discrimination and segregation in industrial relations and extended the job colour bar. The legislation explicitly excluded Africans from the definition of 'employee' so that they could not form or belong to registered trade unions nor take part in Industrial Council or Conciliation Board proceedings. It also sought to prevent whites and Coloureds from working together in the same unions. No new trade union with mixed racial membership could be registered. Where unions with mixed membership already existed they were obliged to form separate branches for their white and Coloured members. The executive committees of such mixed unions were to be exclusively white and no Coloured worker might attend an executive meeting except for interrogation or explanation. The legislation, moreover, gave the Minister of Labour power to instruct the Industrial Tribunal to investigate any industry, trade or class of work with a view to providing for racial job reservation. On the basis of the Tribunal's recommendations, job reservation determinations could be made. They could provide for the complete or partial reservation of any class of work for people of a particular race and could also specify the proportion of his total employees of persons of a particular race that an employer must employ.

Parallel to the series of measures limiting the rights of black and brown South Africans in the towns went others aimed against those Africans living as independent peasants in predominantly white-owned rural areas. The first step was taken with the Prevention of Illegal Squatting Act in 1951 which carried considerably further the spirit of the 1913 Land Act and the 1936 Natives' Trust and Land Act by giving the Minister of Native Affairs powers to compel African tenants to remove from public or privately owned land. Local authorities were given the power to establish resettlement camps to which these displaced Africans could be allocated.

Social and cultural segregation was increased largely by administrative actions. Post offices were required to provide separate entrances for members of different races and separate coaches for different races were provided on the Cape Town suburban railway system where facilities had previously been used in common.

In 1953, however, the right of government to require persons of different race to use separate amenities was successfully contested in the courts on the grounds that this could not be done unless the amenities supplied to the different groups were substantially equal. In response the government passed the Reservation of Separate Amenities Act. Perhaps more than any other apartheid law, this revealed the belief in inherent racial inequality which underlay the whole policy of apartheid. The legislation not only gave the government power to require members of different races to use separate amenities, but also specifically laid down that the facilities provided for the different groups need not be equal.

An example of segregated facilities

In 1957 the State Aided Institutions Act gave power to enforce segregation in libraries and places of entertainment. A Native Laws Amendment Act gave the government power to prohibit the holding of classes, entertainment and even church services if they were attended by blacks in white areas. It was in this general area that apartheid in its first phase was taken to the most extreme, even absurd lengths. Sport was fully segregated and in particular any interracial physical contest in which a black might defeat a white was strictly prohibited. Thus even when a black South African, Jake Tuli, became Commonwealth boxing champion, he was not allowed to compete against whites in his home country. In the pursuit of greater segregation of the races not only benches in public parks but also sections of South Africa's beaches were set aside for people of different colours. In some areas these were demarcated by wire fences. Not only were black-owned taxis forbidden to carry white passengers but ambulances for blacks could not transport white patients even in an emergency. It was even seriously proposed that blood from a member of one race should not be given to a member of another in blood transfusions.

A fundamental principle of apartheid was that the different races should enjoy separate political development. This meant that Africans should have no part in national political life. The most crucial step in this direction had already been taken by the United Party government in 1936 when Africans were removed from the common voters roll at the Cape by the Native Representation Act. This was taken further by the National Party government by the abolition of the Natives' Representative Council, which had dared to stand up to Smuts. Subsequently, the system under which white Natives' Representatives were elected to parliament under the provision of the Natives' Representation Act was also abolished. In place of a voice in national government each African ethnic group was to be given the opportunity to express itself politically in accordance with its own traditions in one or other of the reserve areas which were thus to be developed into Bantustans.

In 1953 the first steps in this direction were taken with the Bantu Authorities Act. This made provision for the establishment of local authorities in the reserves. These would be dominated by chiefs, whose powers were thus considerably increased. As chiefs were appointed by government the increase in their powers was widely resented and the implementation of the legislation led to serious rural resistance.

At the constitutional level it was the position of the Coloured community which faced the National Party government with its most serious problems. Between the wars Hertzog had regarded the Coloured community as an appendage of the white community which should ultimately be absorbed by it. Malan's National Party supporters, with their racist dogma and obsession with white racial purity were, by contrast, determined to segregate Coloureds from whites as strictly as Africans. Coloured political rights at the Cape, however, were protected by one of the entrenched constitutional clauses which could only be altered by a two-thirds majority of both houses of parliament sitting together. Malan's government believed, however, that as the Statute of Westminster had made South Africa a fully independent country its parliament was a completely sovereign body. It could therefore decide by a simple majority to change anything, including the procedures laid down in its own constitution. In accordance with this a law was drafted under which Coloured voters were to be removed from the common roll at the Cape. They would then be registered on a separate roll and allowed to elect four whites to represent them in the House of Assembly, one in the Senate, two on the Cape Provincial Council. This was introduced as an ordinary bill in March 1951 and passed by a simple majority of both Houses sitting separately. A group of Coloured voters tested the validity of the new legislation, however, and the Appeal Court supported their claim on the grounds that parliament, though sovereign, was only parliament when acting in accordance with its own constitution.

The National Party then tried to find a way of getting round the judicial decision. This took the form of a law, the High Court of Parliament Act, making parliament itself a supreme Appeal Court with overriding powers to judge the validity of legislation. After this was passed the High Court of Parliament met and revalidated the Separate Representation of Voters Act. The same group of Coloured voters appealed again, however, and the High Court of Parliament Act was itself declared invalid by the Appeal Court. The issue had by then raised widespread agitation and protest. Even among nationalist-minded Afrikaners there were doubts about the wisdom of overriding the judiciary. Malan let the matter drop but made the question of separate representation of voters part of the National Party's platform for the 1953 election.

After that election Malan approached the subject again. This time he followed the constitutional procedure laid down in the entrenched clause. Two separate attempts to get a two-thirds majority in a joint sitting of both Houses were made but both narrowly failed. After Malan's retirement in late 1954 his successor, Strydom, adopted yet another approach. The Senate was enlarged to eighty-nine members and procedures for the election of senators were modified to ensure an increased nationalist majority. The Appeal Court was then enlarged by the appointment of a number of judges who were well disposed towards the National Party. The government was then able to obtain the required two-thirds majority in a joint sitting of both Houses. The packed Appeal Court dismissed the appeal of a Coloured voter and the Cape's multiracial franchise was finally completely destroyed.

The theory of apartheid with its doctrine that different races should develop along different lines in accordance with their inherent cultural propensities implies that different races require different types of education. This principle was embodied in one of the National Party government's most far-reaching laws, the 1953 Bantu Education Act. The purpose of the legislation, as its author, Dr Verwoerd, the Minister of Native Affairs, explained, was to prevent Africans being given an education which would lead them to aspire to positions which they would not be allowed to hold in white society. This would be bound to happen if their education was under the control of people who believed in racial equality. It would only produce discontented and frustrated individuals. Instead Africans should be given an educational programme designed specifically to give them the skills necessary to serve their own people in the Bantustans and perform the labouring roles which might be required of them by whites. Under the legislation, African education was to be removed from the charge of the Department of Education and placed under the Department of Native Affairs. All African schools, many of which had previously been run by church missions, would be brought under strict government control and would be required to conform to the government-prescribed syllabus. This would involve emphasis on African vernacular language and the inculcation of basic skills. Afrikaans was to be made compulsory along with English in the higher primary schools. Under the Act the immediate management of African schools was placed under the control of African school boards and Africans were expected to pay a higher proportion of the cost of educating their children than in the past.

In 1957 the move towards educational apartheid was taken to its logical conclusion with the introduction of legislation designed to put an end to the situation in which some of the white universities (mainly the University of Cape Town and the University of Witwatersrand) admitted black and brown students to common university programmes with whites. Instead separate universities were to be provided for Indian and Coloured students and for each of the main African ethnic groups. Members of staff of these ethnic universities would be liable to dismissal if they opposed the government's racial policies. The ironically named Extension of University Education Act was vigorously opposed by the South African universities but finally became law in 1959.

The massive reorganisation of south African society envisaged in the government's apartheid programme threatened disruption and suffering for thousands of people. Its openly racist principles were not only bitterly offensive to black and brown political leaders but to idealistic whites also. To enable it to suppress anticipated opposition to its policies the government introduced the Suppression of Communism Act in 1950. The Act not only outlawed the Communist Party in South Africa but defined communism in terms so broad as to cover any call for radical change in South Africa. Persons named as communists under this broad definition could then be banned from participation in political organisations, ordered to remove from their homes or restricted to particular areas of South Africa. It was an important first step in creating the machinery for the systematic suppression of radical opposition.

The impact of baaskap *apartheid on
black and brown South Africans*

The introduction of apartheid in 1948 brought to an end the tendency towards very limited opening up of South African society that had manifested itself during the war and in the immediate post-war years. Probably its most important effect was to help ensure that the growing wealth created by continuing economic growth was not passed on to the black and brown peoples to any significant extent. While industrial growth continued apace, the poor-white problem was virtually eliminated and the living standards of the white population rose steadily. Africans and Coloureds and many Indians continued to live in artificially induced poverty and squalor.

The measures taken to control urban influx limited and distorted the process of urbanisation encouraged by industrial expansion. They artificially held many people back in poverty-stricken circumstances on the reserves or in the white farming areas and made it very difficult for Africans to settle in the towns as family groups, thus increasing the proportion of single male migrant workers. This in turn undermined the stability of family life both in the countryside where wives and children were left for long periods without their husbands, and in the towns, where many women were forced to raise families without stable male support. Some formed informal associations with other solo mothers. One member could then mind the children while the others went out to work.

The pass system in particular not only subjected most Africans to frequent humiliation, but also to constant insecurity and anxiety. As many Africans came into towns in defiance of the regulations, a significant proportion of the population of the black townships lived outside the law, continually at risk of being discovered and arrested. Even an established urban resident, if he left his reference book at home, or mislaid it or had it stolen, could find himself arrested and convicted and hustled off to perform what amounted to slave labour on a prison farm before his family or his employer could find out what had happened to him. The proportion of the black population who experienced arrest and punishment for pass law offences steadily rose. As the police continued and increased the practice of raiding African townships and turning people out of bed at all hours of the night, the bitterness and hatred of the majority of the people towards them was greatly increased.

In these circumstances of poverty, family instability and insecurity, crime and particularly juvenile crime flourished. Gangs of young thugs known as *tsotsis*, many of them the mentally unstable products of appalling home backgrounds, expanded and intensified their activities. Robbing, raping and murdering, they terrorised the population of the African townships. Faced with heightened barriers against their integration with white society, migrant workers openly rejected Western culture and emphasised traditional customs and their rural links. The gap between them and the more Westernised town dwellers, the *kholwa* (school people), increased. In spite of the difficulties they faced, however, the majority of Africans, Indians and Coloureds in the towns retained their balance and their determination to advance themselves and their children through acquiring more skills and knowledge. The poor school buildings and ill-equipped classrooms in the townships were always thronged with eager learners who became increasingly frustrated as the implementation of the Bantu Education Act lowered standards and multiplied the obstacles in the way of individual progress.

On the cultural front government action in removing some of the older townships around Johannesburg destroyed vital centres of cultural life to rehouse their occupants in sterile, barrack-like conditions. Even in these circumstances, however, Africans soon created a host of cultural activities for themselves. Illicit drinking places known as 'shebeens' could never be completely suppressed and served as the focus for much active discussion and cultural interchange. Pop music groups sprang up and flourished. In spite of pitifully inadequate amenities sporting groups developed and occupied the leisure time of some. For many others church activities provided the main focus of cultural and social life. There were the ceremonies of many different independent churches whose rites were often very lively and marked by much singing and dancing, as well as the orthodox services of the established churches. In spite of the poverty, squalor and ugly dreariness of the township environment and the constant fear, both of criminals and of the police, they were probably the most vital centres of social and cultural life in the country.

Among the most serious effects of the development of *baaskap* apartheid was the destruction of hope in peaceful progress through individual effort and its replacement with frustration and anger. While economic progress continued, black and brown South Africans found themselves blocked or severely hindered by deliberate legislation or government action from making the best of new opportunities in the workplace. They saw themselves ever more firmly shut out from common fellowship with whites. Their sense of pride and self-worth was daily more bitterly affronted and insulted by the multiplication of 'whites only' notices.

White opposition to apartheid

In its first years in office the National Party government faced a United Party opposition that was badly weakened by the deaths of Hofmeyr in 1948 and of Smuts in 1950. Under the rather colourless leadership of J.G.N. Strauss and his successors, the United Party – many of whose members shared the race attitudes of the nationalists – failed to produce a convincing alternative to apartheid. Support for the United Party declined throughout the period of *baaskap* apartheid and by the end of the 1950s it had become almost irrelevant to the political life of the country. Only the battle over the attempt to remove the Coloured voters from the common roll at the Cape gave the United Party temporary vitality. The main effort, however, was not made by the United Party itself but by a new extra-parliamentary movement dedicated to the defence of the constitution.

The Torch Commando

In 1951 a number of ex-servicemen, including A.G. Malan ('Sailor Malan'), an Afrikaner who had served in the British Royal Air Force during the Battle of Britain and won a reputation as an air hero, founded the movement to resist nationalist attempts to violate the constitution. The Torch Commando appealed to white Afrikaner ex-servicemen in the first place but soon acquired a rapidly expanding membership among English-speaking white South Africans. It held open mass meetings and demonstrations often in the form of torchlight processions. It attracted large crowds and several serious clashes with National Party supporters took place. For a time civil war between sections of the white population seemed a possibility.

Support for the Torch Commando was, however, mainly based on English-speaking white South Africans' fears for their own language and other rights. Few of the supporters of the movement had much real concern for the rights of Coloured people that were the issue on which the constitutional controversy arose. Thus, though the movement was supposedly dedicated to the protection of Coloured voting rights, no agreement could be reached on admitting Coloureds as members. In November 1951 Coloured ex-servicemen severed their association with the movement in disgust. As soon as the government abandoned its attempt to override the constitution directly, the Torch Commando rapidly declined. Its support for the United Party in the 1953 election failed to prevent the voters' swing to the nationalist government.

In the aftermath of this setback a small number of whites founded the multiracial Liberal Party in 1953 with the aim of working towards a non-racial South Africa. The party included some outstanding intellectuals and had a strong appeal to liberal-minded idealists of all races. For some time it offered significant competition to the African, Indian and Coloured political movements and to more Marxist-orientated white movements for the loyalties of such people. Its voter support among the white electorate was never more than tiny, however. Its members suffered severely from government repressive measures and the party was finally forced to wind up as a result of legislation prohibiting multiracial parties.

Also in 1953, a more radical white group, the Congress of Democrats, was founded. Its membership was always very small. Outside of parliament significant numbers of whites continued to fight for a more just society. One public movement that proved long-lived was a women's movement known as the Black Sash. It began in 1955 when Strydom enlarged the Senate and finally succeeded in overturning the entrenched clause in the constitution protecting Coloured rights. A number of white women with black sashes over their shoulders as a sign of mourning for the constitution posted themselves oustide buildings whenever government ministers were present. The movement subsequently developed into a liberal white women's pressure group concerned with humanitarian and civil rights issues generally.

The introduction of apartheid and the intensification of discrimination at a time of growing political consciousness and rising expectation among black and brown South Africans provoked an organised movement of mass peaceful defiance on a scale far in excess of anything that had ever happened in South Africa before. At the December 1949 conference of the ANC, its militant Youth League triumphed over more conservative tendencies. A 'Programme of Action' to abolish racial discrimination by mass action involving boycotts, strikes, civil disobedience and non-co-operation was adopted. Dr J.S. Moroka was elected as president in place of the more moderate Dr A.B. Xuma. Walter Sisulu, an active member of the Youth League, became General Secretary and a number of other Youth Leaguers were elected to the National Executive Committee. A Council of Action was set up to prepare the implementation of the programme.

The conference took place at a time of deep concern over divisions between black and brown South Africans. Poverty and frustration worsened by deliberate race discrimination had inevitably tended to increase tension between sections of the oppressed populations. Those between Africans and Indians in Natal were particularly acute. Indians formed a very closed community. They tended to monopolise small trading activities to which Africans aspired. Trading largely with Africans they, like others in this business, offered credit on high interest to their hard-pressed clientele. In a social atmosphere poisoned by white assertions of inherent race superiority, they made no secret of their belief in their own superiority to black Africans. In January 1949 a minor incident, in which an Indian trader struck a young Zulu boy, had triggered violent riots between Africans and Indians in Durban. In three days of fighting 142 people were killed and over a thousand were injured.

Leaders of the two communities moved rapidly to heal the breach. While the rioting was continuing the popular Zulu leader, A.G. Champion (previously of the ICU), then president of the Natal branch of the ANC, and Dr Yusuf Dadoo of the Natal Indian Congress issued a joint call to their supporters to help stop the rumours that had started the conflict. Later, in response to a call by the then ANC president, Dr Xuma, thirty-five leaders of the South African Indian Congress and the African National Congress met in Durban to discuss racial intolerance. The riots had paradoxically brought Indian and African leaders closer together than ever before.

At its December 1949 Congress the ANC called for the establishment of joint councils of Africans and Indians to diffuse hostility and build up goodwill. Early in 1950 the ANC, the Transvaal Indian Congress and the

Provincial Branch of the African Peoples' Organisations (the now nearly defunct Coloured people's party) called a one-day strike for 1 May in protest against restrictions placed on two African and one Indian leader who had previously been members of the Communist Party. The strike was also intended to support calls for higher wages and other workers' demands. Some members of the ANC Youth League feared that their Programme of Action was being taken over by non-African and communist influence. Nevertheless, co-operation in mass action was continued with a call for another one-day strike on 26 June. Then in June 1951 planning began for a massive and sustained campaign of passive resistance against discriminatory measures. A joint conference of the African National Congress (ANC) and the South African Indian Congress (SAIC) thus set up a Joint Planning Council with equal African and Indian representation. The plan envisaged a three-stage programme of passive resistance to discriminatory laws. In the first stage a number of carefully selected volunteers were openly to breach selected discriminatory laws in the major cities and welcome arrest. In the second stage, building on the enthusiasm generated in the first, the number of volunteers would be increased. In the third stage the movement would be spread to all urban areas and into the countryside as well. Mass participation of the whole populace would be invited. This would be supported by strikes and demonstrations until the whole system of racial discrimination collapsed.

The campaign began on 26 June 1952 with small batches of volunteers breaking segregation laws and courting arrest. It spread slowly from Port Elizabeth and East London to the smaller towns of the Eastern Cape and from Johannesburg to twelve other cities on the Rand. It got going in Cape Town and a number of centres in the western Cape in August and in September began to make an impact in Bloemfontein and Durban. The campaign steadily gained momentum until October. Protesters went to gaol in hundreds, demonstrating an impressive capacity for discipline and self-sacrifice. Tremendous enthusiasm was generated. ANC membership soared and may have reached a hundred thousand at its high point. In the towns in particular, African political consciousness was aroused to an unprecedented degree. The campaign also attracted considerable attention abroad and contributed to the United Nations General Assembly decision to establish a permanent committee on the racial situation in South Africa.

The government, however, took stern action in a determined effort to smash the movement. On 30 July homes of ANC and SAIC members were raided and papers were seized. In August and September leaders of the movement in the Transvaal, Natal and the Eastern Cape were arrested and charged under the Suppression of Communism Act.

Then, on 18 October, violent rioting broke out in the African township of New Brighton near Port Elizabeth. Similar riots followed in Johannesburg, Kimberley and East London in November. The riots were unplanned, spontaneous outbursts born of pent-up suffering and frustration. The crowds stoned police and burned down government and other public buildings in the townships. In the mood of mass hysteria the crowds in some cases attacked whites who happened to be in the townships, without discrimination. A nurse in East London was one of the six whites killed. In response the police set up road blocks and opened fire with automatic weapons. In the East London locations, eyewitnesses reported seeing and hearing bursts of Sten gun fire throughout the night. The official figure of

Women leaving jail after being imprisoned for taking part in the Defiance Campaign, 1952

about forty killed almost certainly underestimates the true situation. The ruthless response was, however, successful on this occasion in bringing the disturbances to an end very quickly.

The riots almost certainly had no connection with the defiance campaign though the excitement and hope it generated may have increased tension in the townships. They provided the government with an ideal opportunity to smear the movement, however. Though the ANC called for an enquiry which the government refused, many whites held the ANC at least indirectly responsible for the outbursts. In this atmosphere the government issued a proclamation under which anyone (including whites) who influenced Africans to break any laws could be heavily fined or imprisoned for three years. Many Africans were horrified at the violence of the riots and lost enthusiasm for further participation in the defiance campaign. It continued to the end of the year but gradually fizzled out as support dwindled. It had failed to achieve any concession from the government. Indeed the campaign and the riots between them strengthened the government's position by frightening the white population and so contributing to the National Party election victory in 1953.

With the collapse of the mass defiance campaign, the ANC and the SAIC suffered a serious loss of morale. Dr Moroka, the ANC president, lost much support when he pleaded not guilty to offences committed during the defiance campaign instead of welcoming imprisonment. At the end of 1953 he was replaced by Albert Luthuli. Attempts to organise resistance to the forced removals of African settlements in Johannesburg and to combat the Bantu Education Act by providing alternative schooling collapsed. ANC membership suffered a sharp decline. Then at the December 1953 conference a new initiative involving a massive peoples conference to define a charter of liberties for a future South Africa was proposed. Discussions were held with the SAIC, the South African Coloured People's Organisation, and the Congress of Democrats. After many small-scale planning meetings, the Congress of the People finally met at Kliptown in 1955. It was attended by about three thousand people of all races. It adopted a Freedom Charter which pronounced that South Africa belonged to all its inhabitants and called for a non-racial democracy, the removal of all discriminatory legislation, and equal opportunities in education and work for persons of all races. It also called for the nationalisation of the banks, mines and heavy industry and the redistribution of land.

The Congress of the People evoked a dramatic government response. The houses and offices of leading participants were raided and on 5 December 1956 leaders of all the participating race groups were arrested and charged with treason. Though the numbers of those facing charges were successively reduced at different stages of the mammoth trial, thirty were still before the court when proceedings finally ended on 29 November 1961. All the accused were acquitted. Though the government had failed to prove its case against any of them, however, it had kept a substantial portion of the radical leadership of all races out of circulation for a long period. The impact of the trial on the lives and careers of those involved, moreover, demonstrated the heavy penalties which might befall those who expressed radical opinions even if finally found innocent.

Albert Luthuli

Frustration at the apparent impotence of the Congress Alliance in face of government determination provoked internal dissension in the ANC, while it was deprived of much of its top leadership through their involvement in the treason trial. Some members of the Youth League had always been suspicious of co-operation with other race groups in common protest. In particular, they mistrusted white radicals and their socialist ideology. In November 1958 Robert Sobukwe with a number of supporters walked out of the Transvaal Congress of the ANC in protest at the policy of multiracial alliances. In March 1959 the Pan-Africanist Congress (PAC) was formed. Though the PAC rejected co-operation with other race groups and was particularly opposed to radical socialist ideas held by some members of the ANC, its ultimate ideal, like that of the ANC, was a non-racial South Africa. Though limiting membership to Africans only, it subsequently adopted a definition of 'African' under which even whites could and did join the organisation. The formation of the PAC was followed by acute rivalry between it and the ANC for the leadership of African resistance to apartheid.

Though nationwide political protest against apartheid was channelled through the ANC, Africans in different parts of the country offered resistance to aspects of the system in a variety of ways. Some of the most bitter resistance took place in the rural areas. Enforcement of the regulations requiring women to carry passes meant bitter resistance in many areas and was particularly strong in the Hurutshe Reserve of the western Transvaal. Pass books were burned and officials distributing them stoned.

The introduction of Tribal Authorities under the 1951 Bantu Autorities Act also provoked serious resistance. In May 1958 serious rioting broke out in the Pedi country in the northern Transvaal following the deposition of a chief and his replacement by a government nominee in the course of the introduction of a Tribal Authority. In the same year a serious and widespread rural revolt broke out in Pondoland. In opposition to the new system, Mpondo rebels withdrew to the hills and established a 'mountain committee' as a nucleus of an independent alternative government. Huts of government informers were burned and widespread intimidation was employed against all who followed government instructions. White storekeepers were warned to co-operate with the rebels or have their premises boycotted. The insurrection continued for several months and was only suppressed with the use of armoured units and planes.

In the urban areas, in spite of government legislation, African trade union organisation survived and showed itself capable of impressive strike action in support of the ANC political leadership. One of the most effective forms of urban African protest was a prolonged boycott of municipal buses in Johannesburg in protest against an increase in fares. In face of persistent government harassment thousands of Africans walked long distances to work for a prolonged period until the authorities finally gave in. The deep anger and frustration which had burst out in the violent riots of 1952 could not be entirely contained within disciplined movements, however. In 1959 it burst out again in the Durban African township of Cato Manor. There a police liquor raid sparked off serious rioting and nine policemen were killed.

At its annual conference in Durban in December 1959 the ANC decided to launch a mass anti-pass campaign on the 31 March 1960. The PAC then

People fleeing from police fire at
Sharpeville, 21 March 1960

decided to get in first and announced its own campaign for the 21st of that
month. On that day there were widespread demonstrations in which
Sobukwe and many of his followers deliberately broke the pass laws and were
arrested. At Sharpeville a large crowd gathered outside the police station.
Some had come without their passbooks intending to court arrest. Others
had the impression that an important announcement about the pass laws was
about to be made. As the crowd milled around the station some of the police
seemed to have fears that the fence was about to collapse. Suddenly they
opened fire and as the unarmed crowd fled in panic the police continued to
fire into it. Of the sixty-nine people killed most were shot in the back. In
addition 180 people were wounded. The Sharpeville massacre aroused
massive world-wide protest. It marked a major turning point in popular
attitudes to the South African situation in the Western world. So great was
the international reaction that there was a considerable net outflow of
capital from the country until government restrictions on currency movement stemmed the loss. Within South Africa, Luthuli identified the ANC
with the PAC protest. On 27 March he publicly burned his passbook and
called for a national stay at home the next day in mourning for those killed.
The summons met with a wide response. On 30 March, however, the police
struck back with a series of raids and over the next few days over 18 000
people were arrested. Police action on 30 March coincided with outbreaks of
rioting in a number of centres. The PAC led protest movements in Cape
Town and Durban. That afternoon the government declared a state of

emergency in 122 districts of the country. The Active Citizens Force (a white army reserve) was mobilised and employed to seal off the African townships of Langa and Nyanga near Cape Town. On 8 April both the ANC and the PAC were declared illegal organisations.

The opening of armed struggle

In 1961, ex-members of the ANC under the leadership of Nelson Mandela made a last attempt to persuade the government of the need for radical change by peaceful means. They issued a demand backed by the threat of a national strike that a convention of all races should meet to work out a new constitution. The government rejected the demand out of hand and the strike gained only limited support. Most ANC leaders now at last became convinced that there was no hope of achieving political change in South Africa by peaceful means. Mandela went underground and a militant wing of the ANC, Umkhonto we Sizwe (Spear of the Nation), was formed to undertake a campaign of sabotage of public installations in the hope of forcing the white population to recognise the need for change. The ANC leaders' commitment to non-violence was still so strong, however, that the campaign at this stage was to be strictly restricted to sabotage of material installations. Great care was taken to avoid loss of human life. The campaign began on 16 December 1961, the Afrikaners' 'Day of the Covenant'. About twenty sabotage attempts were made on pylons, post offices, gaols, railways and Tribal Authorities' premises. The PAC also formed a fighting organisation called Poqo with a commitment to outright guerrilla warfare. During 1962 and 1963 its members killed a number of policemen and government informers in the western Cape and attempts were also made to kill Chief Kaiser Matanzima and other government-supported chiefs in the Transkei. Both the ANC and the PAC established headquarters outside South Africa with offices in Dar es Salaam, London, Cairo, Algiers and elsewhere. Small numbers of black South Africans began slipping out of the country illegally to join these organisations and to undertake training for guerrilla warfare.

Nelson Mandela before imprisonment

South Africa becomes a republic and leaves the Commonwealth

In the meantime, Verwoerd moved to cap the creation of the legal framework of apartheid by achieving the Afrikaner nationalists' long-cherished dream of making South Africa a republic. The issue was put to a referendum of white voters on 6 October 1960 and secured a clear overall majority. The change in South Africa's constitutional status, however, raised the question of its continued membership of the Commonwealth. The Commonwealth Prime Ministers' Conference in 1960 declared itself unable to decide the question in advance. When South Africa's application for continued membership was considered at the 1961 Prime Ministers' Conference it met so much opposition from leaders of African countries that Verwoerd was forced to withdraw it. On 31 May 1961 the republican constitution came into force. Instead of the British monarch being head of state, represented by a governor-general, there was now a state president chosen by parliament. Like the governor-general before him, however, he had no executive powers in his own right. Government was still carried out by a prime minister and cabinet chosen by and from the majority party in the parliament. Parliament remained exclusively white and guarantees for the equality of the English and Afrikaans languages were retained. South Africa's international situation was modified, however, and its isolation significantly increased by the fact that when it adopted republican status it ceased to be a member of the Commonwealth.

From baaskap *apartheid to separate development*

In the period from 1959 to 1961 when the National Party government was completing the framework of *baaskap* apartheid and crowning its achievements by transforming South Africa into an Afrikaner republic, the fundamental basis of apartheid policy was beginning to change. The main reasons for this were the major changes which had taken and were taking place in the wider world since 1948, the changing economy of South Africa and the need to defuse growing African militancy.

Ever since 1948 South Africa had been the target of continuous international criticism. South Africa, by openly embodying racism in law, increasing inequality by government action and removing rights that had been previously enjoyed, was moving in exactly the opposite direction to the rest of the world. There, with the progress of decolonisation, the yellow, brown and black races were emerging from white rule in the European colonial empires to form independent sovereign nations and to be accepted, nominally at least, as equals in world forums. Until the later 1950s, however, the process was still in its early stages. It had affected Asia much more than Africa. The United Nations was still effectively dominated by the United States and its allies. South Africa, though having to face much criticism, especially over its role in South West Africa, was protected from more than verbal assault by the extent and profitability of Western investment in the country as well as by Western preoccupation with the struggle against communism.

By the end of the 1950s the situation was changing significantly. The independence of Ghana in 1957 brought a strong African voice to the United Nations General Assembly. It also marked the beginning of rapid decolonisation of European colonial empires in Africa. By the end of the 1950s many black states in west and east Africa were on the brink of independence. It was also clear by this time that south Africa's long-cherished aim of absorbing the three High Commission Territories, Basutoland (now Lesotho), Swaziland and the Bechuanaland Protectorate (now Botswana), was never going to be achieved. Like Britain's other African colonial territories they were destined to become independent black nations. South Africa could thus no longer continue to ignore the reality of the sovereign status of black nations. While it had earlier been so contemptuous of black African pretensions to political sovereignty that it had rejected out of hand an invitation from the Ghanaian prime minister, Kwame Nkrumah, to attend the 1956 Pan Africanist Congress in Accra. It now recognised that it must find some basis for peaceful co-existence and co-operation with African states and their leaders. This message was brought home to many white South Africans by the British Prime Minister, Harold Macmillan, in his address to the South African parliament on 3 February 1960 when he spoke of South Africa's need to adapt itself to the 'wind of change' blowing through Africa.

Within the South African economy, moreover, manufacturing had become by far the largest sector. So long as the purchasing power of the majority in

South Africa remained disproportionally low the nation needed to find export markets for much of its production. Increased exports were needed, moreover, to help pay for the high level of imports required for continuing rapid economic growth and technological advance. The new states of Africa appeared to offer the most obvious opportunities for such exports.

At the political level the defiance campaign, the violent outbreaks in rural and urban areas and the reaction to Sharpeville both within and without South Africa not only provoked fiercer oppression but also increased the government's desire to find some way of diverting African political aspirations away from the key issue of control of the South African economic heartland.

The first steps towards a significant change in the character of apartheid came as early as 1959 and were initiated by Dr Verwoerd himself. In 1966, however, he was assassinated in peculiarly dramatic circumstances. A parliamentary messenger who had apparently once been employed as a spy for South Africa walked up to the Prime Minister as he stood on the floor of the House of Assembly and stabbed him to death. The assassin was subsequently declared insane. Verwoerd was succeeded by J.B. Vorster, previously Minister of Justice and architect of some of the most repressive features of South Africa's security system. Under his more pragmatic leadership the second phase in the development of apartheid reached its fullest development.

New policy for the Bantustans

The key to the change in direction of policy was a new approach to the future of the Bantustans. Before 1959 the intention had been that the furthest the Bantustans would be allowed to go was the development of a significant measure of local self-government along tribal lines under white trusteeship. In introducing the Promotion of Bantu Self-Government Bill to parliament in 1959, however, Dr Verwoerd argued that although this was not what white South Africans would have liked, they would have to accept that the Bantustans must be allowed to develop into fully fledged states which might eventually become fully independent nations and members of the United Nations. This would involve breaking up the territory of South Africa into a white state and a number of black states.

However grudgingly adopted, this new policy involved an important change in the basic principles of apartheid. It meant abandoning the idea that different races had inherently different cultural potential, that modern technological civilisation was the cultural expression of the white race alone and that African peoples were destined to express themselves through traditional tribal cultures. It was now accepted in theory at least that the Bantustans were to develop into modern nation states, the sovereign equals of European powers. This meant that open assertion of the inherent inequality of persons of different race was being abandoned. A new way of justifying the white monopoly of power in the economic heartland of South Africa was being prepared. Instead of justifying discrimination against blacks in the heartland of South Africa openly on grounds of race, it would now be done on the grounds that they were citizens of separate states. It was hoped that South Africa's policies could now be made to seem in line with worldwide developments instead of opposed to them. Instead of a system of increased segregation and discrimination, apartheid was to be presented as a system of internal decolonisation.

In setting the African nations of South Africa free, Verwoerd argued, the white man would win his own freedom and the right to retain control of his own country. As Mr G.F. van L. Froneman, chairman of the Bantu Affairs Commission, put it in a speech to the Institute of Citizenship in 1968:

The Government's policy is therefore not a policy of discrimination on the ground of race or colour, but a policy of differentiation on the ground of nationhood of different nations, granting to each self-determination within the borders of their homelands – hence this policy of separate development (Quoted in Desmond, n.d., p.42.)

In opening the way for the constitutional progress of the Bantustans towards eventual independence, moreover, avenues would be created for politically ambitious Africans to seek power and office in these new states. This would divert their attention away from the white-ruled economic heartland. The resentment of Africans in the Bantustans themselves would also be directed against their black governments rather than the government of South Africa as a whole. In accordance with the new image that South Africa sought to present to the world, the word apartheid, which had acquired a bad image in the world at large, was increasingly replaced by the term 'separate development'. The reserves were now referred to as African 'homelands'. The term native was dropped altogether in favour of Bantu.

The idealistic tone of the new approach to apartheid was in serious conflict, however, with the practical situation of the Bantustans. The government had no intention of increasing their area very significantly beyond that provided in Hertzog's 1936 Natives Trust and Land Act. Not only did they in total amount to no more than 13.5 per cent of the total land area of South Africa but the area of individual Bantustans varied considerably from the quite substantial size and resources of the Transkei to tiny Basotho Qwaqwa, arbitrarily designated as the homeland of over a million Southern Sotho-speakers in South Africa. None of them, moreover, could possibly support the populations to be assigned to them. They could only serve as labour dormitories for the white South African economy and as convenient dumping grounds for blacks whose labour was not needed by white employers. Many of them were divided into numbers of fragments separated by white-owned territory. Political independence in such circumstances could be no more than a cruel farce.

Constitutional development of the Bantustans

The first major step towards the constitutional development of the Bantustans came in 1963 when the Transkei was granted a considerable measure of self-government. Ironically, in order to ensure that the Transkei would exercise this authority in accordance with a policy of 'separate development', the government had to exercise its influence to impose a prime minister on the territory in opposition to the majority vote. The self-governing constitution provided that 64 of the 109 seats in the Assembly should be held by chiefs. In the 1963 election Victor Poto who strongly opposed 'separate development' won thirty-eight out of the forty eight elected seats. The support of the chiefs who owed their appointment to the South African government, however, enabled it to ensure that Kaiser Matanzima, a supporter of 'separate development', would become prime minister. Progress in the other Bantustans was much slower. As late as 1971 the Transkei was still the only one to have a Legislative Assembly. Thereafter, however,

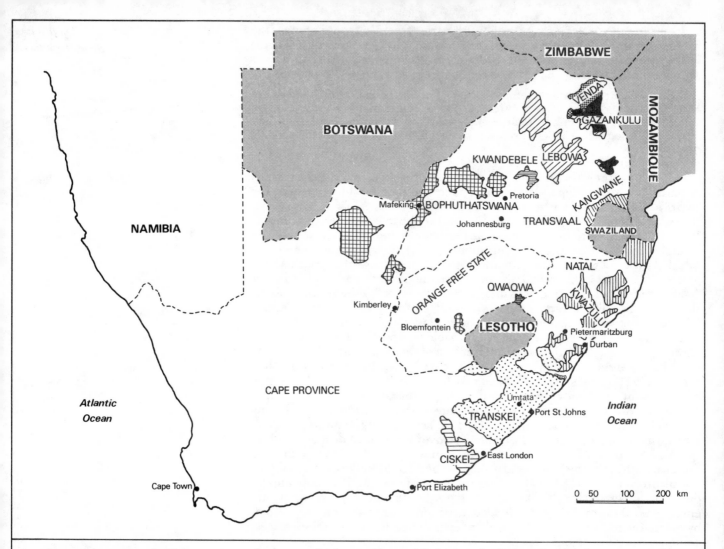

9.1 Contemporary South Africa, showing the Bantustans (Homelands)

Economic development of the Bantustans

these were fairly rapidly established in the Ciskei, Bophuthatswana, Lebowa, Gazankulu, Venda, Basotho Qwaqwa and KwaZulu.

During the period of *baaskap* apartheid the South African government had paid no more than lip service to the idea of developing the African reserves to anything more than the labour reserve areas they had long been. The government's own commission, the Tomlinson Commission, had recommended in 1954 that white investment in the reserves should be encouraged and the government itself spend £104 million sterling in the first ten years to establish industries and create employment there. The government, however, banned white investment in the reserves on the ground that it was contrary to apartheid and in the period 1956–61 it spent only £7.9 million sterling on the territories. With the adoption of the new approach of 'separate development', spending was very considerably increased and the ban on white investments in the area was lifted. Some industrial develop-

214

ment and some mining was started within the Bantustans. Only a small proportion of government expenditure was directed towards genuine industrialisation of the areas or job creation within them, however. Far the greater part went on housing and township development to accommodate the greatly expanded population that was to be forced into or artificially held back within them.

In spite of the theory of 'separate development', the government's answer to the problem of employment in the Bantustans was to encourage the establishment of industries on the borders of the 'homelands'. The black labour force for these industries would commute across the border every day, earning its living in the white area but having its home in the Bantustan. When the 'homeland' in question became independent, workers would automatically become foreigners in South Africa with no citizen rights at their place of work. Industries were encouraged to establish in these border areas by the availability of black labour at lower rates than in the city centres. They were also allowed to employ blacks in a variety of skilled jobs still at that period reserved for whites elsewhere in South Africa. In practice border industries were generally only successfully established at quite short distances from existing major industrial centres. In some cases, indeed, 'homeland' borders were deliberately extended to take in the African townships near white cities. The African township of Umlazi outside Durban, for example, was declared part of KwaZulu in this way. Its people continued to work in Durban as before but now found themselves living on what was planned to be ultimately declared foreign soil.

A major feature of the period of 'separate development' was a new approach towards black African states. This involved not only the more distant states of west and east Africa but the states of Lesotho, Botswana and Swaziland, which lay as enclaves within the borders of South Africa, and the emerging political and bureaucratic elites of the Bantustans as well. In the attempt to establish good relations with Lesotho, Vorster had a personal meeting with Chief Leabua Jonathan in 1966 and was photographed shaking his hand. Similar meetings were held with Seretse Khama of Botswana in 1968 and Prime Minister Makhosini Dhlamini of Swaziland in 1971.

To further the policy official delegates and other important visitors from the black states were accorded a status amounting to that of 'honorary whites'. A select number of the more expensive hotels in the main centres as well as at Jan Smuts International Airport outside Johannesburg were allowed to abandon race segregation and offer accommodation to blacks. This began a gradual, fitful and far from consistent process of reducing racial segregation (so-called petty apartheid). Regulations enforcing segregation in a number of areas, such as the use of park benches, entrances to public buildings and some bathing beaches were abolished or simply no longer enforced. Pressure from the international sporting community which resulted in the exclusion of South Africa from most international competition brought a new look at segregation in this area also. An initial concession was made when a Maori player was accepted as a member of a New Zealand rugby team to play in South Africa. Thereafter the ban on multiracial sport was progressively eroded. It even became possible for boxing matches between whites and blacks to be staged. At the base of the system, however, schools and sporting clubs generally remained strictly segregated and the opportunities and equipment available to would-be sportsmen of different race grossly unequal.

In spite of intense diplomatic efforts including several trips to meet black African leaders by Vorster himself, South Africa's outward-looking policy and its call for dialogue with black African states was fairly widely rebuffed. It did achieve some success, however. The greatest of these was the establishment of formal diplomatic links with Malawi. After a delegation of Malawian leaders had toured South Africa, formal diplomatic relations were opened in 1967. To avoid embarrassing South Africa, Malawi first chose a white as its diplomatic representative in Pretoria but soon afterwards a black Malawian was appointed and accorded the same social privileges as his white fellows in the diplomatic community. Relations with Malawi reached their high point in 1971 when Dr Kamuzu Banda, President of Malawi, made an extensive, highly publicised state visit to South Africa. In return for his friendship South Africa offered Malawi substantial loans and other assistance, notably with the building of a new capital at Lilongwe.

Once separate nationhood rather than race and colour became the base on which discrimination was justified it became much more important to the ruling white elite in South Africa that the great majority of blacks should be made citizens of the Bantustans. To achieve this the principle that blacks could be in the towns only when needed by white employers was to be enforced much more strictly and blacks not needed by the white economy were to be sent to the Bantustans. Urban influx and the distribution of black labour was to be more rigidly controlled and migrant labourers prevented from bringing their families to town and eventually acquiring rights of residence there. In the white rural areas a major move was started to remove the remaining communities of African peasants living on their own land or on that of missions or as tenants on white-owned farms. These so-called black spots were to be eliminated and their people moved beyond Bantustan boundaries. In some cases these boundaries were themselves changed to allow consolidation of the Bantustans into larger blocks. In these cases, too, settled populations were to be forcibly removed.

J.B. Vorster

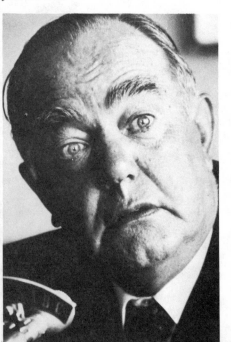

Thus the other face of the relaxation of some aspects of apartheid was a much more drastic implementation of others. The most cruel of these was the forced removal of huge numbers of Africans from the towns and white-owned rural areas to the 'homelands' which involved a disruption of African life on a scale far greater than anything which took place before 1960. In relation to the towns a government circular stated,

It is accepted Government policy that the Bantu are only temporarily resident in the European areas of the Republic, for as long as they offer their labour there. As soon as they become, for some reason or another, no longer fit for work or superfluous in the labour market, they are expected to return to their country of origin, or the territory of the national unit where they fit in ethnically if they were not born and bred in the homeland . . . no stone is to be left unturned to achieve the settlement in the homelands of non-productive Bantu at present residing in the European areas. (Quoted in Desmond, n.d., p.42.)

The category of unproductive Bantu included 'the aged, the unfit, widows, women with dependent children' (quoted in Desmond, n.d., p.43) and other superfluous Bantu resident in European urban areas. With regard to the rural areas, not only independent African peasants but farm workers and

Resettlement camp at Ramatlabama, Bophutatswana

their families living on white farms in excess of continuous requirement were to be moved into the Bantustans.

Though some of these groups had owned their land for as much as a hundred years this gave them no protection. Many had been able to farm and keep cattle in their previous homes. As government admitted, however, 'As a result of a shortage of adequate land it is not possible to settle all these people, together with their cattle, in the homelands on an agricultural basis and consequently it is imperative that, before they are settled in some town or settlement, they must first sell their cattle, sheep and goats' (quoted in Desmond, n.d., pp.49–50). They were thus not only to be forcibly removed to the Bantustans but also deprived of their main source of income. Altogether between one and three million Africans were moved into the Bantustans in this period. The resettlement camps to which they were sent often lacked anything approaching satisfactory accommodation, health or education facilities and were at a great distance from any source of employment. While rural Africans settled there often lost their stock those from urban areas were cut off from friends, relatives and the familiar environment of the towns. They found themselves dumped among strangers in a bleak and unfamiliar environment offering little opportunity for a meaningful life. As the *Rand Daily Mail* reported on the settlement at Morsgat:

Poor, often non-existent facilities; unhealthy and degrading living conditions; additional costs eroding wages that are far too low; the enforced break-up of families. These are the morale shattering hardships responsible for a comment that is heard again and again in Morsgat: 'We have been thrown away' (quoted in Desmond, n.d., p.256.)

Within the towns control over the influx of African workers was tightened further by the 1964 Bantu Laws Amendment Act. This provided for a nationwide network of labour bureaux intended to exercise complete control over the movements of all Africans outside the homelands and to ensure that their labour was distributed precisely in accordance with the needs of white employers. As part of the policy of preventing further

217

permanent African settlement in the towns, African workers were prevented from bringing their families with them. A policy of providing hostel accommodation for single men rather than family homes in the African townships was adopted. Thus, although the African urban population continued to increase, a higher proportion came to consist of short-term labour migrants. In addition to stopping migrant workers settling permanently in the towns, indeed, it was government policy to progressively turn back into migrants those African workers who were already permanently settled in urban centres. In spite of government policy, however, many women did in fact evade the law and leave the 'homelands' to enter the towns with their children to be with their husbands. They thus added further to the large numbers in the townships who were forced to live outside the law in constant fear of being picked up by the police.

The change from *baaskap* apartheid to 'separate development' coincided with the Sharpeville massacre and its aftermath. It came in just as the African nationalist parties, despairing of redress through constitutional means, launched the armed liberation struggle. The measures taken under the new policy, moreover, especially the forced removals and tightened pass law regulations, were bound to rouse African hatred and bitterness to an extreme degree. Their enforcement thus called for a ruthlessly efficient system of political repression by the police.

In response to the opening of the campaign of sabotage by Umkhonto we Sizwe and Poqo, the National Party government introduced a series of measures that progressively extended the powers of the security police and eroded the legal rights of individual citizens. In 1962 the security police were granted the right to detain and hold suspects in isolation for single or successive periods of twelve days without bringing them before the court. In 1963 this was extended to a period of ninety days. In 1965 provision was made for the first ninety-day period to be extended by a further ninety days. Subsequently an indefinite number of such extensions was permitted. Suspects held under the ninety-days' detention system were deprived of access to any legal advice or defence. Wholly in the power of the police, they could be subjected to extreme pressure. Reports of the use of torture in interrogation multiplied and growing numbers of suspects died in mysterious circumstances while held in police custody.

The security police achieved their first triumph in the use of their new powers with the arrest of Nelson Mandela, the leader of Umkhonto we Sizwe. He had gone underground and evaded the police so successfully that he was named 'The Black Pimpernel'. He was finally tracked down and trapped with a number of associates on a farm near Rivonia. Placed on trial he used the occasion to pronounce a devastating condemnation of the South African system. He was sentenced to life imprisonment in 1964. Together with other black political prisoners he was held on Robben Island until 1982 when he was transferred to Polsmoor Prison outside Cape Town. After this initial victory the security police succeeded in penetrating a number of other resistance groups. Radical opponents of the regime were imprisoned, broken down psychologically or forced into exile. In 1968 the security police system was reorganised and centralised around the Bureau of State Security (BOSS). Its powers were further increased at this time and it seemed for a while to have succeeded in repressing all militant opposition to the regime.

In parliament the official United Party opposition continued to be feeble and ineffectual. The introduction of legislation banning multiracial political movements in 1966 led to the dissolution of the Liberal Party. Thereafter Mrs Helen Suzman, the only member of the Progressive Party for a number of years, was the sole spokesman of genuine opposition to the general direction of government policy in parliament. From the government's point of view the most dangerous threat to its position came not from the white liberals but from extreme conservatives within its own ranks. The adoption of the 'outward-looking policy' and the modifications of petty apartheid were deeply disturbing to some members of the party who, like many white South Africans of both language groups, still held to the crude and simple racist beliefs on which *baaskap* apartheid had originally been based.

White opposition in the period of 'separate development'

Within the National Party two schools of thought came to be recognised. These were the hardliners, known as *verkramptes* (the cramped ones) and the more pragmatic and reformist *verligtes* (the enlightened ones). The growing rift was not wholly a matter of ideas. It also reflected the fact that, with the long period of National Party power, leading Afrikaners in all walks of life were increasingly becoming a sophisticated establishment elite. Their interests as well as their life style and culture were drawing away from those of the remaining ranks of Afrikaner manual workers and poor whites. They were, moreover, not so crucially dependent on the votes of Afrikaner workers as they had once been. Within the Cabinet the leader of the *verkramptes* faction was Albert Hertzog who had played a key role in the fight to win over Afrikaner workers for Afrikaner nationalism and to preserve colour discrimination in employment. He held a leading position in a number of Afrikaner cultural organisations including Christelike Kulturaksis (Christian Culture Action) founded in 1964 to fight against liberal tendencies in Afrikaner literature.

The admission of a Maori rugby player as a member of a New Zealand team to play the Springboks in South Africa helped to precipitate open conflict in the National Party in 1968. Hertzog and two of his supporters were dropped from the Cabinet. In September 1969 Hertzog broke from the National Party altogether and formed the Herstigte Nasionale Party (the Restored National Party – HNP) to fight against any modification to classical apartheid. The rebels, however, were unable to win any significant level of support within the *broederbond* and the Afrikaner establishment closed ranks against them, Vorster using the formidable apparatus of BOSS to harass them. He then deliberately called an election early in 1970 before they had been able to organise effectively. The HNP failed to win a single seat and never subsequently succeeded in winning one. It did, however, continue as a significant extra-parliamentary voice condemning government reforms from a standpoint of white racist extremism. The split, moreover, did not mean the end of opposition to reform within the National Party. Many hardliners remained and a loosely defined right wing, sometimes known as Houdende Afrikaners (Afrikaners holding to their principles) emerged. Dr Andries Treurnicht was to become the most outspoken champion of this tendency.

The division of Afrikanerdom: the first split in the National Party

In the short run at any rate the decision by the leaders of both main African nationalist parties to follow the path of armed struggle had disastrous con-

Black opposition to separate development

Chief Gatsha Buthelezi and
Chief Kaiser Matanzima

sequences for organised black opposition within South Africa. It gave the security police the justification for drastic action against black radicals. For a time black political organisation at the national level within South Africa was virtually wiped out and black workers' movements were cut off from political leadership. In spite of laws denying them any legal recognition and outlawing strikes in all circumstances, black trade unionists, however, continued to function and to build up the strength of their organisations. This was to be demonstrated in dramatic fashion in 1973.

With the banning of both ANC and PAC open political activity by blacks was largely confined to the political organisations of the developing Bantustans (homelands). As the essential basis of the separate development policy was the grant of political freedom to the homelands, their political leaders had to be granted the freedom of expression and criticism which would otherwise never have been tolerated. No sooner was a start made towards the implementation of the separate development policy than political problems of this type began to manifest themselves. Kaiser Matanzima was in effect imposed on the Transkei as prime minister by the South African government because of his willingness to co-operate with the separate development policy. To consolidate his position in the territory, however, he needed to expand his political power base among a population the majority of which was deeply hostile to the South African government and its policies. One of his first acts after the grant of self government, therefore, was to reject the basic principle in the South African government's Bantu education policy by insisting on English as the medium for instruction in the Transkei primary schools instead of Xhosa. Subsequently he went on to demand the incorporation of white enclaves within the Transkei and even for extension of the state to take in the Ciskei and the port of East London. He and other homeland leaders also engaged in much criticism of aspects of racial policy in South Africa at large.

Much the most effective and from the government's point of view most exasperating of the 'homelands' leaders was Chief Gatsha Buthelezi of KwaZulu. Not only did he call for major territorial adjustment but openly demanded an end to social and economic discrimination in South Africa as a whole. The 'homelands' political movements thus did not develop into wholly harmless safety valves for African aspirations but as sources of pressure for wider change. Nevertheless, the fact that the 'homelands' leaders derived their power bases and platforms from participation in a system of 'separate development' meant that they were gravely compromised and could not hope to win the political loyalty of the majority of the black population.

Steve Biko and the rise of the black consciousness movement

In 1969 continuing frustration at the consolidation of 'separate development' and the inspiration of the black power movement in the United States led to the emergence of a new nationwide black political movement. In that year Steve Biko led a breakaway of black students from the multiracial National Union of South African Students and founded a black students' organisation called the South African Students' Organisation (SASO). This in turn gave rise to a wider political movement called the Black Peoples' Convention. The black consciousness movement rejected co-operation with white organisations and sought to make African, Indian and Coloured South Africans identify themselves as black in the face of white oppression.

It also rejected the Bantustans and condemned any co-operation with the institutions of 'separate development', building up its strength by creating a network of social and cultural associations. On the surface the racial attitude of the black consciousness movement seemed to mirror those of white racism and to be in harmony with apartheid. The government thus initially adopted a tolerant attitude towards the new movement.

In the 1960s and the first years of the 1970s the system of white domination in the whole of the southern and central African region came under increasing attack. The process began with the triumph of African nationalism in the white-dominated Central African Federation of Southern Rhodesia (now Zimbabwe), Northern Rhodesia (now Zambia) and Nyasaland (now Malawi). As a result of this, instead of going forward to achieve independence as a white-ruled state, the federation was dissolved in 1964. Nyasaland became independent as Malawi in 1964 and Northern Rhodesia as Zambia later the same year. The effects of this were mitigated from the South African government's point of view by the cordial relations it succeeded in establishing with Malawi. The development towards and eventual achievement of independence by Basutoland as Lesotho, the Bechuanaland protectorate as Botswana, and Swaziland were also handled with relative ease by the South African authorities at first, because of the extreme economic dependence of the new states on the white-ruled Republic. When the strongly anti-South African political opposition in Lesotho won the general election in that country in 1970, white officers in the Lesotho army, many with South African links, helped Chief Leabua Jonathan stage a coup to keep himself in power.

More important developments in the long run were the widespread rebellion in Angola and the beginning of the armed freedom struggle in that country in 1961. This was followed by the opening of guerrilla warfare in Mozambique by Frelimo guerrilla fighters in 1964. In Rhodesia (formerly Southern Rhodesia, now Zimbabwe) the collapse of the Central African Federation gave rise to a white backlash which brought the strongly racist Rhodesian Front to power in 1962. Fearing that the British connection would lead to pressure for racial change, the Rhodesian Front demanded independence, which Britain refused. The first Rhodesian Front prime minister, Winston Field, was dropped when he refused to carry the demand for independence to the point of rebellion. He was replaced by the more daring and determined Ian Smith. As Britain still insisted that independence must have the support of the great majority of the whole population of Rhodesia and must rest on four other principles, including unimpeded progress towards African majority rule, Ian Smith took the desperate gamble of unilaterally proclaiming the independence of Rhodesia in November 1965.

Smith's unilateral declaration of independence (UDI) placed him in open rebellion against Britain. It led to the imposition of mandatory United Nations trade sanctions against the rebel colony and it attracted world attention to the area to an unprecedented degree, thereby seriously undermining the stability of the white-ruled bloc. The South African government found itself placed in an awkward position and at first adopted a stance of formal neutrality in the situation. It did not openly recognise or give direct support to the Ian Smith regime but it refused to apply economic sanctions and allowed trade to continue, thus making it possible for the illegal regime to survive. The first attempts by the African nationalist movements of Zimbabwe (ZAPU and ZANU) to counter Rhodesia's UDI by guerrilla action were quickly crushed. By 1972, however, ZANU had built up enough popular support in north-eastern Zimbabwe for freedom fighters infiltrating from Mozambique to establish a significant foothold.

In the 1960s also, South Africa's position in South West Africa (Namibia) underwent significant change. In 1966 the United Nations General Assembly voted to remove the South African mandate to rule the territory. This was subsequently endorsed by the Security Council in 1973. South African administration in the territory thus became illegal under international law. Though the United Nations failed to get South Africa to withdraw its troops from the territory or to establish its own administration there, the call for United Nations sanctions against South Africa became more insistent and more difficult for Western nations to resist. In 1966, moreover, the South West African Peoples' Organisation (SWAPO), despairing of political progress within the country, opened its own armed struggle. Because of the geographical situation the guerrilla war in Namibia was linked almost from the outset with the progress of events in Angola.

The beginning of effective guerrilla warfare in Rhodesia led South Africa to offer more direct aid to the Smith regime and units of the South African police were sent to assist in the war with the freedom fighters. Less open South African assistance was also given to the Portuguese in Angola and Mozambique. Rhodesian, South African and Portuguese military chiefs met repeatedly to plan a common strategy. Down to as late as 1973, in spite of a deteriorating situation in north-eastern Rhodesia and the failure to destroy guerrilla movements in Mozambique and Angola, the forces of white supremacy seemed to be holding their own. With the continuing strength of the South African economy and the close relations between South Africa and Malawi, only Zambia under President Kaunda seemed to stand in the way of the expansion of South African economic and political influence over the whole central African zone.

The final phase & collapse of apartheid

10

The years 1973 to 1974 marked the transition from the policy of 'separate development' to a new approach of multiracial co-option. Part of the background to this was the changing nature of the South African economy. Ever since the period of the mineral discoveries in the nineteenth century the growth of the South African economy had depended very largely on the exploitation of large quantities of exceptionally cheap low-skilled black labour obtained through the migrant labour system. With the advance of technology, however, the needs of industry began to change. To utilise the new equipment most effectively required less unskilled labour – however low its cost – and many more skilled operatives. The number of white workers was inadequate to fill these positions. Their numbers, moreover, were further depleted as whites took advantage of the expanding economy to move from manual work to clerical and administrative posts. Employers thus had to rely increasingly on black and brown workers to perform the more skilled operations the new machinery demanded.

From the early years of *baaskap* apartheid through the period of separate development the advance of black and brown workers up the ladder of industrial skills continued and was quietly permitted by government so long as it did not threaten white jobs directly or raise serious political opposition from white workers. The new needs of industry, moreover, meant that it was becoming less important for employers to pay extremely low wages than it was to have efficient, conscientious and loyal workers. In these circumstances the system of migratory labour was becoming increasingly disadvantageous. To use their work force to best advantage, employers needed to have the continuous service of workers over prolonged periods. It was increasingly important to them also that their workers should be emotionally stable, which meant that they should be able to live with their families in reasonably comfortable and secure circumstances.

The method of obtaining increased continuity of service by sending workers to the Bantustans for short holiday periods only and then allowing them back on permits which specified working for the same employer was widely adopted. This proved an unsatisfactory half-way solution, however, and it was increasingly evident to many major employers that the move from migrant labour to stabilised labour was essential for the future.

The increasing dependence of industry on black and brown workers to carry out skilled operations also meant that the bargaining power of these workers was growing in spite of a legal prohibition on all strike action by

223

blacks. Just how far this had gone and how effectively blacks were organised in spite of the laws denying them the right to recognised trade unions became obvious in 1973. A wave of massive strikes by African workers in Natal and on the Rand rocked the whole economy and precipitated an important shift in policy. Though the strikes were put down – in one case troops were brought in – significant pay increases were granted. The possibility of Africans being allowed some measure of trade union rights, including even the right to strike, was held out. Even more important, Vorster announced that greatly increased educational opportunities for Africans to acquire advanced skills must be made available so that South Africa could make full use of the abilities of all its peoples.

This meant that the government had at last recognised and openly accepted the growing dependence of the economy on black and brown workers not just as unskilled labour but in highly skilled and responsible positions. It meant the abandonment of one of the basic principles of *baaskap* apartheid and separate development. It implied a need to build a new relationship with the black, Indian and Coloured work force which would involve a whole series of further policy changes.

*The revolution in Portugal and the strategic
transformation of the central African region*

In 1974 the entire strategic situation in central Africa was dramatically changed by the outbreak of revolution in Portugal and the collapse of the dictatorship there. The revolution had deep roots in Portugal itself but economic exhaustion, demoralisation and disillusionment arising from the long and fruitless struggle to defeat the African liberation movements in Portugal's African territories played a significant part in precipitating it. To that extent the revolution could be said to have been a victory won by the African freedom fighters of Mozambique, Angola, and Guinea-Bissau. In the aftermath of the revolution Mozambique moved quickly to independence in June 1975 under a government formed by the main liberation movement, Frelimo, headed by Samora Machel.

In Angola the Portuguese collapse was followed by a prolonged struggle for power between three rival liberation movements. In the north of the country inhabited by branches of the Bakongo people, the FNLA, led by Robert Holden, had wide support. In the capital, Luanda, and in a block of territory in the centre of the country occupied by the Mbundu people the radical Marxist-oriented and city-based MPLA could count on majority support. To the south, among the Ovimbundu people of the Benguella plateau, the UNITA movement of Jonas Savimbi had considerable support. With the departure of the Portuguese in 1974, civil war was precipitated by the FNLA which launched a drive southward towards the capital. The FNLA enjoyed the strong support of President Mobutu Sese Seko of Zaire and received much material aid from the United States which was anxious to check the spread of Marxist regimes in Africa. In support of United States policy and with a view to its own position in Angola, South Africa gave open support to UNITA and sent sections of its own forces across the border to help UNITA's northward drive. In response the MPLA gained material support from the Soviet Union while Cuba came openly to its aid and sent large numbers of its troops to Angola. The turning point came in December 1975 when the American Congress, afraid of being drawn into a Vietnam-type situation in Africa, refused to allow United States funds to be used in Angola. With the help of the Cubans

the MPLA rapidly defeated the FNLA and then turned against UNITA and its South African allies who had been advancing rapidly north. The UNITA drive quickly collapsed and South African forces were withdrawn across the border after some losses.

The establishment of radical African governments in Mozambique and Angola transformed the regional strategic situation. The position of the Smith regime in Rhodesia was fatally weakened and appeared to the South African authorities to be no longer viable. South Africa's position in Namibia was also severely compromised and SWAPO was placed in a favourable position to escalate the armed struggle there. The way was at last open through southern Mozambique for African guerrillas to infiltrate South Africa itself.

The Soweto explosion

As the South African government tried to come to terms with the dramatic changes in its immediate external situation it was faced with a massive internal upheaval. The segregated African townships outside the white urban areas had long seethed with pent-up anger and frustration. Nowhere was this more tense or more dangerous than in the huge agglomeration of government-planned African townships to the south west of Johannesburg known as Soweto. Black high-school students felt this frustration to the highest degree. As they struggled to master new knowledge and skills they were painfully aware of the barriers posed to their advancement by the inadequate numbers and training of their teachers as well as lack of equipment and books. On top of this the requirement that not only must they learn Afrikaans as a language as well as English but also accept it as the medium of instruction through which they would have to learn other key

225

subjects like mathematics seemed an intolerable, artificial obstacle to their struggle for advancement. The hope and excitement generated by the dramatic changes in Mozambique and Angola together with expanding job opportunities in the South African economy made the continuation and stricter enforcement of this rule seem a totally intolerable and artificial obstacle.

In June 1976 schoolchildren throughout Soweto staged a massive demonstration against the use of Afrikaans as a medium of instruction. The police used force to disperse the demonstration and it developed into bitter and violent rioting that spread from Soweto to other towns around the Rand and Pretoria and then out of the Transvaal to Natal and the Cape. As the wave of violence spread, moreover, Coloured and Indian youths took part as well as Africans. The riots were far and away the largest outbreaks of racial violence that South Africa had ever seen, far greater in scale than the 1952 upheavals and those which followed the 1961 Sharpeville massacre. Unlike earlier disturbances, moreover, the insurgents did not quickly yield, even to the most drastic use of force. Time and again unarmed youths charged the police through a hail of bullets, displaying a reckless bravery born out of the depths of their bitterness and frustration. No sooner would the upheavals appear to be suppressed than they would flare up again and this continued through the whole of the rest of the year. Even then the relative peace which followed merely masked continuing simmering violence always on the verge of bursting forth again.

In the effort to suppress the upheaval the security forces killed large numbers of young blacks. Hundreds of arrests were made and these were followed by suspiciously large numbers of 'suicides' and unexplained deaths of persons held in police custody. In response large numbers of black youths fled the townships and escaped across South Africa's borders into Botswana or Swaziland. Many of them proved eager recruits for the guerrilla forces of the liberation movements.

Though ANC propaganda and the rhetoric of black consciousness may have had something to do with creating the mood that lay behind the Soweto upheaval the disturbances were neither planned nor controlled by either of the exiled nationalist movements, or by the more recently formed black consciousness organisations. They were spontaneous expressions of anger and frustration led by previously unknown young leaders. So far as the Soweto disturbances were organised at all, they were directed throughout by an association of high-school students. The upheavals and the reaction they met from the police, however, left in their wake a situation very favourable to the expansion of guerrilla warfare. Not only did the liberation movement have access to greatly increased numbers of recruits, but they could now count on strong local support from the mass of the African population. By 1978 guerrilla activity within South Africa's borders was already assuming significant proportions. In 1980 ANC guerrillas demonstrated that their military forces had come of age in terms of the use of advanced technology and sophisticated strategic planning. Using limpet mines, they successfully organised simultaneous bomb blasts at two of South Africa's key oil-from-coal installations at Sasolberg in the Orange Free State and Secunda in the Transvaal.

One response of the South African authorities to the many sided crisis facing them was ferocious repression in the short term and a longer-term massive military build-up. In October 1977 the Christian Institute and seventeen black organisations constituting the entire institutional network of the black consciousness movement were banned. Two newspapers serving African readers, the *World* and the *Weekend World*, were suppressed. World opinion, shocked at these developments, was further horrified at news of the death in prison of the outstanding 'black consciousness' leader, Steve Biko. The police at first claimed that his death was the result of a hunger strike. The inquest revealed, however, that he had died of brain injuries received while in police custody and that before his death he had been kept naked and in chains for a prolonged period.

The spread of guerrilla warfare to South Africa itself and its escalation in Namibia imposed a very heavy burden on South African military manpower. The immense length of the borders through which guerrillas could infiltrate was in itself a major military problem. In response South Africa embarked on a massive escalation of its military capacity both in men and materials. Military spending increased dramatically. The demands on military manpower led to the introduction of two years' full-time military service for all white youths. This was to be followed by periodic service as military reservists up to the age of sixty. Even these measures could not satisfy the need for fighting men. The South African defence forces were thus led to abandon the long-cherished principle that blacks must not be allowed to carry arms and to recruit, train and use black as well as Indian and Coloured troops in armed operations. This military expansion had wide-ranging consequences for other aspects of South African life. Not only did military spending become an ever-increasing burden on the economy but conscription added its influence to that of the falling white birth rate to reduce the number of young whites entering the industrial work force. The dependence of the economy on skilled workers of other races was thus further increased. Military expansion, furthermore, inevitably gave the defence force heads a larger say in the affairs of government and thus began an important change in the way that government operated. The military forces were faced with the problem of trying to prevent the spread of guerrilla activity among a majority population deeply alienated from the system of white domination. They also faced the need to employ significant numbers of black and brown troops at this task. They appreciated that success was impossible unless the loyalty of at least a large part of the black and brown population could be won over. Thus the army commander, Magnus Malan, promoted the doctrine of a total strategy which must be adopted if South Africa were to succeed in the total war of survival which it faced. In addition to heightened military preparation this total strategy involved significant social reform.

The most important element in the new approach to Africans living and working in urban areas was a fundamental change of policy towards that section of the black population actively employed in the white areas. This included mainly those living permanently in the towns and enjoying Section 10 rights but also some living in the Bantustans who commuted regularly to perform skilled work in the white areas. The new policy reflected both the needs of the economy and the political objective of

Repression and militarisation: the martyrdom of Steve Biko

Steve Biko

Changes in policy towards urbanised Africans

227

reducing black hostility in the townships and winning the loyalty of some at least for the defence of the system. It involved the open recognition that urban blacks were a permanent element in the population of the cities. It was also recognised that their services were needed at all levels of the economy, not just in menial roles. Legal obstacles to their performing more responsible highly paid tasks would therefore have to be removed and they would have to be provided with living circumstances which would enable them to be efficient workers and encourage them to be stable and contented city dwellers.

The new approach meant abandoning one of the most basic policies of *baaskap* apartheid and separate development, the idea that the entire black population of urban areas should be regarded as a temporary phenomenon and that the numbers living there permanently should be progressively reduced. It also meant formally abandoning the policy of maintaining a racial hierarchy in industrial jobs by restricting skilled and responsible work to whites only. The system of job reservation had in fact been steadily eroded ever since 1948 but this had been done without openly abandoning the principle and blacks were usually only allowed to take on more advanced work when white workers were moved up still higher. The entire legal system of job reservation, however, was now done away with.

With blacks increasingly performing technically complex roles in industry it was in the interests of management that they should be organised in trade unions with whom formal negotiations could be held. After the 1973 strikes, moreover, government became convinced that greater control might be exercised over African workers by allowing them to form registered unions than by leaving them to organise outside the law. A government commission, the Wiehahn Commission, set up to look into this matter reported in May 1980. In the light of its recommendations legislation was brought in allowing Africans as well as Indians and Coloureds to form trade unions. The restrictions on multiracial trade unions were also reduced. At the same time, however, the regulations for registration gave the authorities wide powers to control trade union activity.

The relaxation of controls over black trade union activity was followed by a massive proliferation of unions, some inside and some outside the new regulations. They were grouped in several rival federations. Open industrial action was taken much more frequently and the wages of blacks, especially those in more skilled situations rose significantly. While in 1971 the average white wage was 20.9 times the average black wage, by 1979 it was only 7 times higher. In spite of this, however, and because of inflation, the difference in rands between the average white and black wage was as great as ever and the majority of black workers in lower-paid jobs continued to receive wages below the minimum subsistence level for a family. To reduce tensions in the townships and develop a more stable work force, the policy of converting settled labour into migrant labour was abandoned and reversed and mines and industries were openly encouraged to stabilise their work forces. One of the most notable examples of this was the Kimberley diamond mines. They had been the first pioneers in the mass use of migrant labour in South Africa and the originators of the closed compound system. They began a programme of full-scale labour stabilisation in 1972 and, while in 1970 86 per cent of their work force had been migrant labourers, by 1979 only 38 per cent were migrants and 62 per cent were stabilised. At the same time the policy of preventing workers bringing their families to town was reversed. Africans living in the towns were given greater security of tenure of their homes. This began in 1976 when provision was made to allow urbanised Africans to obtain leases of up to thirty years on their homes in African townships within white South Africa. The period was subsequently extended to ninety years and then in 1983 a massive scheme was launched to encourage and help urban Africans to buy their homes outright. In response to the report of the Riekerts Committee in 1980, moreover, the rights of urbanised Africans were significantly increased by allowing them to transfer their Section 10 residence rights from one town to another. As part of this programme it was seen to be desirable to give urban Africans a measure of political expression. This was to be confined to the local level, however, and was embodied in the establishment of elected urban councils in the black townships.

With these changes went substantial further relaxation of social apartheid. The number of hotels licensed to serve all races was greatly increased. Many restaurants were also allowed to abandon race segregation. The desegregation of sport was greatly expanded. Not only were matches between teams of different race permitted but South Africa began to field mixed-race teams in international sport. Eventually such mixed-race sport was permitted even at club level though most white clubs continued in practice to remain segregated. The recognition that the economy would need the labour of individuals of all races at high technical levels required the expansion of advanced educational opportunities for black and brown South Africans. Considerably increased resources were put into the expansion of facilities for these race groups in schools, colleges and segregated universities. In addition, the ban on the admission of black and brown students to the white universities was tacitly relaxed by the grant of special permission for students to attend a white university where the courses they wished to pursue were not available at a segregated university. Through the operation of this system the number of African, Coloured and Indian students at the University of Cape Town increased to about one-third of the first year student intake by 1984.

The other side of the new policy of improving the lot and co-opting the loyalties of those blacks needed permanently by the white economy was the more thoroughgoing exclusion of those who were not believed to be so needed. The main instrument for this purpose was to take the idea of 'separate development' to its logical conclusion by making the Bantustans formally independent. Their inhabitants would then become foreign citizens and South Africa would no longer have any formal responsibility for their fate. Their economic dependence on South Africa would ensure the co-operation of the ruling elites of these areas. At the same time, the political ambitions and frustrations of their population would be directed towards their local governments. South Africa could even drop the statistics of that part of its population living in those areas from its own statistical tables. The first homeland government to accept nominal independence was the Transkei in 1976. It was followed subsequently by Bophuthatswana in 1977, Venda in 1979, Ciskei in 1981 and KwaNdebele in 1984.

The South African government's intentions at the international level were frustrated, however, by the fact that no country in the world recognised

The other side of the co-option policy: independence for the Bantustans

the so-called independent nations and under international law they remained part of South Africa. The move to push the Bantustans into formal independence went along with a variety of measures to prevent their populations from entering the white areas. For this purpose heavy penalties were imposed on employers who took on black workers who did not have authority to be in the town. At the same time, forced removals to the Bantustans continued and accelerated. With the use of more advanced technology, moreover, the increased demand for skills went with a reduction in the total number of workers needed. South Africa, which had for so long had an insatiable thirst for cheap black labour, now had an unwanted surplus. The primary role of the Bantustans thus changed from that of labour supply areas to dumping areas for the unemployed. The other side of the stabilisation of labour also meant less opportunity for work on a migrant basis for people in the Bantustans. The introduction of the new policy thus meant that the already significant gap between those with Section 10 rights in the towns and the larger numbers without them would widen rapidly. While for those in steady employment in the urban areas conditions improved somewhat, for those based in or forced into the Bantustans the situation became even worse. They found themselves trapped in hopeless poverty with no hope of escape through employment in the white areas. In some of these areas diseases of malnutrition among children became rampant.

Black opposition after Soweto

The forceful suppression of the black consciousness movement in 1977 left little channel for the legal expression of opposition by the majority of the population. In these circumstances Chief Gatsha Buthelezi became a national figure. Not only did he persistently refuse to accept independence for KwaZulu but continued to attack the white South African social system and to call for a national convention of all races to work out a new constitution for a non-racial South Africa. He extended his power base outside KwaZulu by opening his originally Zulu cultural and political movement Inkatha to Africans of all ethnic groups in South Africa. In 1978 he linked this with a Coloured and an Indian political organisation in the South African Black Alliance. His most impressive initiative came in 1981 when he invited a number of white businessmen and intellectuals to take part in a multiracial committee to draw up an alternative plan for the development of Natal along non-racial lines. Many Africans, however, considered any co-operation with the Bantustan system a betrayal of African interests. They thus rejected Buthelezi as a stooge and a sell-out. A new political movement, the Azanian

Consultations between the South African government and the chief ministers of the eight self-governing homelands, March 1974

People's Party, formed in Soweto in 1979, reflected this spirit. From his senior position in the Anglican Church Bishop Desmond Tutu spoke up boldly and convincingly against the inhumanity of the South African system and called for world pressure to force change on the country.

The National Party entered on the new phase of the development of its policies with a further electoral mandate in general elections held in 1974. That election, however, demonstrated the significant increase in liberal opposition to the government's policies. The Progressive Party increased its strength from one to seven. In a number of United Party constituencies, moreover, conservatives were replaced by genuine opponents of apartheid. Soon thereafter the long-dying United Party finally dissolved itself. Conservatives formed the New Republic Party with a significant base only in Natal. The remainder joined the Progressives. That party now advocated a federal system for a future non-racial South Africa and renamed itself the Progressive Federal Party. It then became the official opposition in the South African parliament.

Though in parliament it was liberal opposition to the government that was growing most rapidly, it was conservative opposition that had the greatest effect on political decision making. The extreme conservative HNP continued in existence. More important was the remaining group of hardliners within the National Party led by Andries Treurnicht. Their opposition was particularly important in blocking proposed constitutional reforms aimed at providing a solution to the political future of the Indian and Coloured communities. This had always posed a thorny, theoretical problem for National Party politicians, as no credible homelands could be ascribed to these peoples. A government commission, the Theron Commission, recommended in 1976 that the Coloureds be, in effect, assimilated to whites. This, however, was too big a reversal of past policy and the long struggle to remove Coloured voters from the voting role for the party to swallow. At the same time, in the post-1974 situation some means of co-opting the loyalty of these groups was held to be desirable and urgent.

In 1977 Vorster thus put forward a plan for major constitutional change aimed at giving Indians and Coloureds a voice in central government but preserving the principle of race separation and assuring continued white supremacy. The scheme involved adding separate Indian and Coloured parliaments to the existing white House of Assembly. The three parliaments would then elect representatives to a multiracial government team in which whites would have a majority. The government would be headed by an executive president with wide powers. The plan was put to the electorate in a general election in 1977. Though the government once again achieved a massive majority, hardliner opposition in its own ranks led to the scheme being temporarily shelved. Instead the Schlebusch Commission was set up to make recommendations on constitutional change. It proposed that the Senate be abolished and replaced by a President's Council consisting of whites, Indians and Coloureds. This would be empowered to make further constitutional proposals and would have advisory authority only. A separate President's Council to cater for urban Africans was also proposed. These plans were accepted and the white upper house disappeared to make way for the new multiracial council. Plans for the separate council for blacks were dropped, however, as no representative blacks could be persuaded to join it.

P.W. Botha, 1986

Important changes in the character and orientation of the National Party government began with the end of Vorster's term in office. In September 1978 he announced his intention to resign on grounds of ill-health. In the contest for the leadership of the National Party Dr Connie Mulder, previously the favourite candidate, was weakened by rumours of a major scandal involving the Ministry of Information which he had headed. He was thus beaten in the party caucus election by P.W. Botha, the Minister of Defence. Botha then became prime minister while Vorster was elected state president.

Soon afterwards the scandal came into the open. Contrary to explicit assurances given by parliament, large sums of government money had been used to buy up an English language newspaper in South Africa for the purposes of government propaganda. Other huge sums had been used for secret operations aimed at gaining influence over publications and buying the goodwill of politicians and prominent personalities in the United States, Britain and Europe. Some of those involved were also accused of having misused some of the funds on themselves. As a result of the scandal Mulder was driven out of the National Party altogether and founded a Conservative Party. It was then shown that Vorster had been privy to some aspects of the affair and he was forced to resign the presidency in disgrace.

Botha's position in the party was significantly strengthened by these developments but he still faced a possible serious rival in the hardliner, Dr Andries Treurnicht, who had taken Mulder's position as leader of the Transvaal branch of the party. A further general election in April 1981 brought the National Party back with a massive majority once more. The Progressive Federal Party, however, made further modest gains while the extreme right-wing HNP raised its share of the vote considerably, though it won no seats. The election did nothing to resolve the power struggle within the party but Botha brought matters to a head by adopting a new version of the triple parliament, multi-constitutional scheme which was proposed by the multiracial President's Council. When he insisted that the scheme would be not only cosmetic but would involve real power-sharing, Treurnicht, who had already voiced his disapproval of rugby between teams of white and Coloured schoolboys, moved a vote of no confidence in Botha's leadership. He lost and was driven out of the party altogether. He and a number of his followers then formed the Conservative Party of South Africa and quickly absorbed Mulder. Unlike the HNP they had a significant voice in parliament from the outset. Outside Parliament the anxieties and sense of betrayal felt by many Afrikaner blue-collar workers, policemen, soldiers and junior officials led to the emergence of a whole series of militant white rightist groups. Some, like the Wit Kommando, engaged in acts of sabotage. The most significant was the Afrikaner Weerstandbeweeging founded by Eugene Terre Blanche in 1973. He was the son of an ex-member of the Ossewabrandwag and his movement adopted similar para-military forms.

*Botha's managerial style of government and
the new dominant elite*

Under Botha's leadership the changes in the style of government already apparent under Vorster rapidly became more pronounced. Botha had been Minister of Defence and on coming to office brought the previous commander-in-chief of the armed forces, Magnus Malan, chief spokesman of the 'total strategy', into the Cabinet as Defence Minister. The National

Security Council came increasingly to be seen as the main source of government policy. It was not only a matter of a larger voice for the military, however. While the National Party caucus lost much of its role in decision making, matters of policy were increasingly referred to Cabinet committees, the majority of whose members were high officials, technocrats and businessmen. South Africa came to be run increasingly by a new political elite consisting of Cabinet ministers and top executives, military chiefs, technical experts, academics and businessmen. Unlike Vorster, moreover, Botha made close contacts with English-speaking businessmen as well as Afrikaners. These changes reflected on the one hand the increasing mobilisation of the South African economy in accordance with the principles of the total strategy and on the other the continuing evolution of the top Afrikaner elite. They had now become a group of men long accustomed to wealth and power, increasingly practising a cosmopolitan culture and at ease with their English-speaking counterparts.

Along with the introduction and development of the policy of multiracial co-option after 1973 went the development of new regional policies in the light of the radically changed situation in the wider central and southern African region. In the immediate aftermath of the collapse of Portuguese colonial authority and its own brief and abortive intervention in Angola, the South African government adopted a peaceful stance towards its new African neighbours. It deliberately refrained from going to the aid of Portuguese settlers in Mozambique when they sought to stage a counter-revolution. It maintained trade links and other forms of co-operation with the African Marxist state. South Africa's main regional policies concerns were concentrated on Rhodesia (Zimbabwe) and Namibia. In both these areas its objective became to secure the establishment of moderate African-led governments which could win acceptance in the international world, end guerrilla warfare in their own countries and, at the same time, serve South African interests by providing a buffer zone holding back African nationalist guerrillas. With regard to Rhodesia the coming of independence to Mozambique quickly convinced Vorster that Ian Smith's white regime was no longer viable in the long run. He thus put South Africa's weight behind efforts to persuade Smith to negotiate the transfer of power with the object of establishing a moderate African government in the country. Though he helped force Smith to release the main African nationalist leaders and to enter into negotiations, however, Smith's own intransigence repeatedly frustrated South Africa's efforts as well as those of Britain and the United States to achieve the negotiated peace they desired.

When in 1978 Smith finally reached agreement with Bishop Abel Muzorewa to create a nominally black-led government but with whites still holding the key levers of power, South Africa gave cautious approval. In the elections held in Rhodesia-Zimbabwe in 1979 the call of the Patriotic Front for a boycott of the polls was largely ignored and the Muzorewa regime was endorsed by a handsome majority. South African confidence was further increased but it wanted to see the new regime gain international legitimacy and the civil war in Zimbabwe brought to an end. It thus welcomed the temporary re-establishment of British authority in preparation for new elections under an independence constitution negotiated in September 1979. It anticipated as did white Rhodesians that Muzorewa would win.

The development of regional policy

Eugene Terre Blanche, leader of the AWB (Afrikaner Weerstandbeweging) which developed Nazi-style symbolism and salutes

In the meantime, South African policy towards Namibia developed along roughly parallel lines. Until 1974 South Africa had persisted in the face of all international opposition in extending apartheid to Namibia. Homelands were defined for African, Khoi, San and Damara communities leaving half of the total area reserved for the small white minority, including most of the territory's mineral wealth and agricultural potential. This white state was destined to be ultimately absorbed into South Africa while the ethnic homelands would be pushed into independence. The 1968 Development of Self-Government for Native Nations in South West Africa Act laid the legal foundations for the creation of ethnic governments in Namibia's version of the Bantustan idea.

In 1974, however, South Africa, with its position in its own region weakened by the Portuguese collapse, faced a renewed onslaught in the United Nations. In the General Assembly it faced a threat of expulsion from the organisation while the Security Council unanimously adopted a resolution calling for the South African government to recognise the territorial integrity and unity of the Namibian nation and withdraw its own administration from the country. In the attempt to placate foreign criticism while still fully preserving white interests, the South African government developed a new approach. Instead of breaking up the territory altogether it now planned to encourage the formation of a federation of ethnic states. This would meet the demands of the United Nations Assembly for the integrity of the national territory to be preserved. At the same time, the federal structure would allow whites to retain control of the wealth of the state. To further this plan a conference of representatives of the various ethnic states met at the Windhoek Turnhalle (Sports Hall) and worked out a federal constitution based on ethnic states.

The Turnhalle proposals were rejected outright by SWAPO, however, and also by the United Nations which established a contact group of five Western nations (the United States, Britain, France, West Germany, and Canada) to press South Africa further on the matter. Under this pressure Vorster agreed that the Turnhalle proposal should be abandoned and elections held under United Nations supervision for a constituent assembly which would work out a constitution for the country. The elections were delayed by disagreements between South Africa and SWAPO over arrangements for the cease-fire and accompanying troop withdrawals. Anxious to test political support for the Turnhalle scheme, in September 1978 Vorster abruptly proclaimed South Africa's intentions to hold elections in the territory under its own auspices. These were held in December. In spite of SWAPO calls for a boycott there was a large voter turnout and the Democratic Turnhalle Alliance won a resounding victory. As with the Muzorewa regime in Rhodesia/Zimbabwe, it seemed as if the Turnhalle scheme had majority support and South Africa could afford to risk an election under United Nations auspices. South African authorities accordingly agreed that the recent election should be discounted and the previously agreed scheme for United Nations supervised elections should go ahead.

South Africa's expectations were rudely shattered, however, when Robert Mugabe's ZANU, the most radical of the contenders, won an overwhelming victory in the elections in Zimbabwe. He was able to form a government including Joshua Nkomo and his ZAPU following in a very junior capacity and to lead Zimbabwe to independence on 18 April 1980. The

Zimbabwe election shattered South Africa's confidence in the probable outcome of a Namibian election. Arrangements for this were therefore stalled on various pretexts and South Africa held on to the territory in spite of the disintegration of the Democratic Turnhalle Alliance and the increasing improbability of finding any credible alternative to SWAPO.

The military problems which this entailed, together with the increasing infiltration of African freedom fighters into South Africa itself, led to the adoption of a more aggressive policy after 1980. This was aimed at destabilising the neighbouring radical African regimes and either replacing them with governments more favourably disposed to South Africa or at least forcing them to stop supporting the freedom fighters in Namibia and South Africa. In Mozambique South Africa gave open support to the Mozambique National Resistance (MNR), an anti-Frelimo guerrilla organisation originally sponsored by the white Rhodesian Intelligence Service. In Zimbabwe South Africa was widely believed to be involved in supporting rebellion by a section of ZAPU in the Ndebele-occupied areas. In Angola South African forces began by raiding SWAPO camps in the south of the country then increasingly openly used their troops to give support to Savimbi's UNITA against the MPLA government. This culminated in 1982-3 with the invasion and prolonged occupation of large areas of southern Angola in an operation code-named Safari. By 1983 these measures had achieved a considerable measure of success. Grave internal economic difficulties in Mozambique compounded by appalling drought which ravaged all of southern Africa severely undermined the Frelimo government's attempts to deal with the MNR guerrilla threat. In Angola also economic problems compounded by the burden of fighting a prolonged civil war and the effects of drought left the MPLA government in a precarious position.

Negotiations between South Africa and the Marxist regimes in both Angola and Mozambique came to fruition early in 1984. In return for a South African undertaking to stop support for the MNR and provide a measure of economic aid, the Mozambique government agreed to enter a non-aggression pact under which it would refuse facilities to the ANC for the prosecution of guerrilla activities in South Africa. The treaty was formally signed by Botha and Machel at Nkomati on 16 March 1984. At a conference in Lusaka an agreement was also reached with the MPLA government in Angola under which South African troops would evacuate the territory and stop supporting UNITA while the Angolan authorities would prevent SWAPO establishing bases on their territory.

The two agreements quickly proved rather precarious. Shortly before the Nkomati accord was reached, South African military authorities supplied the MNR with enough arms to continue in operation for a prolonged period. MNR military activity was in fact stepped up. In Angola the MPLA was not able to eliminate SWAPO bases entirely. South Africa, on the other hand, was not prepared to abandon UNITA altogether and the establishment of genuine peace was held up by the continuing failure to resolve the issue of Namibian elections, the relationship between UNITA, the MPLA and South Africa, and the return of the Cuban forces supporting the MPLA regime. Nevertheless, South Africa had gained something of a breathing space in its border conflicts within which to implement its internal constitutional experiment.

Once the struggle with Treurnicht and the hardliners in the party had been fought and won, Botha determined to press ahead with the multiple parliament plan. The scheme was put to a referendum of white voters in 1983. In spite of the opposition of the hardliners who rejected all power-sharing with other race groups, and of the progressives who denounced the plan for the exclusion of blacks, it was endorsed by a more than two-thirds majority. Only in one area of the northern Transvaal did it fail to get majority white support. The scheme as finally presented involved the creation of a Coloured House of Representatives and an Indian House of Delegates to meet and debate in parallel with the white House of Assembly. The system gave very extensive power to the president, who was to be chosen by an Electoral College made up of members of all chambers but with a big white majority. Not only would he be both head of state and head of government and have power to appoint a national cabinet from members of all three houses but all disagreements between the houses would be resolved by the President's Council. The scheme would thus free the president from close control by parliament. It provided abundant opportunity for the further development of the managerial style of government that Botha had already taken so far under the existing constitutional system. Elections for the Coloured and Indian Houses were held. Botha was elected as the first executive president and the constitution was brought into operation.

The circumstances of its introduction did not augur well for its success as a means of winning the loyalty of Coloureds and Indians. Changes in apartheid had modified some of the discriminatory measures to which these groups had been subject. Some members of these communities had been able to benefit from this and had achieved considerable prosperity. Nevertheless most members of both groups still suffered discrimination that was both impoverishing and humiliating. They might be free to ride with whites on the buses in some cities but they still faced segregation on the trains. They still had to live in segregated townships usually at a long, costly distance from city centres and in less attractive surroundings than the white suburbs. Even on the beaches desegregation was by no means universal. Many Coloureds and Indians thus rejected the new constitutional provisions as a worthless sop. The fact that the introduction of the constitution would make Indian and Coloured youths liable for conscription further undermined the chances of its winning popularity. Calls to boycott the polls orchestrated by a newly formed multiracial federation of anti-apartheid organisations, the United Democratic Front, were thus widely heeded. A large proportion of those eligible to vote refused to register and of those who did only 30 per cent of Coloured voters and 20 per cent of Indian voters actually took part. In Cape Town, the main centre of the Coloured population, only 11 per cent of registered voters, which was 6 per cent of those eligible, actually voted. The introduction of the constitution, moreover, was marked by widespread rioting by both Indians and Coloureds. The greatest weakness of the new system was its failure to provide any voice for the black majority. Government still maintained that urban blacks would find political expression in the homelands though this was in contradiction with the measures already taken to allow them more permanent status in the towns. Blacks regarded the new constitution as an insult. Coming as it did at a time of economic downturn and heightened hardship it sparked off a massive wave of violence in the African townships.

Johannesburg graffiti during the tri-cameral elections

The township rebellions

Thus the introduction of the new multi-racial constitution did not provide the desired reinforcement for the white power establishment but became the point of departure for a massive escalation of internal and external pressures for much more radical change. While the riots in the Coloured and Indian areas died down fairly quickly, demonstrations in the black townships, fuelled by economic hardship, growing unemployment and political desperation, soon exceeded the level of the 1976 Soweto uprising. On 21 March 1984, the twenty-fifth anniversary of the Sharpeville shootings, police opened fire on a peaceful crowd marching through Uitenhage to a commemorative meeting, killing nineteen and wounding many more. Riots and demonstrations multiplied and the crowds openly displayed a total rejection of the legitimacy of the government. They boldly displayed banners and slogans of the banned ANC, gave mass black power salutes, sang ANC freedom songs and danced the toi-toi as a symbol of defiance and anticipated triumph.

There was an important difference between these disturbances and the Soweto uprising. Although largely spontaneous and locally organised in each township, they were initiated in response to the boycott call of the nationwide UDF, they had a largely common ideological inspiration, and made use of common symbols originating from the ANC and disseminated by the UDF. Unlike the Soweto upheaval they involved a large part of the adult population as well as the youth and drew on the organisational resources of the large numbers of local civic associations that had burgeoned in the townships in the aftermath of the suppression of the national 'black consciousness' movement.

Popular anger was directed not only against the state at large but also against the recently created township councils which had been elected by derisory numbers of voters and had infuriated the township population by drastically raising rents. It soon began to take the form of killing black policemen, community councillors, suspected informers or others regarded as collaborators with the regime. Often they were burned to death by having necklaces of burning petrol-soaked tyres placed round their necks.

The declaration of a state of emergency covering wide areas of the country under which the police gained greatly increased powers, and stringent curtailment of media reporting of the disturbances, initially availed little to bring them under control. The number of deaths in township violence actually increased after the state of emergency came into force. Some townships passed out of the hands of the legal authorities into those of a variety of local civic organisations. They imposed a degree of order maintained, together with compliance with strikes and boycotts, through informal 'peoples courts'. Prominent in the organisation and enforcement of these experiments in popular government were groups of radical youths styling themselves 'comrades'. Though the police could make armed sorties into these areas, they were unable to destroy the control of the 'civics' or restore that of the official authorities for a prolonged period.

The disturbances were openly encouraged by the ANC which from Lusaka called on the people to make the townships ungovernable. They were accompanied by guerrilla action on the part of ANC 'freedom fighters'. A number of land-mine explosions took place near the Zimbabwe frontier, a bomb exploded in a Durban shopping centre and rocket attacks were made on an oil-from-coal plant in the Transvaal. They were also accompanied by repeated marches, demonstrations and protests of a more orderly nature by the multiracial United Democratic Front. Church leaders of all races played a prominent role. The Anglican archbishop of Johannesburg, Desmond Tutu, and the Revd Allan Boesak, the coloured president of the World Council of Reformed Churches, acquired wide international recognition for their insistence on the total abolition of apartheid in favour of a democratic order.

Archbishop Desmond Tutu

Faltering reform and tightening sanctions

The Botha government's political response to these mounting pressures was indecisive and contradictory, reflecting the widening divisions within the Afrikaner power elite. Though by this time an important segment of Afrikaner leadership was convinced of the need for radical change, Botha's military and intelligence advisors retained their faith in the 'total strategy' as originally propounded by Magnus Malan. This involved the attempt to destroy the ANC's power bases at home and in the 'frontline states'. A new political order was then to be negotiated with a 'moderate' African leadership which would give blacks living in white areas some representation in the central government system but on the basis of separate representation of racial communities and in such a way as to leave ultimate white control intact. Botha called on African leaders to participate in an open forum to devise a constitutional structure for their representation in central government but, almost simultaneously, many leaders of the United Democratic Front, the most obvious possible moderate negotiating partners but regarded by Botha's advisors as surrogates for the ANC, were arrested and charged with treason. The charges were so insubstantial that most were withdrawn as soon as they were brought to court.

Advance publicity for a speech made by Botha in August 1985 created the impression that some really fundamental measures were to be announced. Apart from the rhetorical pronouncement about South Africa 'crossing the Rubicon', it contained few concrete proposals but rather laid emphasis on government's determination to restore order. International opinion, already aroused by the townships' upheaval and the government's repressive response, now demanded action and western powers began to apply tougher measures against South Africa. European banks restricted loans and the EEC began to implement a number of other economic measures. The United States, however reluctantly, made an important decision of principle in agreeing to impose some, albeit nominal, sanctions.

The Commonwealth Heads of Government Meeting in Nassau, Bahamas in October 1985 adopted an accord calling on the South African government to free Nelson Mandela, lift the ban on the ANC and other parties, and enter into negotiations with the aim of totally dismantling apartheid. An Eminent Persons Group of senior statesmen from a number of Commonwealth countries was set up to visit South Africa, consult all shades of opinion, and urge the regime to follow the line laid down in the accord. The EPG was initially well received in South Africa: it was given freedom to visit the townships and to meet political figures of all races, including Nelson Mandela in prison. The mission was suddenly and brutally aborted by the South African defence forces launching raids into Zambia, Zimbabwe, and Botswana.

The collapse of the EPG initiative heightened international pressures still further. In the United States, Congress over-rode President Reagan's veto to impose additional sanctions. EEC measures were tightened. The rand fell to about half its previous value. The South African economy, burdened by massive military expenditure and the costs imposed by international sanctions, had slowed since the mid-70s to a rate of growth well short of that of the population. It now went into serious decline and the already serious problems of unemployment worsened dramatically.

By 1987 the government finally succeeded in bringing the African townships under a measure of control. Under cover of state of emergency provisions, which were extended to the whole country, thousands of alleged activists, many of them children, were arrested and held for long periods without trial. The use of army units in place of the hated police helped defuse the tension, and the expenditure of large sums on housing and amenities also encouraged the return to a semblance of normality.

By 1986 moreover the enthusiasm of the young 'comrades' was in decline while the domination and thuggery that sometimes accompanied it had long alienated many township residents. It was particularly resented by migrant workers accommodated in the single men's hostels. Not only were they seriously worse off than the permanent township resident but, as 'target workers', were angry and frustrated by forced compliance with strikes and boycotts. Coming from areas where the traditional patriarchal ethos remained strong, they especially resented being pushed around by young boys. The result was the emergence of groups of 'vigilantes' who, often with the complicity of the security forces, attacked the 'comrades' and their supporters. In the massive squatter settlement of Crossroads outside Cape Town, for example, the entire section occupied by the 'comrades' was burned down.

Such conflicts were widespread and were exploited by government in re-establishing some control. In at least one case government hit-men eliminated the leaders of a particularly successful 'civic'. While in most areas these types of conflict were a temporary phenomenon, in the province of Natal they assumed an exceptional scale and long term significance. The resentment of migrant workers against the urban 'comrades', and of Zulu speakers in townships near Durban against Xhosa-speaking immigrants from southern Natal, became identified with the political rivalry between the ANC and Chief Buthelezi's Zulu nationalist movement Inkatha. Conflict here soon assumed the character of a long running local civil war. Elements of the security forces moreover increasingly saw Buthelezi and Inkatha as an ally and helped develop the KwaZulu police as an anti-ANC force.

By 1987 many leaders of white opinion, including not only powerful English businessmen but also much of the Afrikaner elite, had come to the conclusion that a political settlement going well beyond the framework adhered to by Botha and the securocrats was essential. The new attitude acquired a key political base in 1983 when the *verligte* Pieter de Lange took the chairmanship of the Broederbond from the hard-liner Carel Boshoff. Thereafter the organisation became a radical think-tank. White opinion initially concentrated on Chief Buthelezi as a possible negotiating partner. His expressed hostility to sanctions and calls for a non-violent approach to ending apartheid won much white approval. The multiracial *indaba* on the future government of Natal that he had initiated gained him strong support from businessmen in that province. Government's attitude was clear in the wide coverage given him on radio and television. The Progressive Federal Party was also drawn to him and on 21 September 1985 joined Inkatha in an alliance to press for a national convention to frame a new constitution.

By this time, however, most radical white opinion had come to the conclusion that, even if Buthelezi might have a significant role, no genuine political solution could be found without an agreement with the ANC. As the most effective freedom fighting organisation, the ANC had overwhelming support in the townships, in the UDF and the most powerful of black trade union organisations, Cosatu. The first overt move in this direction came in September 1985 when Gavin Relly of the immensely powerful Anglo-American Corporation led a group of businessmen and opposition politicians to a meeting with ANC executive members in Lusaka, Zambia. The following year, while the EPG was visiting South Africa, the Broederbond was circulating a document to its members with a very similar message, advocating the abandonment of group rights, the release of Mandela and negotiations with the ANC. In July 1987 Van Zyl Slabbert led a group of liberal Afrikaners to a meeting with ANC leaders in Dakar, Senegal and thereafter more or less continuous, though initially informal, negotiations were under way. In May 1988 the cabinet itself set up a four-person committee to maintain contact with Mandela who had firmly refused an offer of freedom in return for disowning the 'armed struggle'.

Botha and the securocrats maintain the total strategy

Even at this date Botha and his key advisers clung to the hope that the ANC could be defeated and stability achieved through limited political reforms negotiated with moderate leaders. Their determination was probably strengthened by the results of the 1987 elections to the white House of Assembly: the National Party lost votes both to the Progressives and the Conservatives. The Conservatives gained more seats, however, and became the official opposition. The Progressives, strengthened by the adhesion of some ex-members of the National Party, renamed themselves the Democratic Party. Botha did his best to discourage party members' contacts with the ANC. The UDF was harassed by increasing restrictions and finally effectively banned. It dissolved itself to re-emerge as the Mass Democratic Movement. The programme of limited reform also continued. In 1986 the hated pass system and the whole apparatus of influx control, already collapsing under pressure of illegal urban immigration from the desolate Bantustans, was finally abolished. A system of regional administration representative of all races but based on economic criteria, ensuring white predominance, was developed. The application of the Group Areas Act was modified to allow for some mixed areas. In January 1986 Botha proclaimed that blacks would gain representation in the centre of government, but when the Progressive leader, Van Zyl Slabbert, a month later said this could result in the choice of a black president, Botha rebuked him.

The destabilisation strategy

Along with the mixture of repression and reform at home, Botha's securocrats maintained the tough external policy towards neighbouring black states. In spite of the renewal of the Nkomati Accord and repeated assurances, aid to Renamo, designed to keep Mozambique dependent on South Africa, continued. Direct military action by South African forces, as in the

raids which ended the visit of the EPG, was also undertaken to force neighbouring states into non-aggression pacts with South Africa and enforce the
denial of facilities to the ANC. The SADF's greatest commitment was in
Angola, where the Lusaka accord had given way to renewed invasion of the
southern provinces in support of UNITA and in the attempt to destroy
SWAPO guerrillas' capacity to infiltrate Namibia.

After the October 1986 summit meeting between Reagan and Gorbachev
in Reykjavik, the situation in Angola and Namibia began to be affected by
the changing relationship between the super-powers. The USSR made it
increasingly apparent that it was no longer concerned to dispute Western
hegemony in Africa. As the Soviet threat receded, however, United States
interest in supporting South African defiance of the UN in Namibia and
armed aggression in southern Angola evaporated.

In this atmosphere the Angolan army and its Cuban allies launched a major
offensive aimed at definitively smashing UNITA. Their advance was met
and defeated by South African troops who then committed themselves to
the pursuit of their retreating enemy, seeking to deliver the final blow to
the MPLA's military capacity. South African forces laid siege to the key
Angolan military and airforce base of Cuito Cuanavale but the Cuban and
Angolan forces successfully held out in well-prepared defensive positions.
The South African airforce was unable to maintain command of the air.
While the South African forces were held up around Cuito Cuanavale,
Angolan and Cuban forces advancing on their western flank reached the
Namibia/Angola border and pushed their way eastward along it, opening a
long stretch to renewed SWAPO infiltration and threatening to cut the
SADF's line of retreat. For them to break out of this situation would have
required greatly increased military forces, and high losses of white troops
were predicted. The effective military stalemate allowed the two super-
powers to broker discussions aimed at resolving the entire complex of issues
concerning Angola, the Cubans and Namibia.

This reached fulfilment in a treaty signed in December 1988 under
which South African forces were to withdraw from Angola, while Angola
was to deny military facilities on its territory to the ANC. The Cuban
troops were to be repatriated by July 1991. In Namibia, the UN Security
Council Resolution 435 was to be brought into force from 1 April 1989.
However, even after the arrival of the UN Commissioner for Namibia and
the introduction of the United Nations force UNTAG, the South African
administrator and police continued to play an important role until the election of the Constituent Assembly. SWAPO gained a majority, but short of
the two-thirds required for it to determine constitutional provisions on its
own. A moderate multi-party constitution was adopted and Namibia finally achieved independence under a coalition government on 21 March 1990.

With the resolution of the Namibian problem, international attention
focused on South Africa's internal situation. By 1988 it was clear that while
the South African authorities had succeeded in imposing a measure of order
by sheer force, they could not hope to regain the loyalty of the majority of
the population or defuse concerted international hostility without dismantling apartheid altogether. The ANC, on the other hand, was forced to
come to terms with the fact that there was no realistic prospect of seizing

power through popular insurrection. The USSR was no longer inclined to support the armed struggle but urged negotiations with Pretoria. The decline, followed by the collapse, of Communist regimes in Eastern Europe and finally the USSR itself undermined the credibility of the one-party state and the state-directed command economy. The 1985 party conference in Kabwe, Zambia, marked the high point of enthusiasm for an insurrectionary approach and of the predominance of hard-line SACP members in the ANC executive. But the mood rapidly changed in the direction of favouring negotiations and the acceptance of multi-party democracy together with the persistence of a largely capitalist economic order. Finally, the resolution of the Angolan situation and the loss of the ANC bases there left no real alternative to negotiating with government should the opportunity arise. The ANC thus published draft constitutional proposals demonstrating its moderate negotiating stance. The message that negotiations were an acceptable alternative to insurrection was conveyed to the townships by the UDF. Mandela wrote to Botha suggesting they should meet.

In January 1989 ill health forced Botha to withdraw temporarily from his official duties. The following month he was replaced as party leader by F.W. de Klerk who was thus recognised as his successor in the presidency. Botha temporarily resumed office in May and held a meeting with Mandela in prison, thereby finally acknowledging his crucial importance to South Africa's political future, though he still rejected negotiations with the ANC. He strongly opposed de Klerk's travelling to Lusaka to meet President Kaunda as it might signify willingness to recognise the ANC. When his cabinet supported de Klerk he abruptly resigned in mid-August instead of waiting until the September House of Assembly elections.

In these elections both the Conservative Party and Democratic Party made gains, but the National Party maintained a clear majority and de Klerk was confirmed as State President. He was generally regarded as one of the most conservative of Botha's possible successors, although his brother Willem was a prominent liberal involved in informal negotiations with the ANC. His first pronouncements indicated a determination to maintain the basic apartheid principle of group rights. By this time, however, the internal and external pressures to scrap the entire system were becoming overwhelming. The Bush administration in the United States in particular indicated that further sanctions might be imposed on the already crippled South African economy.

The abandonment of apartheid

On 2 February 1990, in a presidential address on the opening of Parliament, de Klerk astonished the nation and the world by announcing that Nelson Mandela was to be released, the ANC, the PAC, the SACP and the UDF unbanned, and that the government intended to enter into negotiations with a view to the development and introduction of a new constitution based on universal suffrage. It was as yet no more than a declaration of intent. The structures of race discrimination, institutionalised in South Africa since Union in 1910 (and in large part in the previous colonies and republics long before that), and hardened, rationalised, and systematised after 1948, were still substantially intact. Nevertheless an historic and irreversible step had been taken. The demolition of the whole monstrous fabric of apartheid was now on the agenda.

Order or anarchy?

11

Towards the new South Africa

On 11 February 1990 Nelson Mandela emerged from 27 years' imprisonment. His gracious manner and dignified bearing, as he called for discipline and restraint from the huge and rapturous crowds assembled to greet him, gave him immediate recognition as a statesman of international as well as national standing. This was confirmed in the course of an extensive programme of international travel and meetings with world leaders. However, he and the ANC at large faced serious problems in preparing themselves for constitutional negotiations. Having been legally banned for so long it had no organisational network of local branches. The problems of converting spontaneous mass loyalty into disciplined political support were further complicated by differences over ideology and tactics among the top leaders as well as potential conflicts between returning exiles and members who had remained in the country. Keeping the loyalty of the young township

The pictures in Chapter 11, with the exception of that on page 251, are reproduced by kind permission of Reuters from Rich Mkhondo's book *Reporting South Africa*, James Currey, London and Heinemann, Portsmouth (N.H.) 1993

Nelson Mandela and delegates at Soweto stadium after his release

radicals posed exceptionally difficult problems. They were conscious of the important role they had played in the township rebellions, yet in the process they had often missed years of education. There could be few prospects for them in the new South Africa unless they could be persuaded to go back to school. Mandela's personal position and the problems of the ANC in general were further complicated by the trial and conviction of Winnie Mandela for complicity in the murder of a young activist, 'Stompie' Mokoetsie, by members of her personal bodyguard, the 'Mandela football team'. Notorious for an emotional outburst endorsing mob execution by 'necklacing', and deeply unpopular with much of the ANC membership, Winnie had significant support among the radicals and held a number of important positions. Her formal separation from Nelson and her elimination from all offices in the organisation during 1992 effectively ended this problem. However, the greatest of all the ANC's problems lay in the fact that government retained the initiative in the reform process. Until the new political order should be established the ANC could do nothing positive to benefit its supporters. Even to protect their security it would have to appeal to the government and its security forces. Its leverage was restricted to threats to break off negotiations, the organisation of strikes and demonstrations, and the struggle to persuade the international community to maintain economic sanctions.

Winnie Mandela and Joe Slovo after a march to the Union buildings Pretoria

Desmond Tutu touring a camp for refugees from township violence

The government also faced serious political problems. Its policy was vehemently denounced by the Conservative Party and the militant extra-parliamentary movements of the far right including the AWB. Its core political support in the Afrikaner community appeared to be significantly eroding in favour of the Conservatives despite an undertaking that no new constitutional system would be adopted without a prior referendum of white voters. Its position was further complicated by the fact that much of the rank and file of the police and the army was sympathetic to the far right. The special units of the police and of military intelligence, established for and practised in the tactics of destabilisation of the ANC and regimes favourable to it in the frontline states, remained committed to the continuation of the secret struggle with a view to so weakening the ANC that it would be unable to form a government. Within the highest ranks of government the hope that it would be possible to block the ANC and retain a leading position for the National Party through an alliance with Inkatha and other African parties hostile to the ANC, (primarily movements based in the homelands), was strongly held.

Despite their continuing opposition and the mutual hostility and suspicion between the ANC and the National Party, each depended on the co-operation of the other for the achievement of essential objectives. They were obliged to maintain a working negotiating relationship. ANC and government members met for the first time to discuss conditions for the opening of formal constitutional negotiations in May 1990 and again in August when the ANC agreed to suspend its armed struggle in return for the lifting of the state of emergency and other concessions. .

Prospects for an early start to constitutional negotiations were threatened by continuing violence between supporters of Inkatha and the ANC. In August 1990 these disturbances spread from Natal to the townships around the Rand in the Transvaal. They centred on single men's hostels accommodating Zulu migrant workers. The ANC soon became convinced that the violence was being encouraged by a 'third force' and held the government

Mandela, de Klerk and delegates
at the May 1990 talks

responsible for allowing it to continue.

During 1990 much of the traditional social segregation disappeared and, despite some ugly incidents of violence by white extremists, people of all races began to make common use of beaches, swimming baths, hospital wards, railway carriages, hotels, theatres and restaurants. In October, in the Separate Amenities Act, the legal basis for such segregation was formally repealed. Then, at the opening of Parliament on 1 February 1991, de Klerk again seized the initiative in the reform process by announcing that all the remaining legislative pillars of apartheid, including the Group Areas Act and the even more fundamental Population Registration Act, were to be repealed during the session. When this was complete, race would have no significance in law except in the political sphere where existing franchise provisions would remain in force until new constitutional arrangements had been agreed. By this bold move de Klerk outmanoeuvred the ANC which had organised impressive and well disciplined protest marches against the continuance of the racially based Parliament. He also opened the way for the accelerated withdrawal of international economic sanctions. The ANC's continuing pleas for their retention still had support, especially in the Commonwealth, but this was expressed more in resolutions than in practice. African countries proved no less eager than others to expand economic relations. In the sporting field the ANC gave support to the abandonment of boycotts for those sports which adopted genuine non-racial management and participation. In July 1991 the International Olympic Committee agreed to South Africa's readmission.

By the end of June the promised programme of demolishing apartheid's legal structures had been completed. The 1991 school year also saw a significant, though still very partial, beginning of educational desegregation. Under provisions laid down in 1990, government schools for whites were permitted to enrol a proportion of children of other races provided parents of existing pupils gave support. The fact that many white schools were facing crises of falling rolls helped to encourage quite widespread participation in the scheme, especially in the Cape Province. The more expensive white independent church schools went furthest along this road. African enrolment in the previously white universities soared dramatically, resulting in a massive increase in their rolls as well as initiating the racial transformation of their student bodies.

While the legal barriers to social interaction, to individual advancement and to personal freedom were broken down, the actual conditions of life of a very large part of the population, far from improving, continued to deteriorate. As the economy continued to languish in the climate of world recession and local political uncertainty, the level of unemployment neared 40%. Huge numbers of migrants from the hopeless misery of the homelands accumulated in shanty towns of cardboard and black plastic shelters around the major cities. Around Durban alone the numbers of squatters living in utter destitution without the most elementary public services rose to about two million. Millions more lived in similar situations on the Transvaal winterveld and in Crossroads, Khayalitsha and other squatter settlements around Cape Town, making a national total of around seven million. The physical misery, hopelessness and boredom affecting residents in these settlements, as well as the large numbers of unemployed in the more regular townships, fostered appalling levels of criminal violence. They equally fuelled the ongoing political violence, greatly facilitating the activities of *agents provocateurs* of all persuasions. By mid-1991 numbers of whites were being affected by the removal of racial privilege and the continuing economic recession. As many as 20,000 of them were to be found among the huge numbers being fed by hunger relief agencies. Poor whiteism had returned, heightening anxiety and militancy in the ranks of the extreme right.

In spite of the difficulties it faced, the ANC made remarkable progress in 1990 and early 1991 towards building a nationwide network of branches and moulding its massive political support into an organised national movement. In July 1991 it held an impressively well organised National Congress at which a new Executive Committee was elected, successfully fusing new elements with the old guard. Mandela became President while the new Secretary General was the black mineworkers leader, Cyril Ramaphosa. The congress gave the leaders a strong mandate to pursue constitutional negotiations. In addition to strengthening its own organisation the ANC made strenuous efforts to heal the breach between itself and the PAC. A series of meetings took place, culminating in one in Harare, Zimbabwe, at which a full-scale political alliance was projected.

As preliminary political discussions continued, the differing agendas of the government and the ANC began to become clear. The government's aim was a system of power-sharing which would completely protect white economic privilege and job security as well as affording the National Party itself the opportunity to retain a leading role in the new constitutional order. With this in mind, the Party changed its constitution to allow it to

Arms confiscated from a migrant workers' compound

Cyril Ramaphosa

ANC supporters in a Natal township

accept membership from people of all races, and an active campaign was begun to recruit supporters from among conservative elements of the Coloured, Asian, and black communities. To achieve its aims it sought to ensure that the constitution should be drawn up by a multi-party conference where party representation would not depend directly on voter support. The ANC, while prepared to make wide concessions to white interests and fears, was determined to ensure a genuine transfer of power to the majority, opening the way to significant transfers of wealth and programmes of positive job discrimination. It insisted that the constitution should be drawn up by a Constituent Assembly elected by universal franchise, the procedure recently followed in Namibia. In January however, the ANC offered a compromise under which the procedures to be adopted for drawing up the constitution should be worked out by a multi-party conference and this was promptly accepted by government. In February, agreement was reached at a secret meeting between government and the ANC providing for the release of political prisoners and indemnity for returning exiles. The ANC in return formally abandoned the armed struggle.

Despite these preliminary agreements, the opening of the multi-party talks was stalled as a result of the continuing violence between supporters of Inkatha and the ANC and suspicions of government involvement. Meetings between Buthelezi and Mandela were held in January and April, at which the leaders pledged themselves to peace and reconciliation and mechanisms were established to defuse further conflict, but the carnage continued and even intensified. In April the ANC threatened to break off further negotiations unless government took effective action to stop the

Mandela and Buthelezi at a meeting to halt violence

247

killings, and called for the dismissal of Magnus Malan, Minister of Defence, and the Minister of Law and Order, Adriaan Vlok. Government rejected ANC accusations but in July it was revealed that secret payments had been made from government funds to Inkatha. The government's moral standing internationally as well as in South Africa was seriously shaken. Malan and Vlok were demoted to minor cabinet posts but ANC suspicions were not fully dispelled. They were subsequently reinforced by increasing evidence suggesting direct involvement of security forces personnel in a number of instances of major violence.

While the opening of formal talks was delayed, the ANC in May published its preliminary constitutional proposals. These included a directly elected Executive President, a bi-cameral legislature with the lower house elected by proportional representation, a system of regional government with considerable local authority, and a justiciable bill of rights. It continued to insist that the constitution must be adopted by an elected constitutional assembly. After the revelations of government funding of Inkatha, it added the demand that, as government was clearly a party to the conflict, the constituent assembly must function under an impartial interim government. The government's proposals, published in September, also included a bi-cameral legislature, proportional representation for the election of the lower house, regional government and a bill of rights. However, its continuing commitment to power-sharing rather than majority rule was embodied in the extensive powers to be given to regional governments and the upper house. The government's proposals also included provision for a collegiate presidency, giving the leaders of each major community effective veto powers.

The multi-party conference on procedures for the adoption of a new constitution, the Convention for a Democratic South Africa (code named Codesa), finally assembled on 20 December 1991. It was widely representative and included delegates from the 'independent' homelands governments, but the PAC, which had drawn back from completing its alliance with the ANC, refused to attend. In the Codesa talks the government gave way to pressure from the ANC and its allies over the issue of an elected constituent assembly. It was agreed that this would operate as the National Parliament while the constitution was being drawn up and adopted. It was also agreed that a widely representative Interim Government would exercise authority during this period.

Buthelezi and de Klerk

The beginning of formal constitutional negotiations intensified the fears and hostility of the white far right. After the government had been defeated by the Conservative Party in a by-election in the Transvaal constituency of Potchefstroom, de Klerk took a gamble on turning the tables on the far right. He called a referendum of white voters for 17 March 1992 on whether they wished the process of constitutional negotiation to continue. By so doing he also effectively discharged the promise of a referendum of the white electorate before the adoption of a universal franchise constitution. In spite of vigorous campaigning by the Conservative Party and the militant extra-parliamentary movements of the far right, the government received an overwhelming mandate to proceed. The 'yes' votes were well over a two-thirds majority and only one constituency in the entire country, Pietersburg in rural north Transvaal, recorded a 'no' majority.

After its hand had been strengthened by the referendum, government took a tough line in the second session of Codesa talks, insisting on provisions

Police in Soweto:
peace-makers or third force?

which would effectively give it a veto in the Constituent Assembly. The most crucial issue was the majority to be required in that body for the adoption of contested constitutional provisions. Not content with two-thirds which the ANC was willing to accept, government insisted that a 75% majority should be required clause by clause. ANC representatives, in their anxiety to conclude an agreement, went so far as to offer 70% but when this was refused the talks became deadlocked and collapsed. The ANC called on its members to participate in a campaign of mass action to force government to make concessions. Then, on 17 June, a number of residents of the Transvaal township of Boipatong, including women and children, were massacred, apparently by members of Inkatha who had allegedly been brought to the scene in marked police vehicles. De Klerk denounced the killings and went personally to the scene as an expression of sympathy. He met a hostile reception and was forced to withdraw. The police then, apparently without orders, opened fire, killing at least 30 more. In reaction to the killings the ANC publicly broke off bi-lateral discussions with government. It insisted on a series of demands before it would resume participation. These included the fulfilment of earlier undertakings to fence the single men's hostels, to ban the carrying of 'traditional weapons' by Inkatha supporters, and to dissolve police and army units engaged in covert operations. It insisted that de Klerk should take personal responsibility for security. It also made concessions on the constitutional issues a pre-condition for renewed discussions.

The Boipatong massacre aroused widespread international concern. The United States and other western governments brought pressure on de Klerk. In late July, the United Nations Security Council responded to a

Zulu migrant Inkatha supporters

249

Supporters of one of the extreme white right movements, the AWB, awaiting their leader, Eugene Terre Blanche

request by Nelson Mandela by sending a special UN Representative to the country on a fact finding mission. On the basis of his report the Security Council authorised the deployment of a team of UN Observers to monitor political violence in the country. In the first week of August the ANC, together with the SACP and COSATU, launched an impressive campaign of mass action. A two day general strike received overwhelming national support and virtually brought the entire economy to a standstill. This was followed by a series of well disciplined mass demonstrations. By these means the ANC succeeded not only in demonstrating the great extent of its support nationwide, but also in reasserting its leadership over a large section of its constituency in the townships and squatter settlements that, in frustration and disillusionment with the leadership's concessions, had virtually slipped out of its control.

In mid-July de Klerk announced the dissolution of a number of notorious security units. Subsequently a major reorganisation of the police force and the early retirement of a number of senior officers in the Security Services was promised, together with an independent judicial inquiry into allegations of police complicity in political violence. Initial talks towards a resumption of negotiations broke down in August, however, over the government's demand for ANC acceptance of a blanket amnesty for politically motivated crimes which would cover members of the security forces. Government then passed such provisions through Parliament on its own initiative. On 2 September de Klerk told a National Party rally that he was confident that with its black, Coloured, and Asian allies it could win a majority in a universal franchise election. Tension between government and the ANC reached a new peak on 7 September. The ANC launched a march to Bisho, capital of the Ciskei, with a view to toppling the regime of Brigadier Oupa Qozo. When it was stopped by a cordon of Ciskei police, a section of the crowd attempted to push past them and the police opened fire, killing a number of unarmed marchers and wounding a member of its Executive Committee, Steve Tshwete.

During the suspension of formal talks, not all contacts between the government and the ANC had been abandoned. On 20 September it was announced that the ANC had agreed to a summit meeting between Mandela and de Klerk with a view to clearing the way to re-opening negotiations. This meeting culminated on 26 September in the signing of a Record of Understanding. This included a government undertaking to take action on the fencing of migrant hostels and the carrying of traditional weapons. On 30 September the ANC Executive Committee endorsed the pursuit of bi-lateral negotiations with government with a view to the speedy installation of an Interim Government and elections for the constituent assembly. Buthelezi protested loudly, threatening to block any agreement reached without his consent. He went on to hold a conference of his own with representatives of the far right and anti-ANC homelands governments. It appeared that the majority in government had finally decided to abandon alliance with Inkatha and other anti-ANC homelands-based movements in favour of a working coalition with the ANC. The ANC, for its part, declared in November that it would be prepared to agree to a government of national unity which would include the National Party not only for the period of the Constituent Assembly but also for the first five years under the new constitution. It was also prepared to offer guarantees on job security and salary levels to senior government and security forces personnel. Early in December it was announced that the government and the ANC had agreed that elections for the Constituent Assembly should take place as soon as practicable and that a multi-party administration including the ANC would be set up in the meantime. Multi-party talks were to be resumed and were reconvened as the Multi-Party Negotiating Forum (MPNF) in April 1993.

Chris Hani

Inkatha, the Conservative Party and representatives of Bophutatswana and Ciskei meanwhile formed the Concerned South Africa Group (COSAG) in opposition to the National Party/ANC understanding and to fight for full regional autonomy at the talks. Viljoen, ex-chief of Staff, and several other generals dismissed in response to investigations into security forces' involvement in township violence, formed a new grouping of extreme white rightist movements, the Afrikaner Volksfront (AVF). On the eve of the renewed talks, the key ANC/SACP leader and sponsor of the idea of a government of national unity, Chris Hani, was assassinated by a white extremist and each major step taken at the talks was accompanied by renewed outbursts of township violence. A campaign of random terror against whites also began, apparently sponsored by the APLA, the military wing of the PAC.

The Forum nonetheless proceeded to fix the date for elections to the Constituent Assembly for 27 April 1994. It developed a draft Interim Constitution, and in spite of rejection by the COSAG parties, went on to define the Interim Executive Committee. In mid-September the election date and arrangements for its conduct, together with the proposals for the Interim Executive, were submitted to the tri-partite Parliament for legal endorsement. Preparations for the crucial elections remained menaced, however, by continuing township violence, strong opposition by Inkatha and the Conservative Party, and threats of open war by white extremists.

Appendix 1: The enclave states, Lesotho, Swaziland & Botswana

The history of these states known in the colonial period as the High Commission Territories of Basutoland, Swaziland and Bechuanaland Protectorate forms an integral part of the wider history of southern Africa. It has been treated as such in previous chapters. The history of each of these nations however has an internal thread of continuity of its own. These will be explored briefly in this appendix.

The kingdom of Lesotho

The area which now constitutes the independent kingdom of Lesotho is entirely surrounded by South Africa. Most of the territory is rugged and mountainous. There is also, however, a narrow skirt of lower-lying land around the foothills of these ranges. The Orange and Caledon rivers rise in the kingdom and their upper valleys constitute the north-western and south-eastern borders. Before about 1820 the high mountain areas, constituting the greater part of the land area of the kingdom were still inhabited only by small communities of San hunters. Bantu-speaking peoples had already begun to settle the more low-lying land however. The first to do so were an Nguni-speaking people known as the Zizi who crossed over passes in the Drakensberg and entered the upper Caledon valley, possibly about the beginning of the seventeenth century. This group subsequently came to be called the Phetla (pioneers). Later two other chiefdoms of the Zizi group, known as the Polane and Phuthi, also made their way into the territory. The original Nguni-speaking chiefdoms soon split up into a number of independent offshoots widely scattered over the east and south of the country. In the nineteenth century the most powerful of them was the Phuthi chiefdom of Moorosi with its base on a mountain stronghold in the Orange river valley. During the eighteenth century numerous chiefdoms of Sotho-speakers belonging to both the Fokeng and Kwena clusters settled in the upper Caledon valley alongside and outnumbering the Nguni-speaking communities.

The origins of the Lesotho kingdom date from the period of the *lifaqane*, as the *mfecane* is known to Sotho-speakers. (See Chapter 3.) The invasion of the Hlubi, the devastations of the marauding Tlokwa and the impact of Matiwane's Ngwane created the opportunity for the Mokoteli chief, Moshoeshoe, to bring the remnants of many chiefdoms together in a single kingdom. Abandoning his first base on the fortified hill top of Butha Buthe

Boer attack on Thaba Bosiu, 1865

he found in the larger and almost impregnable mountain stronghold of
Thaba Bosiu the perfect base for his nation-building enterprise. To
consolidate his position he relied on careful diplomacy backed by armed
resistance only when he was left with no other recourse. Thus he first paid
tribute to Matiwane who after his victory over the Hlubi became for a time
the most powerful leader in Transorangia. Then, as Matiwane's exactions
became intolerable, Moshoeshoe switched his allegiance to the Zulu and
sought their help against his previous overlord. The strength of his
mountain position enabled him to beat off a direct attack by Matiwane's
forces and another by a passing Ndebele military expedition. It also helped
him to hold his own until he finally gained the upper hand in his long-drawn-
out contest with Sekonyela (son and successor to Mma Ntatisi as leader of
the Tlokwa). Secure in his mountain fastness he was able to hold out against
Kora and Griqua raiders, until, with his encouragement, his people had

253

acquired and mastered the use of the horses and guns which at first made the Griqua so formidable.

This successful combination of diplomacy and defensive strategy enabled Moshoeshoe to preserve large herds which were augmented by successful raids on the Thembu beyond the Drakensberg. In the conditions of insecurity and destitution brought about the *lifaqane*, ever-growing numbers flocked to seek his protection and his patronage. The wealth of his herds enabled him to attach them permanently to his following by loans of cattle under the traditional *mafisa* system. These new followers who came fleeing from the chaos in Transorangia or returning home after a period as refugee workers in the Cape Colony, were attached to the immediate followings of one or other of his brothers or sons. Then as their individual followings expanded these junior members of the royal family moved, or were despatched, to establish their headquarters in strategic positions at a distance from Thaba Bosiu. In this way the territory of the kingdom came to be occupied by a network of settlements directly administered by chiefs of Moshoeshoe's House.

Not all the communities in the kingdom were integrated in this way, however. A number of entire chiefdoms became part of the kingdom retaining their political identity and ruled by their own chiefs under Moshoeshoe's paramountcy. Amongst the chiefdoms were the Phuthi of Moorosi. A raiding party sent by Moshoeshoe had caught him at a weak point when he had just lost much of his cattle to the Thembu. Moshoeshoe's raiders captured a number of Moorosi's young men and in consideration of their safe return he became and thereafter remained a vassal of the Sotho king. The Khoa-Khoa were close allies of Moshoeshoe in his early days. They suffered heavily in the upheavals of the *lifaqane* and were temporarily dispersed after the death of their chief Lethule. His heir, Matela, sought refuge with Moshoeshoe, however, and he subsequently encouraged him to gather the remnants of his people together under his own chiefdomship. Moletsane, the daring leader of the Taung, was another important vassal.

The kingdom lacked the centralising force provided by the military system in the Zulu kingdom. It was always a loosely knit patchwork of largely autonomous communities. It was held together by the ties of kinship and personal loyalties strengthened by the bonds of obligation created by the loan of cattle under the *mafisa* system. These ties were further strengthened by Moshoeshoe's practice of consulting the leading men and holding open *pitso* (consultative assembly) at Thaba Bosiu.

To help him in his dealings with the Griqua and with the advancing whites, Moshoeshoe took the initiative in inviting French evangelical missionaries into his country. With his active encouragement the missionaries opened schools which introduced the Sotho to literacy and Western education generally as well as to their specifically Christian message. Lesotho thus developed a strong foundation of Western education before the beginning of the colonial period. Apart from formal schooling the missionaries also played a part in introducing new agricultural methods and crops to the kingdom, notably the use of the plough and the cultivation of wheat and fruit trees.

In the missionaries Moshoeshoe found diplomatic advisors who were of great assistance in his dealing with white authorities and helped him with his diplomatic correspondence. However, Moshoeshoe was also determined to

Sotho weapons
Casalis, *Les Bassoutas*, 1859

retain his independence and the loyalty of the non-Christian majority of his subjects. He thus never formally adopted the new faith. In spite of the protest of his Protestant missionaries, moreover, he deliberately admitted Catholic missionaries as well as representatives of the Anglican Church to his kingdom. In time the Catholic missions were to acquire an extensive following, and Protestant/Catholic differences became an important element in the history of the country.

By adapting the military and diplomatic skills he had developed in the period of the *lifaqane* to the new threats he faced after the Boers' 'great trek', Moshoeshoe preserved the state he had created through the turbulent period of the Orange River Sovereignty. He twice resisted British expeditions without alienating British sympathy altogether or giving up the aim of securing British protection against his Boer neighbours. After the British abandonment of the Orange River Sovereignty and the creation of the Orange Free State Republic it was once again the combination of diplomacy and the defensive strength of Thaba Bosiu that enabled him to save his kingdom from disintegration. After war with the Orange Free State in 1858 had given him the advantage, he exercised great restraint. Resisting the temptation to overestimate the strength of his position he clung to his conviction that in the long run the survival of his kingdom depended on gaining the protection of the strongest power in the region: the British. He thus accepted the arbitration of the Governor of the Cape, Sir George Grey, even though he was not satisfied that the border award was fair to his people or took adequate account of his victory. The wisdom of his approach paid dividends at the end of the long and desperate struggle with the Orange Free State which began in 1865. This time Moshoeshoe's kingdom was brought to the verge of total disintegration. Only the successful defence of Thaba Bosiu kept it in existence at all while Moshoeshoe desperately appealed to the British for protection. At last in 1868 his prayer was answered when Governor Wodehouse proclaimed British annexation of the kingdom. The continued existence of Lesotho had been secured and Moshoeshoe could die content that his life's work had not been in vain.

Sotho warrior

In annexing Lesotho, Wodehouse had significantly exceeded his instructions. He had only been given the tentative authority to extend British protection over the country and then on the assumption that it would be annexed to Natal. Once the Union Jack had been hoisted, however, Wodehouse declared that to annex the territory to Natal would be impracticable. An unwilling British government was thus left with a new direct dependency. Though the governor succeeded in brazening out his situation he was well aware that his position was weak and that if he involved the British government in further difficulties he might easily be recalled. He could thus not afford to push the Orange Free State too far in the frontier negotiations which followed. The result was that in the second Treaty of Aliwal North the border of modern Lesotho cut off a very substantial part of the original territory of the kingdom and left the Sotho only a narrow strip of fertile land between the rugged high country of the Maluti mountains and the Caledon river.

A major weakness of Lesotho in the second war with the Orange Free State had been that the aged Moshoeshoe had no longer been able to contain the rivalry of his sons and keep them together in a united struggle. Thus in

A breakdown in unity: Cape administration 1871–83

255

March 1866, Molapo (Moshoeshoe's second son by his 'great wife'), who had been established as ruler of the Leribe district, abandoned his father and surrendered to the Free State. He agreed to become their subject and thereby transfer a large part of northern Lesotho to the republic. In the settlement after the British annexation however, this area was brought back to the kingdom. In May 1867, Letsie, Moshoeshoe's eldest son by his 'great wife', had also made a separate peace with the Orange Free State and become their vassal. When Moshoeshoe died on 11 March 1870 there were therefore serious divisions between his sons and none of them had the undisputed confidence and loyalty of the people that Moshoeshoe had enjoyed. Letsie was recognised as paramount but was never able to control effectively Molapo or Masopha, another of his brothers. He was defied even by his own principal heir, Lerotholi.

In 1871 Britain succeeded in persuading the Cape government to take over the administration of Basutoland, as Lesotho was then known. The chiefs drew up a partition arguing that if they were to be brought under Cape laws, the Sotho should have representation in the Cape parliament, but their request was given little serious consideration. The first years of the Cape administration of Lesotho were nevertheless relatively happy and prosperous. The government agent, Charles Duncan Griffith, established a good working relationship with the chiefs. He gradually extended a network of magistrates over the country and in 1872 established the Basutoland Mounted Police (now renamed the Lesotho Mounted Police, it is still the only security force in the country).

Though Basutoland had lost much of its best land, enough still remained to sustain the population at the 1868 level for some time at least. The introduction of the plough and new crops helped to make possible the production of a substantial surplus. For a considerable period Basutoland was the main supplier of food to the diamond fields and sold a great deal of grain in the Orange Free State as well. Basutoland was also a major supplier of labour to the diamond diggings, and the practice of labour migration first became established in the kingdom on a substantial scale in the 1870s.

One of the main attractions of labour in the mines at this stage was the opportunity of buying guns. In this way the Sotho extensively re-armed themselves with more modern equipment. In 1873 Lesotho first became involved in the consequences of white reaction to this African re-armament. When Langalibalele fled from Natal into Basutoland, Griffith offered Molapo a share of the Hlubi herds if he would assist in capturing the refugee chief. Molapo agreed, and sent his son and principal heir, Jonathan, who met Langalibalele and by deception persuaded him to go to Leribe. Here he was arrested and handed over to the colonial authorities.

In 1879 the loyalty of Lesotho chiefs was put under severe strain. They were called upon to assist the Cape forces in attacking Moorosi, who had been driven to rebellion by the high-handed behaviour of the local white magistrate. Although reluctant to assist in action against one of Moshoeshoe's faithful vassals, Letsie and Molapo sent forces which took part in the siege and eventual capture of Moorosi's mountain stronghold. Jonathan commanded the force from the Leribe chiefdom, and when Molapo died in 1880 he was accepted as the successor to him. Having proved their loyalty by this distasteful task of suppressing Moorosi, the Sotho were deeply upset to be informed that the Cape's Disarmament Act was to be applied to them and that they must surrender their guns.

The news was met with widespread resistance from the Sotho though they were not completely united and in Leribe Jonathan supported the Cape government. He lost the loyalty of many of his followers to his brother Joel, however, and was driven from his main stronghold by his relatives. By guerrilla tactics and good use of fortified hilltops the Sotho exhausted the morale and financial resources of the Cape's forces. The Cape government gave up the struggle and agreed to an award arbitrated by the Governor Hercules Robinson under which the Sotho who registered their guns could receive them back. The authority of the Cape government had been so undermined, however, and such bitter conflict had arisen between chiefs, that the government agent who was appointed in place of Griffith was unable to restore order.

The famous General Gordon was briefly called in to reorganise the Cape's forces and subdue the chiefs who persisted in rejecting government authority. He disagreed strongly with the Cape Secretary for Native Affairs, however, and finally resigned, protesting that he was not prepared to fight against people he admired so much. Finally the Cape persuaded the British government to resume direct responsibility for the territory. In September 1883 the Cape Parliament passed a Disannexation Act and the following March, Basutoland, with the overwhelming support of the great majority of the chiefs and people, became once again a direct responsibility of the British imperial government.

The British administration had very limited objectives. Its prime object was to maintain peace within Basutoland and between it and the Orange Free State at minimum expense. So far as possible the Sotho were to pay the costs of administering the territory. The British authorities thus had to rely to a considerable extent on the support of the traditional Sotho authorities. For this reason the administration sought to build up the authority of the Paramount Chief. With such limited resources the administration lacked the means to do much about the economic or social development of the territory. For many years after the unification of South Africa the British administration still expected that the territory would eventually be absorbed into the Union of South Africa. It was only after the Second World War and the election of the National Party government with its apartheid programme that this was finally abandoned. No serious attempt was made towards developing Basutoland as an independent national economy. In these circumstances its development was inevitably shaped by the economic processes which dominated the rest of southern Africa.

The market for Basutoland's grain exports to the diamond fields collapsed after the completion of railway lines from the Cape ports to Kimberley. It became cheaper to supply the diamond fields with grain imported from overseas than with produce brought by ox wagons from Basutoland. Sotho agriculture declined as a result of falling profits, but also as a result of over-exploitation of the soil. As the Sotho were denied the right to own land outside the narrow confines of Basutoland, overcrowding forced many to move into the mountainous back country and cultivate steep slopes which had been regarded as uncultivable in pre-colonial times. Soil erosion became very serious indeed and erosion ravines, *dongas*, became one of the most striking features of the scenery of the increasingly desolated landscape. As agriculture declined and the soil itself was washed away, the growing population became even more heavily dependent on the proceeds of migrant labour in South Africa. From an economic point of view Basutoland became just another African reserve, feeding the white South African economy with ultra-cheap labour while relieving it of much of the social cost of maintaining this work force. The fact that Basutoland was a British responsibility was in some ways beneficial to white South Africa which did not even need to be concerned about administrative costs as it did with its own Native Reserves.

Social inequality

While the majority of the Sotho became increasingly impoverished, chiefs continued to enjoy a privileged position and the proportion of the country's wealth owned and enjoyed by the chiefly elite increased. One reason for this was the continuous increase in the number of chiefs. In the pre-colonial days, as chiefly families increased along with those of their followers, the lesser sons of chiefs would be established in new areas or would break away from the parent community altogether to establish new chiefdoms in unoccupied territory. Once the Sotho were confined within fixed borders, however, the number of chiefs was bound to become disproportionate to the territory available, yet the British administration relied very heavily on the Paramount Chief and his subordinate territorial rulers to maintain the day-to-day administration of the country. To ensure a measure of broad agreement Letsie I, like Moshoeshoe, would summon a *pitso* from time to time to discuss matters of special importance. Such an open and informal forum with no fixed composition or regular meetings was not ideal as an organ of administration. The Resident Commissioner thus pressed for a more formal council to be established to meet regularly once a year. This was agreed in 1889 but it was only finally established during 1903 by Paramount Chief Lerotholi. The council thus formed was made up of a hundred members, five nominated by the Resident Commissioner and the remainder by the Paramount Chief. In March 1910 this council was further formalised as the Basutoland Council with the same membership, except that the Resident Commissioner became President. The formation of a formal council provided the Paramount with a regularly constituted consultative body. Its first act in 1903 was to accept a body of regulations designed to adapt the traditional customs of Basutoland to the changed conditions of the time. Put forward by the Paramount these were known as the 'Laws of Lerotholi'. As constituted, however, the new council was considerably less democratic than the *pitso* of pre-colonial times. It was dominated by the chiefly elite and by the 'sons of Moshoeshoe' in particular. It thus inevitably sought to entrench and protect their interests.

Towards political reform

In 1907 Simon Phamotse, one of chief Jonathan Molapo's councillors at Leribe, founded a Progressive Association. It attracted support from the Western-educated elite made up mainly of teachers and clerks. They wanted to see the country modernised along British lines and transformed in the direction of representative democracy and also wanted traditional courts dispensing customary law replaced by magistrates' courts. They relied on the British administration to achieve these ends. They also gained some support from Jonathan Molapo who was critical of the Paramount's more conservative position. They succeeded in gaining some places in the

Basutoland Council as nominees of the Resident Commissioner but failed to attract significant popular support.

In 1919 a more radical movement, Lekhotla la Bafo, was founded by Josiel Lefolo who had worked as a mineworker in Johannesburg. He was particularly concerned at the Orange Free State's annexation of so much of the former territory of Lesotho and resented the British administration of the kingdom. He campaigned for the re-establishment of an annual *pitso* and then for the reform of the Basutoland National Council to give representation to commoners. Later he argued for a separate council of commoners as the National Council was in effect a House of Chiefs. He had connections with the ICU in South Africa and with the Communist Party of South Africa, which published his reports in the *South African Worker*. In August 1928 J.T. Gumede, then President of the South African ANC, addressed Lekhotla la Bafo's annual conference.

Basutoland suffered severely from prolonged drought between 1931 and 1933. When this was followed by a year of unusually heavy rain, there was extensive flooding, massive soil erosion, heavy stock losses and some outright starvation. A commission led by Sir Alan Pim was sent from England to look into the affairs of the territory. In response to the Commission's 1935 report, the number of recognised chiefs was substantially cut, the system of native courts and administration was overhauled, some financial assistance was given by Britain for anti-erosion works, and proposals were made for the gradual democratisation of local government and the National Council, though these were not implemented until the 1940s.

At the end of the long reign of Paramount Chief Griffith (1913–39) the succession was disputed between Chief Seeiso and his brother Chief Bereng. Seeiso was accepted as Paramount but died in less than a year. Chief Bereng then failed to gain the Resident Commissioner's approval to exercise the regency and this was entrusted to Seeiso's senior wife Mantsebo. In frustration, Bereng attempted to regain power by the use of supernatural means. A number of other chiefs sharing his sense of frustration and feelings of political impotence adopted the same methods, and several ritual murders were undertaken with a view to preparing powerful medicine. In 1948 Chief Bereng was tried and hanged for these activities.

During the period of British rule, the mission churches continued to expand their activities. The tradition of support for and interest in Western education established under Moshoeshoe I was sustained, and the Sotho attained a high level of literacy. During this period the Catholic Church expanded more rapidly than the Protestants who had initially held the lead. In time political differences began to parallel those in religion, with the Protestants tending to be relatively radical and the Catholics relatively conservative.

In 1952 Ngsu Mokhele, who had come in contact with the South African ANC while a student at Fort Hare, established a new political movement – the Basutoland African Congress – pledged to fight for independence. The new party, later known as the Basutoland Congress Party (BCP), absorbed most of the adherents of Lefola's Lekhotla la Bafo but also attracted a much wider following. In resentment against the limitation of the power of the chiefs and the ritual murder trial, the party had the backing of the

259

conservative supporters of the chiefly elite as well as the more radical Westernised elite. In 1954 the movement succeeded in preventing the adoption of proposals made by the Moore Commission for very moderate political progress at local govenment level.

The way was open for more far-reaching change and in 1960 the country received a new constitution. The Basutoland National Council now acquired legislative authority. Half of its members were elected from the members of elected district councils. The rest were made up of chiefs, government officers and nominees of the Paramount Chief. Before the first election to the new body, however, the BCP had split, and in 1958 some two years before the election, Chief Leabua Jonathan (son of Jonathan Molapo) had founded a more conservative, predominantly Catholic party called the Basutoland National Party. In the 1960 elections the BCP nevertheless held the lead at both district and national level. Soon after this the party was weakened by internal squabbles however and at the next election in 1965 it was defeated by the Basutoland National Party. It was this party under the leadership of Chief Leabua Jonathan that led the country to independence as the Kingdom of Lesotho in 1966.

Independent Lesotho

Formal independence and admission to the United Nations and to the Organisation of African unity could not alter the harsh realities of Lesotho's position. It remained wholly surrounded by South African territory and with no independent outlet to the outside world. On the achievement of independence it entered a customs union agreement with South Africa. This enabled the newly independent government to receive a share of the customs dues collected at South African ports. However, the agreement also stipulated the free entry of South African manufactured goods to the kingdom and thus virtually ruled out the possibility of Lesotho developing its own home industries. With an agricultural base grossly inadequate to support its population Lesotho was bound to remain little more than a labour reserve for the white-dominated South African economy.

Indeed, the independence of the country had advantages for South Africa because it ensured that Sotho workers in South Africa were citizens of another sovereign state, foreigners who could be denied political rights in the country where they spent most of their working lives. Independence also meant that South Africa could legitimately reject any responsibility for economic and social conditions in Lesotho and thus entirely avoid contributing towards the welfare in retirement or unemployment of a significant part of the work force employed in white-owned farms, mines and industries. Even the aid which Lesotho began to receive from international agencies could in great part be regarded as a subsidy to South African industry because it helped to keep alive and train workers for South Africa at international expense.

Leabua Jonathan

The 1970 coup

In the period immediately before and after the achievement of independence there was considerable tension between the Prime Minister and King Moshoeshoe II. The King who had the support of the Marema Tlou Freedom Party (a break-away from the BCP) felt that the constitution deprived him of powers that rightly belonged to him. Leabua Jonathan, however, was determined that the King should be no more than a figurehead. In December 1966 the Prime Minister banned a meeting at Thaba Bosiu that was to have been addressed by the King. The crowd was forcefully dispersed with some loss of life. The King was placed under house arrest for some time.

The main opposition to Jonathan came, however, from the BCP. It campaigned vigorously in the 1970 election, attacking Jonathan's attitude to South Africa among other issues. As the results came in it became clear that the BCP had won the election. Jonathan however, relying on the white-officered Lesotho Mounted Police, staged a coup. He declared a state of emergency, suspended the constitution and nullified the election. Ntsu Mokhehle was jailed. The King was placed under house arrest again, and then exiled to Holland for most of the rest of the year. The protection of the courts for individual civil rights was temporarily removed when the Chief Justice appointed by Jonathan suspended his court and returned for a time to South Africa. A number of attempts at armed resistance were made but they were speedily and fiercely crushed by the police paramilitary unit commanded by an Englishman, Fred Roach.

In 1971 Jonathan made the first attempts to heal the divisions created by his coup. Ntsu Mokhehle and other political detainees were released and discussions were held with a view to persuading the BCP and the Marema Tlou Freedom Party to join in a coalition government. Roach was dismissed and declared a prohibited immigrant. The attempt at political reconciliation failed, however, because of Jonathan's refusal to accept the validity of the 1970 election. In 1973 a new move was made with the establishment of an appointed Interim National Assembly to draw up new constitutional proposals. Attempts to persuade Ntsu Mokhehle and his supporters to participate failed once again however.

In January 1974 open revolt broke out. BCP supporters tried to seize arms from a number of police stations and to overthrow the Jonathan regime. The uprising was put down quickly and with considerable severity. An unknown number were killed and 200 were detained. Ntsu Mokhehle and six other BCP leaders fled to South Africa. Thereafter the exiled BCP was assisted by the South African Pan-Africanist Congress (PAC).

In the meantime as Leabua Jonathan tried to consolidate his political hold after the 1970 coup his attitude towards South Africa underwent a major change. Though he had initially adopted a friendly stance towards South Africa and relied on its good will at the time of the coup he increasingly adopted a critical attitude more in tune with the views of the great majority of the population who had firsthand experience of South Africa's discriminatory practices. In 1970 Lesotho and Malawi had been the only African nations in the OAU to abstain from voting on a motion calling on the Western powers to refuse to supply arms to South Africa. In 1971 Jonathan openly supported Vorster's call for a dialogue between the black African states and South Africa. During 1972, however, Jonathan's critical attacks became so sharp that Vorster openly responded. In 1974 Jonathan raised the question of the conquered territories taken by the Orange Free State from Lesotho with the United Nations General Assembly. In 1975 Lesotho vigorously denounced South Africa's 'homeland policy' at the United Nations and the OAU.

Relations between Lesotho and South Africa reached a crisis in 1976 when Jonathan stood firm in refusing to recognise the 'independence of the Transkei'. The Transkeian authorities responded by closing their borders to

Lesotho citizens. Some communities which had no direct links with the main centres in Lesotho were almost totally isolated and in danger of starvation. Jonathan refused to back down, however, and Lesotho received special food aid and other assistance from the EEC and the UN. As he moved towards more open hostility towards South Africa, Jonathan established closer relations with the ANC. This may also have been related to the support given to the exiled BCP leaders by the rival PAC. In contrast to his original stance and to the distress of some of his more conservative capitalist supporters, Jonathan established good relations with the Marxist regime in Mozambique and established diplomatic relations with Yugoslavia, China and the Soviet Union. In 1978 Lesotho was host to an international symposium on human rights focusing mainly on southern Africa.

In addition to these changes in his foreign policy Jonathan made further moves in the attempt to restore internal unity in Lesotho. In 1975 he brought Gerard Ramoreboli, who had previously been a member of the BCP, and Patrick Lehloenya, previously of the Marema Tlou Freedom Party, into his cabinet. This did not prove enough, however, and in 1979 there were further outbreaks of open violence. Once again they were quickly and savagely repressed and many refugees fled to South Africa. In January 1980 nearly 800 were living in a refugee camp near Bethlehem in the Orange Free State. By this time Jonathan's exiled opponents had begun to build up an organised guerrilla force, the Lesotho Liberation Army (LLA). This force soon attracted a measure of support from South Africa as a means of putting pressure on Jonathan to moderate his criticism and stop his own support for the ANC. In July 1981 a fuel depot outside the capital, Maseru, was blown up by LLA mortar fire coming apparently from across the South African border. In October a paramilitary barracks was also shelled from South African territory. In December South African commandos themselves made an attack on the houses of ANC refugees in Maseru, causing considerable loss of life.

In spite of the increasingly independent stand taken by Lesotho towards South Africa on political matters, its economic dependence on the white-ruled republic remained complete. Continued participation in the southern African customs union was unavoidable and though Lesotho established its own currency (the Loti) in 1980 it still remained part of the Rand currency area set up in 1974. In 1981 it received a two million rand loan for agricultural development from South Africa. The largest planned development project, moreover, was a scheme for multiple dams on the Orange River from which water would be sold to South Africa. The changes in the South African economy which brought a decrease in the use of migrant labour further weakened the Lesotho economy which remained overwhelmingly dependent on the earnings of labour migrants.

During 1984 and 1985, tension between South Africa and Lesotho intensified as Chief Jonathan persisted in refusing to accept a joint security treaty or to expel the ANC. South Africa was also disturbed by Lesotho's expanding relations with countries of the Eastern Bloc. Then, in January 1986, South Africa struck a decisive blow. It closed its borders with Lesotho, thus denying the country access to a wide range of essential supplies. This succeeded in triggering a coup by the para-military force under the leadership of Major-General Justin Lekhanya who deposed Chief Jonathan and seized power himself. Party political activity was suppressed. Jonathan died in

April 1987. Lekhanya soon reached agreement with South Africa on security issues, and over 200 ANC supporters were expelled. In 1989 Lekhanya was shown to have been involved in the shooting of a civilian in Maseru, though the Court subsequently cleared him of criminal responsibility. Some members of his military council wanted him removed. He responded in February 1990 by dismissing three members of this council and one of the Council of Ministers. When King Moshoeshoe refused to sanction these changes Lekhanya deprived the monarch of all his constitutional powers. However, with the dramatic changes taking place in South Africa, the position of the Lekhanya regime has become increasingly precarious.

Swaziland

Like Lesotho, the territory of Swaziland is the core area of a pre-colonial African kingdom created at the time of the *mfecane*. The kingdom was founded by Sobhuza I who, after conflict with Zwide, led the Ngwane chiefdom into its new home (see Chapter 4). There it conquered numerous other chiefdoms, some Nguni-speaking, others Sotho-speaking. The young men of these different communities were enrolled in age-regiments that usually only assembled in times of war. However, a proportion of the young men from every community chose continuous service at the king's households, making up a permanent standing army which could be greatly expanded in times of need by calling up the remainder of the members of the age-regiments from their homes.

Through this system, combined with the practice of widespread consultation with the leading men and on important occasions the holding of *pitso* open to all, members of the many original communities came to develop a sense of common loyalty to the kingdom. A complex system of patronage developed which allowed individuals from any community in the kingdom to advance their interests by attaching themselves to one or other of the key figures at the king's court. This also helped to develop the sense of common identity. The form of Nguni language spoken by the core Ngwane clan came to be generally adopted along with other features of their culture.

A peculiar feature of the kingdom was the authority accorded to the queen mother (*indlovukazi*). She actually held ritual seniority over the king (*ngwenyama*). Although he had decision-making authority in all executive matters, she had a recognised right to advise and caution him. Her court was thus an important centre of power. This division of power and authority created a valuable balance for checking the extreme use of royal powers. Under Sobhuza's best-known successor, Mswati, the kingdom expanded substantially and established control of wide areas in modern Mozambique. The name 'Swazi' originates from 'Mswati' and gradually replaced Ngwane as the name by which the members of the kingdom identified themselves.

Nguni huts

As the Boers, the British and the Portuguese extended their authority over areas bordering on the Swazi kingdom, its rulers deliberately avoided military conflict with the whites. The political structure of the kingdom thus survived virtually intact until it passed under European authority at the end of the nineteenth century. Though it avoided military conquest, the kingdom suffered very substantial losses of territory as a result of boundary demarcations imposed by white authorities. The boundary between the Swazi kingdom and the Transvaal was demarcated by a British Royal

263

Commission in 1879-80 during the British administration of the Transvaal. This cut off much land and a considerable population. The South African government has made some provision (though very inadequate) for these people in its KaNgwane Bantustan. Agreement between the British and the Portuguese also cut off extensive areas now included in Mozambique.

Apart from such losses of territory to neighbouring white-ruled states, the Swazi kingdom also suffered from the activities of white concession-hunters. Boers from the Transvaal sought grazing rights. Later, after a minor gold find, British concession-hunters flocked to the court of King Mbandzeni seeking mining, mineral and a wide variety of other economic concessions. The Swazi authorities at first attempted to deal with the white concession-hunters by using the same principles that they applied to Africans. They gave a party of Boers rights to grazing in one part of the kingdom and authorised them to appoint their own local council on the assumption that they would owe allegiance to the Swazi king. This small Boer community soon increased in numbers, rejected allegiance to the Swazi ruler, called the area they occupied the Little Free State and elected one of themselves, J. Bezuidenhout, as president. In 1889 it was incorporated in the Transvaal.

It thus became obvious that whites would not submit to the normal Swazi courts or accept the authority of the Swazi chiefs like other subjects of the kingdom. The Swazi authorities tried to find other ways of governing them. Mbandzeni first made use of the advice of one of the concessionaries, John Thorburn. Then in the attempt to find someone whom he could trust to preserve the interests of his kingdom he turned to Theophilus Shepstone junior, generally known as 'Offy', and in 1886 appointed him adviser to the Swazi nation. Mbandzeni encouraged him to regulate the affairs of the whites with the help of an elected committee. He also trusted his advice on the granting of further concessions, but 'Offy' cheated the Swazi and encouraged the king to continue signing concessions, some of them for himself. Mbandzeni was at least partly aware of the danger of giving these concessions, but he feared the consequences of resistance and openly expressed the view that the whites would take his kingdom in the end anyway. He did try to protect his people, however, by repeatedly declaring that he was not giving away either sovereignty or freehold rights but only temporary rights to make use of land or minerals.

The appointment of Shepstone and the election of a committee known as the White Committee did not bring an end to quarrels and bitterness among the concession-holders. Apart from personal differences, the interests of Boer cattle farmers and English miners conflicted and the two groups were permanently at odds. This conflict between the Boers and the British within the kingdom, together with the large-scale political rivalry between Britain and the Transvaal, helped for some time to preserve the Swazi kingdom. Its independence was recognised in the Anglo-Transvaal Conventions of 1881 and 1884. In 1889 Britain and the Transvaal set up a joint commission to look into the problem of the government of the kingdom. By this time Mbandzeni was dying. In the last year of his life he had sacked 'Offy' Shepstone and replaced him with another concession holder, Allister Miller. It was a change for the worse. 'Offy' had at least shown some restraint but Miller was thoroughly unscrupulous and was responsible for involving the king in outrageous concessions. One, called the Unallocated Lands

Concession, was perhaps the worst. It granted rights to about one-sixth of the total area of the kingdom for an annual rent of only £50.

On the death of Mbandzeni in October 1889 he was succeeded by his son, Bhunu, who took the official name Ngwane V. As the young king was a minor, the queen mother acted as regent until 1894. Meanwhile, the joint commission, after visiting the country, proposed the establishment of a new system of government. This was a triumvirate to consist of one representative of the Transvaal, one of the British government, and 'Offy' Shepstone representing the Swazi kingdom. In March 1890, the British High Commissioner in South Africa, Sir Henry Loch, met President Kruger at Blignaut's Pont to discuss the future of Swaziland. The idea was to trade Swaziland to the Transvaal in exchange for the Transvaal calling off two proposed treks by its citizens into the area of modern Zimbabwe where Rhodes was about to send his pioneer column. In the end Loch drove so hard a bargain that the Transvaal *volksraad* refused to ratify the agreement. In a convention signed on 20 August 1890 therefore, the independence of the kingdom was again confirmed. Under this convention, however, the triumvirate of three white men became the official government of the kingdom. A concessions court was also set up to examine and verify the numerous concessions that had been granted.

In April 1893 the British High Commissioner and Kruger met again and this time it was agreed that if the Swazi queen regent gave her agreement the kingdom would pass under the administrative authority of the Transvaal. The queen regent, however, refused to agree and appealed to Britain. She once more dismissed 'Offy' and appointed a solicitor from Natal, George Hulett, as secretary to the Swazi nation. Though a Swazi deputation visited England and saw Queen Victoria, the cession of Swaziland had become an accepted part of British diplomatic strategy. In spite of all protests a new convention between Britain and the Transvaal was signed in 1894 under which the kingdom became a protectorate of the republic.

Once they had established their administration, the Transvaal authorities introduced heavy taxes. These were first imposed in 1898 and bore very heavily on the people because they came in the aftermath of a rinderpest epidemic which had destroyed most of the Swazi cattle. That same year, Bhunu was charged with murder of a senior *induna*, Mbhabha Sibandze, who had died at the royal household at Zambodze. The young king arrived at the courthouse accompanied by members of his age-regiment in full military regalia. The Transvaal special commissioner, Johannes Krogh, sent the king away, warning him that he would report the matter to Pretoria. The Transvaal now rushed reinforcements to the area while the Swazi regiments prepared for battle. The king's council, however, persuaded the young king not to break with the long-established policy of avoiding conflict with white forces. Instead, Bhunu fled to Zululand and sought British protection. He was sent back and stood trial but the charge of murder was not proved. He was reinstated but subjected to a heavy fine, of which the greater part was to pay the police costs.

With the outbreak of the South African War, Transvaal forces evacuated Swaziland and the kingdom regained almost complete independence. The young king Bhunu died, however, in December 1899 and as his heir was a baby the queen mother once again became regent. At the end of the South African War, Swaziland was at first administered together with the Transvaal; but when the Transvaal was granted self-government in 1906, Swaziland was removed from the Transvaal and placed under the British High Commissioner. This prepared the way for the exclusion of Swaziland from the Union of South Africa in 1910 along with the other two High Commission Territories.

Meanwhile a commission had been established to look once again into the validity of the concessions. In general it gave official recognition to most of the concessions including even the notorious Unallocated Lands Concession. Claims were considerably reduced but the final proclamation issued in 1907 gave nearly two-thirds of the land of the kingdom to whites, leaving only a third to the Swazi. For most of Swaziland's period as a High Commission Territory the authorities assumed that, like Basutoland and Bechuanaland, it would eventually be incorporated in the Union of South Africa. In the case of Swaziland the pressures for this were particularly strong because so much of the country was owned and farmed by white South Africans. With so little land left to them, the Swazi, like the Sotho and Tswana, were driven into labour migration to white South Africa. The territory took on the character of just another underdeveloped labour reserve for the white economy. Even by these standards it was exceptionally backward. At independence it had a literacy rate of only about 30 per cent while over 70 per cent of its population suffered from malnutrition.

As the Swazi kingdom had never been conquered, its traditional political system remained exceptionally strong. Even the age-regiment system survived throughout the colonial period and into independence. The regiments no longer took part in warfare, but every Swazi youth was enrolled in one and they continued to assemble every year on the important ritual occasion of the *Ncwala* first-fruits ceremony. Of all the states built on the Zulu pattern the Swazi is the only one to have retained the military system. It played a very important part in maintaining the strength of the traditional political system and strengthening loyalty to the king and queen mother. During the greater part of the colonial period the traditional authorities retained the political leadership of the nation. They led the struggle to win back the lands lost to the concession hunters by petitions and delegations and by legal action. They also launched appeals for funds which were to be used to buy back land from white owners. During the colonial period, however, the system became increasingly autocratic. The traditional royal council was recognised by the British authorities as the Swazi National Council. It became a body entirely dominated by the king's personal nominees.

Sobhuza II: first political moves

The long regency of the queen mother came to an end on 22 December 1921 when Bhunu's heir, Sobhuza II, came of age and was officially installed as king. He at once launched a vigorous struggle to recover the land of the nation. In December 1922 he led a deputation to London to petition the British government over the issue. When this failed to achieve any result, the matter was taken to court in 1924 and the case proceeded as far as the British Privy Council. Once again, however, the Swazi were disappointed. In 1940 Sobhuza appealed to King George VI for more land and this time the British government did undertake to procure some land for

Swazi settlement. The amount was far too small to satisfy needs, however, and Sobhuza set up the 'Lifa Fund' to buy back more land.

In 1929 Benjamin Nxumalo founded a political discussion group, the Swaziland Progressive Association. But eight years earlier the whites in Swaziland had already gained a voice in a European advisory council. In 1955 the whites petitioned the British Secretary of State to turn this into a legislative council. This request was refused, however, and a few years later Swaziland was caught up in the general movement in Africa towards African self-government and independence. In 1960 the European advisory council, sensing the trend of events, launched an initiative aimed at maintaining a measure of white control. They called for the establishment of a multiracial council with limited legislative powers with substantial representation for the white community. The Swazi National Council protested but without effect. Faced with the prospect of elections, the king decided to found his own political movement. The Imbokodvo National Movement, openly pledged to extreme royalism, was founded and allied closely with the United Swaziland Association, the political movement of Swaziland whites. In the elections Imbokodvo captured all the African seats while the United Swaziland Association took all those reserved for whites.

The overwhelming victory of Imbokodvo at the polls, however, gave Sobhuza the confidence to dispense with his white allies. He now adopted a pan-Africanist attitude and pressed for independence. In 1966 a new constitution was drawn up. Special provision for white representation was dropped. On the other hand the king had power to appoint one-fifth of the House of Assembly and half the members of the Senate. He also had the right to block constitutional changes affecting the monarchy even if they were passed by a two-thirds majority. In the elections held in 1967 Imbokodvo won all the seats so that the country entered on independence in 1968 under a constitution which simply clothed the absolute authority of the king in modern form.

During the colonial period there was considerable agricultural development in Swaziland but mainly on land owned by whites. In the pre-independence period, sugar growing became an important element in the economy. Extensive timber plantations had also been established, some of which were on Swazi native land. In 1964 mining of a limited deposit of very high-grade iron ore at Ngwenya was begun. During the life of the deposit (up to 1979) the ore was exported to Japan and for this purpose a railway was built to Lourenço Marques (now Maputo). This has given Swaziland access to the sea independent of South Africa. Swaziland also developed a certain amount of manufacturing but has been subjected to pressure from South Africa to prevent it from competing with South African firms.

In the elections held in May 1972 an opposition party, the Ngwane National Liberatory Congress succeeded in winning three seats in the Assembly. The Imbokodvo first tried to get one of these members deported on the grounds that he was not a Swazi citizen. The High Court revoked the order but then Imbokodvo changed the law to remove immigration cases from the scrutiny of the court. When the Chief Justice's contract ran out it was not renewed. Still unable to tolerate any opposition to the king, the Imbokodvo majority in the Assembly declared the constitution

Swazi land delegation to London, 1923

Economic development

An absolute monarchy

267

King Sobhuza II

unworkable and placed themselves at the disposal of the king. He thereupon abolished the Assembly and all political parties on the grounds that they were repugnant to Swazi traditions. He continued to rule with the advice of the traditional Swazi National Council.

In October 1978 a new constitutional system was announced. A two-chamber assembly was to be chosen by indirect election based on traditional communities known as *tinkhundla*. These were to elect members of an eighty-man electoral college which would in turn elect forty members to the House of Assembly. Ten further members would be appointed by the king. The electoral college would also choose ten out of twenty members of the Senate. When elected, the two Houses would be restricted to debating government proposals and advising the king.

In the first elections to the electoral college in October 1978 no parties were allowed and even the names of candidates were not made public until voting started. The new system came into full operation in 1979. Thereafter, for the rest of Sobhuza's reign, Swaziland remained an absolute monarchy, governed by the king in consultation with a traditional chiefly council known as the *Liqoqo*, made up of royal princes, other traditional chiefs and favoured commoner allies of the monarch. Royal decisions were subsequently enacted as laws by the parliament or put into execution by the prime minister and cabinet. These came to serve the function of transmitting royal decisions to the civil service for action.

After 1974 the strategic situation of Swaziland was transformed as it came to have a common border with the radical regime in Mozambique, a relationship further strengthened by the railway link to Maputo. Following the Soweto uprisings moreover, Swaziland became a refuge for substantial numbers of refugees from South Africa. The ANC presence in the country became more noticeable and Swaziland came to provide a significant corridor for the infiltration of South African territory by ANC guerrillas.

Since 1979 the South African government had indicated the possibility of transferring two areas with their populations to Swaziland. These were the KaNgwane Bantustan and the Ingwavuma territory of KwaZulu. Transfer of the latter would give Swaziland access to the sea. The transfer would also have served South Africa's purpose of denationalising its black African population, since Swaziland, unlike any of the Bantustans, was internationally recognised as an independent sovereign state. The attraction for South Africa of transferring these particular territories was also enhanced by the fact that the alternative approach to denationalising their populations was frustrated by the refusal of either the KaNgwane or the KwaZulu governments to accept independence from South Africa. Apart from this, the offer to transfer the territories was seen as a bait to persuade the Swazi government to ally more closely with South Africa and suppress ANC activity on its soil. In February 1982 Swaziland agreed to a secret non-aggression pact with South Africa and thereafter began a major clampdown on the ANC.

In the last years of Sobhuza's rule, the prime minister, also a royal relative, Mabandla Dlamini, initiated an enquiry into corruption. When the enquiry extended its activities to investigation of the conduct of the Lifa national land repurchase fund, members of the *Liqoqo* felt threatened. Sobhuza had the enquiry closed but Mabandla had succeeded in winning considerable popular support.

On 21 August 1982 Sobhuza II died and the nation embarked on a prolonged mourning period. During this time key members of the royal family and the *Liqoqo* agreed that the young prince Makhosetive (about twelve years old) who was attending boarding school in England, was the legitimate heir to the throne. In the meanwhile one of Sobhuza's wives, Queen Dzeliwe, would act as regent with the advice of an official advisor, Prince Sosiza, who was to hold a traditional title meaning 'Authorised Person'. They would exercise their authority in conjunction with the *Liqoqo*. With Queen Dzeliwe's support, however, the prime minister made a bid to increase his role and that of the Swaziland parliament. He promised extensive democratic reform. When he met opposition from members of the *Liqoqo*, he had two princes, Mfanasibili Dlamini and Mfanawenkhosi Maseko arrested in February 1983 and charged with sedition. Shortly before the trial opened, however, members of the *Liqoqo* prevailed on the Queen

Regent to dismiss Mabandla who fled to take refuge in South Africa.

Mabandla was replaced by Bhekimpi Dlamini and then on 22 August 1983 Dzeliwe was asked to sign away a very large part of her powers to the Authorised Person, Prince Sosiza. When she refused she was deposed in favour of the young heir apparent's mother, Queen Ntombi Latswala. The young prince was brought home briefly from his English school to be shown to the people and Queen Ntombi signed the document transferring powers to Prince Sosiza. New elections under the *tinkhundla* and electoral college system were then held for parliament. It was effectively purged of all Mabandla supporters. The control of the *Liqoqo* and within this a triumvirate consisting of the two princes, Mfanasibili Dlamini and Mfanawenkhosi Maseko, together with a commoner, George Msibi, was consolidated.

They had been particularly strong supporters of the land transfer scheme but this ran into difficulty in 1982 when it was blocked by a successful court action taken by the KaNgwane and the KwaZulu governments. South Africa then set up a judicial commission but this was dissolved in June 1984 without submitting a report. The South African minister of foreign affairs subsequently promised that the transfer would never be undertaken without the full support of the populations concerned. This did not suffice however to put an end to suspicions that just such action was still contemplated. In the meantime, with the land issue stalled and tension arising from attempts to suppress the ANC at a high level, the country remained in a rather volatile situation.

With the election of a new *tinkhundla* in 1983, the Mfanasibili faction was able to consolidate its position still further, and supporters of Prince Mabandla and Queen Regent Dzeliwe were removed from office. In 1984, however, in-fighting broke out within the ruling clique and the Prime Minister Prince Bhekimpi Dlamini secured the removal of Mfanasibili and Msibi from the *Liqoqo*. On 25 April Prince Makhosetive was crowned as King Mswati III. He moved quickly against the whole clique involved in the deposition of Queen Regent Dzeliwe. In May, Prince Bhekimpi was arrested with Mfanasibili and his associates: they were charged with sedition for their action against the Queen. In November the special tribunal set up to deal with the case found them guilty of treason. In July 1986 Prince Bhekimpi and eight others, but not Mfanasibili, were pardoned. New elections were held for the *tinkhundla* in November 1987. The low poll for the electoral colleges suggested widespread disillusionment with the political system. Calls for a more democratic order continued to be rejected in the name of Swazi tradition.

Botswana

Unlike the other two enclave states, Botswana is not the territory of a single pre-colonial state. Its very extensive territory includes a narrow strip in the east which is relatively well watered and in good years excellent cattle country. The greater part of the country, however, is desert, or semi-desert, though there is some reasonably good grazing land around Lake Ngami in the Kalahari. In the north-western areas of the country are to be found some of the greatest concentrations of wild game of any area in modern Africa. In the nineteenth century, before the establishment of colonial rule, desert areas of the country continued to be occupied, as they are today, by small populations of San hunters. They are known in Botswana as the Sarwa. Many

Tswana warriors
from Keith Johnston, *Africa*, 1878

of their communities lived as clients of Bantu-speaking chiefdoms.

The fertile eastern strip was occupied by a number of Tswana-speaking chiefdoms. In the period before the *mfecane* the Ngwaketse were probably the most powerful. The area around Lake Ngami was the homeland of the Tawana chiefdom. During the *mfecane* the Tswana peoples of the area suffered severely from the marauding activities of a number of wandering hordes, particularly the Kololo of Sebetwane who passed through most of the area on their long migration to the upper Zambezi flood plain. They suffered even more severely from the raids of the Ndebele armies, especially after Mzilikazi had established his kingdom in the relatively near vicinity of the Mosega basin. The defeat of Mzilikazi by the Boers and his relocation in Zimbabwe did not mean an end to the Ndebele danger altogether. Their armies continued to exact tribute in north-eastern districts of the country and to dispute sovereignty over it until the arrival of colonial authority. The replacement of the Ndebele kingdom as a neighbour by the Transvaal Boers, moreover, did not mean an end to threats from that quarter. The continuous expansionist pressure of the land-hungry Boer farmers produced

271

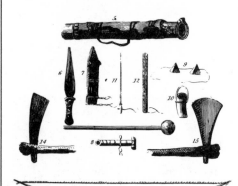

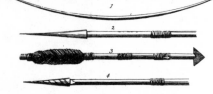

Tswana weapons from
Campbell's *Travels in
South Africa*, 1815

repeated upheavals and tended to push more Tswana peoples into the area of the modern nation.

In the period of the *mfecane* the Ngwaketse suffered particularly severely from Ndebele attacks and lost their predominance, though they remained one of the most powerful chiefdoms in the area. The general effect of the *mfecane* and of the subsequent pressure exerted by the Transvaal Republic was to encourage the tendency towards the formation of larger political units, as smaller chiefdoms sought the protection of more powerful paramounts. The larger chiefdoms in the area thus came to include numerous previously separate groups under their authority. Outstanding amongst the chiefdoms which followed this path were the Ngwato (plural Bamangwato) who became far and away the largest single community in the territory.

By the time that the *mfecane* began affecting the Tswana area, missionary activity was already being undertaken among the southern Tswana by Robert Moffat who had his mission stationed at Kuruman. He played a significant part in the course of the *lifaqane* in this area by helping to persuade the Griquas to drive the Kololo and other groups away from Dithakong, thus sending Sebetwane northward through modern Botswana. He subsequently established a close personal relationship with Mzilikazi. He and his son-in-law, the missionary explorer Livingstone, opened up a route giving access to central Africa running northwards through territory outside the control of the Transvaal Republic. As European influence spread to the area some Tswana chiefs, like Moshoeshoe of Lesotho, cultivated relations with the missionaries to help them cope with the new problems and opportunities brought about by the arrival of the white men. One of these was Chief Setshele of the Kwena who was Livingstone's first convert. Of all the Botswana chiefs, however, it was Kgama, the Christian chief of the Ngwato, who most successfully used the knowledge gained from the missionaries.

British authority over Botswana was established in the course of the 'scramble for Africa'. Action was caused by the desire to preserve a route for Cape and British trade to central Africa along the road which had been pioneered by the missionaries Moffat and Livingstone. This 'Suez Canal' to the north, as Rhodes described it, was threatened by the westward expansion of white adventurers from the Transvaal who, pretending to assist African chiefs in their conflicts, took possession of wide areas of land on which they set up the small republics of Stellaland and Goshen. These republics lay in the southern part of the area occupied by Tswana peoples (that is, south of the Molopo river). It seemed likely that these republics would be absorbed by the Transvaal and pose a barrier to British trade with central Africa. The German annexation of South West Africa (now Namibia) then raised the possibility that the Germans might extend their control eastward to link up with the Transvaal. This would not only shut British influence out of central Africa but pose a threat to the security of the British position at the Cape. Thus after the ex-missionary John Mackenzie and Cecil Rhodes had both failed to persuade the two petty republics to accept a negotiated solution, the British government despatched Sir Charles Warren with a large military force to the area in late 1881.

In January 1885 Warren was given powers to extend British authority over the area between the Transvaal and the area claimed by the Germans as far north as the line of latitude 22°S. Faced with military force the two small republics gave in without a fight. The African chiefs south of the

Moffat preaching to the Bechuana
by Charles Bell

Molopo were also anxious for British protection against Boer expansion. Among the chiefs north of the Molopo, Kgama of the Ngwato was eager for the extension of British protection but wanted the boundary extended further north because it cut his territory in half. Setshele and his son Sebelo of the Kwena and Gaseitswe of the Ngwaketse were less enthusiastic but were persuaded to agree.

The costs of administering the whole of the area threatened to be considerable; white settlers were confined to the area south of the Molopo river, so the area that had been brought under British protection was divided. In September 1885 the area south of the Molopo was annexed as the colony of British Bechuanaland. In 1895 it was transferred to the Cape and is now part of the Cape Province of South Africa. (Reserves set aside within this area of the Tswana peoples have now been incorporated in the Bophuthatswana Bantustan.) The area north of the Molopo river became the Bechuanaland Protectorate. The northern frontier was extended to the Zambezi in 1891-2.

The British government was at first very hesitant to exercise administrative authority within the area. For reasons of expense it preferred to leave the chiefs to administer their own people and to confine its role to preventing the intrusion of Germans or Transvaal Boers into the area. In 1891-2, however, provision was made for the establishment of colonial administration. The protectorate provided the corridor necessary for Rhodes' pioneer column to advance into present-day Zimbabwe. Kgama gave the column considerable help, and his forces helped to defeat the Ndebele. As part of his wide-ranging plans, Rhodes hoped that Bechuanaland would be handed over to the British South Africa Company. Kgama of the Ngwato together with Setshele of the Kwena and Bathoen (successor to Gaseitswe) of the Ngwaketse protested strongly, however, and travelled to England in 1895. The Secretary of State for the Colonies, Joseph Chamberlain, at first refused to alter the decision. The three chiefs, however, addressed numerous public meetings and aroused such widespread sympathy and support that Chamberlain altered his attitude. The protectorate continued under British administration, and the British South Africa Company was instead given a substantial strip of territory to build a railway line to Rhodesia. It was also given an area of land on which it built up, drilled and prepared the force which was to march with Dr Jameson into the Transvaal. The total failure of the Jameson raid and the subsequent Ndebele and Shona rebellions in Rhodesia finally put an end to any prospect of the protectorate coming under the Company, and later, like Basutoland and Swaziland, Bechuanaland was narrowly saved from incorporation in the Union of South Africa at the time of unification. Like the other High Commission Territories it was expected that it would eventually be handed over. There was thus no sense of commitment on the part of the British administration to develop the territories in any way other than as an addition to the South African economy.

From chiefdoms to national politics

In the early days of the protectorate Kgama launched an interesting economic initiative. He bought up a trading company and aimed to acquire a major part of the commerce of the protectorate. He also attempted to prevent his people from being drawn into labour migration by providing work at home. However, the British authorities soon moved in to suppress this enterprise, and the result was inevitable; with minimal capital investment and under the pressures of growing population, taxation and indebtedness, the protectorate followed the familiar path towards agricultural decline, increasing impoverishment and dependence on the earnings of labour migration that characterised colonial Basutoland and Swaziland as well as the native reserves within South Africa.

In spite of this general trend, however, some Africans in the Bechuanaland protectorate still owned considerable numbers of cattle although there was a marked tendency here, as in the other High Commission Territories, for the ownership of cattle to be concentrated in the hands of a small elite. No exact calculations were made in the colonial period but when an agricultural census was undertaken in 1967-8 it showed that nearly half the population owned no cattle at all and 60 per cent of all the cattle in the country were owned by less than 15 per cent of the population.

In 1920 Africans acquired a very limited voice in the overall administration of the protectorate with the formation of a Native Advisory Council. Its members were all nominated by the administration, however. What is more, the tiny number of whites in the country were simultaneously granted an elected advisory council. For many years the white council repeatedly pressed for the incorporation of the territory in the Union of South Africa while the Native Advisory Council continuously opposed the idea.

During much of the colonial period the most outstanding African political leader in the territory was Tshekedi Khama. In 1926 he was made regent over the Ngwato, the largest chiefdom in the protectorate, and began a succession of long and finally successful legal battles with the colonial administration in defence of chiefly authority and the preservation of control over the mineral rights in his chiefdom. In 1925, two years after the death of Kgama, Tshekedi Khama became acting chief of the Ngwato people. An attempt was made to depose him in 1933, after one of his courts ordered a white youth to be whipped for an assault on an Ngwato youth. However, the Ngwato refused to accept the authority of any alternative regent and Tshekedi was soon re-instated.

A more serious political crisis occurred in 1948. Decolonisation was taking its first major step forward in India but South Africa was turning in the opposite direction and accepting the racist doctrine of apartheid. The young heir to the Ngwato throne, Seretse Khama, brought the race issues which dominated southern African thinking to the fore by marrying an English woman, Ruth Williams. Tshekedi opposed his nephew's marriage on traditional grounds; meanwhile the National Party government in South Africa exerted great pressure on the British government to oppose this example of racial integration and this view was supported by the government of Southern Rhodesia. The Labour Party government in Britain gave in to these pressures; the Secretary of State for Commonwealth Affairs, Patrick Gordon-Walker, invited the chief to visit England and then refused to allow him to go home. When he was finally allowed back it was on condition that he did not assume the Ngwato chieftaincy. Seretse was thus encouraged to devote his energies to national politics. The affair gave him tremendous sympathy and support among all the African communities in the protectorate and so helped to launch him on the path to the presidency.

A minor constitutional change was introduced in 1950 when a joint advisory council of whites and Africans was set up, made up of eight members of each race chosen by their respective councils. It was not until 1958 that the decision was made to establish an elected legislative council. Even then the 3200 whites in the territory were given as many seats as the 317,000-strong African population.

Political parties

With the prospect of elections, which were held in 1961, the first African political parties in Botswana came into being. In 1959 L.D. Ratidladi founded the Bechuanaland Protectorate Federal Party. In the following year the Bechuanaland People's Party was founded by one of the country's few graduates, K.T. Motsete, together with Motsamai Mpho, a member of the South African ANC who had been one of the victims of the notorious treason trial (see Chapter 9). The Bechuanaland People's Party was soon to be torn apart, however, in the aftermath of the split of the South African nationalist movement between the ANC and the PAC. One section of the party survived as a relatively radical movement. It took the name Botswana Independence Party for some years, then reverted to the Botswana People's Party.

The confused state of party organisation in the period before 1961 meant that no party dominated the electoral process or controlled the majority of those elected to the legislative council. In January 1962, Seretse Khama, who had been elected to the council in 1961 and had gained the strongest support, founded a new party called the Bechuanaland Democratic Party. He persuaded ten of the twelve recently elected members of the legislative council to join him in this new moderate party. In 1965 a new constitution based on universal suffrage was introduced and in the elections held in the following year Seretse Khama's Bechuanaland Democratic Party was swept to victory.

The independence era

When Botswana achieved independence in September 1966, it faced a disastrous economic situation. Added to the problems of poverty which had matured during the colonial period was the natural disaster of a severe drought which drastically reduced the number of cattle in the country. Not only was Botswana forced to continue to provide cheap labour to the white South African economy, it had even to accept South African food aid and was in no position to exert any significant measure of political independence. Seretse Khama's political problems were made more difficult by the problems arising from UDI in Rhodesia. Not only did Botswana share a very long border with Rhodesia but its railway was part of the Rhodesia/South African railway system. From the beginning Botswana provided a valuable asylum for refugees from the Smith regime in Rhodesia but otherwise it had at first to tread very carefully.

Sir Seretse Khama

In 1967, however, very substantial diamond deposits were discovered in Botswana. These were first exploited in 1971 and this started a major transformation of the nation's economy. Copper deposits had also been found in 1964 at Selebi-Pikwe and in 1973 mining of these began. Though copper production did not prove as profitable as diamond mining and was hit by falling prices, mineral exports easily overtook cattle and cattle products after 1971. Botswana not only acquired a much stronger economy but was also able to provide much more employment for its own manpower than before independence. It thus became a good deal less dependent on South Africa. In this changed atmosphere Seretse Khama built up a close political relationship with President Kaunda of Zambia. Regular air links were established and Botswana broke out of its total dependence on land routes through South Africa by constructing a road to the Zambezi to link up with Zambia. In the later stages of the Rhodesian conflict Botswana played an increasingly important role in bringing pressure on the Smith regime.

Seretse Khama died suddenly in July 1980. He was succeeded in office by his vice-president Dr Quett Masire. Though coming from the Ngwaketse chiefdom, and thus having a much smaller immediate political power base than his predecessor, the new president was able to consolidate his leadership without serious difficulty. With the outbreak of conflict between ZAPU dissidents and government forces in Zimbabwe, Ndebele refugees crossed the border into Botswana in considerable numbers. This created some difficulties in relations between Botswana and Zimbabwe but these were successfully contained. Botswana continued to follow its narrow and difficult path, supporting change in southern Africa in association with the more radical states to the north while remaining still very dependent on South Africa.

Masire's presidency was renewed in September 1984 after elections to the National Assembly had given the ruling BDP a decisive majority. Despite this success the popularity of the party was in decline in urban areas as a result of unemployment and a general economic downturn. In local elections, held at the same time as the general election, the main opposition party the BNF took control of all town councils except Selebi-Pikwe. The ruling party was further weakened by the defection of two members to the BNF. However, internal divisions in the BNF meant that it was unable to make further progress. Elections in October 1989 gave the BDP 31 of the 34 elective seats in the National Assembly and Masire was re-elected for a further presidential term.

Under his leadership the country actively pursued measures to lessen its economic dependence on South Africa. It was an active member of the Southern African Development Coordination Conference (SADCC) set up for this purpose after a conference of five front-line presidents in Botswana in 1979. The headquarters of the organisation was subsequently established in Gaborone. Botswana also persistently resisted pressure and threats from South Africa to enter into a mutual security pact. It was believed to provide an important infiltration route for ANC guerrillas and for these reasons was the subject of a series of armed incursions by South African forces. At the same time strained relations persisted with Zimbabwe over Botswana's refusal to repatriate the ZAPU refugees. After the unity agreement between ZANU and ZAPU in December 1987, however, most of the refugees returned home voluntarily and cordial relations between the two countries were restored.

Appendix 2: Namibia

Namibia, like Botswana, owes its boundaries to the accidents of international diplomacy during the European 'scramble for Africa'. In the north it includes a considerable area of fairly well-watered and densely populated country, the homeland of the Ovambo and other related Bantu-speaking peoples. The greater part of the territory, however, is very arid. Much of the coastline is taken up by the desolate Namib desert. Further inland lies the Kalahari. Outside the area of the desert, the country can support successful pastoral farming although a large area is required to support each animal. The territory is rich in minerals. The sand dunes near the Orange river mouth are the richest source of alluvial diamonds in the world. Copper is another source of mineral wealth. In more recent times uranium has become the most important of the country's resources. Its production constitutes far the greatest single contribution to the total world supply. Numerous smaller deposits of other valuable minerals have also been found. A cold current running along the coast makes the rain fall out at sea, leaving the shore a dry desert. That cold current, however, carries huge shoals of fish, especially anchovies, and this is the basis of a major fishing industry.

Population

The earliest population still to survive in the area are the San hunters and gatherers (see Chapter 1). They were increasingly pushed into the Kalahari by later immigrant peoples, but still remain in significant numbers in the territory and in neighbouring Botswana; the two countries between them provide the homeland for the vast majority of the entire surviving San population of about 50 000. Other early inhabitants were the Damara or Berg-Dama. They are people of Negro physical type but speak a Khoi language and traditionally practised a hunting and gathering economy, though they also smelted iron and copper. In the southern arid areas which constitute far the greater part of the total area the predominant precolonial population consisted of a number of communities of a branch of the Khoi peoples known as the Nama. The main communities resident before the early years of the nineteenth century have come to be known by Afrikaner names as the Rooi Nasie, the Velkskoendraers, Fransmanne, Groot Dode, Bondelswarts and Topnaars. In the northern part of the territory the Bantu-speaking Ovambo and related peoples occupied the area of high rainfall. They practised a mixed pastoral and agricultural economy and probably then as now constituted much the largest population group in the whole

Khoi on the beach at Walfisch Bay
from Johnston, *Africa*, 1878

territory. Further south, another Bantu-speaking people, the Herero, had pushed into the area of Nama occupation. Adapting to the arid conditions, they practised an exclusively pastoral economy like their Nama neighbours.

During the nineteenth century a number of Khoi groups who had been influenced by the Dutch culture of the Cape Colony and had in many cases adopted a form of Afrikaans as their language, crossed the Orange and moved into Namibia. These peoples, known as the Orlams, include the Witboois, the Amraals, the Bersheba and the Bethanie groups. Another such group, marked by a greater degree of European descent and Dutch culture, were the so-called Basters of Rehoboth. They arrived later than the Orlams and settled in an area around the village of Rehoboth in 1870. There they drew up a simple republican constitution and a basic code of laws. Most forceful of all were the nineteenth-century immigrants who were the followers of Jonker Afrikaner, son of the notorious Khoi brigand, Jager Afrikaner, who for so long defied the Cape authorities from his stronghold on an island in the Orange river, before finally being converted to Christianity and receiving a pardon from the governor of the colony.

Jonker Afrikaner

Inter-ethnic conflict and European intervention

Jonker Afrikaner created some unity among the Nama group under his leadership. Using the military advantage of modern weapons, he succeeded in dominating the Herero and reducing them temporarily to tribute-paying clients of the Nama. In 1864, however, the Herero, led by Maherero, appointed the traveller and trader, Charles Andersson, as their commander-in-chief. With further military support from two English traders, Frederick Green and Haybittel, they defeated Jonker Afrikaner's forces and established their own control over the Nama for a time. This was the beginning of a confused period of repeated conflicts interrupted by attempts at general peacemaking. This period of increased warfare and raiding coincided with

Walfisch Bay
from Keith Johnston, *Africa*, 1878

the establishment of traders and missionaries (some of whom supported their missions by trade). As the various African communities parted with their cattle to the traders they attempted to restock their supplies by raiding their neighbours. They also acquired the guns and ammunition to use in such warfare. In 1868 a Nama force robbed Andersson's shop in retaliation for his help to the Herero. Property of the Rhenish mission was also taken and the mission sought protection from the King of Prussia. Twelve years later, in 1880, the German Chancellor, Otto von Bismarck asked the British government whether it was prepared to give protection to German subjects in the area. When Britain failed to reply he prepared to go ahead and establish German authority in the area.

In the meantime, Namibia very nearly came under the authority of the Cape. Maherero, troubled by the problems caused by whites in the area and by news of the approach of a party of *trek boers*, approached the Cape government for protection. A commissioner named W.C. Palgrave was appointed and he made treaties with the Herero and the Rehobothers. The Cape parliament, however, was not prepared to meet the costs of annexation. The only action taken was the British annexation of Walvis Bay in 1878. It was subsequently passed on to the Cape and then became part of the Union of South Africa in 1910.

The German administration of South West Africa

In 1884, a German protectorate was declared over the area surrounding Lüderitz Bay. In 1886 the boundary between what now became German South West Africa and Angola was negotiated with the Portuguese. In 1890 Germany and Britain came to an agreement over the boundary between South West Africa and the Bechuanaland Protectorate. In that agreement the British government gave up the narrow strip of territory known as the Caprivi Strip (in honour of the then German Chancellor, Count von Caprivi). Given to Germany in exchange for German claims on Zanzibar, the corridor was intended to give the Germans access to the Zambezi river. (The population of this area is closely related to that of the Lozi kingdom in Zambia.) The final definition of the boundary also led to the inclusion of some Tswana communities in Namibia.

As the Germans set about establishing their administration, the Herero at first accepted a treaty of protection, but most Nama communities, led by Hendrik Witbooi, refused. A surprise attack was launched against Witbooi in 1890 but he escaped and was only finally forced to surrender in 1894. Other Nama groups were also crushed, but the Germans were still occupied in suppressing an uprising of the Bondelswarts when in 1904 the Herero rose in rebellion. The Herero had seen their lands increasingly taken from them and their herds reduced through trading deals that were little better than theft. Some eight years previously in 1896, the Germans had confiscated large numbers of what remained of the Herero cattle and the following year the rinderpest epidemic killed most of what was left. The Herero uprising strained German forces very severely until reinforcements arrived. Afterwards, with the use of the Maxim gun and the quick-firing Krupp gun, the German forces gained the upper hand. The Herero were forced back into the Waterberg mountains and were decisively defeated there in the battle of

Maharero, chief of the Herero

German colonial life, c. 1903: Margarete von Eckenbrecher and family

281

Hendrik Witboii

Hamakar. In desperation, however, the whole Herero community broke through the German lines and fled into the desert, some making north for Ovamboland, others east to Bechuanaland where many settled as refugees. The Germans could then have negotiated peace on their own terms but a newly appointed commander-in-chief, General Lothar von Trotha, was determine to destroy the Herero for ever. He issued an order calling for the extermination of every Herero man, woman and child; in the meantime the Herero continued a desperate struggle for survival. While the Germans were thus occupied, the old Nama chief, Hendrik Witbooi, now eighty years old, rallied most of the Nama communities for a renewed struggle. After a year of fierce guerrilla warfare, Witbooi was killed in action, and his people buried him secretly on the battlefield to prevent his body falling into German hands. The death of their leader did not break the Nama resistance, however. Witbooi's place was taken by Jacob Marengo and the struggle was maintained for a further two years. By 1907 the Germans had broken all serious resistance and a large proportion of the surviving Herero and Nama were herded into prison and labour camps.

Eventually, however, the Germans began to realise that their extermination policies were rapidly destroying the resources of cheap labour which were the only hope for profitable development of the colony. So the killing was stopped and the emphasis of German policy was shifted towards pushing the survivors into the work force. A system of passes was introduced and vagrancy laws were used to punish Africans who avoided white employment. The Herero had all their lands confiscated and although they had previously been a purely pastoral people they were denied the right to keep any cattle at all.

South West Africa (Namibia) under South African rule

The creation of the South African Mandate

The German administration of South West Africa was ended by South African forces in the early stages of the First World War (see Chapter 8). Smuts intended to annex the territory to South Africa. However, since he had played a major role in creating the system of international mandates, he found himself forced to agree that South Africa should administer the country under a Class C Mandate from the League of Nations. Under the terms of the mandate South Africa was bound to promote to the utmost the material and moral wellbeing and the social progress of the inhabitants of the Territory. South Africa had also to submit annual reports to the League of Nations Permanent Mandates Commission.

The hopes felt by the African peoples that their lands would be restored to them under the Mandate were very soon disappointed. The system for maintaining white domination and the exploitation of black labour developed in South Africa was simply extended to the new territory. Thus, instead of giving land taken from the Germans back to African communities, it was handed out to whites from South Africa. This pattern of colonisation was actively encouraged and whites who set up farms in the territory were heavily subsidised. In 1926 the white population was nearly double what it had been in 1914 even though about 6000 of the German population had left the country. Others remained and continued to form a significant part of the white population although this became predominantly Afrikaner in origin and language. At the same time as South Africa was explaining to the League of Nations Mandates Commission that it was quite impractical to

Ovambo workmen during a meal break
in the Otavi mines, 1908

return the Herero's ancestral lands, great efforts were being made to encourage a group of about three hundred *trek boers* who had migrated to Angola to take up farms in the territory. Apart from the desire to make land available to white South African farmers the Union government wanted to ensure that the African population of the territory would be available as very cheap labour for the white farmers and mining companies.

The greater part of the country outside Ovamboland continued to be known as the 'police zone'. Africans from outside this zone were not allowed to enter it except as labourers on contract. The police zone included the areas of white settlement and diamond and other mining development. Within this area the Herero and Nama communities were given reserves sufficient only to provide some support for their families at bare subsistence level. A large proportion of the active males would thus be forced to supplement the returns of farming in the reserves by going out to work on the white farms or in the mines. To reinforce the necessity to go out and work for the whites, taxes were also imposed, creating an unavoidable need for cash.

In the period from the First World War to 1948 the supreme authority in South West Africa was the Administrator, a civil servant appointed by the South African government. Within the police zone, however, considerable authority was exercised by a Legislative Council, elected by whites in the territory only. Outside the police zone, the area occupied by the Ovambo and related Bantu-speaking peoples was treated as a labour reserve. There was the absolute minimum of development. Unlimited authority was exercised by the Administrator, who was given the title 'great chief'. This authority was exercised through four native commissioners. African chiefs and headmen were used as government agents. The government gave them far greater powers over their own people than they had had in the traditional political systems. It also treated them as government servants who could be dismissed and replaced if they did not serve their masters' interests.

As populations increased and practically no development was undertaken, Africans were forced on to the labour market in ever-increasing numbers.

The style of Mandate administration: social effects

283

Africans from the northern territories became by far the largest element in the work force of the whole territory. Within their home areas the fact that the majority of active males were caught up in the migrant labour system worsened the decline of the agricultural economy and the quality of family life in the same way as in native reserves in South Africa. In addition, Africans working on white farms, in the mines or in the towns of South West Africa were subject to a pass system and labour regulations similar to those of South Africa. They also suffered the same residential, social and educational segregation and discrimination.

The repression of the Bondelswarts

Throughout the period down to the Second World War, South Africa was regularly criticised by the Permanent Mandate Commission. One incident in particular served to give its administration of South West Africa very adverse international publicity. The Bondelswarts, one of the Orlam communities that had migrated into the country from the Cape in the nineteenth century, had in 1896 fought alongside the Nama leader, Hendrik Witbooi, in his struggle against German forces. Though savagely crushed, they resumed the struggle in 1906 but were once again defeated. The Germans then imposed a treaty on them. They were left with only a fraction of their original lands and had to agree to supply labour to the government and white employers. Their most outstanding leader in the armed struggle, Abraham Morris, had a price placed on his head and fled as a refugee to South Africa. When South African forces invaded South West Africa, Morris served as a guide and was given a rifle in recognition of his services. The South African conquest, however, brought little improvement for the Bondelswarts. The South African authorities, far from giving their land back, confirmed the treaty which the Germans had imposed.

The Bondelswarts supplemented the produce of farming by hunting with the help of dogs. To break their economic independence and force them out to work for whites, therefore, in 1922 the government raised the tax the Germans had imposed on the Bondelswarts dogs by four times. The Bondelswarts were already living on the edge of extreme poverty and starvation according to an official report. They tried to earn the money for the dog tax by selling cattle and carting wood. Many could not raise the sum and 140 were convicted and fined. At that moment, Morris decided to return from South Africa with a number of other refugees. He did not seek official permission, and this was treated as a serious offence although he handed his gun back to the police when asked. The police summoned the Bondelswarts to hand him over. When they refused, the South African army, with bomber support, attacked the community. In five days the Bondelswarts were completely crushed.

South African schemes to absorb or partition South West Africa

At the end of the Second World War Smuts planned to absorb South West Africa into the Union of South Africa. In May 1946 the white Legislative Assembly in Windhoek passed a motion calling for the incorporation of the territory in South Africa. A public relations exercise was then undertaken purporting to show that the indigenous peoples also favoured the move. Chiefs (who were appointed by and could be removed from office by government) were asked to give their opinion on the matter and their affirmative answers were then put forward as being representative of the views of all their people.

The issue was then put to the United Nations General Assembly. The South African proposal met with widespread opposition, however. India, already involved in open conflict with South Africa in the Assembly over the treatment of Indians in South Africa, led the attack. It was supported by the Soviet Union and the Eastern bloc, the Latin American states, and the Arab-Asian bloc. The attack focused on South Africa's practice of racial discrimination. The Rev. Michael Scott provided evidence against the South African proposal on behalf of the Herero. Dr Xuma, the president of the South African ANC, travelled to New York and called on the Assembly to reject the proposal on the grounds of racial discrimination within South Africa. Even the British representative questioned the benefit the people of South West Africa would derive from incorporation, considering the racial discrimination practised in South Africa itself. South Africa's so-called referendum in the territory was rejected as a wholly inadequate way of testing the true opinion of the indigenous population. South Africa's request was rejected and Smuts was asked to place the territory under the international trusteeship system of the United Nations and to prepare a trusteeship agreement. Smuts would not, however accept that the United Nations was the legal successor to the defunct League of Nations with respect to the Mandate and refused to enter into a trusteeship agreement. He did, however, promise to submit reports on South Africa's administration of the territory to the United Nations and to continue to administer the country 'in the spirit of the existing mandate'.

The difficulties which Smuts encountered in the United Nations provided useful fuel for the National Party's election campaign in South Africa in 1948. The National Party professed the intention of rejecting the authority of the United Nations altogether and incorporating the territory in South Africa unilaterally. In 1949 a major step in this direction was taken by providing six seats in the South African House of Assembly and four in the Senate for the white population of South West Africa. It stopped short at this, however, and did not proceed to open defiance of world opinion by declaring unilateral incorporation of the territory. Indeed over time, the South African government came to accept the United Nations's standing in respect to the territory, at least implicitly, even though it exposed South Africa to repeated embarrassment and criticism. Though it did not reject the right of the United Nations to concern itself with the territory altogether, however, South Africa continued to apply its apartheid policies there in spite of the hostility of world opinion.

As apartheid in South Africa changed from its classical (*baaskap*) form to 'separate development' the new approach was applied to Namibia also. The new programme was worked out by a South African government commission set up in 1962 under the chairmanship of F.H. Odendaal. The 1964 Odendaal Report was prepared in close collaboration with Dr Verwoerd. The new scheme relinquished the idea of incorporating the whole of South West Africa as an integral part of South Africa. Instead, the country was to be prepared for eventual partition. The Native Reserves for the African community, the Khoi, San and Damara, were to be developed into self-governing and eventually independent 'homelands'. The economic heartland of the territory containing about 50 per cent of its total area and most of its mineral wealth together with a great part its agricultural potential would be reserved as a homeland for the white minority. When the ethnic 'homelands' eventually attained their independence this white 'homeland' would be incorporated with the white core of South Africa.

Under pressure from the United Nations in 1964 Verwoerd promised that the plan would not be put into immediate effect. In fact, however, the South African government went ahead with it and in 1968 provision was made for the creation of self-governing authorities in the ethnic 'homelands' by the Development of Self-Government for Native Nations in South West Africa Act. Under this Act, Bantustan-type systems were established for a number of the Native Reserves including Ovamboland, Damaraland, Hereroland, Okavangoland and East Caprivi. In 1969 the South West Africa Affairs Act transferred many powers from the whites-only territorial assembly in Namibia to the South African assembly.

In response to the spread of apartheid in South West Africa, politically conscious Africans formed a number of movements of which SWAPO (the South West Africa People's Organisation) gained the widest support. Its closest rival, SWANU (the South West African National Union), declined after 1966 until it retained a hold only on a section of the Herero. In that same year, 1966, SWAPO abandoned hope that international pressure would bring a speedy and peaceful solution and launched a guerrilla struggle against South African forces in South West Africa. So long as Angola remained under Portuguese control this struggle was kept up under great difficulties. SWAPO freedom fighters, however, did begin to develop skills in guerrilla tactics and won growing support from the Ovambo people in particular.

United Nations protest and its effects

In the United Nations, pressure on South Africa over South West Africa steadily increased as more African nations joined the world body. As early as 1960, Ethiopia and Liberia had instituted proceedings against South Africa in the International Court of Justice for failing to carry out the terms of the UN Trusteeship agreement in South West Africa (see Chapter 9). In July 1966, the International Court finally announced its decision. By a narrow majority it decided that regardless of the case itself (on which it passed no judgements) the action must fail because the plaintiffs, Ethiopia and Liberia, had no 'legal standing' in the matter. South Africa was jubilant at this result; but it produced a wide sense of shock and disappointment among African nations in particular. So great was the international sense of outrage aroused by the judgement, indeed, that it had the opposite effect from what might have been expected. Instead of granting South Africa a breathing space, it prompted the United Nations to take further action.

While in South West Africa itself SWAPO launched an armed struggle against South African forces, the United Nations General Assembly passed a resolution in October 1966, terminating the UN Trusteeship agreement on the grounds that South Africa had failed to fulfil its obligations. The Assembly resolution declared that South West Africa was under the direct responsibility of the United Nations. In 1968 the Assembly decreed that the territory should in future be called Namibia. In 1969 the United Nations Security Council gave its support to the Assembly's decision and called on South Africa to withdraw from Namibia. In 1971 the International Court of Justice confirmed the legality of the Assembly's action in withdrawing the mandate from South Africa and declared the Security Council decision on Namibia legally binding on all members of the United Nations. South Africa refused to obey the Security Council's decision or to admit United Nations administrators to the territory, so the United Nations Secretary-General was empowered to hold discussions with the South African government on how the United Nations decision could be best implemented and Namibia led to genuine independence.

In 1971 the grievances of African workers in Namibia were dramatically revealed by a massive strike of Ovambo contract workers who stopped work and demanded to be sent home. The strike, which temporarily paralysed the economy of the territory, resulted in some limited improvements in working conditions. More significantly, however, it greatly reinforced Ovambo political consciousness and strengthened SWAPO's power base in Ovamboland. From 1972 to 1973 the United Nations Secretary-General, Kurt Waldheim, and his deputy, Dr A.M. Escher, pursued negotiations with South African Prime Minister Vorster over the future of Namibia. While the South African government assured the United Nations officials that it would do nothing to undermine the unity and integrity of the territory, it still continued to implement its apartheid schemes. In 1973 the South African parliament passed a Development of Self-Government for Native Nations in South West Africa Amendment Act providing for self-government in Ovamboland and Eastern Caprivi; this was clearly a further step towards breaking up the territory into a series of 'independent' ethnic states.

In response to South Africa's handling of the Namibian situation, the United Nations Security Council decided in December 1973 that further negotiations should be broken off. The UN General Assembly supported this decision and went a step further by recognising SWAPO as the true voice of the Namibian people. United Nations pressure on South Africa increased still further in 1974 while the collapse of Portuguese imperialism altered South Africa's strategic situation.

A move to expel South Africa from the United Nations was overruled only by France, Britain and the United States who used their privilege of veto in the Security Council, and in December 1974 the Security Council unanimously adopted a resolution calling on South Africa to recognise the territorial integrity and unity of the Namibian nation and withdraw its own administration from the country. In response, the South African government abandoned the attempt to implement apartheid completely by breaking up the territory as earlier suggested by the Odendaal Report. Instead it now sought to establish a federal system for the country based on the ethnic 'homelands'. This would formally preserve the unity of the country but in practice leave the whites in effective control over the greater part of its resources. Ethnic balancing within the federal government could be expected to give the white minority sufficient opportunity to maintain most of their privileges. To further this approach a multiracial conference made up of representatives from the various ethnic communities was summoned in 1975. It met at the Windhoek Turnhalle, and worked out a federal constitution based on ethnic representation. To assist the work of the conference and give its results a better public image some of the social aspects of apartheid were abandoned.

The work of the Turnhalle Conference, however, was totally rejected by

SWAPO. After the MPLA victory in Angola and the collapse of South African intervention there, SWAPO was able to expand its guerrilla struggle a great deal, strengthen its political influence among the Ovambo people (the largest single ethnic community in Namibia) and win growing support from others. The United Nations also rejected the Turnhalle Conference; as a result the Western powers feared a showdown in the United Nations and a call for economic sanctions against South Africa which they would find difficult to resist. In the hope of avoiding this the United States, Britain, France, West Germany and Canada formed a contact group which began negotiations with the South African government in August 1977. In response, Vorster agreed to abandon the Turnhalle proposals. Instead he agreed that elections should be held in the territory under United Nations supervision. The elections were to be held on a 'one man–one vote' basis for a constituent assembly which would then work out a constitution for the country. The South African government and SWAPO, however, were each afraid that electoral arrangements might favour the other. Disagreements persisted over the numbers and role of United Nations troops to be introduced to the territory for the election period. South Africa refused to reduce its troops until an effective cease-fire had been achieved. SWAPO was reluctant to lay down arms until South African troop levels were reduced.

On 20 September 1978, however, Vorster completely cut across his earlier agreement with the United Nations and proclaimed his intention of holding elections under South African supervision in December, an obvious first step towards pushing Namibia into independence on the basis of the Turnhalle constitutional proposals. When the December elections came, SWAPO's call for a boycott proved ineffective and about 80 per cent of the voters turned out at the polls. The groups who had negotiated the Turnhalle constitution formed an alliance called the Democratic Turnhalle Alliance (DTA) and this party won a resounding victory. Under threat of international sanctions, however, South Africa agreed that further elections would be held under United Nations supervision and a new assembly elected. With the massive DTA victory in the December poll there seemed every reason to believe that it would easily defeat SWAPO in an open poll.

South African reactions to Namibia's future

Little over a year later, in the light of ZANU's sweep to victory in Zimbabwe, it was felt that the DTA's victory in Namibia might be as insubstantial as Muzorewa's in Zimbabwe. South Africa, deeply shocked by events in Zimbabwe, kept delaying agreement on the final details of arrangements for the United Nations-sponsored elections. On the other hand, although a provisional DTA government was established and allowed to exercise considerable authority, the South African government also held back from pushing Namibia into unilateral independence. It still proclaimed its intention of allowing the United Nations-sponsored elections once agreement could be reached on the details.

During the prolonged political stalemate which followed, SWAPO guerrilla activity increased and its political support among the African population of Namibia expanded. South African forces hit back repeatedly against guerrilla bases in Angola and gave increasingly open aid to Jonas Savimbi's UNITA in its guerrilla struggle against the MPLA government of Angola. This in turn increased the dependence of the MPLA on the support of Cuban troops. With the support of the Reagan administration in the United States, South Africa increasingly insisted on the withdrawal of the Cubans as a precondition for a general settlement which would allow United Nations-sponsored elections to be held in Namibia. The escalating cross-border raids by South African forces culminated in 1983 in a massive invasion code-named 'Operation Askari' after which South African forces occupied and held wide areas of southern Angola for a prolonged period.

Within Namibia itself the Democratic Turnhalle Alliance splintered and declined. Elections in the ethnic states in 1981 showed that it was rapidly losing popularity. During 1982 serious friction developed between the DTA Council of Ministers and the Administrator General of the Territory appointed by the South African government. This came to a head in 1983 when Dirk Mudge and the Council of Ministers resigned. The Administrator General dissolved the National Assembly and resumed direct rule of Namibia.

The decline of the DTA took place against the background of a drastic downturn in the economy of the country. In the 1970s the economy had been buoyant and possession of Namibia profitable to South Africa. By 1981 however this situation had been dramatically reversed. As a result of general world depression, the price of luxury products, gem diamonds and the fur made from lambs' skins known as karrakul fell sharply. Prices for copper and uranium oxide were also severely depressed. Farming by both whites and Africans was drastically affected by prolonged drought and the growing insecurity resulting from the guerrilla war. White farmers began abandoning Namibia in increasing numbers. The fishing industry was severely damaged by overfishing in the 1970s. By 1981 the catch had fallen to a quarter of peak production and was probably still too high to be sustained. By 1983 South African subsidies to Namibia were running at around 300 million rand per year without counting the very much greater cost of its military defence.

Early in 1984 lengthy negotiations between South Africa and the MPLA government in Angola which paralleled those between South Africa and Mozambique culminated in a conference in Lusaka. An accord was reached under which South African troops were to be completely withdrawn from Angolan territory and South Africa was to stop military support for UNITA. In return the MPLA government would ensure that SWAPO was not allowed to use bases on its territory from which to conduct its guerrilla struggle in Namibia. Provision was made for a joint South African and Angolan Commission to monitor the implementation of the agreement. The way appeared open for a general settlement which would allow the long delayed United Nations-sponsored elections to be held in Namibia. At a subsequent conference, however, representatives of SWAPO and the South African government failed to reach agreement. The issue of the withdrawal of the Cubans further impeded a general settlement. The withdrawal of South African troops was not completed. South African support for UNITA continued. On the other side the MPLA authorities would not or could not prevent SWAPO continuing to use Angolan territory as a base for their infiltration of Namibia. Within the territory South Africa in 1984 and early 1985 encouraged the development of a new grouping of anti-SWAPO parties made up of DTA and five other internal parties. The idea that this Multi-Party Conference (MPC) might be allowed to form a transitional government was openly canvassed.

SWAPO demonstrators

In the hope of giving this some legitimacy attempts were made to persuade SWAPO to join the grouping. In March 1984 the veteran Namibian political leader, Toivo ja Toivo, and a number of SWAPO activists were freed from Robben Island. In May, talks between the internal parties in Namibia and SWAPO were held in Lusaka under the joint chairmanship of President Kaunda and South Africa's Administrator General of the Territory. SWAPO held out for the full implementation of Resolution 435, however, and the talks collapsed.

South Africa then proceeded to establish a regime based on the MPC with a view to its leading the country to independence as a federation of ethnic communities. A 'Transitional Government of National Unity' with a National Assembly and a cabinet all appointed from among the membership of the MPC parties was inaugurated on 17 June 1985. It promptly established a constitutional committee to draw up an independence constitution. However, the new regime failed to gain international acceptance. It was internally divided and came into conflict with its prime sponsor when its constitutional proposals did not provide the safeguards for community rights which the South African government required.

During 1986 and 1987 the stalemate in Namibia continued, with South Africa insisting with US support on linking the implementation of Resolution 435 to the withdrawal of Cuban forces from Angola. During this period strikes and protests intensified and in 1987 SWAPO was able to undertake significant guerrilla activity in white farming areas. This was met by brutal repression by South African forces, most notoriously by the strong arm covert action Koevoet (Crowbar) unit. The SADF now committed itself on a larger than ever scale to the invasion of southern Angola in support of UNITA. The crucial turning point came early in 1988 with the military stalemate at the siege of Cuito Cuanavale occurring at a time of rapid change in the relations between the world super-powers.

This facilitated the opening of negotiations jointly sponsored by the USA and USSR, culminating in a wide ranging agreement finally signed on 22 December 1988. This provided for the withdrawal of South African forces and the repatriation of the Cubans from Angola, and opened the way to the implementation of Resolution 435 in Namibia.

The UN Transitional Assistance Group (UNTAG), established to oversee elections for a Constituent Assembly, began to arrive in the Territory in February 1989. Martin Ahtisaari, the UN Special Representative, arrived on 31 March. He faced an immediate crisis as substantial numbers of SWAPO forces crossed the border from Angola under arms in contravention of the agreements, though possibly as a result of an administrative misunderstanding. South Africa threatened to abandon the entire arrangement if its forces were not allowed to leave their camps to resist the intrusion, and Ahtisaari was obliged to concede. After a brief flare up the transitional process continued. South African forces, formally reduced to 1500, were confined to their camps as were those of SWAPO. South Africa retained very significant influence in this period, however, as the UN force, cut down well below the originally agreed size for economy reasons, was heavily dependent on South Africa for essential supplies. Moreover, the South African Administrator retained responsibility for the maintenance of law and order, and the Koevoet unit, though formally absorbed into the police, remained widely deployed.

In the elections held in the second week of November, SWAPO won a working majority of 41 of the 72 seats, but not the two-thirds majority required to pass constitutional provisions. The draft constitution, adopted in February 1990, provided for a multi-party democracy, an Executive President, an independent judiciary and a Bill of Rights. SWAPO leader Sam Nujoma was chosen as the first president. The Constituent Assembly was then constituted as the first parliament and independence was celebrated on 21 March 1990 in the presence of many foreign dignitaries, including South Africa's President de Klerk.

Bibliography

Chapter 1

Alberti, Ludwig, *Account of the Tribal Life and Customs of the Xhosa in 1807, translated by Dr William Fehr from the original manuscript in German of the Kaffirs of the south coast of Africa* (Cape Town: Balkema, 1968)

Birmingham, David and Marks, Shula, 'Southern Africa', in Roland Oliver (ed.), *The Cambridge History of Africa*, Vol. 3 (Cambridge: Cambridge University Press, 1977), pp. 567–620

Clark, J.D., *The Prehistory of Southern Africa* (Harmondsworth: Penguin, 1959)

Clark, J.D., 'Prehistory in southern Africa', in J. Ki-Zerbo (ed.), *General History of Africa*, Vol.1 (London: Heinemann, 1981), pp. 487–529

Denbow, James, 'A new look at the later prehistory of the Kalahari', *Journal of African History*, vol. 27, no. 1 (1986), pp. 3–28

Elphick, Richard, *Kraal and Castle: Khoikhoi and the Founding of White South Africa* (New Haven: Yale University Press, 1977)

Elphick, Richard, *Khoikhoi and the Founding of White South Africa* (Johannesburg: Ravan Press, 1985)

Fagan, Brian M., *Southern Africa during the Iron Age* (London: Thames & Hudson, 1965)

Hall, Martin, *The Changing Past: Farmers, Kings, and Traders in Southern Africa, 200–1860* (Cape Town: David Philip, 1987; London: James Currey, 1987)

Hammond-Tooke, W.D. (ed.), *The Bantu-speaking Peoples of Southern Africa* (London: Routledge & Kegan Paul, 1974)

Harinck, Gerrit, 'Interaction between Xhosa and Khoi; emphasis on the period 1620–1750', in Leonard Thompson (ed.), *African Societies in Southern Africa* (London: Heinemann, 1969), pp. 145–69

Legassick, Martin, 'The Sotho-Tswana peoples before 1800', in Leonard Thompson (ed.), *African Societies in Southern Africa* (London: Heinemann, 1969), pp. 86–125

Marks, Shula, 'The traditions of the Natal "Nguni"; a second look at the work of A.T. Bryant', in Leonard Thompson (ed.), *African Societies in Southern Africa* (London: Heinemann, 1969), pp. 126–44

Marks, Shula and Atmore, Anthony, 'The problem of the Nguni: an examination of the ethnic and linguistic situation in South Africa before the Mfecane', in David Dalby (ed.), *Language and History in Africa* (London: Cass, 1970), pp. 120–32

Oliver, Roland and Fagan, Brian M., 'The emergence of Bantu Africa', in J.D. Fage (ed.), *The Cambridge History of Africa*, Vol. 2 (Cambridge: Cambridge University Press), pp. 342–409

Peires, J.B., *The House of Phalo. A History of the Xhosa People in the Days of Their Independence* (Johannesburg: Ravan Press, 1981/Berkeley and Los Angeles: University of California Press, 1982)

Peires, J.B. (ed.), *Before and After Shaka: Papers in Nguni History* (Grahamstown: Institute of Social and Economic Research, Rhodes University, 1981)

Phillipson, D.W., *The Later Prehistory of Eastern and Southern Africa* (London: Heinemann, 1977)

Schapera, I., *The Khoisan Peoples of South Africa: Bushmen and Hottentots* (London: Routledge, 1930)

Schapera, I., *Government and Politics in Tribal Societies* (London: Watts, 1956)

Schapera, I. and Farrington, B. (eds), *The Early Cape Hottentots* (Cape Town: Van Riebeeck Society, 1933)

Wilmsen, E, *Land Filled with Flies: A Political Economy of the Kalahari* (Chicago: University of Chicago Press, 1989)

Wilson, Monica, 'The hunters and herders', in Monica Wilson and Leonard Thompson (eds), *The Oxford History of South Africa*, Vol. 1 (Oxford: Clarendon Press, 1969), pp. 40–74

Wilson, Monica, 'The Nguni people', in Monica Wilson and Leonard Thompson (eds), *The Oxford History of South Africa*, Vol.1 (Oxford: Clarendon Press, 1969), pp. 75–130

Wilson, Monica, 'The Sotho, Venda and Tsonga', in Monica Wilson and Leonard Thompson (eds), *The Oxford History of South Africa*, Vol.1 (Oxford: Clarendon Press, 1969), pp. 131–82

Chapter 2

Elphick, Richard and Giliomee, Hermann (eds), *The Shaping of South African Society, 1652–1820* (London: Longman, 1979)

Katzen M.F., 'White settlers and the origins of a new society, 1652–1778', in Monica Wilson and Leonard Thompson (eds), *The Oxford History of South Africa*, Vol. 1 (Oxford: Clarendon Press, 1969), pp. 187–232

MacCrone, I.D., *Race Attitudes in South Africa. Historical, Experimental and Psychological Studies* (London: Oxford University Press, 1937)

Marais, J.S., *Maynier and the First Boer Republic* (Cape Town: Miller, 1944)

Marks, Shula and Atmore, Anthony (eds), *Economy and Society in Pre-industrial South Africa* (London: Longman, 1980)

Marks, Shula and Gray, Richard, 'Southern Africa and Madagascar', in Richard Gray (ed.), *The Cambridge History of Africa*, Vol. 4 (Cambridge: Cambridge University Press, 1975), pp. 384–468

Mentzel, O.F., *A Geographical and Topographical Description of the Cape of Good Hope* (3 vols, ed. H.J. Mandelbrote, Cape Town: Van Riebeeck Society, 1921–44)

Neumark, S. Daniel, *Economic Influences on the South African Frontier 1652–1836* (Stanford: Stanford University Press, 1937)

Peires, J.B., *The House of Phalo. A History of the Xhosa People in the Days of Their Independence* (Johannesburg: Ravan Press, 1981/Berkeley and Los Angeles: University of California Press, 1982)

Saunders, Christopher and Derricourt, Robin (eds), *Beyond the Cape Frontier. Studies in the History of the Transkei and Ciskei* (London: Longman, 1974)

Spilhaus, M. Whiting, *South Africa in the Making, 1652–1806* (Cape Town: Juta, 1966)

Van Reenen, D.G., *Die Joernaal van Dirk Gysbert van Reenen 1803* (tr. into English by J.M.L. Franken and I.M. Murray, ed. W. Blommaert and J.A. Wild, Cape Town: Van Riebeeck Society, 1937)

Van Riebeeck, J., *The Journal of Jan Van Riebeeck* (ed. H.B. Thom, 3 vols, Cape Town: Van Riebeeck Society, 1952–8)

Chapter 3

Davenport, T.R.H., 'The consolidation of a new society: the Cape Colony', in Monica Wilson and Leonard Thompson (eds), *The Oxford History of South Africa*, Vol. 1 (Oxford: Clarendon Press, 1969), pp. 272–333

Elphick, Richard and Giliomee, Herman (eds), *The Shaping of South African Society, 1652–1820* (London: Longman, 1979)

Freund, William M., 'The eastern frontier of the Cape Colony during the Batavian period (1803–1806)', *Journal of African History*, vol. 13, no.4 (1972), pp. 631–45

Freund, W.M., 'Race in the social structure of South Africa, 1952–1836', *Race and Class*, vol. 18, no. 1 (1976), pp.53–67

Hutton, C.W. (ed.), *Autobiography of Sir Andries Stockenstrom, Bart.* (2 vols, Cape Town: Juta, 1887/ Cape Town: Struik, 1964)

Legassick, Martin, 'The frontier tradition in South African historiography', in *Collected Seminar Papers on the Societies of Southern Africa in the 19th and 20th Centuries*, Vol. 2 (London: Institute of Commonwealth Studies, University of London 1971), pp. 1–33

Lichtenstein, Henry, *Travels in South Africa in the Years 1803, 1804, 1805 and 1806* (2 vols, ed. A. Plumtre, Cape Town: Van Riebeeck Society, 1928–30)

MacCrone, I.D., *Race Attitudes in South Africa. Historical, Experimental and Psychological Studies* (London: Oxford University Press, 1937)

Macmillan, W.M., *Bantu, Boer and Briton: The Making of the South African Native Problem* (rev. edn, Oxford: Clarendon Press, 1963)

Marais, J.S., *Maynier and the First Boer Republic* (Cape Town: Miller, 1944)

Marks, Shula and Atmore, Anthony (eds), *Economy and Society in Pre-industrial South Africa* (London: Longman, 1980)

Moodie, Donald, *The Record or a Series of Official Papers Relative to the Condition and Treatment of the Native Tribes of South Africa* (1st edn, Cape Town, 1838-41, Amsterdam: Balkema, 1960)

Peires, J.B., *The House of Phalo. A History of the Xhosa People in the Days of Their Independence* (Johannesburg: Ravan Press, 1981 /Berkeley and Los Angeles: University of California Press, 1982)

Philip, John, *Researches in South Africa* (2 vols, London: J. Duncan, 1828)

Robinson, A.M. Lewin (ed.), *The Letters of Lady Anne Barnard to Henry Dundas from the Cape and Elsewhere* (Cape Town: Balkema, 1973)

Wilson, Monica, 'Co-operation and conflict: the eastern Cape frontier', in Monica Wilson and Leonard Thompson (eds), *The Oxford History of South Africa*, Vol. 1 (Oxford: Clarendon Press, 1969), pp. 233–71

Chapter 4

Bonner, P.L., 'Classes, the mode of production and the state in pre-colonial Swaziland', in *Collected Seminar Papers on the Societies of Southern Africa in the 19th and 20th Centuries*, Vol. 8 (London: Institute of Commonwealth Studies, University of London, 1977), pp. 31–41

Cobbing, Julian, 'The evolution of Ndebele Amabutho', *Journal of African History*, vol. 15, no. 4 (1974), pp. 607–31

Cobbing, Julian, 'The Mfecane as alibi: thoughts on Dithakong and Mbolompo', *Journal of African History*, vol. 29, no. 3 (1988), pp. 487–519

Delius, Peter, *The Land Belongs to Us: the Pedi polity, the Boers and the British in the nineteenth century Transvaal* (London: Heinemann, 1983)

Fuller, Claude, *Louis Trigardt's Trek Across the Drakensberg 1837–1838* (ed. Leo Fouche, Cape Town: Van Riebeeck Society, 1932)

Hall, Martin, 'Ethnography, environment and the history of the Nguni in the eighteenth and nineteenth centuries' in *Collected Seminar Papers on the Societies of Southern Africa in the 19th and 20th Centuries*, Vol. 8 (London: Institute of Commonwealth Studies, University of London, 1977), pp. 11–20

Hamilton, Carolyn, *The Mfecane Aftermath* (Johannesburg: University of the Witwatersrand Press, forthcoming)

Isaacs, Nathaniel, *Travels and Adventures in Eastern Africa* (ed. Louis Herrman, 2 vols, Cape Town: Van Riebeeck Society, 1936–7)

Kirby, Percival R. (ed.), *The Diary of Dr Andrew Smith, 1834–1836* (2 vols, Cape Town: Van Riebeeck Society, 1939–40)

Kirby, Percival R. (ed.) *Andrew Smith and Natal* (Cape Town: Van Riebeeck Society, 1955)

Kuper, Hilda, *An African Aristocracy: Rank Among the Swazi of Bechuanaland* (London: Oxford University Press, 1947)

Lye, William F., 'The Difaqane: the Mfecane in the southern Sotho area, 1822–24', *Journal of African History*, vol.8, no.1 (1967), pp. 107–31

Meintjes, Johannes, *The Voortrekkers: The Story of the Great Trek and the Making of South Africa* (London: Cassell, 1973)

Morris, Donald R., *The Washing of the Spears: A History of the Zulu Nation under Shaka and its Fall in the Zulu War of 1879* (London: Cape, 1966)

Omer-Cooper, J.D., *The Zulu Aftermath: A Nineteenth-Century Revolution in Bantu Africa* (London: Longman, 1966)

Omer-Cooper, John, 'Aspects of political change in the nineteenth-century Mfecane', in Leonard Thompson (ed.), *African Societies in Southern Africa* (London: Heinemann, 1969), pp. 207–29

Omer-Cooper, J.D., 'The Nguni outburst', in John E. Flint (ed.), *The Cambridge History of Africa*, Vol. 5 (Cambridge: Cambridge University Press, 1976), pp. 319–52

Omer-Cooper, J.D., 'Has the Mfecane a future? a response to the Cobbing critique', *Journal of Southern African Studies*, vol. 19, no. 2 (1993)

Peires, J.B. (ed.), *Before and After Shaka: Papers in Nguni History* (Grahamstown: Institute of Social and Economic Research, Rhodes University, 1981)

Rasmussen, R. Kent, *Migrant Kingdom: Mzilikazi's Ndebele in South Africa* (London: Collings, 1978)

Sanders, Peter, *Moshoeshoe: Chief of the Sotho* (London: Heinemann, 1975)

Smith, Alan, 'The trade of Delagoa Bay as a factor in Nguni politics 1750–1835', in Leonard Thompson (ed.), *African Societies in Southern Africa* (London: Heinemann, 1969), pp. 171–89

Stuart, James and Malcolm, D. McK. (ed.), *The Diary of Henry Francis Fynn* (Pietermaritzburg: Shuter & Shooter, 1950)

Thompson, Leonard, 'Co-operation and conflict: the Zulu kingdom and Natal', in Monica Wilson and Leonard Thompson (eds), *The Oxford History of South Africa*, Vol. 1 (Oxford: Clarendon Press, 1969), pp. 334–90

Thompson, Leonard, *Survival in Two Worlds: Moshoeshoe of Lesotho 1786–1870* (Oxford: Clarendon Press, 1975)

Walker, Eric A., *The Great Trek* (4th edn, London: Black, 1960)

Webb, C. de B. and Wright, J.B. (eds) *The James Stuart Archive of Recorded Oral Evidence Relating to the History of the Zulu and Neighbouring Peoples* (6 vols in progress, Pietermaritzburg: University of Natal Press, 1976–)

Chapter 5

Brookes, Edgar H. and Webb, Colin de B., *A History of Natal* (Pietermaritzburg: University of Natal Press, 1965)

De Kiewiet, C.W., *British Colonial Policy and the South African Republics, 1848–1872* (London: Longmans Green, 1929)

Eybers, G.W. (ed.), *Select Constitutional Documents Illustrating South African History, 1795–1910* (London: Routledge, 1918)

Galbraith, John S., *Reluctant Empire. British policy on the South African Frontier, 1834–1854* (Berkeley and Los Angeles: University of California Press, 1963)

Halford, S.J., *The Griquas of Griqualand: A Historical Narrative of the Griqua People, Their Rise, Progress and Decline* (Cape Town: Juta, 1949)

Midgley, J.F., 'The Orange River Sovereignty (1848–1854)', in *Archives Year Book for South African History*, Vol.2 for 1949 (Pretoria: Government Printer, 1949)

Ross, Robert, *Adam Kok's Griquas: A Study in the Development of Stratification in South Africa* (Cambridge: Cambridge University Press, 1976)

Sanders, Peter, *Moshoeshoe: Chief of the Sotho* (London: Heinemann, 1975)

Slater, Henry, 'The changing pattern of economic relationships in rural Natal 1838–1911', in *Collected Seminar Papers on the Societies of Southern Africa in the 19th and 20th Centuries*, Vol. 3 (London: Institute of Commonwealth Studies, University of London, 1973), pp. 38–52

Thompson, Leonard, 'Co-operation and conflict: the high veld', in Monica Wilson and Leonard Thompson (eds), *The Oxford History of South Africa*, Vol. 1 (Oxford: Clarendon Press, 1969), pp. 391–446

Thompson, Leonard, *Survival in Two Worlds: Moshoeshoe of Lesotho 1786–1870* (Clarendon Press: Oxford, 1975)

Trapido, Stanley, 'The origins of the Cape franchise qualifications of 1853', *Journal of African History*, vol. 5, no. 1 (1964), pp. 37–54

Trapido, Stanley, 'The South African republic, class formation and the state, 1850–1900', in *Collected Seminar Papers on the Societies of Southern Africa in the 19th and 20th Centuries*, Vol. 3 (London:

Institute of Commonwealth Studies, University of London, 1973), pp. 53–65

Trapido, Stanley, 'Aspects of the transition from slavery to serfdom: the South African Republic 1842–1902', in *Collected Seminar Papers on the Societies of Southern Africa in the 19th and 20th Centuries*, Vol. 6 (London: Institute of Commonwealth Studies, University of London, 1976), pp. 24–31

Tylden, G., *The Rise of the Basuto* (Cape Town: Juta, 1950)

Walker, Eric A., *The Great Trek* (4th edn, London: Black, 1960)

Chapter 6

Agar-Hamilton, J.A.I., *The Road to the North: South Africa, 1852–1886* (London: Longman Green, 1937)

Ballard, Charles, 'John Dunn and Cetshwayo: the material foundations of political power in the Zulu kingdom, 1857–1878', *Journal of African History*, vol. 21, no. 1 (1980), pp. 75–91

Bundy, Colin, *The Rise and Fall of the South African Peasantry* (London: Heinemann, 1979; James Currey 1988)

Davenport, T.R.H., *The Afrikaner Bond: The History of a South African Political Party, 1880–1911* (Cape Town: Oxford University Press, 1966)

De Kiewiet, C.W., *The Imperial Factor in South Africa: A Study in Politics and Economics* (Cambridge: Cambridge University Press, 1937)

Doughty, Oswald, *Early Diamond Days: The Opening of the Diamond Fields of South Africa* (London: Longman, 1963)

Duminy, A.H. and Ballard, C.C. (eds), *The Anglo-Zulu War. New Perspectives* (Pietermaritzburg: University of Natal Press)

Etherington, Norman, *Preachers, Peasants and Politics in Southeast Africa 1835–1880. African Christian Communities in Natal, Pondoland and Zululand* (London: Royal Historical Society, 1978)

Etherington, Norman A., 'Labour supply and the genesis of South African confederation in the 1870s', *Journal of African History*, vol. 20, no. 2 (1979), pp. 235–53

Flint, John, *Cecil Rhodes* (London: Hutchinson, 1976)

Goodfellow, C.F., *Great Britain and the South African Confederation, 1870–1881* (Cape Town: Oxford University Press, 1966)

Guy, Jeff, *The Destruction of the Zulu Kingdom: The Civil War in Zululand, 1879–1884* (London: Longman, 1979)

Lehmann, J., *The First Boer War* (London: Cape, 1971)

Morris, Donald R., *The Washing of the Spears: A History of the Zulu Nation under Shaka and its Fall in the Zulu War of 1879* (London: Cape, 1966)

Schreuder, D.M., *The Scramble for Southern Africa 1877–1895: The Politics of Partition Reappraised* (Cambridge: Cambridge University Press, 1980)

Slater, Henry, 'Land, labour and capital in Natal: the Natal Land and Colonisation Company 1860–1948', *Journal of African History*, vol. 16, no. 2 (1975), pp. 257–83

Tylden, G., *The Rise of the Basuto* (Cape Town: Juta, 1950)

Van Jaarsfeld, F.A., *The Awakening of Afrikaner Nationalism 1868–1881* (Cape Town, 1961)

Chapter 7

Blainey, G., 'Lost causes of the Jameson Raid', *Economic History*

Review, vol. 18 (1965), pp. 350–66

Denoon, D., *A Grand Illusion: The Failure of Imperial Policy in the Transvaal Colony During the Period of Reconstruction 1900–1905* (London: Longman, 1973)

Flint, John, *Cecil Rhodes* (London: Hutchinson, 1976)

Galbraith, John S., *Crown and Charter: The Early Years of the British South Africa Company* (Berkeley: University of California Press, 1974)

Johnstone, Frederick, *Class, Race and Gold: A Study of Class Relations and Discrimination in South Africa* (London: Routledge & Kegan Paul, 1976)

Keppel-Jones, Arthur, *Rhodes and Rhodesia: The White Conquest of Zimbabwe 1884–1902* (Montreal: McGill-Queen's University Press, 1983)

Kruger, P., *The Memoirs of Paul Kruger* (London: T Fisher Unwin, 1902)

Marais, J.S., *The Fall of Kruger's Republic* (Oxford: Clarendon Press, 1961)

Marks, Shula, *Reluctant Rebellion. The 1906–8 Disturbances in Natal* (Oxford: Clarendon Press, 1970)

Mendelsohn, Richard, 'Blainey and the Jameson Raid: the debate renewed', *Journal of Southern African Studies*, vol. 6, no. 2 (1980), pp. 157–70

Pakenham, Thomas, *The Boer War* (London: Weidenfeld & Nicolson 1979)

Phimister, I.R., 'Rhodes, Rhodesia and the Rand', *Journal of Southern African Studies*, vol. 1, no. 1 (1974), pp. 74–90

Pillay, Bala, *British Indians in the Transvaal: Trade, Politics and Imperial Relations, 1885–1906* (London: Longman, 1976)

Porter, A.N., *The Origins of the South African War: Joseph Chamberlain and the Diplomacy of Imperialism, 1895–99* (Manchester: Manchester University Press, 1980)

Ranger, T.O., *Revolt in Southern Rhodesia, 1896–7* (London: Heinemann, 1967)

Schreuder, D.M., *Gladstone and Kruger: Liberal Government and Colonial 'Home Rule' 1880–85* (London: Routledge & Kegan Paul, 1969)

Schreuder, D.M., *The Scramble for Southern Africa 1877–1895: The Politics of Partition Reappraised* (Cambridge: Cambridge University Press, 1980)

Slater, Henry, 'The changing pattern of economic relationships in rural Natal: 1838–1914', in *Collected Seminar Papers on the Societies of Southern Africa in the 19th and 20th Centuries*, Vol. 3 (London: Institute of Commonwealth Studies, University of London, 1973), pp. 38–52

Thompson, L.M., *The Unification of South Africa, 1902–1910* (Oxford: Clarendon Press, 1960)

Trapido, Stanley, 'Landlord and tenant in a colonial economy: the Transvaal 1880–1910', *Journal of Southern African Studies*, vol. 5, no. 1 (1978), pp. 26–58

Trapido, Stanley, 'South Africa in a comparative study of industrialisation', in *Collected Papers on the Societies of Southern Africa in 19th and 20th Centuries*, Vol. 2 (London: Institute of Commonwealth Studies, University of London, 1972), pp. 50–61

Van der Poel, Jean, *The Jameson Raid* (Cape Town: Oxford University Press, 1951)

Warwick, Peter (ed.), *The South African War: The Anglo-Boer War 1899–1902* (Harlow: Longman, 1980)

Warwick, Peter, *Black People and the South African War, 1899–1902* (Cambridge: Cambridge University Press, 1983)

Chapter 8

Ballinger, M., *From Union to Apartheid: A Trek to Isolation* (Cape Town: Juta, 1969)

Bundy, C., *The Rise and Fall of the South African Peasantry* (London: Heinemann, 1979; James Currey, 1988)

De Klerk, W.A., *The Puritans in Africa: A Story of Afrikanerdom* (London: Collings, 1975)

Hancock, W.K., *Smuts* (2 vols, Cambridge: Cambridge University Press, 1962–8)

Hancock, W.K. and Van der Poel, Jean (eds), *Selections from the Smuts Papers* (6 vols, Cambridge University Press, 1966–73)

Horwitz, Ralph, *The Political Economy of South Africa* (London: Weidenfeld & Nicolson, 1967)

Houghton, D. Hobart, *The South African Economy* (Cape Town: Oxford University Press, 1964)

Johnstone, Frederick, *Class, Race and Gold. A Study of Class Relations and Racial Discrimination in South Africa* (London: Routledge & Kegan Paul, 1976)

Kadalie, Clements, *My Life and the ICU. The Autobiography of a Black Trade Unionist in South Africa* (London: Cass, 1970)

Karis, Thomas and Carter, Gwendolen M. (eds), *From Protest to Challenge: A Documentary History of African Politics in South Africa 1882–1964* (4 vols, Stanford: Hoover Institution Press, 1971–7)

Kruger, D.W. (ed.) *South African Parties and Policies 1910–1960* (London: Bowes & Bowes, 1960)

Moodie, T. Dunbar, *The Rise of Afrikanerdom: Power, Apartheid and the Afrikaner Civil Religion* (Berkeley: University of California Press, 1975)

O'Meara, Dan, *Volkskapitalisme: Class, Capital and Ideology in the Development of Afrikaner Nationalism 1934–48* (Cambridge: Cambridge University Press, 1983)

Pachai, Bridglal, *The South African Indian Question, 1860–1971* (Cape Town: Struik, 1971)

Palmer, Robin and Parsons, Neil (eds), *The Roots of Rural Poverty in Central and Southern Africa* (London: Heinemann, 1977)

Paton, Alan, *Hofmeyr* (Cape Town: Oxford University Press, 1964)

Plaatje, Sol T., *Native Life in South Africa Before and Since the European War and the Boer Rebellion* (New York: Negro Universities Press, 1969)

Roux, Edward, *Time Longer Than Rope: A History of the Black Man's Struggle for Freedom in South Africa* (2nd edn, Madison: University of Wisconsin Press, 1964)

Serfontein, J.H.P., *Brotherhood of Power: An Exposé, of the Secret Afrikaner Broederbond* (London: Collings, 1979)

Simons, H.J. and R.E., *Class and Colour in South Africa 1850–1950* (Harmondsworth: Penguin, 1969)

Stultz, Newell M., *Afrikaner Politics in South Africa 1934–1948* (Berkeley: University of California Press, 1974)

Trapido, Stanley, 'The origin and development of the African political organisation', in *Collected Seminar Papers on the Societies of Southern Africa in the 19th and 20th Centuries*, Vol. 1 (London:

Institute of Commonwealth Studies, University of London, 1971), pp. 89–111

Trapido, Stanley, 'South Africa in a comparative study of industrialisation', in *Collected Seminar Papers on the Societies of Southern Africa in the 19th and 20th Centuries*, Vol. 2 (London: Institute of Commonwealth Studies, University of London, 1972), pp. 50–61

Trapido, Stanley, 'Liberalism in the Cape in the 19th and 20th centuries', in *Collected Seminar Papers on the Societies of Southern Africa in the 19th and 20th Centuries*, Vol. 4 (London: Institute of Commonwealth Studies, University of London, 1973), pp. 53–66

Van der Horst, S., *Native Labour in South Africa* (London: Cass, 1971)

Walshe, Peter, *The Rise of African Nationalism in South Africa. The ANC 1912–52* (London: Hurst, 1970)

Wilkins, Ivor and Strydom, Hans, *The Broederbond* (New York and London: Paddington Press, 1979)

Wilson, Francis, *Labour in the South African Gold Mines 1911–1969* (Cambridge: Cambridge University Press, 1972)

Wilson, Monica and Thompson, Leonard (eds), *The Oxford History of South Africa*, Vol. 2 (Oxford: Clarendon Press, 1971)

Chapters 9 and 10

Adam, Heribert, *Modernizing Racial Domination. South Africa's Political Dynamics* (Berkeley: University of California Press, 1971)

Adam, Heribert and Giliomee, Hermann, *Ethnic Power Mobilized: Can South Africa Change?*

Africa Confidential (London, fortnightly)

Africa Research Bulletin (Exeter, monthly)

Baldwin, Alan, 'Mass removals and separate development' *Journal of Southern African Studies*, vol. 1, no. 22 (1975), pp. 215–27

Biko, Steve, *I Write What I Like* (London: Heinemann, 1978)

Brookes, E.H. and Macaulay, J.B., *Civil Liberty in South Africa* (Cape Town: Oxford University Press, 1958)

Carter, Gwendolen M., *The Politics of Inequality. South Africa since 1948* (London: Thames & Hudson, 1958)

Carter, Gwendolen M., *Which Way is South Africa Going?* (Bloomington: Indiana University Press, 1980)

Carter, Gwendolen M., Karis, Thomas and Stultz, Newell M., *South Africa's Transkei. The Politics of Domestic Colonialism* (London: Heinemann, 1967)

Carter, Gwendolen M. and O'Meara, Patrick (eds), *Southern Africa in Crisis* (Bloomington: Indiana University Press, 1977)

Davenport, T.R.H., *South Africa: A Modern History* (London: Macmillan, 1977)

Davidson, Basil, Slovo, Joe and Wilkinson, Anthony R., *Southern Africa: The New Politics of Revolution* (Harmondsworth: Penguin, 1976)

Desmond, Cosmas, *The Discarded People* (Braamfontein: Christian Institute of South Africa, n.d./Harmondsworth: Penguin, 1971)

De St Jorre, John, *A House Divided: South Africa's Uncertain Future* (New York: Carnegie Endowment for International Peace, 1977)

First, Ruth (ed.), *No Easy Walk to Freedom..Articles, Speeches and Trial Addresses of Nelson Mandela* (London: Heinemann, 1965)

Gerhart, Gail M., *Black Power in South Africa: The Evolution of an Ideology* (Berkeley: University of California Press, 1978)

Giliomee, Hermann, *The Parting of the Ways: South African Politics 1976–82* (Cape Town: Philip, 1982)

Good, Robert C., *UDI. The International Politics of the Rhodesian Rebellion* (Princeton: Princeton University Press, 1973)

Hirson, Baruch, 'Rural revolt in South Africa 1937–1951' in *Collected Seminar Papers on the Societies of Southern Africa in the 19th and 20th Centuries*, Vol. 8 (London: Institute of Commonwealth Studies, University of London, 1977), pp. 115–32

Hirson, Baruch, *Year of Fire, Year of Ash. The Soweto Revolt: Roots of a Revolution?* (London: Zed Press, 1979)

Horwitz, Ralph, *The Political Economy of South Africa* (London: Weidenfeld & Nicolson, 1967)

Johnson, R.W., *How Long Will South Africa Survive?* (London: Macmillan, 1977)

Kane-Berman, John, *South Africa: The Method in the Madness* (London: Pluto Press, 1979)

Karis, Thomas and Carter, Gwendolen M. (eds), *From Protest to Challenge: A Documentary History of African Politics in South Africa 1882–1964* (4 vols, Stanford: Hoover Institution Press, 1971–7)

Kuper, Leo, *Passive Resistance in South Africa* (London: Cape, 1956)

Lane, P., *Apartheid and the Homelands in South Africa: A New Zealander's View* (Wellington: New Zealand Institute of International Affairs, 1981)

Legassick, Martin, 'Legislation, ideology and economy in post-1948 South Africa', *Journal of Southern African Studies* vol. 1, no. 1 (1974), pp. 5–35

Legum, Colin, *Vorster's Gamble for Africa: How the Search for Peace Failed* (London: Collings, 1976)

Legum, Colin, *Southern Africa, the Year of the Whirlwind* (London: Collings, 1977)

Legum, Colin (ed.), *Africa Contemporary Record* (annually, London, 1969–)

Lipton, Merle, 'Men of two worlds, migrant labour in South Africa', *Optima*, vol. 29, nos 2/3 (1980), pp. 72–201

Luthuli, A.J., *Let My People Go* (London: Collins, 1962)

Martin, David and Johnson, Phyllis, *The Struggle for Zimbabwe: The Chimurenga War* (London: Faber, 1981)

Mayer, P., *Townsmen or Tribesmen* (Cape Town: Oxford University Press, 1961)

Mbeki, Govan, *South Africa: The Peasants' Revolt* (Harmondsworth: Penguin, 1964)

Meredith, Martin, *The Past is Another Country. Rhodesia: UDI to Zimbabwe* (London: Deutsch, 1979)

Patterson, S., *Colour and Culture in South Africa. A Study of the Status of the Cape Coloured People within the Social Structure of the Union of South Africa* (London: Routledge & Kegan Paul, 1953)

Rees, Mervyn and Day, Chris, *Muldergate. The Story of the Info Scandal* (London: Macmillan, 1980)

Sobel, Lester A. (ed.), *Rhodesia/Zimbabwe 1971–77* New York: Facts on File, 1978)

Temkin, B., *Gatsha Buthelezi: Zulu Statesman* (Cape Town: Purnell 1976)

Thompson, Leonard and Butler, Jeffrey (eds), *Change in Contemporary South Africa* (Berkeley: University of California Press, 1975)

Van der Berghe, Pierre L., *South Africa: A Study in Conflict* (Middletown: Wesleyan University Press, 1965)

Wilson, Francis, *Migrant Labour. Report to the South African Council of*

Churches (Johannesburg: South African Council of Churches and
SPRO-CAS, 1972)

Wilson, Monica and Thompson, Leonard (eds), *The Oxford History of
South Africa*, Vol. 2 (Oxford: Clarendon Press, 1971)

Wolpe, H., 'Capitalism and cheap labour-power: from segregation to
apartheid', *Economy and Society*, vol. 14 (1972)

Woods, Donald, *Biko* (London: Paddington Press, 1978)

Chapter 11

Cobbett, W., and Cohen, R. (eds), *Popular Struggles in South Africa*
(London: James Currey, 1988)

Pauw, Jacques, *In the Heart of the Whore: the Story of Apartheid's Death
Squads* (Halfway House, Transvaal: Southern Books, 1992)

Appendix 1

Africa Confidential (London, fortnightly)

Africa Research Bulletin (Exeter, monthly)

Bonner, Philip, *Kings Commoners and Concessionaires: Evolution and
Dissolution of the Nineteenth Century Swazi State* (Cambridge:
Cambridge University Press, 1983)

Burman, Sandra, *Chiefdom Politics and Alien Law: Basutoland Under
Cape Rule, 1871–1884* (New York: Africana Publishing Co., 1981)

Carter, Gwendolen M. and Morgan E. Philip (eds), *From the Front
Line: Speeches of Sir Seretse Khama* (London: Collings, 1980)

Grotpeter, John, *Historical Dictionary of Swaziland* (Metuchen:
Scarecrow Press, 1975)

Hailey, W.M., *The Republic of South Africa and the High Commission
Territories* (London: Oxford University Press, 1963)

Haliburton, Gordon, *Historical Dictionary of Lesotho* (Metuchen:
Scarecrow Press, 1977)

Halpern, Jack, *South Africa's Hostages. Basutoland, Bechuanaland and
Swaziland* (Harmondsworth: Penguin, 1965)

Khaketla, B.M., *Lesotho 1970: An African Coup Under the Microscope*
(Berkeley: University of California Press, 1972)

Kuper, Hilda, *The Swazi: A South African Kingdom* (New York: Holt,
Rinehart & Winston, 1964)

Kuper, Hilda, *Sobhuza II: Ngwenyana and King of Swaziland* (London:
Duckworth, 1981)

Legum, Colin (ed.), *Africa Contemporary Record*
(annually, London, 1969–)

Lye, William F. and Murray, Colin, *Transformations on the Highveld:
The Tswana and Southern Sotho* (Totowa: Barnes & Noble, 1980)

Matsebula, J.S. M., *A History of Swaziland* (Cape Town: Longman
Penguin, 1976)

Palmer, Robin and Parsons, Neil (eds), *The Roots of Rural Poverty in
Central and Southern Africa* (London: Heinemann, 1977)

Parsons, Neil, *The World of Khama* (Historical Association of Zambia,
Pamphlet No. 2, Lusaka, 1972)

Parsons, Q.N., '"Khama & Co." and the Jousse trouble 1910-1916',
Journal of African History, vol. 16, no. 3 (1975), pp. 383–408

Potholm, Christian P., *Swaziland: The Dynamics of Political
Modernization* (Berkeley: University of California Press, 1972)

Sanders, Peter, *Moshoeshoe: Chief of the Sotho* (London: Heinemann,
1975)

Schapera, I., *Tribal Innovations: Tswana Chiefs and Social Change

1795–1940 (London: Athlone Press, 1970)

Selwyn, Percy, *Industries in the Southern African Periphery: A Study of
Industrial Development in Botswana, Lesotho and Swaziland* (London:
Croom Helm, 1975)

Sillery, A., *The Bechuanaland Protectorate* (Cape Town: Oxford
University Press, 1952)

Sillery, A., *Sechele: The Story of an African Chief* (Oxford: George
Ronald, 1954)

Sillery, A., *Founding a Protectorate: History of Bechuanaland 1885–1895*
(The Hague: Mouton, 1965)

Sillery, A., *Botswana: A Short Political History* (London: Methuen,
1974)

Spence, J.E., *Lesotho, the Politics of Dependence* (London: Oxford
University Press, 1968)

Thompson, Leonard, *Survival in Two Worlds: Moshoeshoe of Lesotho
1786–1870* (Clarendon Press: Oxford, 1975)

Wallman, Sandra, *Take Out Hunger. Two Case Studies of Rural
Development in Basutoland* (London: Athlone Press, 1969)

Wallman, Sandra, 'Conditions of non-development in Lesotho',
Journal of Development Studies, vol. 8, no. 2 (1972), pp. 251–62

Wallman, Sandra, 'The modernization of dependence, a further note
on Lesotho', *Journal of Southern African Studies*, vol. 3, no. 1 (1976),
pp. 102–7

Appendix 2

Africa Confidential (London, fortnightly)

Africa Research Bulletin (Exeter, monthly)

Bley, Helmut, *South West Africa Under German Rule 1894–1914*
(London: Heinemann, 1971)

Drechler, Horst, *'Let Us Die Fighting'. The Struggle of the Hereros and
Nama Against German Imperialism (1884-1915)* London: Zed Press,
1980)

First, Ruth, *South West Africa* (Harmondsworth: Penguin, 1963)

Goldblatt, I., *History of South West Africa from the Beginning of the
Nineteenth Century* (Cape Town: Juta, 1971)

Katjavivi, Peter H., *A History of Resistance in Namibia* (London: James
Currey, 1988)

Legum, Colin (ed.), *Africa Contemporary Record* (London, annually,
1969–)

Segal, Ronald and First, Ruth (eds), *South West Africa: Travesty of
Trust* (London: Deutsch, 1967)

Serfontein, J.H.P., *Namibia* (London: Collings, 1977)

Index

Abdurahman, Dr A., 162, 179
Abolition of Passes and Consolidation of Documents Act (1952), 197
Abrahams Kraal, battle of (1900), 145
Active Citizens Force, 210
African Claims in South Africa (ANC), 186
African elite, 141, 161, 162, 258, 260
African franchise *see* franchise
African Methodist Episcopal Church, 161
African Mineworkers' Union, 187
African Native National Conference (1909), 156
African nationalism, 218, 219-21; development of, 160-3; between the wars, 178-81; in Second World War, 186-7; armed liberation struggle, 210, 218, 219-20, 226; black consciousness movement, 220-1; Soweto disturbances 225-6; *see also* ANC; PAC
African (native) reserves, 135, 159, 163, 175, 191, 196, 200, 202, 213, 258, 266; establishment of Tribal Authorities, 200, 208; in Namibia, 283, 285-6; *see also* Bantustans
African People's Organisation (APO), 156, 162, 179-80, 206
Afrikaanse Nasionale Studentebond, 174
Afrikaner, Jager, 31, 32, 37, 279
Afrikaner, Jonker, 279
Afrikaner, Klaas, 31
Afrikaner Bond, 119, 134-5, 141, 142, 155
Afrikaner Cultural Association, 190
Afrikaner language (Afrikaans) and culture, 167, 173-4, 176-7, 194, 202, 219, 225-6, 279, 282
Afrikaner nationalism, xii-xiii, 80, 119, 134, 150, 160, 161, 171, 173-4, 175-8, 189-92; ideology, 176, 177; *voortrekker* centenary celebrations, 177; appeal of Nazi ideology, 182, 184; wartime, 181-2, 183-4, 185; *see also* apartheid; Broederbond
Afrikaner Party, 184, 192, 193
Afrikaners (Boers), 21, 34, 69, 70, 233, 282; Great Trek, xiii, 35, 43, 65, 69, 70, 71-8, 82, 93, 149, 160, 176, 256; racial attitudes, 72; trekker government, 75-6; and Zulus, 78-81; annexation of Port Natal by, 80; Day of the Covenant, 80, 177, 210; Battle of Blood River, 80-1, 84; developments after Great Trek, 82-8; in Transorangia, 86-7; and Orange River Sovereignty, 89-90; notables, 97, 149, 151; *bywoners*, 97, 111, 127, 149, 171; goldmining, 126-9; South African War, 126, 128, 144-8; and Swaziland, 133-4, 248-9, 263, 264, 265; in Cape, 134-5, 142; Milner's distrust of, 142; Vereeniging peace conference (1902), 146-7; poor-whites and unemployed, 149-50, 167, 171-2, 175, 177, 193-4, 202; political parties, 151, 152; and Union of South Africa (1910), 154-60; and First World War, 165-7; and Rand rebellion (1922), 171-2; and Second World War, 181-4; anti-semitism of, 182; Torch Commando, 204; new dominant elite, 233, 239; liberal group seeks political settlement with ANC, 239-40; erosion of support for Nationalist Party by, 244; *see also*

apartheid; Cape Colony; Dutch; Natal; National Party; Orange Free State; Transvaal
agents provocateurs, 246
age-regiment system (*butho*), 15, 53-4, 55, 56-7, 58-60, 66, 67, 68, 113, 114, 133, 265, 266
Aggrey, J.E.K., 179
agriculture/farming, xiii, 8, 101, 102, 140, 148, 158, 159, 171; Bantu, 10-11; Cape, 18, 19, 20, 21-5, 134, 135; loan farms system, 25, 46, 47; Bastard farmers, 31; quit-rent system, 46-7; 1820 settler scheme, 47; expansion across the Orange, 49-51; in Natal, 86, 152-3; *bywoner* tenants, 97, 111, 127, 149, 171; share-cropping, 102, 166; Glen Grey Act (1894), 35; Lands Act (1913), 163, 164, 169, 199; Lesotho, 256, 257-8, 260, 262; Swaziland, 267; Botswana, 270, 274; Namibia, 278, 279, 284, 289; *see also* cattle; land
Ahtisaari, Martin, UN Special Representative, 290
Albany, 47
Algoa Bay, 37, 38
All-African Convention, 180-1, 186-7
Almeida, Francisco de, 17
Amraals, 279
ANC (African National Congress), xiii, 161, 163, 167, 168, 169, 178, 179, 180, 181, 187, 189, 207-8, 219, 226, 235, 237, 238, 241-2; establishment of, 181, 186; Youth League, 186, 205, 206, 208; 'Programme of Action', 205, 206; and mass defiance campaign, 205-6, 207; treason trial, 207-8, 275; split within, and formation of PAC, 208; banning of, 210, 220; armed liberation struggle (guerrilla activity), 210, 218, 219-20, 226, 227, 235, 237-8, 244; and police repression, 218, 220; township disturbances encouraged by, 237; rivalry and conflict between Inkatha and, 239, 244, 247-8; and Lesotho, 255, 262-3; and Swaziland, 269, 270; and Botswana, 275, 277; and Namibia, 285; white liberals seek agreement with, 240; Kabwe Conference (1985), 242; abandonment of apartheid and Government negotiations with, 242, 243-51; lifting of ban on (1990), 242; and release of Mandela, 242, 243, 244; reorganisation of legal party, 243-4, 246; National Congress (1991), 246; Mandela elected president of, 246; release of political prisoners, 247; armed struggle formally abandoned by, 247; Convention for Democratic South Africa (1991), 247, 248-9; and Boipatong massacre, 249; formal talks with government broken off by, 249; campaign of mass action, 250; police open fire on marchers in Bisho, 250-1; Mandela and de Klerk summit meeting, 251; bilateral negotiations with government resumed, 251
ANC Congress, Annual, 186, 205, 207, 209
Andersson, Charles, 279, 280
Andries-Ohrigstad settlement, 95
Anglo-American Corporation, 240
Anglo-Transvaal Conventions (1881/1884), 264
Angola, 3, 4, 63, 222, 226, 242, 281, 283, 286, 288-9; civil war and Independence, 224-5, 233;

South African policy towards, 222, 224, 233, 235, 241, 288, 290; Cubans in, 224-5, 235, 241, 289, 290; Safari operation, 235; SADF raids into, 241, 288, 290; 1988 Treaty between South Africa and, 241
Angra Pequena Bay, 124
Anti-Coloured Affairs Department Movement, 186-7
apartheid, xi, xii, xiii, 193-242, 285; National Party's policy of, 189-92; doctrine of, 190-1, 196; classical (*baaskap*), 193-211, 214, 219, 222, 224, 228, 285; separate development, 193, 200, 212-21, 222-3, 228, 229, 285; multiracial co-option, 193, 228-30, 233; legal framework, 196-202; sporting, 200, 215-16, 219, 229; educational, 201-2, 203, 207, 220, 229, 246; white opposition to, 204-5, 219, 239-40; black and brown opposition to, 205-10, 219-21; Bantustans, 212-15, 216, 217, 229-30, 231, 234, 240, 248, 261, 273; modifications of 'petty', 215, 216, 219; police repression, 218; in Namibia, 234, 282, 285, 286, 287; social, 229, 245; abandonment of, 242, 245-51; *see also* racial discrimination/ segregation
Archbell, James, 66, 69, 75
Arnot, David, 103
Asiatic Land Tenure and Indian Representation Act (1946), 189
Asiatic Law Amendment Ordinance (1906), 164
AWB (Afrikaner Weerstandbeweeging), 232, 233
Azanian People's Party, 231
baaskap (classical) apartheid, 193-211, 214, 219, 222, 224, 228, 285
Bakongo, 224
Balfour Declaration (1926), 173
Ballinger, W.G., 179
Bambatha, Chief of the Zondi, 153, 155
Bambandyanalo, 8, 11
Banda, Dr Kamazu, 216
Bantu Authorities Act (1953), 200, 208
Bantu Education Act (1953), 201-2, 203, 207
Bantu Laws Amendment Act (1964), 217
Bantu-speaking peoples, xi, 3, 4, 5, 7, 8, 10-16, 73, 252, 271, 278-9; Nguni, 8-10; Sotho-Tswana, 10; social, economic and political organisation, 10-15; chiefdoms, 11-15; patterns of expansion, 15-16; Khoisan relations with, 16, 26
Bantustans ('homelands'), 201, 212-15, 216, 221, 223, 227, 230, 231, 248, 261, 273; new policy for, 212-13, 220; constitutional and economic development of, 213-15; forced removals of Africans to, 214-15, 216-17; black political activity in, 220, 230-1; formal independence for, 229-30; and Swaziland, 264, 269, 270; in Namibia, 234, 285-6, 287; illegal urban immigration from, 240
Bapedi Union, 162
Barend-Barends, 50, 63, 67, 75
Barends family, 31

Barkly, High Commissioner Sir Henry, 103-4, 108, 109
Barnato, Barney, 122
Barotseland, 58, 63
Basotho Qwaqwa homeland, 213, 214
Bastards (Basters), 31, 41, 279; *see also* Griqua
Basuto Association, 162
Basutoland *see* Lesotho
Basutoland Congress Party, 259-60, 261, 262
Basutoland National Council, 258, 259, 260
Basutoland National Party, 24-5, 260
Batavian Republic (1803-6), 41-2, 46
Bathoen, Chief of the Ngwaketse, 274
Batty, A.F., 178
Baviaanskloof mission, 39
Beaumont Commission, 163
Bechuanaland *see* Botswana
Bechuanaland Democratic Party (BDP), 276, 277
Bechuanaland People's Party, 275
Bechuanaland Protectorate Federal Party, 275
Beit, Otto, 122, 128
Belgians, 133
Benguella plateau, 224
Bereng, Chief, 259
Bergenaars, 50
Bersheba, 279
Bethanie, 279
Bethelsdorp, 41, 43, 48
Bethlehem Lesotho refugee camp, 262
Beyers, General C.F., 166
Bezuidenhout, Frederik, 44
Bezuidenhout, J., 264
Bhaca, 68, 84
Biggar, Robert, 80
Biko, Steve, 220; death in prison of, 227
Bisho, police open fire on ANC marchers at, 250-1
Bismarck, Otto von, 280
Blaauwkrantz river, 79
'Black Circuit' (Cape Circuit Court), 44
black consciousness movement, 220-1, 226, 230; banning of (1977), 227
Black People's Convention, 220
'Black Peril' election (1929), 174-5
Black Sash, women's movement, 205
black townships, xiii, 194, 203, 208, 210, 218, 225, 227-9, 236, 250; Soweto disturbances (1976), 225-6; security of tenure of homes, 229; and violence in, 236-7, 246; rebellions, 237, 244; government control of, 239; vigilante groups in, 239; unemployment in, 246; *see also* urban population
Blanke Werkers Beskermingsbond, 190
Blignaut's Point meeting (1890), 265
Bloem, Jan, 29-30, 32, 52, 66, 67, 75, 76
Bloem II, Jan, 30, 67
Bloemfontein, 87, 88, 94, 143, 145, 162, 206
Bloemfontein Convention (1854), 91, 93
Blood River, battle of (1838), 80-1, 84, 113, 176, 177
Blood River Territory, 112, 113, 114
Boers *see* Afrikaners
Boesak, Revd Allan, 238
Boipatong massacre (1992), 249
Bondelswarts, 278, 281, 284; massacre of (1922), 170, 284
Bophuthatswana (Bantustan), 214, 273; formal independence for (1977), 229
Boshoff, Carel, 239
Boshoff, Jacobus, 94, 96

BOSS (Bureau of State Security), 218, 219
Botha, Johannes, 75
Botha, Louis, 151, 152, 159, 160, 164, 166, 167, 168
Botha, P.W., 232-3, 235, 236, 238, 239, 240, 242; Mandela's meeting with, 242; resignation of (1989), 242
Botswana (formerly Bechuanaland Protectorate), xi, 1, 3, 4, 5, 10, 63, 68, 77, 136, 137, 145, 148, 157, 211, 221, 226, 252, 266, 270-7, 278, 281, 282; British annexation of (1885), 124, 272-4; incorporated into Cape Colony (1895), 124, 158, 273; and separate development, 215; labour migration from, 274; political developments, 274-6, 277; Independence (1966), 276; economic development, 276, 277; and foreign policy, 275, 276
Botswana People's Party, 275
Bourke, Acting-Governor, 48
Bowler, Louis P., 133
Brand, J.H., President of Orange Free State, 96, 109, 110
Bresler, *Landdrost* of Graaf-Reinet, 36, 37
British/English, 233, 234, 239, 263, 287, 288; occupation of Cape (1795-1802), 34, 35-41; and reoccupation of Cape (1806), 42-4; 1820 settler scheme, 47; Ordinance no. 50, 48-9, 72; at Port Natal, 60, 61, 62, 68, 69, 76, 78, 80; and Xhosa war of resistance, 69-71; and Queen Adelaide Province, 70-1, 73; and Great Trek, 70, 71-7, 83; and Zulus, 78, 80, 81, 112-16, 119; battle of Tugela river, 80; legislation over trekker lands, 83-4; annexation of Natal by (1845), 85-6; 'War of the Axe' (1846-7), 87; annexation of 'ceded territory', 82; and British Kaffraria, 88, 89, 92-3; and Orange River sovereignty, 88, 89-91, 255; Sand River and Bloemfontein Conventions, 90-1; and changes in policy, 91-2; Orange Free State, 94-5; annexation and administration of Lesotho, 98-9, 116, 120, 255, 256-8, 259; and diamond mines, 103-5; confederation policy, 108-10, 112, 119; annexation of Transvaal (1877), 110-11, 119-20; Pretoria Convention (1881), 120; London Convention (1884), 124; and Bechuanaland Protectorate, 124, 272-4, 275; St Lucia Bay annexed by, 125; and goldmining, 126, 131; and Cecil Rhodes, 131-3, 134-41; and Swaziland, 134, 263-4, 265, 266-7; conquest of Matabeleland, 136; Jameson Raid, 138, 141; South African League, 141; Chamberlain seeks control of Transvaal, 141; and Milner's confrontation with Transvaal, 142-4; South African War, 144-8; post-war reconstruction, 148-50; political and economic developments, 151-4; and Union of South Africa (1910), 154-60; and First World War, 165-7; and Second World War, 181-8; and Rhodesia, 221-2, 233, 234-5; and Namibia, 280-1, 285; Caprivi Strip ceded to Germany by (1890), 281; *see also* Cape; Natal; Transvaal
British Bechuanaland, 124, 173
British East India Company, 17-18, 19
British Kaffraria, 88, 89, 92-3
British South Africa Company, 132, 133, 136, 137, 139, 140, 274
British South Africa Police, 137
Broederbond (Brotherhood), 167, 173-4, 176-8, 183, 184, 189, 190, 192, 195, 219, 239, 240

broedertwis (brother quarrels), 183
Bronkhorst Spruit, 119
Broome Commission, 185
Bruintjies Hoogte, 33, 38
Bulawayo, 136, 140
Bulhoek Israelites, massacre of (1920), 169-70
Buller, General, 145
Burger, Jacobus, 95
Burgers, D.F., President of Transvaal, 105, 109, 110
Bushman-Hottentots, 6; *see also* San
Butha-Buthe mountain, 64, 252
Buthelezi, Chief Gatsha, 220, 230-1, 239-40, 247, 248, 251
butho, see age-regiments
Buysvolk, 43
bywoner (client tenants), 97, 111, 127, 149, 171
Calata, James A., 181
Caledon, Governor, 43
Caledon river/valley, 63, 65, 252, 255
Camdebo, 33, 34
Campbell-Bannerman, Sir Henry, 152
Cape Colony (now Cape Province), xii, 1-2, 9, 10, 53, 60, 63, 65, 67, 68-9; establishment and early development, 17-34; first European settlements, 17-22; slave labour and expansion in farming, 22-5; colonial expansion, 25-6; Khoisan reactions to Europeans, 26-30; racial attitudes, 30-2, 72; and Coloureds, 30-1, 92, 105, 107, 141, 155-7, 198-9, 200-1; last years of Company rule, 32-4; 1795-1834: 35-51; first British occupation (1795-1802), 36-41; Christian missionaries, 38-41; Batavian Republic (1803-6), 41-2; and return of the British (1806), 42-4; struggle for the *zuurveld*, 44-7; 'ceded territory', 45-6, 69, 70; judicial reform, 47-8; expansion across the Orange, 49-51; Xhosa war of resistance, 69-71; and Queen Adelaide Province, 70-1, 73; Great Trek out of, 35, 71-7; 'War of the Axe', 87-8; constitutional developments, 91-2; 'colour-blind' franchise, 92; Parliament created (1853), 92; diamond mining, 101, 103-5, 106-7, 109; responsible government status for, 105, 108; administration of Lesotho, 105, 116, 256-7; confederation policy, 108-9, 110, 112, 119; Sotho resistance: the 'Gun War', 116-18, 120; Bechuanaland incorporated into (1895), 124, 273; customs union 130-1, 134, 148; political tactics of Rhodes in, 134-5, 140-1; and South African War, 140-8; Union of South Africa (1910), 154-6; franchise, 155-7, 162, 163, 172, 174, 175, 179, 200-1, 204; political activity in, 161-2; Afrikaner nationalism, 176-7; and Namibia, 280-1
Cape Midlands, Boer invasion of (1899), 145
Cape Mounted Police, 108
Cape Native Voters' Association, 180
Cape of Good Hope Punishment Act (1835), 51, 83, 87
Cape Patriots, 32
Cape Provincial Council, 181
Cape Regiment, 43
Cape Town, 22, 23, 36, 37, 38, 43, 47, 60, 101, 130, 137, 155, 178, 198-9; University of, 202, 229; resistance to apartheid in, 206, 209; squatter settlements, 246
Caprivi Strip, 281
Carnarvon, Lord, 104; confederation scheme of,

108-10
Cathcart, Governor, 91
Cato Manor township, riots in, 208
cattle/stockraising, 64, 76, 77, 140, 254; Bantu 8, 11, 12, 13, 14; Khoi, 5, 7, 24; Cape Colony, 24-5, 46, 47, 49-50, 51; *trek boers*, 25, 47, 73, 280, 283; 1820 settler scheme, 47; expansion across the Orange, 49-50; Zulu, 59, 61, 63, 78, 79, 80, 81, 274, 280; foot and mouth disease, 80; Xhosa cattle killing tragedy, 93, 111, *rinderpest* epidemic, 140, 149, 265, 281; Bechuanaland, 274; Namibia, 280, 281
Cattle Commando (*Beestekommando*), Boer, 81, 84, 85
ceded territory (neutral strip), 45-6, 51, 69, 70, 88
Central African Federation, 221
Central South African Railways, 148
Cetshwayo, Zulu chief, 113-16, 124-5, 153
Cewa, 68
Chamberlain, Joseph, 137, 138, 139, 141, 142-3, 148, 151, 274
Champion, A.W.G., 178, 179, 205
Charlestown, 129
Chavonnes, Governor, 22, 24
Chinese miners, 150, 152, 171
Christelike Nasionale Onderwys, 150
Christelike Kulturaksis, 219
Christian Institute, banning of (1977), 227
Chunu, 60, 61
Cilliers, Sarel, 71, 75, 80
circumcision, 15, 24
Ciskei, 111, 214, 220; formal independence for (1981), 229; police open fire on ANC marchers in Bisho, 250-1
Clark, Sir George, 91
click languages, 7-8, 9
Clothing Workers' Union, 189, 190
coalminers, 164, 165
Codesa *see* Convention for a Democratic South Africa
Coillard, François, 133
Colenso, Bishop, 124
Colenso, battle of (1899), 145
Colesberg, 26, 129, 130
Collins, Captain, 44, 46, 49
Coloured Affairs Department, 186
Coloured Persons' Rights Bill (1926), 172
Coloureds, xiii, 30-1, 101, 171, 202, 204, 224, 226, 227, 228, 231, 250; in Cape Colony, 30-1, 92, 105, 107, 141, 155-7, 198-9, 200-1, 204, 236; franchise, 92, 155-7, 162, 172-3, 191, 200-1, 204, 231, 236; wartime, 166, 186-7, discrimination against, 189-90, 196, 197, 203-4, 205, 236; and Group Areas Act, 198-9; Universities for, 202, 229; joint non-white opposition to apartheid, 205-6, 230-1; President's Council, 231-2, 236; and multiracial constitution, 236-7
commandos, Boer, 28-9, 33, 38, 74, 76, 77, 78, 79-80, 81, 94, 110, 145-6
Commonwealth, South Africa leaves (1961), 210-11
Commonwealth Heads of Government Meeting, Nassau (1985), 238
Communist Party (SACP), 180, 186, 206, 242, 250, 259; members expelled from ICU, 178, 179; outlawed (1950), 202
Congo Free State, 133
Congress of Democrats, 205, 207

Congress of the People (Kliptown 1955), 207; Freedom Charter of, 207
Conservative Party, 232, 242, 244, 248; wins Potchefstroom by-election, 248
conscription, 227
Consolidated Gold Fields of South Africa Ltd, 123, 128, 131, 136
Convention for a Democratic South Africa (Codesa, 1991), 248-9
copper mining, 276, 278, 289
COSATU, 240, 250
Council of Policy, Dutch, 20, 22, 36
Cradock, Governor, 43, 44, 46
Cradock's Pass, 69
Craig, General, 36
Creswell, Frederick, 149-50, 152
Crocodile river, 15
Cronje, Professor, 190
Crossroads squatter settlements, 246
Cubans in Angola, 224-5, 235, 241, 289, 290
Cuito Cuanavale base, 241; seige of, 290
customs unions, 130-1, 134, 148, 154, 262
Dadoo, Dr Yusuf, 205
Damara or Berg Dama, 4, 234, 278, 285
Daniel's Kuil, 50
Day of the Covenant, Boers, 80, 177, 210
De Beers Consolidated Mines Ltd, 122, 123, 128, 136
De Buys, Coenraad, 32, 37, 38, 41, 43, 69
De la Rey, J.H., 168
De Lange, Pieter de, 239
De Wet, C.R., 166
Defence Association, 107
Delagoa Bay, 52, 53, 54, 55, 60, 74, 75, 95, 106, 110, 125, 127, 141; given to Portugal (1875), 109; railways, 127, 129-30, 145, 149, 154
Democratic Party, 240, 242
Democratic Turnhalle Alliance, 234, 235, 288, 289
Derdepoort meeting (1849), 95
Desmond, Cosmas, 216
Development of Self-Government for Native Nations in South West Africa Act (1968), 286; Amendment to (1973), 287
Dhlamini, Makhosini, 215
diamond fields/mining, 101-5, 106-7, 109, 120, 121-3, 128, 158, 228-9, 256, 257; dry diggings, 101, 103; Keate awards: British annexation of, 103-5: industrial revolution in, 121-3; in Botswana, 276; in Namibia, 278, 289
Dias, Bartholomew, 17
difaqane see mfecane
Dingane, Zulu king, 61, 62, 64, 67, 68, 76, 77, 78-9, 80-1, 84, 133
Dingiswayo of the Mthethwa, 54, 56, 57, 116
Dinizulu, Zulu king, 125, 153, 154, 155
Disraeli, Benjamin, 105
Dithakong, 60, 272
Dlamini, Bhekimpi, 270
Dlamini, Mabandla, 269-70
Dlamini, Mfanasibili, 269, 270
Dominion Party, 175, 181, 185
dongas (erosion ravines), 257
Donkin, Acting-Governor, 45
Doppers, 75
Drakensberg, 1, 8, 15, 56, 60, 62, 75, 85, 96, 111, 252, 254
drought, 49, 51, 53, 235, 259, 276, 289
Du Bois, W.E.B., 161
Dube, Revd John, 161, 162

Dundas, Acting-Governor, 38, 41
Dunn, John, 113, 114, 116
D'Urban, Governor, 69-70, 71, 76, 81
Durban (formerly Port Natal), 55, 60, 62, 68, 69, 76, 78, 80, 81, 239; squatter settlements around, 246
Dutch, 6, 7, 17, 35, 141, 279; early settlement in Cape Colony, 18-34; conflicts between Company and, 20-2, 32, 34; and slave labour, 22, 23; farming expansion, 22-5; colonial expansion, 25-6; Khoisan reaction to presence of, 26-30; development of commandos, 28-9; racial attitudes, 30-2; last years of Company rule, 32-4; Xhosa resistance against, 33-4; Batavian Republic, 41-2; *see also* Afrikaners
Dutch East India Company, 18, 20-2, 24, 25, 27, 32-4, 37, 72
Dutch Reformed Church, 20, 75, 76, 176, 190
Dwane, Revd James, 161
Dzeliwe, Queen, Regent of Swaziland, 269-70
East Caprivi, 286, 287
East London 101, 130, 178, 179, 206-7, 220
Eastern Europe, collapse of Communist regimes in, 242
Eckenbrecher, Margarete von, 281
education, 239, 244; Milner's anglicization policy, 149, 150; African, 161, 203, 223, 225-6, 229, 284; apartheid legislation, 201-2, 203, 207, 220; and relaxation of apartheid, 228-9, 245; Lesotho, 254, 259
Edwards, William, 40
EEC (European Economic Community), 262; economic sanctions against South Africa, 238, 239
Einiqua, 5
Ekonomiese Volkskongres, 178
eku-Pumelini, 66
elections: Transvaal (1907), 152; first union (1910), 159; 1915: 166; 1920: 167; 1921: 167; 1929 ('Black Peril'), 174-5; 1933: 175; 1943: 185; 1948: 188, 192, 194, 285; 1953: 194, 195, 201, 204; 1958: 194; 1970: 219; 1974: 231; 1977: 231; 1981: 232; 1987: 240; 1989: 242
em-Gungundhlovu, 79, 80
Emigrant Tembuland, 111
EPG (Eminent Persons Group), collapse of mission to South Africa of, 238-9, 240, 241
Erasmus, *veldkornet*, 38
Erasmus family, 75
Escher, Dr A.M., 287
Ethiopian Movement, 161
Extension of University Education Act (1959), 202
Fagan Commission (1946-8), 188
FAK (Federasie van Afrikaanse Kultuurverenigings), 174, 176, 177, 190, 195; Volkskongress (1944), 190, 191
Faku, Pondo ruler, 61, 85, 125
False Bay, 19
Faure, *landdrost* of Swellendam, 34, 36
Ferreira, Petrus Hendrik, 33
Field, Winston, 221
First World War (1914-18), 165-7, 171, 282, 283
FNLA, Angola, 224, 225
Fokeng *see* Kololo
Fort Hare, 161, 244
Fort Peddie, 70

t Salisbury, 134
t Victoria, 136
.ort Wiltshire fair, 45
Fourie, Jopie, 166, 176
Fourteen Streams, 129
France, French, 35, 234, 287, 288; Huguenots in
    Cape, 19-20; missionaries, 62, 98, 133, 239
franchise (voting rights), non-white, 135, 147,
    162, 163, 164, 172, 174, 179; Coloureds, 92,
    155-7, 162, 172-3, 191, 200-1, 204, 231,
    236; Indians, 163
Franchise and Ballot Bill (1892), 135
Fransmanne, 278
Fredericksburgh, 45
free blacks, 30, 31
Frelimo, 221, 224, 235
Frere, Sir Bartle, 110, 112, 114, 115-16, 118,
    119
Froneman, G.F. van L., 213
'frontier ruffians', 32
Froude, J.A., 106, 109, 110
Fynn, Henry, 60
Gabarone, 277
Gandhi, Mahatma, 163, 164
Gardiner, Captain Allen, 68
Gaseitswe, Chief of the Ngwaketse, 124, 273,
    274
Gatsrand, 80
Gaza kingdom, 57, 68
Gazankula homeland, 214
Gcaleka, Gcalekaland, 15, 70, 111, 112, 125
Genadendal mission, 39
George VI, King of England, 266
German South West Africa see Namibia
Germans, 19, 20, 138, 280, 281-2
Ghana, 211
Gladstone, William E., 119
Glasgow Missionary Society, 39
Glen Grey Act (1894), 135
Glenelg, Lord, 71
gold fields/gold mining, 8, 78, 101, 121, 123,
    125, 126-9, 131, 136, 137, 149, 158, 164,
    175, 194, 264; initial changes caused by, 126-
    7; the nature of the Rand deposits, 127-8;
    labour force, 128, 129, 148, 149-50, 165, 170-
    1, 187; and wages, 148, 149, 185, 187; see also
    Witwatersrand
gold standard, abandonment of (1933), 175
Gonaqua chiefdom, 16, 29
Gonema, Chief of the Gorona, 28
Gorbachev, Mikhail, 241
Gordon, General, 120, 257
Gordon-Walker, Patrick, 275
Goshen, 124, 272
Gqunukwebe Xhosa, 16, 26, 29, 34
Graaf-Reinet, 34, 36, 38, 41, 69, 71, 75
Grahamstown, 44, 45, 85
Grahamstown Journal, 76
Great Fish river, 3, 6, 9, 15, 26, 29, 33-4, 36, 38,
    42, 44, 69, 70
Great Trek, Boer, xiii, 35, 43, 65, 69, 70, 71-8,
    82, 93, 149, 160, 176, 255; military tactics,
    73-4; early trekker groups, 74-5; trekker
    government, 75-6; leaders of, 76-7; *voortrekker*
    centenary celebrations (1938), 177
Green, Frederick, 279
Grey, Governor Sir George, 92-3, 94-5, 96, 111
Greyshirts, 182
Griffith, Charles Duncan, 256, 257

Griffith, Colonel, 118
Griffith, Paramount Chief, 259
Griqua, 63, 64, 65, 66, 67, 76, 77, 86-7, 96, 103-
    4, 111, 112, 118, 253, 254, 272; rise of, 31-2,
    41; Hartenaar revolt, 43; split into three
    states, 50; white settler relations with, 50-1
Griqualand East, 111, 112, 120
Griqualand West, 105, 106-7, 108, 109, 110, 112,
    145
Griquatown, 32, 50
Grobler, Piet, 132
Groot Dode, 278
Group Areas Act (1950), 198-9, 240; repeal of, 245
Guinea-Bissau, 224
Gumede, James, 180, 259
'Gun War', Sotho, 118, 120
Gundwane Ndiweni, *induna*, 77
Gwanda, 77
Hamakar, battle of, 281-2
Hamu, 116
Hani, Chris, 251
Hartenaars, revolt of, 43, 50
Harts river, 29, 30, 43, 101
Havenga, N.C., 184, 194
Haybittel, 279
heemraden (urban councils), 20, 71, 76
Herero, 10, 279, 280, 281-2, 283, 285, 286
Hertzog, Albert, 190, 219
Hertzog, J.B., 151, 160, 166, 180, 181, 183-4,
    200; Afrikaner nationalism under, 160;
    segregation policy, 163, 172-3, 174, 175, 178-
    9, 213; 'Black Peril' election (1929) won by,
    174-5
Het Volk Party, Transvaal, 151, 152, 159
High Commission Territories see Lesotho
    (Basutoland); Botswana (Bechuanaland);
    Swaziland
Hintsa, 52, 70
Hlakoane, 63
Hlubi, 55, 56, 60, 62, 64, 107-8, 252, 253
HNP (Herstigte Nasionale Party), 219, 231, 232
Hoffman, Josiah, 94
Hofmeyr, Jan, 119, 134-5, 189, 204
Holden, Robert, 224
homelands see Bantustans
Hopetown, 101
Hottentot armed force see Cape Regiment
Hottentot corps, 37
Hottentots see Khoi-Khoi
Hottentots Holland, 19, 27-8, 43
Huguenots, 19-20
Hulett, George, 265
hunger relief agencies, 246
Hurutshe, 67, 76, 77
Husing, Henning, 21, 22
ICU (Industrial and Commercial Workers' Union),
    169, 178-9, 180, 259
ICU Yase Natal, 179
Ilanga lase Natal (newspaper), 162
Imbokodvo National Movement, 267-8
Imbumba Yama Afrika, 161
Immorality Act (1927), 172; Amendment to
    (1950), 196
Imperial Conference: 1911: 160; 1922: 173
Imvo Zabantsundu (newspaper), 161-2
Independent ICU, 179
Independents, 167
Indian Community, xiii, 180, 224, 226, 227, 231;
    in Natal, 86, 163, 185, 189, 205; in Boer

Republics, 86, 163-4; franchise, 163;
    discrimination against, 163-4; 185, 188-9,
    191, 198, 203-4, 236, 285; non-violent
    resistance (*Satyagraha*) by, 164; Pegging Act
    (1943), 185, 189; Group Areas Act
    (1950),198; universities for, 202, 229; riots
    between Africans and, 205; joint non-white
    opposition to apartheid, 205-6, 230-1;
    President's Council, 231-2, 236; and
    multiracial constitution, 236-7
Indian Relief Act (1914), 164
indunas, 12, 13, 58-9, 60, 61, 77, 81, 265
Industrial Conciliation Act (1956), 199
influenza epidemic, 169
Ingongo, 119
Inhambane, 17, 74, 95
initiation groups, 14-15, 53-4
Inkatha movement, 230, 240, 244; rivalry and
    conflict beween ANC and, 239, 244, 247-8;
    PFP alliance with, 240; government's secret
    involvement with, 247-8; Boipatong massacre,
    249
Innes, James Rose, 161
International Court of Justice, 286
International Olympic Committee, South Africa
    readmitted to (1991), 245
Iron Age peoples, 4, 7-16
Isaacs, Jan, 76
Isandhlwana, battle of (1879), 115, 116, 119
ISCOR (Iron and Steel Corporation),172
Islam, 39
Israelites, Bulhoek, 169-70
ivory trade, 24, 25, 52-3, 60, 74
Izi Yendane (Zulu *butho*), 59-60
Jabavu, D.D.T., 180, 181
Jabavu, John Teno, 156, 161, 162
Jameson raid (Dr Jameson), 137, 138-9, 140,
    141, 274
Jan Smuts International Airport, Johannesburg,
    215
Janssens, General J.W., 41-2, 43
Jere, 57
Jervis, Captain, 81
Jobe of the Sithole, 59-60
Johannesburg, xi, 127, 130, 137, 138, 145, 146,
    148, 152, 164, 177, 181, 186, 203, 206, 207;
    forced removal of Africans from, 197-8, 203,
    207; boycott of buses, 208
Johannesburg Chamber of Mines, 128
Johnston, Harry, 133
Joint Councils of Europeans and Africans, 179
Joint Planning Council, non-white, 206
Jonathan, Chief Leabua, 215, 221, 260-2
Jonathan Molapo, 256, 257, 258, 260
Jong Suid Afrika (Young South Africa), 167
Joubert, Piet, 119, 134
Kadalie, Clements, 178-9
Kalahari, 1, 8, 16, 63, 68, 270, 278
Kalaka, 10
KaNgwane (Bantustan), 264, 269, 270
karroo (semi-desert), 2, 26
Kat river, 45-6, 69
Katanga, 133
Kaunda, President Kenneth, of Zambia, 222,
    242, 276, 290
Keate awards (1871), 104-5
Kei river, 51, 70, 88, 112
Keiskamma river, 29, 45, 69, 88
Kemp, General Jan, 166

Kgalagadi, 16
Kgama, Chief of Ngwato, 67, 124, 137, 272, 273, 274
Kgatla chiefdoms, 15-16, 52
Khamiesberg, 31
Khoa-Khoa, 254
Khoi-Khoi (Hottentots), xi, 5-7, 9, 10, 11, 12, 16, 18, 45, 48, 69, 73, 80, 234, 278, 279, 285; labour force in Cape, 22, 24, 28, 43-4, 48; Dutch barter trade with, 24; reactions to European presence, 26-30, 34, 38; racial attitudes towards, 30, 31, 32; under British occupation 36, 37, 38, 41; Christian missionary activity among, 38, 39, 41, 43; revolt in Eastern provinces, 37, 41; and labour laws, 43-4; Ordinance no. 50: 48-9; massacre of Bondelswarts, 170, 268
Khoisan peoples, 5-8, 9, 10, 14, 16, 26-30, 31, 32
kholwa (school people), 203
Khumalo, 66
Kimberley, 107, 122, 125, 206, 228, 257; siege of, 145
King, Dick, 85
King, Lieutenant, 60
Kitchener, Lord, 145
Klerk, F.W. de, 242, 248, 250, 291; succeeds Botha as president, 242; announces abandonment of aparteid (1990), 242, 245; Mandela's talks with, 245; calls for referendum of white voters, 248; denounces Boipatong massacre, 249; summit meeting with Mandela, 251
Klerk, Willem de, 242
Klerksdorp meeting (1902), 145
Koevoet (Crowbar) unit, 290
Kok, Adam, II, 50-1, 96
Kok, Adam, III, 86-7, 88, 91
Kok, Cornelius, II, 50
Kok family, 31, 50
Kololo (formerly Fokeng), 63, 68, 252, 271, 272
kommissie raad (council), 84
Kooaneng mountains, 62, 64
Kora (or Korana), 5, 63, 64, 65, 66, 67, 76, 253
Kosi Bay, 133, 134
Kreli, Gcaleka chief, 112
Krogh, Johannes, 87
Kruger, Paul, xiii, 75, 119, 120, 124, 125, 129, 130, 133, 134, 136, 138, 141-2, 143, 145, 265
krygsraad (council of war), 75, 84
Krynauw, Jan, 87
Kuruman mission station, 66, 67, 272
KwaNdebele, 229
KwaZulu, 214, 215, 220, 230, 239, 269, 270
Kwena, 15-16, 67, 77, 124, 137, 252, 272, 273, 274
laagers, Boer, 74, 75, 80, 115
labour, 183, 185; Indian, 86, 164; Creswell's white labour policy, 149-50, 152; white labour unrest (1913-14), 164-5; poor whites, 149-50, 167, 171-2, 175, 177, 193-4, 202; Chinese miners, 150, 152, 171; race relations in Rand mining work force, 170-1; Rand Rebellion (1922), 171-2; labour, African, 22, 24; slave, 22, 23, 24, 43; Khoi, 22, 24, 28, 43-4, 48; shortages, 43, 48, 86, 102-3, 149, 183; migrant, 103, 154, 159, 170-1, 194, 197, 202, 203, 216, 218, 222, 223, 228-9, 230, 239, 240, 244, 256, 258, 260, 262, 266, 274, 284; indentured, 110; diamond miners, 122-3; gold miners, 128, 129, 149, 170-1; Glen Grey Act (1894), 135; exploitation of, 148, 149-50, 170, 222, 282; wages, 148, 149, 167-9, 170-1, 185, 186, 187, 228; wartime, 185, 186, 187; and separate development (Bantustans), 213, 214, 215, 216, 217-18, 230; and multiracial co-option, 222, 228-9; in Namibia, 282-4, 287; see also apartheid; strikes; trades unions
Labour Party, South African, 159, 166, 172, 181, 185, 192
Labour Party, Transvaal, 152, 174
Ladysmith, relief of, 145
Laing's Nek, 119
Lake Malawi, 57
Lake Ngami, 124, 270, 271
Lala, 16
land, land tenure, 68, 72, 82, 111, 124, 140, 149, 163, 171, 175; British legislation over trekker, 83; grazing, 53, 72, 74, 133; in Natal, 84, 85-6, 152-3; in Transvaal, 97, 149; Glen Grey Act, 135; bywoner tenants, 97, 111, 149, 171; African purchase of, 163, 175; Native Service Contract Act (1932), 174; Natives' Trust and Land Act (1936), 175, 178, 191, 199; Asiatic Land Tenure Act (1946),189; Prevention of Illegal Squatting Act (1951), 199; forced removals of Africans to Bantustans, 216-17; in Namibia, 266- 7; see also agriculture; labour
Land Act (1913), xiii, 163, 164, 169, 199
land bank, 151
landdrost (Boer magistrate), 20, 26, 28, 33, 34, 47, 69, 76, 80, 84, 95
Langa township, 210
Langalibalele affair, 107-8, 256
Lansdown Commission, 187
Laurier, Sir Wilfred, 160
Laws of Lerotholi, 258
League of Nations, 167; Mandate system, 167, 282, 284, 285
Lebowa homeland, 214
Lefolo, Josiel, 259
Lehana, 117
Lehloenya, Patrick, 262
Lekhotla la Bafo, 259
Lekhanya, Major-General Justin, 1986 coup of, 262-3
Leolu mountains, 15, 62, 68
Leopold of Belgium, King, 133
Leribe, 256, 258
Lerotholi, Paramount Chief, 256, 258
Lesotho (formerly Basutoland), xi, 1, 3, 9, 10, 62, 64, 68, 88, 89, 99, 105, 116, 120, 147, 148, 157, 211, 221, 252-63, 266, 272, 274; establishment of kingdom, 64-6, 252-5; war between Orange Free State and, 97-8, 255-6; British annexation of (1868), 98-9, 255, 256-8, 259; and Cape administration (1871-83), 105, 116, 256-7; labour migration from, 256, 258, 260, 262, 274; Phuthi rebellion, 116-18; 'Gun War', 118, 120; rearmament of, 256-7; British resume administration of (1883), 257-8; and economy, 257-8, 260, 262; social inequality, 258; and political developments, 258-62; Independence (1966), 260; and 1970 coup, 261; and foreign policy, 261-2; South Africa closes borders with (1986), 262
Lesotho Liberation Army (LLA), 262

Lesotho Mounted Police (formerly Basutoland Mounted Police), 256, 261
Lethule, Chief of Khoa-Khoa, 239
Letsie I, Sotho chief, 117, 118, 256, 258
Lettow-Vorbeck, Gen. P.E. von, 166
Lewanika, Lozi king, 133
Liberal Party, 204
Lifa national land repurchase fund, 267, 269
lifaqane, 252, 254, 255, 272; see also mfecane
Limpopo river, 1, 77, 133
Lindley, Daniel, 67
lineage groups, Bantu, 11-12, 13-14
liqoqo, Swazi chiefly council, 269-70
Little Free State (in Swaziland), 264
Livingstone, David, 63, 103, 272
loan farms system, 24-5, 46, 47
Lobengula, Ndebele king, 131-2, 133, 136, 139-40
lobola (bridewealth), 11, 13, 89
Loch, Sir Henry, 134, 137, 265
Lochner, Frank, 132-3
London confederation conference (1876), 109-10
London Convention (1884), 124, 141, 143
London Missionary Society (LMS), 31, 39, 40-1, 48, 66
Lourenço Marques see Maputo
Louw, Jacobus Gideon, 36
Lozi, 63, 103, 133, 281
Luanda, 224
Lüderitz Bay, 165, 281
Lusaka Accord, 241
Luthuli, Albert, 207, 209
Lydenburg, 95, 96, 121
Lyttelton, Alfred, 151, 152
maatschappij (Boer company), 73, 76
Macartney, Governor of Cape Colony, 36
Machel, Samora, 224, 235
Macingwane, 60, 61
Mackenzie, John, 124, 272
McLuckie, William, 66, 69
MacMahon, Marshal, 106, 109
Macmillan, Harold, 211
McMurdo, E., 129
Macomo, 69
Mafeking, relief of, 145, 147
mafisa system, 11, 64, 254
Magaliesberg mountains, 1, 75, 96
Magaye, of the Cele, 59-60
Magersfontein, battle of (1899), 145
Maguire, Rochfort, 132
Maherero, Chief, 279, 281
Mahlatule famine, 53
Maitland, Governor, 87
maize, 10, 86, 176
Majuba Hill, battle of, 120
Makaba, 66
Makana (Nxele), prophet, 44-5, 89
Makhosetive, Swazi prince, 269, 270; crowned King Mswati III (1984), 270
Makwana, 75
Malan, A.G., 204
Malan, Dr D.F., 174, 176, 177, 183, 184, 192, 193, 194-5, 200, 201
Malan, Magnus, 227, 232, 238, 248
Malawi (formerly Nyasaland), 7, 57, 58, 63, 68, 222, 261
Malay community in Cape Colony, 22, 39
Malungwane hills, 77
Maluti mountains, 255

...ndela, Nelson, 210, 242, 247, 250; arrest and imprisonment of, 218; calls for release of, 238, 240; Botha's meeting with, 242, 243-4; Winnie's formal separation from, 244; negotiations with de Klerk, 245; becomes president of ANC (1991), 246; Buthelezi's meetings with, 247; summit meeting between de Klerk and, 251

Mandela, Winnie, 243; trial and conviction of (1991), 244

Manganja, 63

Mangwato, 52, 68

Mantsebo, 259

Mapumelo uprising, 153

Mapungubwe, 8, 11

Mapupa, 57

Maputo railway, 129, 267, 269

Maqomo, Chief, 45-6

Maquassie mission station, 63

Marema Tlou Freedom Party, 260, 261, 262

Marengo, Jacob, 282

Marico river/valley, 15, 67, 76, 77, 96

Maritz, Gert, 69, 71, 75-76, 77, 80

Maritz, Colonel S.G., 166

marriage: 59; Nguni, 9; Sotho-Tswana, 10; Bantu, 11, 14; Bantu-Khoisan intermarriage, 16; mixed, 30-1, 196

Maseko, 57, 58

Maseko, Mfanawenkhosi, 269, 270

Maseru, 262, 263

Mashonaland, 131-2, 133, 134, 135, 136, 139-40; see also Zimbabwe

Masire, Dr Quett, 276, 277

Masopha, 256

Mass Democratic Movement (MDM), 240

Matabeleland, British conquest of, 136

Matanzima, Chief Kaiser, 210, 213, 220

Matela, Chief of Khoa-Khoa, 254

Matiwane, 55-6, 60, 61, 62, 63, 64, 252, 253

Matiwane's Kop, 62, 79, 80

Matopos mountains, 77, 140

Mauch, Carl, 101, 131

Mayer, Lukas, 125

Maynier, H.C.D., 34, 36, 37-8, 41, 44, 72

Mbandine, King of the Swazi 133-4

Mbandzene, King of the Swazi, 264-5

Mbelebele, 78

Mbopha, induna, 61

Mbulazi, 113

Mbundu, 224

measles epidemic, 80

Mehlokazulu, 114, 153

Melville, John, 50

Mentzel, I., 24

mercenaries, white, 123, 125

Merriman, John, 155

mfecane ('unlimited warfare'), xi, xiii, 52, 53, 55-6, 61-8, 72, 73, 82, 89, 263, 271, 272

Mfengu, 62, 70, 88, 111-12

Mhlangane, 61

Mhlatuse River, 55; battle of (1818), 57, 58

Middleburg conference (1901), 146

migrant labour, African, 103, 154, 159, 170, 183, 194, 197, 202, 203, 216, 218, 222, 223, 228-9, 230, 239, 240, 244, 246; from Lesotho, 256, 258, 260, 262, 274; from Swaziland, 266, 274; from Botswana, 274; in Namibia, 284

migration: of the mfecane, 61-8, 72, 73; Boer Great Trek, 71-7; Ndebele, 77-8

Miller, Allister, 264

Milner, High Commissioner Sir Alfred, 142-4, 148-9, 150, 151, 154, 163, 164

Mines and Works Act (1911), 172

Mines and Works Amendment Act (1926), 172

Mineworkers' Union, 190

missionaries, Christian, 38-41, 43, 44, 48, 63-4, 65-7, 68, 69, 71, 72, 76, 78, 85, 98, 131, 133, 161, 254-5, 259, 272, 280

Mist, Commissioner-General, J.A. de, 41-2

Mkhize, 55, 60

Mlangeni, Xhosa prophet, 89

Mobutu Sese Seko, President of Zaire, 224

Moffat, John Smith, 132

Moffat, Robert, 63, 66-7, 69, 77, 78, 103, 131, 272, 273

Moffat Commission (1918), 168

Mokhele, Ntsu, 259, 261

Mokoetsie, Stompie, 244

Mokoteli, 64, 252

Molapo (son of Moshoeshoe), 256

Moletsane, 60, 61, 63, 90, 239

Molopo, Sotho Chief, 108

Molopo river, 29, 124, 272, 273

Molteno, J.C., 105, 108-9, 110, 112

Mome Gorge, battle of, 153

Mooi river, 78

Moordspruit river, 79

Moore Commission, 260

Moorosi, Chief of the Phuthi, 116-18, 252, 254, 256

Moravian missionaries, 39

Moroka, Dr J.S., 205, 207

Moroka, Chief of Rolong, 75

Morris, Abraham, 284

Mosaka, Councillor Paul, 187

Mosega, 76, 77, 78, 271

Moshoeshoe I, King of Lesotho, xiii, 62, 64-6, 67, 68, 86, 87, 88, 89-90, 91, 94, 96, 97-9, 252-6, 258, 272

Moshoeshoe II, King of Lesotho, 260-1, 263

Motlume, Chief, 52

Motsete, K.T., 275

Mozambique, 7, 9, 11, 57, 61, 68, 91, 103, 130, 131, 132, 133, 136, 221, 222, 225, 226, 262, 263, 264, 269; Independence (1975),193, 224, 235; South African relations with, 222, 233, 235, 240, 289

Mozambique National resistance (MNR),235

Mpande, 81, 84, 86, 113

Mpangazita, 56

Mpezeni, 136

Mpho, Motsamai, 275

MPLA, Angola, 224, 225, 235, 241, 288-9

Mpomdomise, 118

Msene, 57, 58

Msibi, George, 270

Msiri, Yeke King, 133

Mswati, Swazi King, 55, 133, 263

Mswati III, King of Swaziland, 270

Mthethwa, 54, 56, 57, 61

Mudge, Dirk, 289

Mugabe, Robert, 234

Mulder, Dr Connie, 232

'Muldergate' affair, 232

Multi-Party Conference (MPC), Namibia, 289-90

multiracial constitution, introduction of (1983), 236-7

multiracial co-option, 193, 222, 228-30 233

Muzorewa, Bishop Abel, 233, 234, 288

Mzilikazi, 62, 63, 66-7, 69, 75, 76, 77, 78, 131, 132, 133, 271, 272

Mzinyathi river, 55

Nama, 278, 279, 280, 281, 282, 283

Namib desert, 278

Namibia (formerly South-West Africa), xi, 1, 3, 4, 5, 10, 69, 124, 188, 189, 194, 211, 222, 227, 233, 234, 235, 241, 278-91; German annexation (1884) and administration, 124, 272, 281-2; South African Mandate rule, 167, 188, 222, 225, 282-4; massacre of the Bondelswarts (1922), 170, 284; UN pressure/sanctions against, 222; and SWAPO movement, 222, 225, 234, 235, 241, 286, 287, 288, 289, 290-1; apartheid in, 234, 282, 285, 286, 287; Turnhalle Conference (1975), 234, 287-8; and Bantustans, 234, 285-6, 287; multi-party constitution adopted by, 241; mineral deposits, 278, 285, 289; population, 278-9; inter-ethnic conflict and European intervention, 279-80; British cede Caprivi Strip to (1890), 281; pass system, 282, 284; 'police zone', 283; South African schemes to absorb or partition, 284-6; UN withdraws Mandate from South Africa, 286-7; renamed Namibia (1968), 286; 1971 strike, 287; Multi-Party Conference, 289-90; Transitional Government of National Unity (1985), 290; 1989 elections won by SWAPO, 290-1; Independence (1990), 241, 291

Nande (Shaka's mother), 60

Napier, Governor, 81, 85, 87

Nata river, 77

Natal, 1, 5, 8, 52, 55, 60, 61, 62, 81, 88, 91, 92, 98, 106, 112, 116, 125, 130, 141, 185, 226, 239, 240, 244, 255; Boer settlement, 68, 73, 75, 76-7, 78, 79; and Boer Republic of Natalia, 84-5, 93, British annexation of (1845), 85; land and settlement schemes, 85-6; Indian community, 86, 163, 185, 189, 205; Langalibalele affair, 107-8; South African War, 145; economic developments, 152-4; Bambatha's rebellion, 153; and Union of South Africa (1910), 154-60; African political activity, 162, 178, 179; and riots between Africans and Indians, 205; African workers' strikes (1973), 224

Natal Indian Congress, 163, 185, 189, 205

Natal Native Congress, 162

Natal Provincial Council, 189

National Convention (1908-9), 155-6; franchise proposals, 155-7, 162

National Party, South African, 160, 166, 167, 173, 174, 175, 176, 181, 182, 185, 257, 275; Labour Party's alliance with, 72; 'Black Peril' election (1929) won by, 174-5; Purified, 176-7, 183, 194; Reunited, 183-4; New Order movement, 184; struggle between Ossewabrandwag and, 184; apartheid policy, 189-242 passim; 1948 election won by, 192; in South-West Africa, 194; Afrikaner Party joins (1951), 194; split within, and HNP breakaway, 219; and hardliners, 219, 231, 236; post-1978 government, and white opposition, 231-6; new multiracial President's Council, 321-2, 236; Muldergate affair, 232; Botha government, 232-3, 236, 238-9, 240-1; 1987 elections, 240; de Klerk succeeds Botha

as leader of, 242; 1989 elections, 242; abandonment of apartheid and negotiations with ANC, 242, 243-51; power-sharing policy of, 246-7; secret involvement with Inkatha, 247-8; Convention for a Democratic South Africa, 247, 248-9; defeated by Conservative Party in Potchefstroom by-election, 248; wins referendum (1992), 248; Boipatong massacre (1992), 249; ANC breaks off formal talks with, 249; amnesty for politically motivated crimes, 293; de Klerk and Mandela at summit meeting, 251; bi-lateral negotiations resumed with ANC, 251
National Scouts, Boer, 146
National Security Council, 232-3
National Union of South African Students, 220
Nationalist Party, Transvaal, 152, 159
Native Administration Act (1927), 172
Native Advisory Council, Bechuanaland, 274-5
Native Affairs Act (1920), 180
Native Electoral Association, 161
Native Labour (Settlement of Disputes) Act (1953), 199
Native Laws Amendment Act: 1937: 175; 1952: 196; 1957: 200
Native Recruiting Corporation, 170
Native Representation Act (1936), 175, 200
Native Representative Council, 175, 181, 187, 189, 191; abolition of, 200
Native Resettlement Act (1956), 197-8
Native Service Contract Act (1932), 174
Native Vigilance Association, 162
Natives' Trust and Land Act (1936), 175, 178, 191, 199, 213
Natives (Urban Areas) Act (1923), 169
Natives (Urban Areas) Amendment Act (1930), 174
Nazi ideology, appeal to Afrikaner nationalists, 182, 184, 233
Ncapayi, Chief of the Bhaca, 61, 84, 85
Ncwala first-fruits ceremony, Swazi, 266
Ndebele, 10, 62, 63, 64, 66-7, 68, 74, 75, 76, 82, 101, 103, 124, 131-2, 136, 139-40, 235 253, 271, 272, 274, 276; status groups, 77-8; uprising (1896), 140
Ndlambe, 15, 34, 42, 44-5, 51, 52, 70
Ndlela, 81
Ndondakasuka, 113
Ndwandwe, 54, 55, 56, 57, 59, 60, 61, 66
'necklace' murders, necklacing, 237, 244
Netherlands South African Railway Company, 127, 129, 130
New Brighton, 206
New Klipfontein, 164
New Order, 184
New Republic, 125
New Republic Party, 231
Ngeto of the Qwabe, 64
Ngoni kingdoms, 57, 58, 59, 63, 66, 68, 136
Ngqika, 15, 32, 37, 38, 40, 41, 45, 52, 69, 70, 111, 112
Nguni-speaking peoples, 8-10, 11, 12, 13, 15, 16, 53-4, 62, 64, 68, 78, 133, 257, 263; rise of the northern Nguni states, 54-9
Ngwaketse, 30, 52, 66, 67, 271, 272, 274, 276
Ngwane V (Bhuna), King of the Swazi, 265
Ngwane (later Swazi), 54, 55-6, 57, 60, 62, 64, 252, 263

Ngwane National Liberatory Congress, 267
Ngwato, 77, 101, 124, 132, 137, 272, 273, 274
Ngwenya iron-ore mining, 267
Nkandla 153
Nkomati treaty (1984), 235, 240
Nkomo Joshua, 234
Nkulumane, 77, 132
Nkrumah, Kwame, 211
Non-European Unity Movement, 187
Nongalaza, *induna*, 81
Nonqause, Xhosa prophetess, 93
notables (Afrikaner landowners), 97, 149, 151
Nthatsi, Mma, Queen of Tlokwa, 62, 64, 253
Ntombi Latswala, Queen, 270
Nxaba, 57, 58
Nxumalo, Benjamin, 267
Nyanga township, 210
Nyasaland *see* Malawi
Nyuswa, 55
OAU (Organisation of African Unity), 260, 261
Oberholzer, Jan, 49-50
Odendaal Report (1964), 285, 287
Ohlange Institute, Natal, 161
Okavangoland, 286
Olifants river, 5, 6
Operation Safari (1982-3), 235
Operation Askari (1983), 289
Orange Free State, 1,10, 49, 62, 68, 91, 130, 164, 166, 174, 194, 226, 255, 256, 257, 259; British annexation (as Orange River Sovereignty: 1848-54), 88, 89-91; formation and early history, 93-5, 96; war between Lesotho and, 97-8, 255-6; diamond mining, 103, 104-5, 109; and British confederation policy, 109, 110, 119; customs union between Cape and, 130-1; Transvaal's relations with, 142; British annexation (as Orange River Colony: 1900), 145, 148; granted self-government (1907), 152; joins Union of South Africa (1910), 155-60; Land Act (1913), 163; First World War, 166; *see also* South Africa
Orange River, 1, 3, 5-6, 10, 16, 29, 30, 31-2, 37, 39, 41, 43, 62, 65, 69, 71, 74, 76, 86, 88, 91, 252, 262, 278, 279; expansion across, 49-51
Orange River Colony, 162; annexed by British (1900), 145, 148
Orange River Colony Congress, 162
Orange River Sovereignty, 89-91, 255; British annexation (1848), 88; and abandonment of (1854), 91
Orangia Unie (United Orangia) Party, 151, 152, 159
Ordinance no. 50: 49, 72
Orlams, 31, 279
Ossewabrandwag (Ox-Wagon Sentinel), 177, 182, 184, 189, 232
Ovambo, Ovamboland, 10, 278-9, 282, 283, 286, 287, 288
Ovimbundu, 224
Owen, Francis, 68
Ox-Wagon Trek (1938), 177, 183
Paardeberg, battle of (1900), 145
PAC (Pan-Africanist Congress), xiii, 208, 219, 261, 262, 275; Sharpeville massacre (1959), 209; banning of, 210, 220; armed liberation struggle, 210, 219-20; HQs established outside South Africa, 210; lifting of ban on (1980), 242; ANC heals breach with, 246; refuses to attend Codesa talks, 248
Palgrave, W.C., 280

Pan Africanist Congress, Accra (1956), 211
Paris Evangelical Society, 65
Paris Peace Conference (1919), 167,168
Parker, Stafford, 103
pass laws, 148, 168, 169, 183, 185, 203, 208, 240; passive resistance campaign against, 168, 178; wartime campaign against, 186; 1952 Act, 197; mass campaign against (1960), 209; and Sharpeville massacre, 209; in Namibia, 266, 268
passive resistance (non-violent action), 164, 180, 189, 206, 210
Die Patriot (newspaper), 110
Patriotic Front, Rhodesia, 233
Pedi, 15, 52, 53-4, 66, 68, 95, 110, 111, 208
Pegging Act (1943), 185, 189
Phamsotse, Simon, 258
Phetla (Zizi), 252
Philip, Dr John, 48, 50, 69-70, 88
Philippolis missionary station, 50, 63
Phuthi, 237, 239; rebellion, 116-18
Phuting, 63
Pienaar, frontiersman, 31
Pietermaritzburg, 81, 84, 85, 108
Pietersburg (Transvaal), 248
Pim, Sir Alan, 259
Pirow, Oswald, 184
pitso (Bantu meetings), 13, 254, 258, 263
Plaatje, Solomon, 147, 163
Platberg mission station, 63
Plettenberg, Governor van, 26, 29
Polane chiefdom, 252
police repression, 218, 220, 227
Polsmoor Prison, Cape Town, 218
Pondo, Pondoland, 55, 60, 61, 62, 68
Pongola river, 55, 57, 59
poor-whites, 149-50, 167, 171-2, 175, 177, 193-4, 202, 246
Poplar Grove, battle of (1900), 145
Population Registration Act (1949), 196, 245
Poqo (PAC fighting organisation), 210, 218
Port Elizabeth, 101, 130, 178, 206
Port Natal *see* Durban
Port St Johns, 125
Portuguese, 11, 60, 63, 74, 95, 110, 140, 149, 263, 264; in Mozambique, 11, 17, 57, 91, 95, 106, 109, 129, 132, 136, 224, 233; Transvaal's extradition treaty with, 141; revolution in Portugal (1974) 193, 224; and collapse of colonial authority, 224, 233, 234, 287; in Angola, 224, 233, 281, 286
Potchefstroom, 78, 95, 96, 119; Conservative Party wins by-election at (1992): 248
Potgeiter, Andries Hendrik, 71, 75, 76-7, 78, 79-80, 84, 95, 96
Poto, Victor, 213
President's Council, multiracial, 231-2, 236
Pretoria, 15, 96, 119, 143, 181, 226, 243
Pretoria Convention (1881), 120
Pretorius, Andries, 77, 80, 81, 84, 93, 94
Pretorius, Martinus Wessels, 93, 94, 95-6, 103
Prevention of Illegal Squatting Act (1951), 199
Progressive Association, Lesotho, 258
Progressive Federal Party, 230, 232, 240; alliance with Inkatha (1985), 240; *see also* Democratic Party
Progressive Party, Cape, 140-1, 159
Progressive Party, South African, 219, 231, 232
Progressive Party, Transvaal, 152, 159

Prohibition of Mixed Marriages Act (1949), 196
Purified National Party, 176-7, 183, 194
Qozo, Brigadier Oupo, 250
Qwabe, 55, 57, 58, 60, 61
Queen Adelaide Province, 70-1, 73, 76
Quilimane, 17
quit-rent system, 46-7
racial discrimination/segregation, xii, 147, 159, 166, 170-1, 188, 190, 199, 228, 285; in Cape Colony, 30-2, 49, 72, 135; Ordinance no. 50: 49, 72 trekker policy, 85, 86; Glen Grey Act (1894), 135; Rhodes's attitude to, 135, 140-1; Land Act (1913), xiii, 163, 169; against Indians, 163-4, 185, 188-9, 191, 198, 203-4, 205, 236, 285; Hertzog's policy, 172-3, 174, 175, 178-9; Immorality Act (1927), 172, 196; destruction of Cape franchise (1936), 175; wartime, 183, 185, 186; against Coloureds, 189-90, 196, 197, 203-4, 205, 236; social and cultural, 196, 199, 229; Reservation of Separate Amenities Act (1953), 199; educational, 201-2, 203, 207, 220, 229; mass defiance campaign against 205-7; sporting, 200, 215-16, 219, 229; in Namibia, 234, 282, 284, 285; see also apartheid; black townships; franchise; pass laws; urban population
railways, 101, 109, 110, 127, 129-30, 134, 136, 137, 148, 149, 154, 190, 257, 267, 276
Ramaphosa, Cyril, Secretary-General of ANC, 246
Ramoreboli, Gerard, 262
Rand see Witwatersrand
Rathateng, 15
Ratidladi, L.D., 275
Ratlou, Chief of the Rolong, 29
Reagan, US President Ronald, 239, 241, 289
reddingsdaadbond, 177, 195
referendum of white voters (1992), 248
Reform Committee, Johannesburg, 138
regional policy, South African, 221-2, 224-5, 233-6, 240-1
Rehoboth, Rehobothers, 279, 280
Relly, Gavin, 240
Renamo, 240
Representation of Natives Bill, 172-3, 180
Reservation of Separate Amenities Act (1953), 199
Responsible Government Party, Transvaal, 152
Retief, Piet, 69, 76, 77, 78-9, 81
Reunited National Party, 183-4
Reykjavik Summit Meeting (1986), 241
Rharhabe, 15, 52
Rhenish mission, 280
Rhodes, Cecil, xiii, 121, 122, 123, 124, 128, 130, 131-41, 149, 162, 265, 272, 274; becomes Prime Minister of Cape, 130, 135, 136; expansion into Rhodesia by, 131-4, 136, 139-40; political tactics in Cape, 134-5, 140-1; and plot to overthrow Transvaal government, 136-9
Rhodes, Herbert, 121
Rhodesia see Zambia; Zimbabwe
Rhodesian Front, 221
Rhodesian Intelligence Service, 235
Riekerts Committee (1980), 229
rinderpest epidemic, 140, 149, 255, 281
Roach, Fred, 261
Robben Island prison, 45, 108, 218, 290
Roberts, General, 145
Robinson, Commissioner Hercules, 120, 137,

138, 142, 257
Rolong, 29, 30, 52, 63, 65, 67, 75, 76, 77, 89, 90
Rooi Nasie, 278
Roos, Tielman, 174, 175
Rorke's Drift, 115
Rothschild, Lord, 122
Rozwi kingdom, 57, 58, 68, 77, 78
Rubusana, Walter, 156, 162
Rudd concession (Rudd, Charles), 132, 136, 140
Ruyter, runaway, 29
Sachs, Solly, 189
St Lucia Bay, 81, 125
Saldanha Bay, 18, 19
Salisbury, Lord, 137
San (Twa or Bushmen), xi, 3-5, 6, 7, 12, 16, 24, 25, 26, 27, 30, 31, 32, 34, 36, 40, 50, 234, 252, 270, 278, 285
Sand river, 75
Sand River Convention (1852), 90, 91, 93
Sandile, Xhosa chief, 16
Sanlam group, 176
Santam group, 166, 176, 177
Sarwa, 270-1
Sasolberg bomb blast, 226
Satyagraha campaign, Ghandi's, 164
Sauer Committee, 191
Savimbi, Jonas, 224, 235, 288
Scanlen, Thomas, 120
Schlebusch Commission, 231
Schmidt, Georg, 39
Schoemansdal, 75
Schoon, Robert, 66, 69
Schreiner, W.P., 141, 155, 156-7
Scott, Revd Michael, 285
Sebelo, of the Kwena, 273
Sebetwane, 63, 271, 272
Sechele, Chief of the Kwena, 124, 137
Second World War (1939-45), 178, 181-7, 188, 257, 284
Secunda bomb blast, 226
Seeiso, Chief, 259
Sekhukhuni, Pedi chief, 110
Sekonyela, 62, 64, 65, 78, 79, 89, 253
Sekwati, Chief, 66, 95
Selbourne, Lord, 151
Selbourne memorandum, 154-5
Selebi-Pikwe copper mines, 276
Seleka-Rolong, 63
Seme, Pixley Ka Izaka, 162, 180
Sena, 17
Senzanghakona, Chief, 55, 116
Separate Amenities Act, repeal of (1990), 145
separate development (apartheid), 193, 200, 212-21, 222-3, 224, 228, 229, 285; Bantustans, 212-15, 216, 217, 229-30, 231; and black African states, 215; outward looking policy, 215-16, 219; forced removals and tightened labour controls, 216-18; police repression, 218; white opposition to, 219; black opposition to, 219-21
Separate Representation of Voters Act, 201
Seretse Khama, 215, 275, 276
Setshele, Chief of the Kwena, 272, 273, 274
Shaka, Zulu chief, xiii, 56-61, 66, 153
shantytowns, 169, 183, 188
Sharpeville massacre (1959), 209, 212, 218, 226, 237
'shebeens', 203
sheep, 5, 19, 25, 73
Shepstone, Theophilus, 86, 108, 110, 113, 132

Shepstone, Theophilus, Jr (Offy), 133-4, 264, 265
Sherlock, Major, 38
Shona, 10, 57, 77, 78, 101, 132, 139-40, 274; uprising (1896-7), 140, 274
Sibandze, induna Mbhabha, 265
Siganenda, Chief of the Cube, 153
Sikhunyane, 57, 60
Silver Jubilee Conference (ANC: 1937), 181
Simons Town, 36
Sisulu, Walter, 205
skepsels (coloured servants), 31
Slabbert, Van Zyl, 240
Slachter's Nek uprising, 44, 72
slaves, slave labour/trade, 22, 23, 24, 43, 55, 63, 69, 73; runaway, 29; of mixed descent, 30; emancipation of, 35, 47, 48, 49, 70, 110; Christian conversion of, 38, 39
smallpox, 28
Smit, Erasmus, 76
Smith, Dr Andrew, 69
Smith, Sir Harry, 70, 88, 90, 91
Smith, Ian, 221, 222, 225, 233, 276
Smithfield Treaty (1855), 94
Smuts, Jan, 143, 151, 152, 155, 159, 160, 164, 165, 166-7, 169, 173, 174, 181, 182, 185, 186, 187, 204, 282, 284, 285; 1943 election won by, 185; and UN, 185, 188-9, 285; 1948 election lost by, 192
Sobhuza I, King of the Swazi, 54, 55, 81, 133, 263
Sobhuza II, King of the Swazi, 266-9
Sobukwe, Robert, 208, 209
Somerset, Governor, 47, 50
Somerville, Commissioner, 38
Soshangane, 57, 61, 74
Sosiza, Prince, 269, 270
Sotho speakers, 9, 10, 11, 52, 55, 62, 63, 64-5, 66, 86, 88, 89, 94, 96, 97-9, 120, 133, 252-63, 266; Phuthi rebellion, 116-18; 'Gun War', 118, 120; Basotho Qwaqwa 'homeland' of, 213; social inequality, 258; see also Lesotho
Sotho-Tswana, 10, 11, 12, 13, 15, 16, 29, 63, 77, 78
South Africa, Republic of: establishment of (1960), 210; leaves Commonwealth (1961), 210-11; and development of regional policy in central and southern Africa, 221-2, 224-5, 233-6, 240-1; and Mozambique, 222, 233, 235, 240, 289; and Namibia, 222, 233, 234, 235, 241, 282-91; and Angola, 222, 224, 233, 235, 241, 288-9; military expansion, 227; total strategy doctrine, 227, 232, 238, 240; post-1974 constitutional changes, 231-3; P.W. Botha becomes Prime Minister (1978), 232-3; and 'Muldergate' affair, 233; multiracial constitution introduced, 236-7; State of Emergency, 237, 239; and Lesotho, 261-3; and Swaziland, 269, 270; and Botswana, 275, 276, 277; economic sanctions against, 238, 245, 288; radical whites seek political settlement, 239-40; see also apartheid
South Africa, Union of, 281; formation of (1910), 154-9, 164; first governments, 159-60; and First World War, 165-7; and post-war political developments, 167-9; Independence, 173; Second World War, 181-7; and United Nations, 185, 188-9, 285, 286; becomes Republic (1960), 210; exclusion of Swaziland, Basutoland and Bechuanaland from, 266, 274,

275; Mandate rule in South-West Africa, 167, 188, 222, 225, 282-4
South Africa Party, 160, 166, 167, 175, 176, 181
South African Air Force, 241
South African Black Alliance, 230-1
South African Coloured People's Organisation, 207
South African Communist Party *see* Communist Party
South African Defence Forces (SADF), raids into neighbouring states by, 238, 240-1, 290; 'Operation Askari' in Angola (1983), 289
South African Development Coordination Conference (SADCC), 277
South African Indian Congress, 180, 205, 206, 207
South African Institute of Race Relations, 179
South African League, 141
South African National Party, 159, 160
South African Native Affairs Commission (1903-5), 148, 163
South African Native College, Fort Hare, 161
South African Native Congress, 162
South African Native Convention, 162
South African Republic *see* Transvaal
South African Security Services, de Klerk's reform of, 250
South African Students' Organisation, 220
South African Trades Union Congress, 179
South African War (1899-1902), 126, 128, 144-8, 149, 152, 160, 162, 164, 265-6
South African Worker, 259
South West African Affairs Act (1969), 286 *see also* Namibia
Southey, Lieutenant-Governor Robert, 103, 107
Soviet Union, 224, 241, 242, 262, 285, 290; collapse of Communist regime, 242
Soweto, 198, 231, 249; disturbances (1976), 225-6, 237, 269; Mandela's return to, 243
sporting segregation/desegregation, 200, 215-16, 219, 229, 245
Sprigg, Gordon, 112, 118, 119, 120
Springboks, 219
squatter settlements, 246, 250
State Aided Institutions Act (1957), 200
Statute of Westminster (1931), 173, 200
Steelpoort river, 66
Stellaland, 124, 272
Stellenbosch, 20, 26, 28, 33; Afrikaans University of, 195
Steyn, Hermans, 75
Steyn, President of Orange Free State, 142, 151
Stockenstroom, Commissioner Andries, 48, 71
Stockenstroom, Judge, 109
Stone Age, 3, 4
Stormberg, battle of (1899), 145
Stormberg Spruit, 49, 51
strandloopers, 6
Strauss, J.G.N., 204
strikes, 206; African, 167-8, 169, 178, 185, 187, 191, 199, 208, 223-4, 237; white labour, 152, 164, 165, 167, 171-2, 189-90; in Namibia (1971), 287, 290
Struben, Frederick and Henry William, 125, 126
Strydom, J.G., 195, 201, 205
Strydpoort, 74
Sundays river, 26
Suppression of Communism Act (1950), 202, 206
Suzman, Mrs Helen, 219
Swakopmund, 165

SWANU, 286
SWAPO, xiii, 222, 225, 234, 235, 241, 286, 287, 288, 289, 290, 291
Swazi National Council, 266, 267, 268
Swaziland, Swazi, xi, 10, 54, 68, 81, 125, 147, 148, 157, 211, 221, 226, 252, 263-70, 274; creation of kingdom, 55, 263; military system (age-regiments), 55, 263, 265, 266; concession hunters and frontier losses, 133-4, 264-5, 266; and separate development, 215; systems of government, 263, 265, 266, 267-70; becomes Protectorate of Transvaal (1894), 265; and High Commission Territory (1906), 266; labour migration from, 266, 274; Independence (1968), 266, 267; economy, 267; South African secret non-agression pact with (1982), 269; and foreign policy, 269, 270
Swaziland Progressive Association, 267
Swellendam, 26, 34, 36
Taaibosh, Gert, 63
Tanzania, 57, 58, 68
Tas, Adam, 21, 22
Tati goldfields, 78, 101, 103, 121
Tau, Chief of Rolong, 29, 52
Taung, 63, 66, 75, 254
Tawana, 67, 124, 271
taxation, 97, 111, 153, 185, 265, 274, 283, 284
Tembu, 60
Tembu Church, 161
Terre Blanche, Eugene, 232, 233
Tete, 17
Thaba Bosiu, 64, 67, 91, 94, 97, 253-4, 255, 260-1; Treaty of (1866), 97
Thaba Nchu, 64, 66, 75, 90
Thembu, 61, 62, 64, 111, 118, 125, 254
Theopolis mission, 43
Theron Commission (1976), 231
Thlaping, 29, 39, 63, 76
Thonga, 9
Thorburn, John, 264
Thuli, 55
Tile, Nehemiah, 161
tinkhundla (Swazi assembly), 269, 270
Tlokwa, 62, 64, 89, 252, 253
Toit, J.D., ('Totius'), 190
Toit, S.J. du, 119, 134
Toivoja Toivo, 290
Topnaars, 278
Torch Commando, 204
total strategy doctrine, 227, 232, 238, 240
Toutswemogola, 8, 11
Touwfontein meeting (1845), 87
trades unions: white, 152, 164, 165, 189-90, 199; African, 169, 178-9, 186, 187, 189-90, 191, 208, 224, 228; multiracial, 189, 190, 199, 228; black unions' opposition to separate development, 220; and multiracial co-option policy, 228-9
Transkei (later Fingoland), 1, 111, 118, 120, 135, 174, 210, 213, 220; self-governing constitution (1963), 213; and formal independence (1976), 229; and Lesotho, 261-2
Transorangia, 30, 56, 62-3, 64-5, 69, 71, 73, 75, 78, 253, 254; *see also* Orange Free State
Transvaal, 1, 2-3, 5, 8, 9, 10, 15, 52, 63, 66, 67, 68, 69, 75, 86, 95, 96-8, 112, 113, 114, 115, 116, 123, 125, 131, 132, 135, 141, 164, 166, 176, 226, 236, 238; Boer settlement, 69, 73, 74, 75, 76, 78, 82, 88, 90, 91, 95, 96; and unification of South African Republic (1856), 95-7; diamond

mining, 103-5; British annexation of (1877), 110-11, 119-20, 263-4; and British confederation policy, 109-10, 119; anti-British rebellion, 119-20; Pretoria Convention (1881), 120; Kruger elected President of restored Boer Republic, 120; London Convention (1884), 124; New Republic joins (1886), 125; gold mining, 126-9, 131, 137; railways, 127, 129-30; and Swaziland, 133-4, 248-50; *uitlanders'* opposition, 136-7; Rhodes's plot to overthrow government of, 136-9; and Jameson raid, 138, 141, 274; Kruger consolidates his position, 141-2; Milner's policy, 142-4, 148-50; South African War, 144-8, 265-6; and British annexation of (1900), 145, 148-9; white unemployment and poverty, 149-50; and political developments, 151-2; granted self-government (1906), 152, 154; joins Union of South Africa (1910), 154-60; African political activity, 162, 167-9; squatter settlements, 246; and Swaziland, 263-4, 265, 266; and Botswana, 271-2
Transvaal Congress, 162
Transvaal Indian Congress, 205-6
Transvaal Local Government Commission (Stallard Commission: 1922), 169
Transvaal National Union, 136-7
Transvaal Responsible Government Association, 152
Treason Trial (1956-61), 207-8, 275
Treaty of Aliwal North: First, 94, 97; Second, 99, 255
Treaty of Amiens (1802), 41, 42
trek boers, 25, 47, 71, 280, 283
Treurnicht, Dr Albert, 219
Treurnicht, Dr Andries, 231, 232, 236,
Tribal Authorities, 208, 210
Trichardt, Louis, 70, 73, 74-5
Trotha, General Lothar von, 282
Tshekedi Kgama, 275
Tshukwe languages, 5
Tshwete, Steve, 251
Tsonga, 125, 134
Tswana, 10, 11, 12, 13, 52, 63, 67, 103-4, 123, 124, 147, 266, 271-2, 273, 281
Tswapong hills, 77
Tugela River, 55, 59, 60, 61, 79, 80, 81; battle of (1838), 80
Tulbagh, Governor Ryk, 30
Tuli, Jake, 200
Turnhalle Conference (1975), 234, 287-8
Tutu, Archbishop Desmond, 231, 238, 244
Twa *see* San
Tyali, 69
Uitenhage, police open fire on demonstration in (1984), 237
uitlanders, 126, 127, 136-8, 141, 143
Ulundi, 114; battle of, 116
Umfolozi river, 59, 81
Umkhonto we Sizwe (ANC), 210, 218
Umlazi township, 215
Umzimkula river, 55, 60, 61
Umzimvubu river, 79
Unallocated Lands Concession, Swaziland, 264-5, 266
unemployment, 149-50, 167, 172, 175, 230, 246
Union Defence Force, 165
Unionist Party, South African, 159, 166, 167

UNITA (Angola), 224, 225, 288; South African support for, 224, 225, 235, 241, 289, 290

United Democratic Front, 237, 238, 240, 242; *see also* MDM

United Laagers, Port Natal annexed to the, 80

United Nations, 185, 188-9, 211, 212, 233; sanctions against Rhodesia, 221, 222; and Namibia, 222, 234, 241, 285-8, 289, 290; and Lesotho, 260, 261, 262; and Angola, 241; sends fact-finding mission to South Africa, 249-50; call to expel South Africa from (1974) 287

United Party, South African, 175, 180, 181, 183, 184, 185, 189, 192, 200, 204, 219, 231

United States, 211, 224, 235, 239, 241, 250, 287, 288, 290

United Swaziland Association, 267

United Transkeian Territories General Council (the Bunga), 174

universities: separate ethnic, 202; relaxation of apartheid at, 229, 246

UNTAG (UN Transitional Assistance Group), 241, 290

uranium, 194, 278

Urban Areas Act (1923), 169

urban population, urbanisation, 22, 171, 183, 186, 188, 230, 236; segregation and influx control of Africans, 159, 160, 174, 175, 191, 196-8, 202-3, 216, 217-18; shantytowns, 169, 183, 188; boycott of buses, 208; changes in policy towards, 227-9; squatter settlements, 246; *see also* black townships; pass laws

Uys, Dirk, 80

Uys, Piet, 69, 77, 79-80

Vaal River, 5, 6, 15, 29, 30, 31, 50, 62, 63, 66, 67, 75, 76, 78, 86, 88, 90, 93, 94, 101, 130

Van der Kemp, J.T., 40, 41

Van der Stel, Simon, 19, 20, 22, 30

Van der Stel, Willem Adriaan, 20, 21, 22

Van Jaarsveld, Adriaan, 33-4, 37

Van Meerhof, Pieter, 30

Van Onselen, xi

Van Pittius, Gey, 124

Van Reenan, D.G., 23

Van Rensburg, Commandant, 38

Van Rensburg, Janse, 70, 74

Van Rensburg, J.F.J., 184

Van Rensburg, W.C.J., 96

Van Rheede, Commissioner, 30

Van Riebeeck, Jan, 18, 30

Vasco da Gama, 17

Vechtkop, 75

veldkornets, 20, 28, 36, 47, 76, 80, 84, 97

Velkskoendraers, 278

Venables, Henry, 67

Venda, 10

Venda homeland, 214; formal independence (1979), 229

Vereeniging Peace Conference (1902), 146-7, 162

Vergelegen estate, Van der Stel's, 20, 21

Verwoerd, Dr Hendrik, 195, 202, 210, 212-13, 285, 286; assassination of (1966), 212

Vet river, 75, 76, 78

Victoria, Queen, 113, 119, 125, 265

Viervoet Hill, battle of, 90

Village Deep mine, Rand, 150, 169, 187

Villiers, Sir Henry de, 142

Visser, Floris, 36

Vlok, Adriaan, 248

'Voice of the People' (Dutch burgers), 37

volksraad (Boer elected council), 73, 75, 76, 81, 84, 85, 93, 94, 95, 96, 119, 126-7, 129, 138, 141, 142, 143, 265

Voortrekker Movement, 174

voortrekkers, 176; centenary celebrations (1938), 177; *see also* Great Trek

Vorster, J.B., 212, 215, 216, 219, 224, 232, 233, 234, 261, 287, 288

Wade's vagrancy ordinance, 72

Waldheim, Kurt, 287

Walfisch Bay, 279, 280

Walvis Bay, British annexation of (1878), 281

'War of the Axe' (1846-7), 87-8

Ward, Sir Joseph, 160

Warden, Major, 87, 88, 89, 90, 91, 97

Warden Line, 89, 91, 94

Warren, General Sir Charles, 124, 272

Washington, Booker T., 161

Waterberg mountains, 1, 281

Waterboer, Chief Andries, 50, 103-4, 109

Weekend World, suppression of, 227

Weichardt, Louis, 182

Wernher, Beit & Co., 128

Wesleyan Methodist Missionary Society, 39, 63, 65-6, 161

West Germany, 234, 288

wheat production, 18, 22, 23

White Committee, Swaziland, 264

Wiehahn Commission (1980), 228

Wikar, H.J., 16

Williams, Ruth, 275

Winberg, 76, 78, 84, 94

wine industry, Cape, 19, 21, 22, 23, 119, 134, 176

Winterberg, 69, 70

Wit Kommando, 232

Witbooi, Hendrik, 281, 282

Witboois, 279

witchcraft, 13, 79

Witwatersrand gold fields (Transvaal: Rand), xii, 101, 123, 125, 126, 131, 136, 137, 167, 187, 206, 225, 226, 244; labour exploitation, xii, 148, 149-50, 167; nature of deposits, 127-8; planning uprising of *uitlanders*, 137-8; African wage reduction, 148, 149; white unemployment and poverty, 149-50, 167; Chinese mine labour, 150, 152; white trade unionists' strikes, 152, 167; struggle for African rights (1918-20), 167-9, 178; race relations in mining work force, 170-1; African labour strikes (1973), 224

Witwatersrand Native Labour Association, 149, 170

Witwatersrand University, 202

Wodehouse, Governor, 98-9, 255

Woeke, Maritz Hermann Otto, 34

Wolseley, Sir Garnet, 108, 116, 119, 124

women/girls, xi, 30; Bantu, 11, 15; Zulu, 56, 57; Black Sash movement, 205; and pass laws, 208

Wonderfontein congress (1879), 119

World, suppression of, 227

World Council of Reformed Churches, 238

Xesibe chiefdoms, 125

Xhosa, 15, 16, 26, 32, 36, 60, 61, 62, 79, 87, 89, 147, 220, 239; resistance wars, xiii, 26, 29, 33-4, 37-8, 42, 44-6, 69-71, 72-3, 111; chiefdoms, 52; and struggle for the *zuurveld*, 44-5, 69; and 'ceded territory', 45-6, 69, 70; 'War of the Axe' (1846-7), 87-8; uprising in British Kaffraria (1850-2), 89; cattle killing by, 93, 111

Xuma, Dr, 186, 189, 205, 285

Yao slave raiders, 63

Yoalaboholo mountains, 62, 64

Zaire, 224

Zambezi river, 8, 17, 57, 58, 63, 68, 136, 149, 271, 273, 276, 281

Zambia (formerly Northern Rhodesia), 3, 7, 58, 68, 222, 240, 276, 281

Zambodze, 265

ZANU, Zimbabwe, 222, 234, 277, 288

ZAPU, Zimbabwe, 222, 235, 276, 277

Zanzibar, 281

Zeekoe river, 26, 49

Zibhebhu, 116, 125

Zihlandlo of the Mkhize, 59-60

Zimbabwe (formerly Rhodesia), 5, 7, 10, 57, 68, 77-8, 101, 103, 139, 148, 221-2, 246, 265, 271, 274, 288; British expansion into, 131-4, 136, 139-40, 149; Shona and Ndebele uprisings (1896), 140; Smith regime and UDI, 221-2, 225, 233; South African relations with, 222, 233, 234-5; Mugabe wins elections, 234-5, 288; and Independence (1980), 234; and Botswana, 275, 276, 277

Zizi, 10, 252

Zondi, 153

Zoutpansberg, 1, 10, 43, 68, 69, 74, 75, 94, 96, 97

Zulus, Zululand, 52-61, 62, 68, 74, 76, 77, 78, 82, 84-5, 86, 110, 112-16, 124-52, 153, 154, 176, 177, 205, 253, 254, 265; and *mfecane* wars and migrations, 61-8; massacre of Boers by, 78-9; battle of Tugela river, 80; and battle of Blood river, 80-1; military organisation (age-regiments system), 53-4, 56-7, 58-60; faction struggles, 113; British War with (1879), 114-16, 119; and battle of Isandhlwana, 115-16; Inkatha movement, 230, 239, 240, 244, 247-8, 249

zuurveld ('sour grazing'), 26, 29, 34, 36, 37, 38, 42, 49, 51; struggle for, 44-5, 46, 69; 1820 settler scheme, 47, 49

Zwartkopjes, 87

Zwart Ruggens, 33

Zwengendaba, 57-8

Zwide of the Ndwandwe, 54, 55, 56, 57, 60, 62, 66, 263